Discovering Jewish Music

Support for the publication of this book
is provided by
The Lucius N. Littauer Foundation

and

Bonnie and Michael Slobodien
Dedicated *l'dor v'dor*
In honor of our parents,
Lillian and David Slobodien and Dena and Nathan Richmond
who taught us the value of *tzedaka,*
and our children,
Richard Haim, Sarah Margalit, and Elana Rachel,
with whom we are blessed to share
a love for music and a devotion to Judaism.

Discovering
Jewish Music

Marsha Bryan Edelman

THE JEWISH PUBLICATION SOCIETY

 Philadelphia   2003 • 5763

The Jewish Publication Society
2100 Arch Street
Philadelphia, PA 19103

Composition by Sasgen Graphic Design
Design by Adrianne Onderdonk Dudden

Manufactured in the United States of America

03 04 05 06 07 08 09 10 10 9 8 7 6 5 4 3 2 1

Library of Congress Cataloging-in-Publication Data
Edelman, Marsha Bryan
Discovering Jewish music / Marsha Bryan Edelman.
p. cm.
Includes bibliographical references (p.) and index.
ISBN 0-8276-0727-X (audio CD included)
1. Jews--Music--History and criticism. 2. Music--History and criticism. I. Title
ML3776.E44 2003
780'.89'924--dc21

       2003004398

~ Dedicated, with Love

To my mother, Judith Helene
Phillips Bryan, ז״ל , who shared with
me her love of music; to my grandparents, Jack and Rose Phillips, ז״ל ,
from whom I learned to love Jewish
life; and to Eliezer, Raphael, Yehudit
and Yonatan, whom I fervently hope
will embrace both.

Contents

Preface   ix

1 In the Beginning: Children of Yuval   1

2 Into the Diaspora   11

3 The Art of Jewish Music   39

4 Emancipation, Enlightenment, and Evolution   53

5 From *Kodesh* to Concert: Jewish Music Confronts Modernity   71

6 All the World's a Stage: The Story of Yiddish Theater   95

7 Synagogue Music in America   125

8 Jewish Music on the Concert Stage   149

9 Building the Jewish State   187

10 Popular Music of the New State   221

11 Popular Music in America   249

Notes   279
Glossary   335
Key Figures in the History of Jewish Music   349
Selected Bibliography   359
List of Musical Illustrations   373
Index of Musical Illustrations   387
Index   391

Preface

Nearly all Jews (and many outside the faith) have had an experience of something they call "Jewish music," whether in the synagogue, at a life-cycle celebration, or on the concert stage. Close examination of these variant expressions of "Jewish culture" will reveal enormous differences among them, and attempts to reach consensus on what "Jewish music" really is will yield as many opinions as there are voices in the discussion.

This book attempts to answer a slightly different question: How have the values and traditions of Jewish people been reflected in music produced around the world and throughout history? Because Jewish people have lived as a minority culture within larger communities, Jews have "borrowed" aspects of the majority culture along the way. This has led to the creation of more than one kind of music, in more than one language.

Admittedly, there have been other books that have tried to tell the story of Jewish music. First on the scene, and most comprehensive, was Abraham Zvi Idelsohn's *Jewish Music,* a one-volume compilation based upon his monumental ten-part *Thesaurus of Hebrew Oriental Melodies.* Subsequent books have covered much of the same ground, from a variety of perspectives and for a range of potential audiences. What new ground does this book intend to explore?

One of the most important contributions of this book is its comprehensive examination of the 20th century. From our vantage point in these early days of the 21st century, we can see clearly that the last

100 years have been revolutionary on a variety of fronts, including the profusion of music that was produced in Europe, North America, and especially Israel. As theological reforms begun in the 19th century continued to affect the century that followed, synagogue music underwent significant change. The 20th century also saw the evolution of an entirely new genre, with the development of Jewish art music for the concert stage. At the same time (and as in every other time and place), folk and popular music continued to give voice to "the people." Brief but plentiful musical illustrations throughout the book provide written examples of the music discussed, but even more valuable is the accompanying CD recording that provides the reader with an opportunity to hear and appreciate the wide range of what is called "Jewish music."

It would have been impossible, however, to chart a coherent course for "Jewish music" by simply beginning at the dawn of the 20th century. The last 100 years did not happen in a vacuum—Jewish people have been producing music for more than 3,000 years. So it is that this book begins "in the beginning" and explores the earliest music of the Jews and the evolution of rabbinic attitudes that impacted on Jewish musical life for hundreds of years. We also discover the many ways in which Jewish music evolved in spite of the checkered history of the Jewish people—and to a large extent, because of it.

Does this book cover every work by every composer who has claimed to write "Jewish music?" Certainly not. Fortunately, the number of contributors to the field of Jewish music is long—and growing longer by the day. Decisions on whom to include were based on an examination of the music and musicians who made a difference in the world of Jewish music, whose work charted new territory and had an impact on that which followed.

This book also chose to focus on music that, in the words of noted musicologist Curt Sachs, was written "by Jews, for Jews, as Jews."[1] It is a well-documented fact that Jewish people have been disproportionately represented among the writers of music for Tin Pan Alley, the Broadway stage, and even the rock and roll scene. Notwithstanding claims that some of this music was influenced by the Jewish backgrounds of its composers, however, it was not created for an exclusively, or even primarily, Jewish audience. Even more obviously, the significant accomplishments of a host of Jewish composers, instrumentalists, and vocalists may be a positive reflection of their successful integration into "mainstream" life, but it does not reflect any contribution to Jewish culture. Tragically, the rejection of some composers and performers because of their Jewish backgrounds has also been a fact of history, but it does not confer upon the music they produced a stamp of "Jewish" content (no matter what their detractors may have claimed).

This book is designed for all readers. One need not be able to read music or be conversant in musical theory or music history to understand and appreciate the information here. In its pages the reader will find a clear discussion of the development of Jewish music and intelligible explanations of musical issues, without the jargon and technical detail of books intended only for professional musicians. Aspects of Jewish life and ritual that are intimately connected with the development of Jewish music are also explained so that all readers can follow the scope and sequence of Jewish history, using the development of music as a helpful catalyst for understanding and discovery.[2]

Discovering Jewish Music is the product of many years of study and the distillation of years of teaching. I have learned from all of my students and hope this volume will make a contribution to those who follow them, as well as to independent readers eager to discover the "joys of Jewish music." I am also profoundly grateful for the encouragement and material assistance I have received from colleagues, family, and friends. Dr. Rela Mintz Geffen, who has been my mentor as well as my "sister," was the first to read each chapter, and offered substantive advice and critique based upon her wide base of knowledge and her vantage point as the ideal, prototypical, "intelligent, non-musician reader." This book would not have been written without her. I am also enormously indebted to Cantor Deborah Tanzer-Cohen for the painstaking hours she spent transcribing the many musical illustrations in this volume. She has gone from being my student to my colleague, and she has always been my friend.

I am pleased to acknowledge the cooperation of the many publishers and producers whose valuable works are excerpted in this volume. In particular, I am appreciative of the many living composers and performers whose work is included here and on the accompanying CD. I hope their generosity will be rewarded by increased support for their work.

I would like to thank the editors and staff of The Jewish Publication Society. Their enthusiasm for this project and their patience in seeing it to fruition have been a source of inspiration. My final thanks are reserved for those nearest to me, who have provided the greatest encouragement, and made the greatest sacrifices to see this book in print. To my father, Emanuel Bryan; my husband, Herb; and my children, I extend my gratitude and my love. ~

Marsha Bryan Edelman
September 18, 2002 / 12 Tishre 5763

1 ~
In the Beginning: Children of Yuval

Music in the Bible

Most readers are familiar with the sequence of events described in the early verses of the Book of Genesis. In six days God creates the universe and all that is in it, resting on the seventh. Adam and Eve, the first humans, eat from the tree of knowledge and are expelled from the Garden of Eden. Adam works hard to till the soil while, in pain, Eve bears her children. Jealous over God's acceptance of his brother Abel's offering and rejection of his own, Cain kills Abel. What follow next are somewhat lesser-known accounts of the wandering Cain; of Lamekh, the next man to shed another's blood; and following a long list of "begats," the popular tale of Noah and the ark. Those who continue from this point will discover more of the history of the ancients—but they will already have missed a very important footnote in the development of humankind. Hidden among those "begats" is the record of the birth of Jubal: "He was the ancestor of all who play the lyre and the pipe" (Gen. 4:21). Jewish tradition thus records music as the earliest art form, one basic to human nature. In fact, Jubal's father Lamekh composed the first song when he boasted that God would protect him, an accidental murderer, for 77 generations (Gen. 4:23–24).

Lamekh's improvisatory song belongs to a large category of secular music mentioned frequently in the rest of the Bible, including the songs that young David sang to soothe the troubled King Saul and the songs lauding the victories of King David, Jephthah, Deborah, and others.

The most famous biblical song, however, is Moses' "Song at the Sea," a quasi-liturgical ode of thanksgiving following the Israelites' safe crossing of the Red Sea (Exod. 15:1–18). Indeed, the Sabbath on which this passage is read in the synagogue is known as Shabbat Shirah (Sabbath of Song).[1] In fact, Moses' song enjoys year-round familiarity, for it has been incorporated into the daily morning liturgy.[2]

Music in the Temple

In later books of the Bible, as well as in early rabbinic writings, liturgical music plays a larger role than it did during the desert era recorded in the Pentateuch. The Book of Chronicles (whose anonymous author, apparently a priest or Levite, may even have been a member of the Temple choir or orchestra) elaborates on important ritual celebrations, including the role music and musicians played in them.

I Chronicles 15:16–28 describes the festivities held when David brought the Holy Ark to Jerusalem. Some 288 musicians playing lyres, lutes, and cymbals headed the parade. I Chronicles 25 contains a detailed listing of which family groupings were assigned to particular instruments. Moreover, when Solomon became king and assigned responsibility for building and supervising the work of the Holy Temple, he followed his father David's instructions, appointing 4,000 of the Levites to praise the Lord with "instruments which I devised for singing praises" (I Chron. 23:5). At the actual dedication of the finished Temple (II Chron. 5), 120 priests added trumpets to the musical celebrations. Much later, following the destruction of the First Temple, Babylonian exile, and return to Jerusalem under Nehemiah, Second Temple ritual featured the playing of flutes on festive occasions.

Clearly, music has been part of Jewish life and Israelite ritual from the beginning of recorded history, but how did this music sound? Obviously, without recordings or even a system of musical notation for this ancient music, we will never know exactly how the music of Israel sounded in those early years. However, we do know something about the quality of the sound and the form that some Temple compositions might have taken.

I Chronicles 25 describes the Levitical "orchestra" as being comprised of lyres, harps, and brass cymbals. The latter instruments were not the large clanging plates of contemporary marching bands, but rather small finger cymbals known in Hebrew as *mitziltayim*. The lyre *(kinnor)* and harp *(nevel)* are more challenging to imagine. Smaller and larger harps were common instruments of the ancient Near East; "how small" and "how large" are questions that remain to be answered. We can distinguish the two by envisioning handheld instruments (such as those that angels are depicted playing in Renaissance artworks) and the larger harps featured in symphony orchestras. The larger variety were usually played by hand; the smaller instruments were played with a plectrum, or pick. (In I Sam. 18:10, young David is described as entertaining a brooding King Saul by playing this smaller lyre "with his hand" in an apparent display of virtuosity.)

The chronicler does provide us with some additional cryptic information about these harps. The smaller lyres were "set to *alamoth*"; the harps were "on the *sheminith*" (I Chron. 15:20–21). The meaning of these descriptions is unclear. The term *alamoth* generally refers to "maidens," but women have not been definitively associated with Temple musical practices.[3] The assumption is, therefore, that these were high-pitched instruments, whose sound could be likened to the singing voices of young women. The *sheminith,* or "eighth," would appear to refer (somewhat anachronistically) to the octave of the modern eight-note scale. The word refers, therefore, to an instrument pitched approximately one octave lower than its counterpart, apparently parallel to the voices of the (male) singers of the Temple choir.

These two puzzling terms, *alamoth* and *sheminith,* each occur in one other place with musical association: the Book of Psalms. It is known that psalm singing figured prominently in the liturgy of the Temple ritual,[4] and much can be learned about musical practices in the Temple from an examination of the psalm texts.

The Psalms

The psalms are full of references to singing and the playing of instruments. Among the best known is the final chapter, Psalm 150,[5] whose closing verses exhort:

Praise Him with blasts of the horn;
    praise Him with harp and lyre.
Praise Him with timbrel and dance;
    praise him with lute and pipe.
Praise Him with resounding cymbals;
    praise Him upon loud-clashing cymbals.
Let all that breathes praise the LORD. Hallelujah.

Psalm 150 reiterates the importance of music in ancient Israelite worship and offers a list of instruments known to have been popular at the time. In addition to the harps, lyres, and cymbals played by the Temple orchestra, the "lute and pipe" included in the list were played by laymen and were normally used for secular purposes. Even more interesting is the inclusion of the "timbrel and dance," since both are associated with women. However, the last line of the psalm clearly invites all of humankind to join in the praise. In fact, it has been suggested that the psalm offers a sort of "stage direction" indicating the sequence in which the various instruments should enter the performance;[6] the growing crescendo reaches its peak with the entrance of human voices.

In I Chronicles 6, we read that David's chief musicians are Heman; Asaph, on his right; and Ethan, on his left. These three led groups of Levitical choristers and instrumentalists when the Ark was brought to Jerusalem, and continued to preside over musical proceedings at the completion of the Temple. The literary structure of many of the psalms is consistent with the notion that the texts were divided among the singers in particular ways. "Responsorial" and "antiphonal" singing, still common forms of worship for many religious communities, are indicated.

In responsorial worship, the main body of text is chanted by a precentor (or choir); the congregation (or secondary choir[s]) chants a simple response. Various liturgical passages utilize this form. The *amen* answer to a blessing is one example, as is the response to the Priestly Blessing (variously scripted as *amen* or *ken yehi ratzon*, "may it be Your will"). Many religious poems (called *piyyutim*) of the Middle Ages also adopted this form, including this early text discovered in the Cairo Genizah:[7]

> Who stood on Mt. Horeb, absorbing the content of "Remain [here]
>   with me" (Deut. 5:28)—as Moses?
> Who led My flock in the desert, bringing forth water by saying
>   "Spring up, O well" (Num. 21:17)—as Moses?
> Who asked Me for mercy saying "Renounce the plan [to punish Your
>   people]" (Ex. 32:12)—as Moses?...[8]

This example from the High Holy Day liturgy (with refrains at the beginning and end of each section) is more familiar:

> The Supreme King! God Who dwells on high,
>   Who is powerful on high,
> May the strength of His hand be exalted—
> *La'adei ad yimlokh* [forever shall He reign].[9]

Psalm 136 also provides an example of this form, utilizing a slightly more ambitious response:

> Praise the LORD; for He is good,
> His steadfast love is eternal.
> Praise the God of gods,
> His steadfast love is eternal.
> Praise the LORD of lords,
> His steadfast love is eternal.
> Who alone works great marvels,
> His steadfast love is eternal.
> Who made the heavens with wisdom,
> His steadfast love is eternal.
> Who spread the earth over the water,
> His steadfast love is eternal....

The same refrain is used in the opening verses of Psalm 118:

> Praise the LORD for He is good,
> His steadfast love is eternal.
> Let Israel declare,

"His steadfast love is eternal."
Let the house of Aaron declare,
"His steadfast love is eternal."
Let those who fear the LORD declare,
"His steadfast love is eternal."

Since prayer books did not exist and most people were not versed in the liturgy, responsorial singing was likely the only option for participation by the common Israelite pilgrim to Jerusalem. Levites, who served five-year apprenticeships before being elevated to the choir at the age of 30, were the singers of antiphonal psalms, in which entire verses might have been alternated between choirs. The regular rhythms of Psalm 148, as well as the recurring use of the word *"hallelu"* (praise) make these verses perfect for antiphonal singing:

Halleluyah! Praise the LORD from the heavens; praise Him on high.
 Praise Him, all His angels; praise Him, all His hosts.
Praise Him, sun and moon; praise Him, all bright stars.
 Praise Him, highest of heavens, and you waters that are above
  the heavens....

Psalm 113 begins the *Hallel* service recited on festivals. Virtually all of the melodies popularly used for this text take advantage of the rhythmic structure of these lines to create a song that alternates between cantor and congregation:

Hallelu avdei Adonai   O servants of the LORD, give praise;
Hallelu et shem Adonai   praise the name of the LORD.
Yehi shem Adonai mevorakh   Let the name of the LORD be blessed
Me-atah ve'ad olam....   now and forever....

The Hebrew acrostic poem that is Psalm 145 (liturgically preceded by a rabbinic text that quotes the last verse of Psalm 144) makes it a similarly easy text to share antiphonally in contemporary synagogues:

Aromimkha elohai hamelekh va'avarakhah shimekha le-olam va'ed
 (I will extol You, my God and King, and bless Your name forever

and ever.)
Bekhol yom avarakheka va'ahalelah shimekha le-olam va'ed
(Every day will I bless You and praise Your name forever and ever).

Clearly, when modern congregations are invited to "sing responsively" with the cantor, they are engaging in an ancient, albeit misnamed, practice.

The opening verses of many of the psalm chapters seem to offer us the most information regarding Israelite musical practice—if we could only break their codes! These lines, called "prescriptions," are short sentences that, while designated "verse one," actually precede the main body of the text. Some appear to ascribe authorship, and/or provide additional information regarding the circumstances that inspired the psalm's composition. Psalm 3, for example, begins with the statement "A psalm of David, when he fled from his son Absalom."

Other prescriptions provide semi-elaborate "stage directions" to the Levitical musicians. Psalms 120–134 are all designated "Song of Ascents" *(Shir ha-Ma'alot)*. The pageantry of Temple ritual may have provided for the chanting of these specific psalms while the high priest slowly ascended the Temple mount.[10] Psalm 4 begins, "For the leader; with instrumental music. A psalm of David" inviting the Temple orchestra to join in the ritual.

And then there is Psalm 46, beginning "For the leader of the Korahites; on *alamoth*." Is this another reference to an instrument? (Perhaps that smaller harp?) If so, then prescriptions with parallel forms would appear to be referring to other, unknown instruments: the *gitith* (Psalm 8), *ayyeleth-hashahar* (Psalm 22), *shoshannim* (Psalm 45), *mahalath* (Psalm 53), *yonath-elem-rehokim* (Psalm 56), and others. We have already noted that there are many references throughout the Bible and the Talmud to the instruments played in ancient Israel; none of these mystery instruments is ever mentioned. It is far more likely, then, that the prescriptions are telling us that these psalms are to be chanted to well-known, popular tunes of the same name.

The practice of elevating local folk songs to ritual status by adapting their melodies to liturgical texts is commonplace throughout the world. This practice, called "contrafaction," is a useful means of keeping a popular tune in the repertoire even if its accustomed text falls out of favor. Many *piyyutim* of the Middle Ages followed this pattern, and the Hasidim of Eastern Europe made the practice a "holy mission" by elevating and adapting even non-Jewish tunes for the service of God.

Ancient Roots, Eternal Questions

Knowing, or even presuming, that we have correctly interpreted the cryptic psalm prescriptions does not tell us anything about the sound of this music—only that at least several tunes were in use during the Temple period. Despite limited knowledge, most musicologists assume that ancient Jewish musical tradition is at the root of all contemporary Jewish music (at least for synagogue ritual). Some ethnomusicologists have tried to deduce some of the qualities of original Jewish musical practice—if not the actual notes themselves—by studying music of the Babylonian[11] and Yemenite Jews, Jewish groups that had limited contact with their non-Jewish countrymen and at the same time were isolated from influences of later Western musical developments. Scholars have assumed that the traditions of these earliest Diaspora communities remained faithful to the essence of Temple practice. However, we need to take into account certain factors before concluding that there is, indeed, any discoverable "true" and uniquely Jewish musical tradition.

First, there is the question of the reliability of oral transmission. On the plus side, we can assume that the liturgical traditions of Israel were passed down through the generations with great care. After all, this sacred knowledge entrusted to the priestly clan constituted an ongoing link with our ancestors, enabling the possibility of continuity with God.

On the other hand, it is likely that transmission was, at best, inconsistent. Even with the best of intentions, some pitches are likely to have been remembered improperly; the tunes might have been subconsciously changed in an attempt to "correct" or "improve" upon the legacy. Moreover, the Babylonians and Yemenites were not deaf. While they may have had limited formal contact with other musical traditions in the last 1,200 years, they could not have failed completely to overhear the chanting of some local *muezzin* calling the Islamic faithful to prayer. Occasional lullabies, work songs, or children's rhymes must also have penetrated the Jewish community and subconsciously altered the holy traditions.

We began our search presuming one unique Jewish musical tradition just waiting there for us to discover it. However, this is not necessarily—or even likely—the case.

Let us assume, for practical purposes, that the history of the Jewish people and their liturgical practices began following the Exodus from Egypt. The clan of 70 "persons that were of Jacob's issue" (Exod. 1:5), which entered Egypt, left several generations later as some 600,000 (Exod. 12:37)—plus associated family members. Rabbinic lore (Midrash) relates that the Israelites merited redemption because during their 210-year sojourn in Egypt they kept their identities as Hebrews and retained their unique Hebrew names. Does this mean that they were not susceptible to the influences of Egyptian culture? Of course not. According to the rabbis, only the tribe of Levi is credited with having continuously maintained adherence to the faith of Abraham, Isaac, and Jacob; many of the rest of the Israelites are said to have adopted most Egyptian ritual and cultural practices[12]—and these would certainly have included music.

By the time the Israelites chronicled in the Book of Joshua settled in Canaan, they had shed the psychological mantle of Egyptian slavery but likely not the culture itself. Moreover, their desert sojourn, conquest of Canaan, and continuing interaction—for good and for bad—with neighboring peoples of the ancient Middle East brought the Israelites into constant contact with foreign cultures and their music. The harps and lyres depicted on Israelite coins and the mosaic floors of ancient synagogues are the same instruments found on Phoenician, Assyrian, and Babylonian artifacts. The Talmud describes Egyptian music as "raucous" and Greek song as "erotic"— but how different could they really have been?

Closer to our own time, we know (despite what most conventional music history books say) that the roots of Gregorian chant and the Catholic mass (ostensibly the starting point for the development of modern Western music) were heavily influenced by the music best known to the early church fathers: the music of the Jewish synagogue. Human experience is thus marked by constant interchanges of cultural experience. The resulting cross-pollination enriches each civilization—but it also makes it harder for anyone to untangle unique roots.

Where do we go from here? If all there is to say about Jewish music is that it owes some debt to all other musical traditions with which it has come into contact, and that it is therefore a constantly evolving (but never unique) art form, then why a book devoted to discovering Jewish music? Is there really any such thing at all? Or have we been trying to answer the wrong question?

Perhaps it is a mistake to try to define "Jewish music," but there has always been "music of the Jews," and this is the subject we will look at together, considering the many influences that have affected Jews in many different times and places. Having accomplished this investigation, we will be in a better position to understand the Jewish musical present, and to appreciate the variety of its forms and expressions.

2~
Into the Diaspora

If the dedication and worship services at the Jerusalem Temple marked the peak of Jewish musical performance in the ancient world, then the destruction of that Temple at the hands of the Romans in 70 C.E. marked the nadir of Jewish music history and practice. With the Temple gone, the elaborate ceremonies surrounding daily, Sabbath, and festival offerings also came to an end.

Destruction of the Temple, however, meant much more than an end to sacrificial offerings. To acknowledge the loss of both their Temple and Jewish national autonomy (in the absence of a functioning Jewish rabbinical court, or Sanhedrin), the rabbis invoked a ban on public musical performance.[1] The Levitical choirs and the instruments that had enhanced Jewish rituals were silenced by rabbinic decree. The same prohibition of musical celebration was imposed upon synagogue practices as well.[2]

If the rabbinic ban on music had been uniformly and universally enforced, this volume on the history of Jewish music would be exceedingly short. Fortunately, the rabbis underestimated the power of music in the lives of the people. Mothers continued to sing to their babies, children invented nursery rhymes, and laborers of all stripes continued to whistle while they worked. Folk music, the music of the people, could not be silenced.

To be sure, synagogues—even without an instrumental tradition—continued to play an important role in Jewish communal ritual. During the time of the Temple, delegations known as *anshe ma'amad,* representatives of the people, were regularly sent to Jerusalem from outlying regions to be present at the sacrifices and pray for their people. As an added benefit, they absorbed as much as possible of the Levitical singing and helped ensure that synagogue singing conformed to the musical practices of the Temple. Now a somewhat circumscribed connection to those practices provided an important emotional link to the Temple traditions. Furthermore, the Rabbis were forced to concede that music would need to play a role in the evolution of new ceremonies and liturgy to take the place of Temple rites. In the centuries to come, synagogue rituals would be organized with the help of two important musical tools: cantillation and *nusaḥ*.

Cantillation, Biblical Chant

Cantillation (from the Latin *cantare,* meaning "to sing") is the practice of chanting from the biblical books in the Jewish canon. The practice goes back to the time of Ezra, when the Jewish people returned from their Babylonian exile following the destruction of the first Temple (about 510 B.C.E.).[3] Realizing that the people had stopped observing the laws of the Torah, Ezra took it upon himself to read portions of the Law every time he could assemble an audience. Sabbaths and festivals provided obvious opportunities; so, too, did market days, when large groups would gather to buy, sell, and catch up on local news. Market days were Mondays and Thursdays, and so, to this day, the Torah is read publicly at least three times each week.[4]

Of course, Ezra did not have the benefit of modern acoustics, microphones, or even the undivided attention of his congregation. Ezra stood in the marketplace surrounded by squawking chickens, braying animals, and unruly children, and competed with the sounds of life. Exaggerating the highs, lows, and cadences of normal speech, Ezra projected the holy texts in a style caught somewhere between speaking and full-blown singing.

Ezra did not read the Torah in the manner common today. In fact, it is assumed that he differentiated only the beginnings, middles, and ends of verses. The notion of chanting the Bible was an evolving one that gradually became accepted and musically more elaborate. By the second century, Rabbi Akiva (ca. 50–135 C.E.) demanded that the Torah be studied—by means of chant—on a daily basis (B. Sanhedrin

99a). Rav (third century) is quoted in several Talmudic discussions as understanding Nehemiah 8:8 (in which Ezra's public reading is described) as referring to punctuation by means of melodic cadences. Johanan (d. 279) of the Tiberias Academy is credited with fixing the notion that it is not only customary, but required, that the reader use the proper musical chant. He states categorically, "Whosoever reads [the Torah] without melody and the studies [Mishnah] without song, to him may be applied the verse (Ezek. 20:25): 'Moreover I gave them laws that were not good, and rules by which they could not live'" (B. Megillah 32a).

We must note that the biblical texts available to Ezra, to the Rabbis of the Talmud, and even through the sixth century, were like the Torah scrolls in use today: devoid of any vowels, punctuation, and grammatical indicators. Ezra and those who followed him depended upon an oral tradition for their understanding of the proper pronunciation and accentuation of the sacred texts. As chanting became more widely practiced, a system of hand signals common in the ancient Near East began to be employed. This system, called "chironomy," required an assistant to the reader to use gestures of the hand and fingers to visually illustrate the proper musical rendition of the text.

Much later, in the second half of the first millennium, a group of largely anonymous Masoretes ("conservators of the tradition") redacted the oral tradition inherited from Moses. These scholars noted the missing vowels, punctuation, and grammatical organization into the text using a set of 28 symbols called "neumes" *(te'amim)*.[5] Later the neumes were also used to provide musical direction to the reader. Simple (and sometimes more complex) melodic patterns were attached to each symbol to provide for a fully detailed rendition of the biblical text. As the system became more elaborate, chironomy became of increasing importance, since readers were now compelled to provide more sophisticated musical renditions based upon varying combinations of these neumes. Moreover, while the neumes appeared in various versions of the Bible acceptable for study purposes, it remained customary to chant publicly from a non-punctuated scroll. Chironomy remained commonplace in the time of the Masoretes and through the eleventh century and has enjoyed some renewed interest in our time.

Today, it is more common for readers to commit the musical patterns to memory, just as they also learn the proper pronunciation and accentuation. Fortunately, only the five books of the Torah and the scroll of Esther read on Purim require such memorization. The prophetic selections read as *haftarot* on Sabbaths and festivals, the Book of Lamentations chanted on the Ninth of Av, and the scrolls read on the pilgrimage festivals of Pesaḥ, Shavuot, and Sukkot (The Song of Songs, Ruth, and Ecclesiastes, respectively) may be chanted from fully notated texts.

Notwithstanding the devastation that came with the loss of Judaism's spiritual center, the new primacy of the synagogue revived Jewish worship. Synagogues were no longer second-class houses of worship, and Jewish ritual was democratized to allow for near-equal participation by all segments of the (male) population.[6] *Sheliḥei tzibbur,* literally "emissaries of the community," took turns acting as precentor, leading the gathered worshipers in prayer. But what prayers?

The Emergence of Nusaḥ

The story of the evolution of the modern prayer book is a long one on which many volumes have been written. In fact, the story continues to this day, since, unlike the Torah or Talmud, the prayer book *(siddur)* was never formally canonized. Literally hundreds of different prayer books have been compiled, and new texts continue to be issued to suit the ever-changing needs of modern congregations. What has emerged over time is a basic *matbeah shel tefillah,* an overarching core for Jewish prayer that helps to structure all services. In and around this *matbeah* are various prayers that distinguish the daily morning, afternoon, and evening services from each other, as well as from the more elaborate rituals of Sabbaths and festivals.

More germane to the subject of our inquiry is the parallel evolution of musical traditions to distinguish these same services, or sections thereof—a system known as *nusaḥ.*[7] The prayer leader utilizes prescribed scales and even melodic patterns to be sure that daily services sound different from Sabbath services; morning services sound different from afternoon and evening services; the early morning *Birkhot ha-Shaḥar* and *Pesukei de-Zimrah* (literally "blessings of the dawn" and "passages of song") sections sound different from the main body of the morning *Shaharit* service, and so forth. The proper utilization of *nusah* guarantees that a Jewish "Rip van Winkle" could sleep for 20 years and identify the service to which he had awakened just by its musical motifs.[8]

The foregoing discussion might lead the reader to conclude that Jewish services the world over represent a single tradition: All biblical passages are cantillated in a manner inherited from Ezra, while liturgical selections are governed by *nusah*. In fact, this summary is only partially correct—and a rather small part of a very complicated story.

One Bible, Many Chants–One People, Many Voices

Let's return to the subject of cantillation. We have already mentioned that different books of the Bible are read on different occasions. What was left unsaid is that the music also differs on each occasion. On the one hand, Hebrew remains Hebrew, and the neumatic patterns underlying the linguistic structure of the text remain constant from one biblical book to the next. On the other hand, the musical patterns assigned to each neume differ from one book, or occasion, to the next. We find, for example, that the chanting of Esther on Purim sounds very different from the chanting of The Song of Songs on Passover. However, The Song of Songs, Ruth, and Ecclesiastes are all chanted according to the same patterns. Since each of these is read on a pilgrimage festival, the liturgical similarities that bind those three festivals extend as well to their musical traditions.[9]

Furthermore, each Sabbath and festival service includes a prescribed reading from the Pentateuch and a selection from one or more books of the Prophets. Prophetic readings all follow the same musical patterns while differing from Pentateuchal passages. Selections from the first five books of the Bible all sound the same, whether read on a weekday, Sabbath, or festival, but the sections read on the mornings of Rosh Hashanah and Yom Kippur are chanted according to a distinctive High Holy Day mode. The Book of Lamentations, read on the Ninth of Av, is read according to its own

Liturgical Occasions and Their Associated Biblical Readings

BIBLICAL PASSAGES	OCCASION	STYLE OF CHANT
Selections from the Pentateuch	Morning services on Mondays, Thursdays, Sabbaths; all major and minor festivals (except Rosh Hashanah, Yom Kippur, and Simḥat Torah); afternoon services on Sabbaths, fast days, and major festivals	Torah Chant
Passages from Prophets	Sabbaths and festivals (following Pentateuchal readings); afternoon service on Yom Kippur and other fast days	Haftarah Chant
Esther	Evening and morning services of Purim	Esther Chant
The Song of Songs	Passover (practices vary; most often the Sabbath of Passover at morning services)	Three Festivals Chant
Book of Ruth	Shavuot (practices vary; most often morning services)	Three Festivals Chant
Book of Ecclesiastes	Sukkot (practices vary; most often the Sabbath of Sukkot at morning services)	Three Festivals Chant
Lamentations	Evening services on the Ninth of Av	Eikhah (Lamentations) Chant[10]
Excerpts from Genesis and Leviticus: final reading from Deuteronomy and opening passages from Genesis	Morning services on Rosh Hashanah and Yom Kippur; evening and morning services on Simḥat Torah	High Holy Day Chant

distinctively mournful chant. In total there are six different musical systems for reading from the Bible, all of which utilize the same grammatical neumes, as shown in the table on page 16.

We have already learned that different worship services, and even segments of services, are bound by different musical motifs. This correlates well with our understanding of the distinctions among biblical books and their renditions—but it is still not the whole story. We are not simply discussing subdivisions and variations of one unified Jewish ritual practice. In fact, there is no "one" Jewish ritual practice and there has not been since shortly after the destruction of the Second Temple.

Following the destruction of the First Temple, the Jewish people were exiled to Babylonia. Many chose to stay there even after permission was granted them to return to Jerusalem. After the loss of the Second Temple there was further exile, both spiritual and physical, that continues into the twenty-first century. Jews no longer live in one country, or even one region. During the past 2,000 years, there has hardly been a place on earth that Jews have not inhabited at one time or another, though always as a minority presence.

Constant interaction with other communities has subjected Jewish musical practice to a host of foreign influences that have left their mark on Jewish tradition. Over time, three distinct Jewish communities emerged: Separate Oriental, Sephardic, and Ashkenazic practices in ritual, liturgical, and musical custom bind Jews living (or descended from those who once lived) in countries under Arab influence, the Iberian Peninsula (and its immediate neighboring regions), and Central and Eastern Europe, respectively. Even within these broad divisions, local variations took on important significance—especially in music. Today we can count tens, if not hundreds, of versions of Jewish tradition that each community considers "authentic" and "correct." All still distinguish musically among the biblical books and liturgical occasions, so cantillation and *nusaḥ* continue to govern traditional Jewish music—but in many different forms.

Oriental Communities

In Chapter 1 we discussed the notion that the music of the Babylonian and Yemenite communities constitutes the oldest continuous Jewish tradition and that in contemporary form is a presumed link to the ancient Temple practices. To a large extent, the same could be said about the music of Jews from Syria, Egypt, Iran, and other modern Arab countries. Certainly to the ear of an untrained (Western) listener, the similarities among these musical traditions is striking, and, indeed, more unites these traditions than separates them. Bearing in mind that Jews from different communities in this region find much that distinguishes them from their cousins, we can nevertheless speak in generalized terms about the music of the Orient.

The concept of *nusah,* with its prescribed scales and melodic patterns, emerged naturally through Jewish interaction with the Arab world. The "Great Tradition" that defines Islamic musical practice is based upon an elaborate body of *makamat,* or modes. These *makamat* differentiate liturgical themes as well as specific occasions, just as *nusah* defines Jewish prayer. The custom of the Orient is to use short, somewhat repetitive phrases of limited range and predominantly stepwise motion for syllabic, musically perfunctory chanting of text. Daily services need to be short so that worshipers can focus on their busy workday routines. (How much more is this true of the Islamic faithful who are called to prayer five times each day!) This does not, however, preclude the festive use of melisma, whereby an individual word (or even syllable) will be drawn out with the intonation of many pitches. Sabbaths and festivals are occasions for more melismatic treatment of the text, since refraining from work on those occasions means more time available in the synagogue.

Example 2.1 Syllabic passage

Example 2.2 Melismatic passage

Traditionally, women and men in the Orient do not socialize together publicly, either in ritual or in secular life. The separation of the sexes has produced bodies of musical repertoire whose topics and languages are particular to the men and women who sing them.

Men sing in Hebrew (although their unique dialect is heavily accented by the surrounding Arabic). Their songs are nearly all of a liturgical or quasi-liturgical nature and are sung in large gatherings of men on Sabbath and festival afternoons. The Yemenite community has produced an anthology of religious poetry called the *Diwan* that is very popular and whose texts have been set to a variety of melodies. It is customary to sing successive verses of the same text to excerpts from several of these different tunes, so that each tune remains familiar, and so that the full renditions of what are often very lengthy poems do not become monotonous. Liturgical poetry, known as *piyyut,* is extremely popular in the Middle East, and some of the texts not included in the prayer book have gained near-obligatory status as part of home-based rituals. The chanting of table songs, known as *zemirot,* following Sabbath and festival meals has extended beyond the Oriental communities, though it is not usually as prolonged an activity in the West.

Women of the Orient generally sing in a unique Judeo-Arabic that distinguishes Jewish songs from those of the surrounding population in linguistic, if not musical, style. Women sing in small groups while they work at household chores. Some of the most famous women's songs surround life-cycle events, in which women are active, if separate, participants. Celebrations of births, circumcisions, and engagements take on extra drama through the distinctive ululation that marks the women's joy. The weeklong henna ceremonies preceding an Oriental wedding are filled with specially choreographed activities (coffee at the home of the bride's future mother-in-law, public dressing of the bride in ritual garb, and so forth) and a large body of song transmitted orally from mother to daughter.

Oriental music of both men and women makes use of a system of quarter-tones that are unknown in the West.[11] Western listeners frequently mistake the correct performance of Eastern musical passages for inexact pitch production and/or the result of the ("unpleasant") nasal quality of Eastern singers. In fact, the broader musical pallet available to Oriental vocalists results in its distinctive color that might continue to distinguish all Jewish music today, were it not for other events.

The Jews of Sepharad

One of the most significant of those events was the conquest of the Iberian Peninsula by the Ottoman Empire in 711 C.E. The Arab foray into Spain and Portugal brought Jewish immigration to those regions. The period from the 8th through the 11th centuries came to be known as a "Golden Age" in which Jewish literary, economic, and ritual life flourished throughout the region. Moorish culture defined Spanish art and architecture as well, and Jewish music continued to reflect the style of its host community.

All of that changed with the Crusades and Christian domination of Europe following the defeat of the Ottoman Empire in 1099. While this was to have distinctly unfortunate consequences for most of Jewish life, it had an interesting effect on Jewish demography and, ultimately, on Jewish music.

Life under Islam had been generally benevolent for the Jews. Recognizing the common patriarchy of Abraham (father to both Isaac and Ishmael), Muslim rulers accepted Jews as a religiously misguided, but tolerable, presence in their lands. All non-Muslims were known as *Dhimmi,* protected by the government and allowed freedom of religion, although with certain restrictions. Synagogues were not allowed to tower over mosques; Jews themselves were limited to riding donkeys instead of horses, lest they themselves tower over the

Muslim faithful. The *Dhimmi* had some obligations to their protectors—including paying taxes and providing auxiliary services to the military (in which they were otherwise prohibited from serving)—and were required to maintain distinctive dress to keep themselves recognizably separate from the Muslims. (At various times this included the wearing of yellow hats and/or badges on all clothing, a practice adopted by Christian oppressors in later years.) Such minor reminders of second-class citizenship did not generally detract from Jewish life, however, and the Jews remained loyal to their Muslim benefactors.[12]

The prospects for life under Catholicism were not so clear. Many Jews chose not to take their chances with an unknown, but potentially hostile, commodity and returned in large numbers to the Arab lands of their origin. The Jewish musical culture of these still-Oriental communities remained basically untouched by its European experience.

Other Jews chose to remain in Spain. They had lived there for generations, adjusted to the climate, owned land and other property, and felt more than geographically distant from the Middle East. How bad could life under Catholicism be?

Immediately, life changed in some very important ways. The primacy of the church in Catholic life became apparent, and while Jews continued to play an important role in Spanish economic, political, scientific, and cultural life, their status sank to a much-more-distant second place. As 1492 approached, the compulsion of Catholic authorities to enforce their own version of Church doctrine on the masses forced a further erosion of Jewish status, leading ultimately to the famous expulsion.[13]

On the other hand, the Oriental Jews who remained in Spain through most of the fifteenth century were present to witness two significant and interrelated developments in the history of music: the emergence of Western music and harmony as we know them today, and, alongside the growing power of the Catholic Church, a flowering of secular culture.

Since the first Catholics were actually liberal Jews, the development of Catholic music and liturgy was much influenced by Oriental Jewish practice. So-called Gregorian chant (named for the sixth century Pope during whose reign the music was canonized) is not far removed from Jewish chant, with its emphasis on syllabic recitation and step-wise motion. *Credo in unum dei* (I believe in one God) received a trinitarian slant in Catholic doctrine but is obviously related to the Jewish *Shema* ("...the LORD is One"), while *Sanctus, Sanctus, Sanctus* was exactly translated into Latin from its original Hebrew text: *Kadosh, Kadosh, Kadosh...*("Holy, holy, holy is the LORD God of Hosts...").

The Jewish antecedents to Catholic liturgy and ethnomusicological similarities between Jewish and Christian musical traditions were unknown to Spanish commoners of the Middle Ages. Despite the increasing convergence of Sephardic[14] *nusaḥ* and Catholic chant, occasional converts between the two religions were more likely to be distracted by the myriad distinctions separating Jews and Catholics than to have made any profound discoveries of common roots. Most others simply kept to their own side of the religious divide, without even exhibiting any real curiosity about the "other."

The emergence of secular music changed attitudes and exposures. Wandering minstrels began to appear on street corners and in the marketplace singing tales of warrior maidens, Spanish castles, and lost loves. Jewish passersby could not help but overhear these songs and assimilate their melodies into Jewish life. These folk-style songs were the inspiration for a large repertoire of Spanish *romanceros*, folk ballads in Ladino[15] recreating many of the same, totally non-Jewish stories in that uniquely Jewish combination of Spanish and Hebrew. The sounds of Spain crept into Jewish ritual life as well, providing tunes for synagogue liturgy and for home-sung *zemirot*. In one well-known example, a Ladino love song, "La Rosa Enflorece," provided the tune for the Sabbath evening poem, *Tzur mi-Shelo Akhalnu*.[16]

La ro - sa en - -flo - re - - - -ce en el mez - - - de Mai

Example 2.3 From "La Rosa Enflorece"

The rose is blooming in the month of May
My soul is clouded, distressed by love.

Tzur mi - she- lo - - - a - khal - - - -nu ba - re - khu e - - - mu - nai

Example 2.4 From *Tzur mi-Shelo*

The Rock from Whose [bounty] we have eaten! Bless Him, my faithful
friends—
we have eaten our fill and left over—according to the LORD's word.

Did the rabbis approve of this growing Jewish interest in Spanish
music? Probably not. The ban on music imposed following the
Temple's destruction had not been lifted, and any unnecessary
involvement with music was considered frivolous.

Was rabbinic approval (or lack thereof) an issue in medieval
Spain? Again, probably not, for two reasons. Since, as we have seen
above, Jewish and early Catholic (read "Western") music already had
much in common, the rabbis probably did not recognize the incursion of Spanish culture as a distinctly foreign presence. New melodies
for all manner of religious texts were constantly being produced. In
many communities it became customary for the officiating *hazzan* to
improvise both a new text and its melody, in spontaneous praise of
God. People are always products of their environment. The influence of Spanish music on Jewish ritual was probably gradual and
subconscious.

The purely secular songs, serving no religious purpose, and with
no connection to the Jewish community at all except their language,
might have occasioned some rabbinic wrath—or at least a disap-
proving frown—but for one important quality about them: Many of
the Ladino songs were sung by and for women.

Although there were certainly exceptions,[17] women in medieval
Spain occupied themselves primarily with the care of home and children. While men had reason to perfect their Arabic, Spanish, and
other languages of politics and commerce, women remained
cocooned in the exclusive sorority of other women and the Ladino
language. They sang as they worked at the cooking, cleaning, and
nurturing chores that filled their time. Ladino was primarily an oral

language,[18] and these songs became the vessels transmitting Sephardic culture from one generation to the next.

Not surprisingly, women's songs in Ladino reflected the concerns of women. The same universal experiences that define all human life—birth, love, work—found expression among the Jewish women in Spain but often with uniquely Jewish detail. Women sang graphic songs in praise of the laboring mother who had given birth to a son who would be entered into the covenant by the *mohel* (ritual circumcisor) and then grow into a learned Jew, steeped in Torah. They sang lullabies to those same sons, encouraging them to recite the *Shema Yisrael* before retiring to sleep. They yearned for spare moments in which to embroider beautiful clothing with which to honor the Sabbath. Their special efforts to prepare culinary delights for Jewish festivals are recorded in songs describing the recipe for Hanukkah *burmuelos*.[19] The traditional *Havdalah* ceremony separating the Holy Sabbath from the work days ahead concluded with a prayer for a good week—in which husbands and sons would go to the synagogue wrapped in tallit and tefillin. While Jewish women were fond of singing "foreign" songs of Spanish lovers in the hills of Cordoba and Barcelona, they also sang of their more realizable hopes: that the Jewish man of their dreams would carry them up a ladder of gold to the marriage canopy under which they would begin a life together filled with *mazal bueno* (good fortune) and happiness.

Example 2.5 From "Durme, Hermozo Hijico"

Sleep, sleep beautiful son, sleep with pleasure.
Close your shining eyes and sleep with pleasure.
You will go to school and you will learn the law.

Example 2.6 From "Scalerica de'Oro"

A ladder of gold, of gold and ivory
So the bride can go up to take her wedding vows.
  [Chorus] We've come to see, we've come to see
  May they have joy and prosper and always be happy.
The bride has no money, may they have good fortune. [Chorus]
The bride has no riches, may they have good fortune. [Chorus]

The Sephardic experience produced one other genre of song that is not only distinctly Jewish, but also unique to the Jews of Spain: songs of Jewish heroes. Life in Catholic Spain meant continual exposure to Christian festivals, including celebrations in honor of the "Saint of the Day."[20] Traditional Jews, who venerated their biblical ancestors but recognized their mortal failings, could not "compete" in this atmosphere. The Jewish community responded by creating songs extolling the virtues of figures like *Moshe Rabbenu* (Moses) that could be sung appropriately on festivals associated with the Torah and the Lawgiver (including Shavuot and Simḥat Torah). The Spanish community made a point of inserting the names of Moses and Aaron into the well-known Passover song, "Eḥad Mi Yode'a."[21] The best-known example, though, is a song that made its way into the "secular" repertoire, sung for no reason other than to express Jewish joy and pride. "Cuando El Rey Nimrod" borrows a rabbinic midrash[22] to explain the special circumstances surrounding the birth of the patriarch Abraham:

Example 2.7 From "Cuando El Rey Nimrod"

> When King Nimrod was walking in the fields
> He looked to the heavens and at the stars.
> He saw a holy light over the Jewish quarter,
> A sign of the birth of Abraham, our father.
> > Abraham, our father, dear father,
> > Blessed father, light of Israel.

The popularity of this song is attested to not only by its ubiquity in the Sephardic world, but also by the custom of the Jews of Morocco, who have contrafacted this melody and now use it for the chanting of "Shalom Aleikhem"[23] preceding the Friday evening meal.

The observation that Moroccan Jews have a particular musical custom reinforces our earlier assertion that there are many local variants within the larger traditions. In the case of Sephardic culture, the mass expulsion of the Jews from Spain in 1492 (and Portugal five years later) created a near-instant challenge to the integrity of Sephardic custom. Unlike prior exiles, in which the Jews were either sent en masse to a particular locale (for example, Babylonia after the destruction of the First Temple) or gradually made their way to any one from among a homogeneous group of neighboring countries (for example, following the loss of the Second Temple), the Jews of Iberia took a variety of routes, scattering their cultural traditions in many directions. The southern route finally took some Jews back to ancestral homes in Arab lands including Turkey and Morocco, while others landed in such disparate communities as France, Italy, Greece, Albania, and the former Yugoslavia. Those who chose a northern route were well accepted in Amsterdam, ultimately traveling from there to England, South America, and, finally, North America.[24]

The challenge for these now far-flung communities was to ensure the preservation and transmission of their cultural heritage to subsequent generations—without the aid of recording devices or even musical transcriptions. That Sephardic communities in Greece, France, and Morocco should have their own distinctive traditions comes as no surprise. Many of these local variations—from "traditional" foods to the incursion of words in Greek, French, and Arabic into the Ladino language—were directly inspired by the larger cultures in which Sephardic Jews now live. New songs in Ladino, unique to each individual Sephardic community, bear the imprint of the Jews' continuing confrontation with the larger, non-Jewish world around them.

Example 2.8 From "Mama, Mirame Las Gambas"

Mama, look at my legs, they hurt from so much dancing.
When I do the Charleston my heart is full of joy.

On the other hand, the extent to which the Sephardic communities succeeded in retaining their Spanish heritage across geographic and generational boundaries is both remarkable and enlightening. Though it was only in the twentieth century that serious research into the origins and history of many of the Ladino and other songs of the Sephardic community was begun, we can learn much from the presence of particular song themes, or even the same melody itself, among widely separated communities. When Moroccan and Turkish Jews sing songs of Spanish warrior maidens, and when Greek and Yugoslavian communities extol the beauties of Barcelona, it is clear that these songs must have a common origin in Spain, prior to 1492. While these songs have no significance to Jews of other ethnic backgrounds, there is no doubt that the tenacity of the old traditions and songs is due to the strong attachment of the Sephardic community to its special cultural history and identity.

Ashkenazic Jewry

Jews who found their way to Central and Eastern European countries are referred to collectively as "Ashkenazim," from *Ashkenaz,* the Hebrew word for Germany, whose language and culture colored the lives of Jews throughout the region. Factors affecting the music of Ashkenazic Jews are not different from those of the Oriental or Sephardic Jews discussed above; Ashkenazic Jews merely settled in different regions and were therefore subject to different musical influences. Ethnomusicological analysis of Arabic *makamat* and Eastern European prayer modes reveals some remarkable similarities. At the same time, Ashkenazic music shares much with the decidedly Eastern strains of Gypsy and Tartar communities with whom they came into contact.

Ashkenazic music also borrowed extensively from the more Western influences surrounding it. For instance, German folk ballads of the Middle Ages had a profound effect on synagogue song, providing the model for the creation—and contrafaction—of individual liturgical motives and a body of "traditional" tunes known as *mi-Sinai* melodies. Their name (literally "from Sinai") implies much greater antiquity than these tunes can justly claim, since it is known that the tunes emerged in Germany between the eleventh and fifteenth centuries. Moreover, unlike the Torah text that all Jews share (notwithstanding varying levels and interpretations of commitment) these so-called Sinaitic melodies resonate exclusively for Ashkenazic Jews. For many of them, however, the *mi-Sinai* melodies define the "correct" chants for texts including *Avot* (from the Sabbath *Amidah)* and *Kol Nidre,* and the label refers less to their purported origin than to the extent to which they have entered the hearts of Ashkenazic worshipers.

Ba - rukh a - tah - A - do - nai E - lo - hei - nu v'e - lo-hei a -vo-tei - - nu

Example 2.9 From Sabbath morning *Avot*

Kol nid - re - v' - e - sa - rei - va - ha - ra -mei v'-ko - na - mei v'-khi -nu -yei

v' - ki - nu - sei u - - - - - shevu ot -

Example 2.10 From *Kol Nidre*

Example 2.11 From High Holy Day *Ma'ariv* melody

And then there was Yiddish. Jews from Germany, Romania, the former Czechoslovakia, Hungary, or any of the former Soviet states developed many local customs and attitudes that distinguished them from each other, but they did share a common language. A merger

A Comparison of Arabic Makamat and Ashkenazic Modes

Allowing for the differences between the Oriental quarter-tone scales and the Western scales based exclusively on combinations of whole and half steps, the Arabic *makam Bayat* is virtually identical with the Ashkenazic *Magen Avot* mode (and the old Dorian church mode).

This mode is used in the Arabic world for especially joyous songs, while Ashkenazic Jews use it for a variety of occasions ranging from festive Sabbath songs to lamentations on the Ninth of Av. In one more recent example of cross-cultural sharing, a popular Palestinian song in the *Bayat* mode notated by ethnomusicologist Abraham Zvi Idelsohn (1882–1938) in the early twentieth century has "crossed over" and, in more strict metrical form, been appropriated for use as a popular Israeli folk dance:

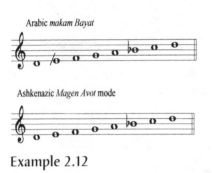

Arabic *makam Bayat*

Ashkenazic *Magen Avot* mode

Example 2.12

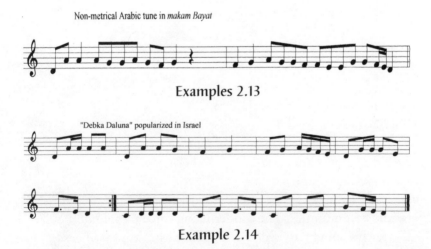

Non-metrical Arabic tune in *makam Bayat*

Examples 2.13

"Debka Daluna" popularized in Israel

Example 2.14

The Arabic *makam Siga* shares much of its tonal vocabulary with the Ashkenazic *Hashem Malakh* mode. The Arabic mode, however, behaves more like the ancient ecclesiastical Phrygian mode, while *Hashem Malakh* has the characteristics of a major scale at its lower end and the qualities of a minor scale in its upper register (that notably exceeds the traditional octave).

Arabic *makam Sasgar*, though strongly resembling the Western major scale, is used in the Orient for tunes of a serious nature. Its Jewish counterpoint, the Ashkenazic *Viddui* mode, is best known in its usage for penitential prayers, yet utilizes its major cast to affirm truth and the redemptive opportunities provided by genuine repentance.

Example 2.15

The collection of pitches known in the Arab world as *makam Hijaz,* and among Ashkenazic Jews as the *Ahavah Rabbah* mode, is distinguished by its use of the augmented second.

The distinctive sound of this interval, with its half-step resolution, is used in both communities for songs and prayers of extremely heartfelt emotion.

Example 2.16

The special poignancy of that interval seemed to express the pain, poverty, and persecution experienced by the Jewish people during their sojourn in Eastern Europe, and as such, this mode attained special popularity—especially among the

Example 2.17

Hasidic communities. The modernizing force of Solomon Sulzer and others who sought to redeem Jewish music from such excesses (see Chapter 4) took special care to eliminate the overuse of the *Ahavah Rabbah* mode in Jewish worship. As a result, this mode, while still favored within the Eastern European tradition, is virtually absent from the musical practice of western Ashkenaz.

of Middle German and Hebrew, Yiddish provided a flavor and inflection in which European Jewish culture flourished for nearly 1,000 years. It also lent a rhythm and cadence that would have a distinctive influence on the musical traditions of these regions, effectively sundering the musicological links between Jews of the East and these new residents of the West.

Like ballads of every community, Yiddish folk songs tell the human story. Tales of childhood, of loves won and lost, of poverty, of sorrow, and of joy comprise the repertoire of the Ashkenazic Jewish communities. Even beyond the songs for Sabbath and festival celebrations, some ostensibly secular songs have decidedly Jewish content. "My child will learn Torah, he'll be the writer of holy books, a good man, and a pious Jew" establishes a clearly Jewish agenda and turns a generic lullaby into an expression of Jewish values. A song lamenting the inevitability of potatoes in the diet of Eastern Europe points out that a potato *kugel* (pudding) helps to celebrate the Sabbath—and provides some relief from the monotony of impoverished, potato-filled menus.

Many other songs, though, fail to pass any test of Jewish content. "Tum Balalaika," with lyrics like, "Play balalaika, we'll all be merry" not only carries no Jewish value concept, but also poses silly riddles in a song that seems to encourage the performance of music, despite continuing rabbinic attitudes to the contrary. "Gey Ikh Mir Shpatzirn" (I Go Out for a Stroll) even mocks contemporary morality, telling the tale of a young woman who goes out (alone!) for a walk and encounters and develops a relationship with a young man.

Ge-zunt iz di bes-te skhoy - re mein kind vet ler - nen Toy - - - - re

Example 2.18 From "Unter dem Kind's Vigele"

Health is the best reward, my child will learn Torah.
He will always learn Torah, he will write holy books.
A good and pious man he will be, God wills it for him.

Example 2.19 From "Bulbes"

Sunday, potatoes, Monday, potatoes,
Tuesday and Wednesday, potatoes.
Thursday and Friday, potatoes,
Sabbath, for a change, a potato pudding,
Sunday, back to potatoes.

Example 2.20 From "Tum Balalaika"

A young man sits and thinks, thinks and thinks the whole night.
Whom should he marry, whom should he not marry?
[Chorus] Play, balalaika, we'll all be joyous.

Young lady, young lady, I would like to ask you:
What can grow, grow without rain?
What can burn without being consumed?
What can yearn, crying without tears?
   [Chorus]
Silly young man, why must you ask?
A stone can grow, grow without rain.
Love can burn without being consumed.
A heart can yearn, crying without tears.
   [Chorus]

Example 2.21 From "Gey Ikh Mir Shpatzirn"

I went out strolling....I met a young man.
He said he would wed me...but not before the summer.
The summer has come...but he hasn't wed me.
Now he finally wants to marry me...but I don't want to know him!

The music of Ashkenaz also reflects the somewhat different social and political climate of Central and Eastern Europe. Jews there never experienced the prolonged acceptance and tolerance enjoyed by their Oriental and Sephardic cousins. Rather, Ashkenazic Jews were repeatedly victimized by their anti-Semitic neighbors. More like the Oriental Jews than the Sephardim, who scattered among a variety of host communities, the Ashkenazim wandered within an essentially homogeneous area. The continuous transplantations provided a fertile arena for shared musical practices, as Jews from one region mingled with another. Such constant shifting of populations kept musical traditions in continuous evolution and resulted in multiple variants of the same basic texts and tunes.

Social factors within the community also contributed to an elasticity of musical tradition. Rabbinic prohibition on the public performance of music remained in effect but was relaxed for three occasions: weddings, consecrations of new synagogue sanctuaries, and dedications of new Torah scrolls. Since none of these occurred with any regularity in Eastern Europe, the prospects for gainful musical employment in any one town were quite dim. From at least the early seventeenth century, itinerant musicians known as *klezmorim* traveled throughout Eastern Europe, performing at celebrations within the Jewish community and outside it.[25] Since the essential requirement was that one be able to dance to the music, the listeners rarely cared what particular tunes were being played. As a result, Jewish music was performed at non-Jewish parties, while non-Jewish tunes became extremely successful at Jewish events. Eventually much of this exchanged repertoire became part of the "tradition" of the respective communities, without its origin being within the conscious knowledge of the listeners, or even the musicians who provided it.

Hasidism and Jewish Music

A combination of external events and internal Jewish politics also played a major role in expanding Ashkenazic Jewish music. One particularly difficult era in Jewish history was the period 1648–1658, during which Bogdan Chmielnicki governed Poland. Thousands were killed in vicious pogroms and the survivors were plunged into intense despair. One Jewish tradition predicts that the Messiah will arrive when the suffering of the people is at its greatest. Many felt that the time was ripe for deliverance, and thousands were convinced that it had indeed arrived with the appearance of Shabbatai Zevi,[26] who proclaimed himself the Messiah and attracted hordes of followers—only to devastate them when he converted to Islam. Reeling from their experience, his erstwhile followers—and even those who had merely stood back and observed his effect upon the community—were returned to their misery.

Adding insult to this injury was the stratification that existed within the Jewish community. Extreme poverty kept all but the very wealthy—or those whose brilliance could attract wealthy patrons—from devoting their lives to study in schools of higher Jewish learning called yeshivot. The small minority of yeshivah students represented a Jewish elite, an "upper class" of Jews, whose greater knowledge was presumed to be accompanied by greater piety and spirituality and a much better relationship with the Almighty than that to which ordinary working folk could aspire.

Rabbi Israel ben Eliezer (ca.1700–1760) stepped into the breach in the late 1730s, revealing himself as a charismatic wonder-worker[27] and champion of the average person. Combining aspects of kabbalistic thought with his own teachings, Rabbi Israel became known as the Ba'al Shem Tov, (the "owner of the Good Name") or Besht (B'Sh'T). Violently opposed by leaders of the yeshivah world and ultimately excommunicated by the Vilna Gaon[28] for his nontraditional teachings, the Besht attracted many followers with his assertion that sincerity and a strong desire to commune with the Almighty could raise one to spiritual heights.

Among the Ba'al Shem Tov's claims was the notion that music could be an especially potent medium for the expression of human emotion and communication with Heaven. The Besht shared the kabbalists' view that music was synonymous with joy, and that joy was the force that could overpower evil—including one's own evil inclination *(yetzer ha-ra)*. Words were unnecessary; a pure melody, called a *nig'n* (from the Hebrew *nigun,* "melody") could express this joy. The kabbalists taught that any human creation had a spark of divinity within it, so even a non-Jewish melody had the capacity to glow brightly if used "properly."

Example 2.22 From Nig'n attributed to the Ba'al Shem Tov

In addition to personally composing many *nigunim* still sung today, the Ba'al Shem Tov and the Hasidic masters[29] who followed him "borrowed" foreign melodies and adapted them for service to the Almighty. This contrafaction enriched the repertoire of the Jewish community both consciously and subconsciously. The entire controversy itself between the Hasidim and those who rejected their approach (called *Mitnaggedim,* literally "opposers") yielded another enrichment of the Yiddish repertoire: parody songs by leaders of the opposition that made fun of the relationship between the Hasidic rebbe and his students. In an ironic twist, the Hasidim rejected the sarcasm inherent in these songs and embraced them as their own. Subsequent generations with no relationship to either side continue to sing these songs as simply part of the repertoire of Eastern Europe.

Az der Reb-be lakht   un   az der Reb-be lakht   la-khn al-le Ha-si - dim

Example 2.23 From "Az der Rebbe"

When the rabbi laughs, all the Hasidim laugh.
When the rabbi sings, all the Hasidim sing.
When the rabbi dances, all the Hasidim dance.
When the rabbi speaks, all the Hasidim sleep.

Notwithstanding "borrowings" by *klezmorim* and Hasidim, Ashkenazic Jewish music continued to observe the rabbinic ban on music for its own sake. However, as Western music continued to evolve, the gulf between Western practices and synagogue song widened—and the challenges to Jewish musical integrity and continuity increased. A similar scenario was not being played out in the Oriental or Sephardic worlds, though. In neither of those communities did secular music undergo as fundamental an alteration as it did in the West—and therefore, neither Oriental nor Sephardic Jewish music has undergone much change. It will therefore be our challenge in the chapters that follow to explore Ashkenazic Jewry's continuing confrontation with the West and the evolution of Ashkenazic notions of Jewish musical "tradition."

3 ~
The Art of Jewish Music

Chapter 2 dealt with the emergence of three different ethnic communities and described the distinctions in textual content and musical style among the traditional songs of Oriental, Sephardic, and Ashkenazic Jews. However, much of our previous discussion has dealt with folk music: the spontaneous, anonymous creation of songs with universal appeal and simple-enough musical content to allow virtually anyone to learn and sing them. Most of what we refer to as "traditional" falls into this category, whether the music is for secular or liturgical purposes. Thus, quasi-liturgical chants from the Yemenite *Diwan,* the "warrior maiden" ballads of the Jews from Spain, and the *mi-Sinai* tunes of *Ashkenaz* are all part of our heritage of folk music.

The alternative to folk music is art music: music consciously created by one composer trained in sophisticated musical practice and normally involving one melody (or shorter melodic fragment) presented with harmonic accompaniment (either vocal or instrumental). Frequently art music involves a more complex musical structure than would be found in the typical repeating verse-chorus pattern of folk song. In the case of instrumental music, a short theme may be subjected to embellishment, variation, or other forms of development. The first-movement theme of Beethoven's familiar Fifth Symphony provides a useful example of how short musical ideas called "motives" can be developed into a satisfying work of art. The last movement of his Ninth Symphony, featuring Goethe's "Ode to Joy," illustrates the successful symphonic treatment of a melody with text. The singable theme of Schubert's Eighth *(Unfinished)*

Symphony demonstrates what can happen to a longer instrumental theme, this one a kind of song without words.

Is there art music among the Jews? Yes, but it emerged on the scene relatively recently and only in certain communities. There are two good reasons. For one thing, art music is an essentially Western creation. In the East, the melodic line is primary; harmony as we know it (the coincident sounding of two or more different pitches) does not exist.[1] Instruments do frequently accompany singers or play in combinations without vocalists, but that accompaniment is either purely percussive (rhythmic drumming, for instance, without the intonation of pitch) or duplicative (in which the melodic line is played by two or more instruments with different tone qualities). Oriental melodies are often highly embellished, with improvisatory segments woven into the fabric of a familiar tune at the discretion of the performer. The "art" of Eastern music exists in the successful manipulation of melody, and so each performance produces a spontaneous new composition unlikely to be repeated in its exact form. Surrounded as they were by Eastern musical sounds, Oriental Jews had neither "foreign" models to imitate nor reason to produce art music.

A distinguishing characteristic of art music is its existence, on at least some level, as music for the sake of the music itself. When the Rabbis prohibited musical performance after the destruction of the Second Temple, they effectively preempted the development of art music. This ruling presented no problem for Oriental Jews. They limited themselves primarily to music for liturgical, or quasi-liturgical, functions and had no conflict with rabbinic attitudes.

Jews in the West lived in a very different cultural milieu. In church-dominated Central Europe, artistic musical renderings of liturgical texts spilled over into the creation of secular choral works called "madrigals" and a variety of instrumental dance forms. By the time the Renaissance offered its musical fruits to the world, the discrepancy between Western cultural practices and Jewish tradition begged for resolution. Nowhere were rabbinic attitudes toward music found more frustrating than in seventeenth century Italy. Talented Italian composers like Palestrina and Monteverdi[2] created a national cultural climate against which Jewish musical tradition stood in impoverished contrast.

Salamone Rossi and Synagogue Choral Music

The Jews of Renaissance Italy enjoyed intermittent tolerance by various rulers of the autonomous city-states that dotted the northern province. Many achieved prominence as court instrumentalists, singers, dancers, and actors. Salamone Rossi (ca.1570–ca.1628) was the last and most distinguished example. In 1587, he began his long association with the Gonzagan Court, initially as a singer and violist. He soon became the leader of Duke Vicenzo I's court musicians and directed an instrumental ensemble probably composed of Jewish musicians.[3] He also became a leading composer,[4] pioneering the musical form known as the trio sonata.[5]

Rossi's great claim to Jewish musical fame came with his publication in 1623 of *Ha-Shirim Asher li-Shelomo,*[6] a collection of 33 psalms, hymns, and other liturgical poems set for combinations of from three to eight voices and intended for use on festive synagogue occasions. In publishing these works, Rossi relied heavily on the endorsement of his friend Rabbi Leon (Judah Aryeh) Modena.[7] Modena (1571–1648) had issued a responsum in 1605 that, after years of prohibition, provided halachically derived approval for the performance of choral works in the synagogue.[8] Modena's own choir at his synagogue in Ferrara seems to have established a precedent. But how did the music sound?

There are at least six musical traditions among the various Jewish communities of Italy, including variations of Ashkenazic and Sephardic practices. While there are substantial differences among them, all share an Eastern cast. In Rossi's day, this Eastern orientation precluded harmonization according to the prevailing Western styles.[9] Rossi was faced with two choices: Give up his goal of creating art music for the synagogue or abandon the traditional *nusah* that limited his musical options. Rossi chose the latter.[10]

An initial hearing of Rossi's music confirms the impression that Rossi "sold out" to the conventions of his day. Worse, most lay listeners would assert that his music sounds like "church music." Since much of the extant music of the period was, in fact, composed for the church, (and since many contemporary churches—as well as secular choral societies—continue to perform this repertoire), this impression is not without foundation. However, bearing in mind not only the restrictions under which Rossi worked, but also the assumption that music of the Jews has always borrowed from the surrounding culture, it is only fair to take a second look at the claim that Rossi has indeed written "Jewish music."

First, let's examine Rossi's texts. If we are willing to accept songs of warrior maidens as Jewish simply because they are sung in Ladino, then we must certainly give Rossi credit for setting traditional Jewish texts. One could argue that anything intended for use in the synagogue or Jewish ritual life must be Jewish, no matter what it sounds like. All 33 of the selections in *Ha-Shirim Asher li-Shelomo* pass this test.

Let's look at Rossi's setting of Psalm 137. This psalm, describing the exile to Babylonia after the destruction of the First Temple, is familiar to many[11] and has been set to music often by non-Jewish composers from Palestrina to the present. Interestingly, all of those non-Jewish settings limit themselves to just the first few verses of the text:

Al naharot bavel	By the waters of Babylon
Sham yashavnu	there we sat,
gam bakhinu	sat and wept,
bezokhreinu et tziyon	as we thought of Zion.
Al aravim betokhah	There on the poplars
talinu kinoroteinu	we hung up our lyres.

Other composers continue with these lines:

Ki sham she'elunu shoveinu	[F]or our captors asked us
divrei shir	there for songs,
Vetolaleinu simḥah	our tormentors, for amusement:
Shiru lanu mishir tziyon	"Sing us one of the songs of Zion."
Eikh nashir et shir Adonai	How can we sing a song of the Lord
Al admat nekhar.	on alien soil?

This picture of the Jewish nation, conquered and wailing, suits Christian theology. However, this is not the entire story. The very next verses constitute a "Jewish pledge of allegiance" (offered to this day by Israeli soldiers upon their induction into the army):

Im eshkaḥeikh Yerushalayim	If I forget you, O Jerusalem,
tishkaḥ yemini	let my right hand wither;
Tidbak leshoni leḥiki	Let my tongue stick to my palate
Im lo ezkereikhi	if I cease to think of you,
Im lo a'aleh et Yerushalayim	if I do not keep Jerusalem in memory
al rosh simḥati.	even at my happiest hour.

This is a very different Jewish people, resolute in its commitment to remember Zion (and ultimately return to her). It is no wonder that Christian composers neglected these verses—but the psalm doesn't end here either. It concludes with three of the most vindictive passages in Jewish scripture, an exhortation to the Jews not only to recover from their national trauma but also to enact punishment of those who would oppress them:

Zekhor Adonai livnei Edom	Remember, O Lord, against the Edomites
et yom Yerushalayim	the day of Jerusalem's fall;
ha'omerim aru, aru	how they cried, "Strip her, strip her
ad hayesod bah.	to her very foundations!"
Bat Bavel, hasheduda	Fair Babylon, you predator,
ashre sheyishalem lakh	a blessing on him who repays you in kind
et gemuleikh shegamalt lanu	what you have inflicted on us;
Ashre sheyoḥez venipetz	a blessing on him who seizes
et olalayikh	your babies
El ha-selah.	and dashes them against the rocks!

This is not a pretty picture. Most Jews would rather the psalm conclude with its commitment to Jerusalem. But that's not what the psalmist wanted and neither did Rossi. For the first time in history, Psalm 137 was set in its entirety. It took a Jewish composer to do it.

Psalm 137 is not an example of Rossi's best work.[12] It is, however, an example of work that could only be done by a sensitive Jewish composer.

There are other examples of Rossi's special settings of his Jewish texts. Taking just one, we can look at the opening bars of his Psalm

146. *Halleluyah,* the first word of the text, is actually a combination of two words: *hallelu,* ("Praise" in the *tzivu'i,* or commanding tense) and *"Yah,"* (one of many names for the Divine). Rossi's psalm is set in the key of A minor. If we accept the stereotypical notion that the minor mode is a "sad" one, then we should certainly switch to the "happy" major mode for the enunciation of God's name—and that is exactly what Rossi does.

Example 3.1 From *Halleluyah, Halleli Nafshi* (Psalm 146)

There is one more of Rossi's compositions that merits discussion here: his setting of *Barekhu.* This selection consists of a one-line "call to prayer" that announces the official start of the service proper,[13] followed by the congregation's response to the leader's call:

Leader: *Barekhu et Adonai hamevorakh*	Bless the LORD, the blessed One.
Cong.: *Barukh Adonai hamevorakh*	Blessed is the LORD, the blessed One
leolam va'ed	for all eternity.

Although the traditional *nusaḥ* for this passage varies from one occasion to the next, the precentor's line is always extended, literally calling the faithful to prayer with a drawn-out invitation (lest the call be so brief that one might miss it). The Ashkenazic custom for Sabbath evening is to chant an especially melismatic rendition:

Example 3.2 From *Nusaḥ* for *Barekhu* on Sabbath evening

The congregation's response, on the other hand, is normally a perfunctory, syllabic chant, reflecting the obedient acceptance of the charge to praise God (as well as the more limited musical ability of the typical congregant).

Example 3.3 From congregational response to *Barekhu* on Sabbath evening

Rossi's composition is in two very different sections. The precentor's "call to prayer" is melismatic and polyphonic. Melismatic phrases (interestingly, a frequent attribute of Eastern music) were part of the normal order of performance during the Renaissance; individual words were exaggerated through elongated articulations of several notes for each syllable of text.[14] The polyphonic (literally, "many sounds") style allowed each vocal line its own integrity; each part is musically interesting to the singer and listener, and no one part predominates over the others. The result is a layering of musically equal, semi-autonomous lines.[15]

Example 3.4 From Rossi's *Barekhu*

The one moment of this opening section in which Rossi abandons both melisma and polyphony is in his setting of the word *"Adonai."* There is only one God, and that Name must be clearly enunciated to all; even Renaissance convention allowed for clear articulation of certain texts. Notwithstanding his desire to create beautiful music, the purpose of Rossi's composition was to set a prayer text, and like all good liturgical composition, his music is always subservient to the meaning of the text.[16]

Example 3.5 From Rossi's setting of God's name in *Barekhu*

The musical alternative to polyphony that Rossi uses in his setting of God's name is "homophony" (literally, "same sound"). This style distinguished the Baroque era in the same way that polyphony characterized the Renaissance. Homophony also distinguishes the second section of Rossi's *Barekhu* from the first. The worshipers respond to the precentor's call to prayer in a clipped, syllabic chant. The congregation is as unschooled and unrehearsed in musical chant as the precentor is expert. Rossi exploits the emerging new style to distinguish the choral "congregation" from the preceding "precentor" and utilizes the homophonic style throughout the second section of the composition—that is, until he reaches the text *le-olam va'ed,* "for all eternity" (or as some translate this text, "forever and ever"). Child of the Renaissance that he is, Rossi cannot resist the urge to paint these words literally, and so he not only reverts to a more polyphonic style but repeats these words, not "forever" but three times—more than enough to make his point.

Example 3.6 From the *"congregation's"* response in Rossi's *Barekhu*

Rossi's selection of this particular text for choral performance might be considered as inappropriate inasmuch as it seems to remove the traditional roles from both precentor and congregation; in fact, it appears to render both parties mute as the chorus takes over. Unfortunately, there is little information extant regarding the manner in which this piece—or any of the other *Ha-Shirim*—was performed. It is likely, though, that the *ḥazzan* participated as a member of the choral ensemble, thus fulfilling his accustomed role.

Additional insight on this subject can be gleaned from careful examination of Rossi's scores. In his setting of *Barekhu,* Rossi notates a double bar at the conclusion of the "leader's" (polyphonic) passage, before the entry of the choral "congregation"—a clear indication of an intended break in the music. This is consistent with Rossi's practice in another setting that would normally involve congregational participation: the Sephardic *Kedushah* (known as *Keter*) in which the composer repeatedly stops the music with that same double bar and even refrains from setting texts that the congregation would have been accustomed to singing. It now becomes apparent that Rossi had no intention of appropriating the congregation's role in the service but, rather, of enhancing those portions where the precenter would have chanted alone.[17]

Similarly, in his setting of *Barekhu,* while Rossi distinguishes the style of chanting that the precenter and congregation would typically have employed, he does not appropriate the congregation's accustomed role. Instead, the choral "response" would have followed the congregation's own chanting of *Barukh Adonai hamevorakh.*[18]

In this one, short selection, we can see Rossi, the master composer, standing at the end of one musical era, (the Renaissance) and the beginning of the next (the Baroque). We also see Rossi, the proud,[19] knowledgeable Jew, making an important contribution to the Jewish community of his day and to Jewish music history as well.

Ordinarily, when one creates something of lasting import, it is imitated by others and becomes the subject of innovation and improvement in generations that follow. What impact did Rossi's music have on future Jewish composers? In the short term, none at all. All trace of Rossi disappears in or about 1628, when his last collection of songs was published. Despite the assertion (in Modena's introduction to the collection) that the *Ha-Shirim* was variously suitable for performance in the synagogue, the study hall, the house of a bride and groom, and private homes, there is no clear indication that any of the *Ha-Shirim* were regularly used in this way even during Rossi's time, let alone in the absence of the composer's urging and encouragement. Whether overnight or somewhat more gradually, Rossi's music faded from practice. In fact, were it not for the chance nineteenth-century discovery of a complete set of Rossi's part books,[20] all knowledge of Rossi's contribution to Jewish music might well have disappeared.

The Emergence of Art Music in Western Europe

On the other hand, attitudes toward artistic musical performances within the framework of Jewish communal life were gaining some limited acceptance, predominantly in other parts of Sephardic Europe. During the 17th and 18th centuries, a number of isolated musical works were written by composers of Jewish and non-Jewish origin, for a variety of Jewish texts and occasions. Between 1628 and 1639 Leon Modena headed a Jewish music academy in Venice whose extensive repertoire contributed to the ceremonies on Simḥat Torah and other festivals. In 1681 a Venetian Jewish fraternal organization called the Shomrim la-Boker (Morning Watchmen) commissioned Christian composer Carlo Grossi (1634–1688)[21] to compose a work celebrating the anniversary of its founding. The resulting *Cantata ebraica in dialogo* was set for a solo singer, four-part choir, and instrumental accompaniment. The Hebrew text takes the form of a conversation between a "passerby" (the soloist) and the "watchmen" (the

Example 3.7 From "Sova Semaḥot" chorus from *Cantata ebraica*

chorus) gathered for early morning rituals. It reveals that the organization was founded on the festival of Hoshana Rabbah[22] and is devoted to prayer and good deeds performed in service to the Jewish community. Manuscripts are also extant for Hoshana Rabbah cantatas written for a similar Zerizim[23] fraternity of Piedmont in 1732, 1733, and 1735. The complete score exists for musical ceremonies surrounding the inauguration of a new synagogue in Siena in 1786, and partial scores have also been preserved from ceremonies held there in 1796 to consecrate new Torah scrolls.

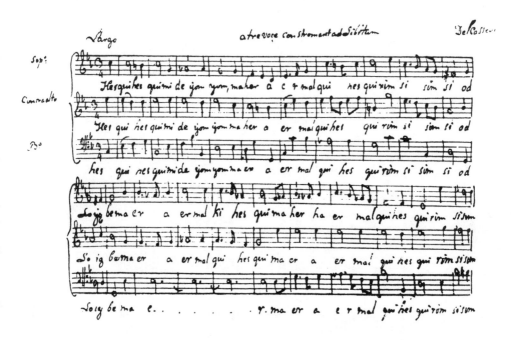

Example 3.8 From a copy of the original score for "Ḥishki Ḥizki" by Abraham Caceres

Jewish art music appears to have been performed even more extensively in the Sephardic synagogues of Amsterdam. Only textual evidence from the seventeenth century remains, but several important musical documents from the eighteenth century give testimony to elaborate art music performances for Shavuot, Simḥat Torah, and certain special Sabbaths. Celebrations of fraternities, weddings, visits to the synagogue by members of royalty, and competitions held in conjunction with the appointment of new cantors were occasions for cantatas and other important musical works. Music by a Jewish composer, Abraham Caceres (first half of eighteenth century); Cristiano Giuseppe Lidarti, an Italian gentile (1730–after 1793); and a variety of other known and anonymous composers had an important impact on the Amsterdam tradition that continues to the present.

In Southern France, a cantata known as *Canticum Hebraicum,* written by an otherwise unknown Louis (Ludovico) Saladin between 1680–1700 for the celebration following a circumcision ceremony, had a similar effect. Sections of the composition became "folklorized" over time, transformed from elaborate selections for three soloists, chorus, and orchestra to popular melodies for single-voiced congregational chant, still performed during circumcision rituals in the Comtat Venaissin district of Provence.

Example 3.9 From "Yeled ha-Yulad" in *Canticum Hebraicum* by Ludovico Saladin

Considering then-prevalent rabbinic attitudes toward music, it is remarkable that the Jewish communities of the West should have found resources and recourse to art music. It might at first seem problematic to note the prevalence of nontraditional musical styles and sounds in ritual and quasi-liturgical celebrations and ceremonies of various Jewish communities. The predominance of music by non-Jewish composers might also raise questions regarding the validity of this music as a true expression of the Jewish people. However, we have already seen that Jewish music has been influenced by a variety of outside musical forms and flavors. Since art music is an intrinsically non-Jewish genre, it is to be expected that early forms of Jewish art music would take their cues from existing models, no matter what their (theological) orientation. More impressive, though, is the fact that, despite negative reinforcement from rabbinic authorities, individual Jews should nevertheless have been driven to commission and create new forms of Jewish musical expression. At least one measure of their success is in the extent to which the masses have adapted these sometimes esoteric creations, made them their own (even in simplified form), and incorporated them into the ever-evolving repertoire of Jewish musical tradition.

4 ~

Emancipation, Enlightenment, and Evolution

The existence of art music in Sephardic Europe testifies to the somewhat liberal tendencies of rabbinic authorities in those communities to find grounds for accepting, and even encouraging, the creation of sophisticated musical forms. Equally necessary to these developments were the relatively benign social climates in those regions that allowed some Jews to develop the human and material resources necessary to mount their sometimes-elaborate musical productions.[1]

Neither of these conditions existed for the Jews of Ashkenaz. The rejection by the *Mitnaggedim* of the Hasidic notion that music could play an important role in the emotional and devotional life of the Jew illustrates the rigidity with which traditional, negative views of the role of music were upheld in mainstream Ashkenazic rabbinic circles. Just as significantly, the Jews of Central and Eastern Europe had neither the opportunity to learn the craft of music nor the wherewithal to produce serious performances. Jewish folk music gave expression to communal values embodied in holiday observances and personal celebrations, but it also reflected cultural, as well as financial, impoverishment, exacerbated by the twin realities of omnipresent anti-Semitism and political disenfranchisement.

But at least for the Jews of Central Europe, many of the conditions and limitations on Jewish life and culture changed as a result of the French Revolution. The *liberté, egalité,* and *fraternité* won by the French proletariat was extended to Jewish residents of the realm, and the changing political tides soon washed onto German shores as well. Jews enjoyed the educational as well as political benefits of the more open society. They crowded into universities and conservatories that had been closed to them in the past and quickly took up important roles in intellectual and cultural society. The coincident dissolution of the *kehillah*,[2] by means of which the Jewish community had governed itself since the Middle Ages, led to a significant weakening of rabbinic authority over the masses. For the first time since the destruction of the Jerusalem Temple and the termination of Jewish autonomy in Israel, Jews could claim individual citizenship in a state. Many turned their backs on the religious establishment and embraced secular society with a vengeance. Participation in all aspects of Jewish religious life declined, and while some chose to simply disengage from the Jewish community, others rejected it completely and converted to a Christianity that, in then-modern society, imposed few obligations while offering the blessing of full membership in "the real world."

It should come as no surprise that many in the rabbinic establishment chose not to accept the new status quo. Still, some were forced to concede that, by comparison, the isolationist attitudes and arcane rites of Jewish tradition could not compete in the open marketplace of freethinking ideas and unending political, economic, educational, and cultural opportunities. In particular, ancient Jewish ritual practices stood in pale contrast to the enlightened modern church. The church offered participatory rites punctuated by the singing of moving hymns by the congregation and impressive performances by professional choirs singing the glorious music of Bach and Mozart—complete with stirring instrumental accompaniment. The synagogue offered unaccompanied Eastern chants known only to a limited inner circle of "whining" *ḥazzanim*, recited in an antique, literally backward, and virtually incomprehensible language. How could Judaism hope to compete on such a stage?

The only possible answer was to reformulate Judaism to suit the sensibilities of the modern era. That meant an overhaul of ritual—and especially music. First to go was traditional *nusaḥ*. The replacement of much of the Hebrew liturgy with prayers in the vernacular (German or French) made it easy for the reformers to demand new musical settings of these texts. In some cases, new melodies were composed. When the "new" texts were actually vernacular treatments of Old Testament psalms that had already been set by church musicians, synagogue reformers had no problem inviting these settings into the Jewish service. Chorales and hymn tunes by Christian as well as Jewish composers mingled indiscriminately in the reformed temples.

Example 4.1 From "Allgegenwart" (Omnipresence) included (without attribution) in a hymnal published in Stuttgart in 1836[3]

God is in the heights, also in the depths is the LORD.
Where people beg to Him; where the angels look, He is there.
What I think in my thoughts close to me, from all limitations it
    is free.
In every space He enclosed the world with His hands
And all their ends were created by Him.

This new appreciation for the importance of music in contemporary ritual life led to innovations in musical presentation that extended well beyond language or choice of melody. By the early nineteenth century, Jewish day schools included music reading and part-singing in their curricula, enabling a better-trained laity to take an active and sophisticated role in congregational singing. Academies trained new synagogue professionals in modern music theory and harmony, replacing the *ḥazzanim* of old. In the mode of Johann Sebastian Bach, *kantor* of his Leipzig church, Jewish "cantors" became officiating soloists and music directors who presided over choral performances, complete with organ accompaniment.

The principle underlying these radical revisions in Jewish musical practice was clear. With greater access to secular musical styles and performances, Jewish congregants now expected their music to rise to the level of the surrounding culture. Unfortunately, merely replacing traditional Jewish musical chants and chanters with more modern fare did not guarantee quality. Bach, the prototypical *kantor*, was a genius; not everyone who aspired to Jewish musical leadership could be expected to be a beautiful singer, a talented conductor, and a master composer! Moreover, there was a noticeable price to pay for abandoning tradition. *Nusaḥ* had provided a form and structure to synagogue ritual, helping to define the Jewish seasons. In addition, despite regional variations, the homogeneity of Ashkenazic musical tradition guaranteed that travelers—or displaced populations— could find accustomed rituals anywhere they went. The abrogation of time-honored Jewish liturgical practice created musical anarchy, with little of serious enough quality to compensate for the loss of spiritual succor once offered by familiar tunes.

The Contributions of Solomon Sulzer

Solomon Sulzer (1804–1890) single-handedly changed the course of nineteenth-century Reform musical practice. Born into a traditional Austrian household, Sulzer enjoyed the dual advantages of home-based familiarity with ancient Jewish musical custom and the secular musical training available in his time to a young Jew with musical talent.[4] Sulzer began his cantorial career at the age of 16, officiating in his native Hohenems, then ascending to the position of chief cantor of the Great Synagogue in Vienna in 1826. That prominent position, combined with his beautiful singing voice, brought him great renown within the Jewish community and beyond. Sulzer became a favorite performer in the salons of Vienna, coming to the attention of Franz Schubert and Franz Liszt.[5] Liszt overcame his own anti-Semitism to visit the synagogue in order to hear Sulzer preside, and pronounced himself spiritually moved by the experience.[6] Schubert's untimely death in 1828 at the age of just 31 cut short his association with the younger musician. However, Schubert became close enough to Sulzer to accept his invitation to write a composition for the synagogue. Schubert's setting of Psalm 92, *Tov le-Hodos,*

Example 4.2 From *Tov le-Hodos* by Schubert

appeared in the first volume of Sulzer's magnum opus, *Schir Zion,* published in 1840.

Sulzer recognized the need to modernize Jewish musical practice. Left to his own preferences, he would have gone much further in promulgating such reform. However, Sulzer also recognized the role *nusaḥ* had played in synagogue life, and he respected the desire of the masses to hold fast to the *mi-Sinai* melodies that pervaded so much of the liturgy. Thus, his solo passages remained largely faithful to the traditional Ashkenazic modes, but were purged of the operatic excesses that had crept into much cantorial practice in the previous century. In his choral writing, though, Sulzer straddled the roles of reformer and conservator. Constrained by still-prevailing harmonic conventions, Sulzer abandoned conventional *nusaḥ* and wrote in the style of his times, often reminiscent of the music of his friend, Schubert (though rarely approaching its quality). At the same time, in several instances Sulzer felt compelled to create a new *nusaḥ,* composing works for the entire musical calendar in hopes that his unique melodies for Sabbaths, festivals, and other liturgical occasions might come to replace the motives of the previous era.

Ironically, some of Sulzer's best-known and most ubiquitous melodies were actually intended to be used as special ceremonial fare. Sulzer's "Torah Service for Festivals" provides a prime example. Among the texts included in that service are the Jewish credo, *Shema Yisrael* ("Hear, O Israel, the LORD our God, the Lord is One") and *Ki mi-Tziyon* ("For out of Zion shall come the Torah, and the word of the LORD from Jerusalem"). The setting of each of these short texts opens with an identical motive:

Shema yis- ra - el
Ki   mi -tzi - yon

Example 4.3 From opening motives of *Shema* and *Ki mi-Tziyon*

Sulzer expected this motive to be heard only in conjunction with the Torah service on the pilgrimage festivals of Pesaḥ, Shavuot, and Sukkot. He could not have anticipated that these two melodies would become so beloved—albeit in folklorized fashion—that they would become regular parts of daily worship. However, Sulzer's singing was envied by his cantorial contemporaries, who went to great lengths to emulate his personal dress, his hair style, and even his gold-topped walking stick. The publication of *Schir Zion* made it possible for them to sing his music, if not approach his ability as a singer. Indeed, *Schir Zion* filled a significant vacuum in Reform musical practice. Before long, Sulzer's music was being heard throughout Europe, and his melodies, sans choral accompaniment, even crossed the barrier into traditional synagogues.

Most cantors—and their congregants—were eager to make new music by a Jewish composer a part of their services, but not all cantors were capable of adapting. Prior to the nineteenth century, *ḥazzanim* either learned their craft by rote, absorbing the sounds of the synagogue through their regular attendance there or, at best, studying with a senior *ḥazzan* (usually a father or uncle). Music theory, choral conducting, accompanying skills, and even music reading were not abilities that one tended to pick up "along the way." Asher Lion (1776–1863) of the Reform temple in Berlin was one such "*ḥazzan-cum*-cantor." While his beautiful singing pleased his congregants, they were eager to hear Cantor Sulzer's music in their temple—but Lion could not read the music. Fortunately for him, Louis Lewandowski was available to help him.

Louis Lewandowski Continues the Reforms

Louis Lewandowski (1821–1894) was born in Poland. Following his mother's untimely death when he was 12, Louis was sent to Berlin with letters attesting to his musical aptitude, but with little money. He became a *singerl*,[7] singing soprano for Asher Lion, and he enjoyed a warm relationship with the veteran *ḥazzan,* but he had no desire to follow him into Jewish music. Fortunately, through Lion, the young Lewandowski came to the attention of Alexander Mendelssohn, a cousin in the famous Mendelssohn family,[8] who recognized the youth's talents and agreed to finance Lewandowski's musical studies in Berlin. Indeed, Lewandowski, who excelled in his studies at the Berlin conservatory and actually ranked first in his class, hoped to become "the Jewish Mendelssohn," a successor to the renowned non-Jewish musician.[9]

With the furor over the publication of Sulzer's *Schir Tzion,* the Orthodox Asher Lion was forced by popular sentiment to bring the new music into his synagogue. Unfortunately, Sulzer's music was published in four clefs,[10] and poor Lion, with only limited musical skills, was barely able to read just one clef. Lion remembered his young *singerl,* now studying in Berlin, and implored him to solve the "mystery" of Sulzer's music. Lewandowski wisely transcribed Sulzer's music into the treble clef that Lion could manage and agreed to help Lion direct his new chorus. When the veteran Lion retired, his congregation engaged a talented younger *ḥazzan,* Abraham Jacob Lichtenstein (1806–1880), to succeed him. Lewandowski was then called upon to provide choral arrangements for Lichtenstein.

Two stories compete to explain Lewandowski's decision to commit his time and energies to the music of the synagogue. According to one, Lewandowski actually suffered a nervous breakdown that brought his conservatory studies to an end and forced him to look for a nondemanding, part-time job to support himself during his recovery. In another story,[11] Lewandowski complained to his teacher about the time his synagogue work was taking from his quest to become a composer of secular, symphonic music. This teacher is said to have discouraged Lewandowski from aspiring to the stature (and talent) of Mendelssohn and instead urged him to do what he could for Jewish liturgical music. However it happened, the match between Lewandowski and the synagogue could not have been more fortuitous; Louis Lewandowski's first claim to fame is as the first Jewish choral director.

Lewandowski's ambition drove him beyond the role of mere interpreter of someone else's work; his own compositions demonstrated his excellent training and (notwithstanding his teacher's apocryphal criticism) his exceptional talent. Although Lewandowski studied with Sulzer for six months, the younger musician's work departed significantly from that of the older master. For one thing, Lewandowski was not a cantor. While he had great understanding and sensitivity for that role (and a keen sense of the practical reality that guaranteed his employment as long as his patron cantor's vocal talents were sufficiently displayed), Lewandowski favored the choral medium in his work. He demonstrated great affinity for the traditional melodies of his youth (of which he was constantly reminded by immigrants from Poland who sought the more tolerant social climate of emancipated Germany), and his harmonic style and gift of melody were appealing to a broad public. The young musician also exhibited a spirit of innovation that satisfied the most ardent reformers of his time.

Lewandowski was lured away from his studies with Sulzer in Vienna by the invitation to become choir director of the new Oranienburgerstrasse Shul in Berlin. (Lichtenstein was appointed cantor there at the same time.) The permanent installation of an organ in that refurbished Berlin temple, complementing liturgical reforms authored by Abraham Geiger,[12] provided Lewandowski with further inspiration. He was among the only Jewish composers of his time to truly understand the complexities of writing for the organ, and his skill in that regard became a vital aspect of his work.

During their overlapping lifetimes, Lewandowski was largely eclipsed by Sulzer's personal power and significant achievements. Sulzer's prominence as a cantor of exceptional vocal prowess cast him onto center stage, while Lewandowski's role as choral conductor was essentially behind the scenes. Ironically, the timing of Sulzer's major publications both contributed to and coincided with the transitions in Lewandowski's life: As noted above, the 1840 publication of *Schir Zion*'s first volume created the original need for a choral conductor; the 1866 publication of *Schir Zion*'s second volume provided a new flood of music that guaranteed that Lewandowski's early years in his new position of choir director would again be dominated by the music of Sulzer. The younger composer had ideas of his own, though, and interspersed his work among the compositions of the elder master. Among his major works, *Kol Rinah Utefillah* (for one and two voices, 1871), *Todah W'simrah* (for four voices, soloists, and optional organ accompaniment, 2 volumes, 1876–1882), and *18 Liturgische Psalmen* (for solo, choir, and organ, n.d.) contained music for the entire liturgical year. Indeed, Lewandowski's music has survived on an equal footing with Sulzer's and has enjoyed the same backhanded, if well-intended, compliment: Melodies by Lewandowski have been folklorized into common usage by worshipers across the full spectrum of ritual practice.

Example 4.4 From *Od Yenuvun* in the conclusion of Psalm 92 by Lewandowski

Naumbourg and French Reforms

While the political roots that led to Jewish emancipation had first taken hold in France, liturgical reform there took a backseat to activity from its western neighbor. The winds of German ritual innovation did ultimately blow into France, and Paris became a center of musical change, chiefly through the person and activity of Samuel Naumbourg (1815–1880).

Naumbourg was born in Bavaria, a descendant of nearly 10 generations of South German *ḥazzanim*. He received his music education in Munich and sang in the synagogue choir of Maier Kohn.[13]

After serving as a choirmaster in Strasbourg, Naumbourg arrived in Paris in 1843. In 1845, through the direct intervention of noted opera composer Jacques Fromenthal Halevy,[14] Naumbourg was appointed first *ḥazzan* at the synagogue in Rue Notre-Dame-de-Nazareth. There he was authorized by the French government (as well as the synagogue officials) to conduct a thorough reform of liturgical music practices that had fallen into disorder following the 1832 death of Israel Lovy, the synagogue's last well-known *ḥazzan*.

Naumbourg was interested in preserving the synagogue's (and his own) traditional practices while effecting significant modernization. His 1847 *Zemirot Yisrael* includes volumes for the Sabbath and the High Holy Days; Volume 3, *Hymnes et Psaumes* was added when the work was reissued in 1864. Many of the selections, for *ḥazzan* and two-to-four-voice choir (with some organ accompaniments), are based upon traditional material, often from Naumbourg's native south Germany. Other selections and arrangements include melodies by his predecessor Lovy, as well as compositions by his contemporaries Halevy and Jacob Meyerbeer.[15] (Works by the latter, as well as Naumbourg's own works in their style, bear a more-than-passing resemblance to the Parisian grand opera then popular.) Naumbourg also published *Aguddat Shirim* in 1874, a collection of traditional synagogue melodies that included some western Sephardic material as well as a long preface on the history of Jewish religious music. Naumbourg's reputation as a scholar was further augmented by his 1877 publication (with Vincent D'Indy) of Rossi's work under the title *Cantiques de Salamon Rossi.*

This combination of conservation, scholarship, and innovation earned Naumbourg great popularity in his era. Indeed, his influence at the time was comparable to that of Sulzer and Lewandowski. The relatively smaller size and comparative isolation of the French Jewish population from the larger Ashkenazic Jewish community yielded lesser renown for its adopted son. However, Naumbourg's music remains a pillar of the French synagogue today, and some of his more grandiose compositions are staples of the concert repertoire in the West.

By the time of their deaths in 1880, 1890, and 1894, the music of Naumbourg, Sulzer, and Lewandowski, respectively, had transformed synagogue music in Central Europe. Not only were the

Example 4.5 From *Se'u Shearim* by Naumbourg

reforms popularized by their rabbinical collaborators firmly entrenched in the ritual psyche of the synagogue, but the music of these three giants of the nineteenth-century synagogue—in one form or another—had found a permanent place in the repertoire of Western congregations of all philosophical perspectives. Although the political climate that permitted such innovation had not spread eastward, the external influences that had affected the music of Central European synagogues—art song and opera in particular— were no less familiar and popular in the major Jewish communities, especially in Russia. Somewhat later and less dramatically—but no less impressively—Jewish musical traditions in Eastern Europe also confronted the modern era.

Modern Synagogue Music in Eastern Europe

Baruch Schorr (1823–1904) brought the music of Sulzer to his synagogue in the Hasidic heartland of his native Lemberg. After beginning his career as a child singer with the choirs of Bezalel Schulsinger and Yeruchom Blindman,[16] he served a Bessarabian[17] congregation as cantor from 1846 to 1848. Following a series of other positions, Schorr returned to Lemberg in 1859 and served there until 1890. In that year, the versatile composer appeared on stage to take a bow following the performance of his Yiddish operetta, *Samson*. In the uproar that followed, Schorr was suspended from his Orthodox congregation for a period of four weeks, a reprimand that offended him so deeply that he left for New York, where he served the Attorney Street Synagogue for five years. The Lemberg community eventually missed his improvisations and the innovative choral compositions that had so stirred their emotions and invited him back. Schorr returned to Lemberg in 1896 and served there until he died while officiating at services on the last day of Passover, 1904. During his last years, the talented composer also penned commentaries on the Pentateuch *(B'chor Schorr)* and Ecclesiastes *(Yisron L'chochmah)*.

Nissan Blumenthal (1805–1903) was the first to adopt Western ways, utilizing a smooth bel canto[18] style that replaced some of the coloratura and other excesses of his contemporaries. Blumenthal, self-taught during his early years in Iasi, Romania, accepted his first cantorial position in Berdichev in 1826. Jewish settlers from Brody, Galicia, organized the first *chor-schul* (choral synagogue) in Odessa in 1840 and engaged Blumenthal as their first chief cantor. The coincident publication of Sulzer's *Schir Zion* spurred the popularity of four-part singing. Blumenthal's music emphasized the inspirational and emotional qualities that Hasidic music had stressed in other Eastern

European corners, but without the cantorial excesses that had lowered musical standards in the region. Indeed, Blumenthal's music is generally considered to have raised the standards of synagogue song in Russia.

Example 4.6 From *El Erekh Apayim* by Schorr

Blumenthal was succeeded at the Broder Shul in Odessa by Pinchos Minkowsky (1859–1924). Born into a distinguished family with musical and scholarly roots, Minkowsky sang in his father's choir as a youth but was urged to become a rabbi. He ultimately combined his musical and Jewish knowledge by becoming a cantor in his native town of Belaya Tserkov (Ukraine) in 1875. He contin-

Example 4.7 From *Avinu Malkeinu* by Blumenthal

ued his musical studies with Nissan Spivak (1824–1906), a leading exponent of the "classical" Eastern European synagogue song, and later studied with teachers of voice, counterpoint, and composition. Minkowsky briefly served congregations in Kishinev and Kherson in Bessarabia before arriving in Odessa in 1884, only to depart for a five-year stint in America. Minkowsky returned to Odessa in 1890 and remained with the Broder Shul until about 1919, before permanently immigrating to the United States. While his scholarly contributions to Jewish music eclipsed his musical talents,[19] the installation of an organ and the creation of a women's chorus during his association with the Broder Shul made a lasting impact and clearly established the music of reform in Eastern Europe.

The choir director at the Broder Synagogue under both Nissan Blumenthal and Pinchos Minkowsky was David Nowakowsky (1841–1921). Nowakowsky was born in a small village near Kiev and sang in the *chor-schul* in Berdichev for ten years, during which time he studied harmony, counterpoint, and composition. Nowakowsky was appointed choirmaster in Odessa in 1870 but was stifled somewhat during the early part of his career by personality clashes with Blumenthal. His association with Minkowsky (to whom he also taught harmony) was more fruitful, and during this period Nowakowsky realized his full potential as a conductor and composer.

Example 4.8 From *Ḥatsi Kaddish* for Friday evening by Minkowsky

Example 4.9 From *Pesaḥ Lonu Sha'ar* by Nowakowsky

While both men espoused a commitment to the purity and dignity of synagogue music, their reforms imposed significant change on the traditional service.

Nowakowsky published relatively little of his music. *Shire David,* with music for the *Kabbalat Shabbat* service, and *Shire David-Tefilot Neilah* (1895) contain only a small number of his compositions. Indeed, there are those who challenge the suitability of his often lengthy works for the synagogue. One of his best-known compositions, *Adonai Zekhoronu Yevorekh,* while written for the *Hallel* service on the pilgrimage festivals, has actually enjoyed its greatest popularity on the concert stage. Still, Nowakowsky is regarded as among the most "Europeanized" of the Eastern European composers and contributed much to the westernization of synagogue music within the Pale of Settlement.

The last, and by some accounts, the finest of these Russian reformers was Eliezer Gerovitsch (1844–1914). The Kiev-born composer remained in his hometown studying traditional Jewish texts and general studies until 1862, at which point—and against his family's wishes—he traveled through Berdichev and Odessa and became an apprentice to Cantors Spitzberg (a pupil of Sulzer) and Blumenthal. Through them, he became acquainted with the repertoire of the classical German synagogue, including the music of Sulzer and Lewandowski. Gerovitsch ultimately enrolled in the St. Petersburg Conservatory and received a thorough music education, including harmony and counterpoint. With his exceptional tenor voice, Gerovitsch was appointed to the coveted post of chief cantor of St. Petersburg, but the harsh climate there had a deleterious effect on his health and his voice. In 1887, Gerovitsch moved to the less prestigious—but healthier—post of cantor in Rostow-on-the-Don and remained there until his death.

Gerovitsch's published works—*Shirei Tefillah* for Sabbath, pilgrimage festivals, and the High Holy Days; and *Shirei Zimra* for Yom Kippur and the New Year—demonstrate his solid musical training and originality. In particular, his music uniquely combines the Eastern European traditions of *minhag ashkenaz* (despite his earlier exposure to more westernized fare) and the Russian nationalist tendencies he learned at the conservatory. In this manner, Gerovitsch, while writing exclusively for the synagogue, anticipated the activities of the next generation of St. Petersburg students who would complete the transition of Jewish music to the realm of art music and the concert stage.

Example 4.10 From *Tal Ten* by Gerovitsch

5 ~

From Kodesh to Concert:
Jewish Music Confronts Modernity

Whether in sporadic appearances in Sephardic Europe or in its emergence in some innovative temples, through the early twentieth century the incidence of composed art music in the Jewish community remained clearly linked to Jewish religious life. The limited number of formally trained Jewish musicians either plied their trade in entirely secular spheres or, as we have seen, intersected with the Jewish community only for ritual purposes. The enhancement of life-cycle ceremonies and enrichment of synagogue services did nothing to overcome the rabbinic bias against the creation of music "for its own sake" that was in place since the destruction of the Second Temple, nor did it generate either a demand or an audience for any other form of sophisticated Jewish music. Those Western European Jews who, in increasing numbers, did succeed in winning places in conservatories and later on concert stages, did so by estranging themselves, at least professionally, from their religious roots.[1]

Despite the adoption by some synagogues of some of the reformist tendencies (and the new "classical" synagogue compositions) the Jews of Eastern Europe never benefited formally from the political or social freedoms enjoyed by their Western brethren. Indeed, in Russia, most Jews were limited to residence within a Pale of Settlement,[2] and only individuals with particular skills and/or political connections could gain entrance to the cities and the educational and cultural opportunities they offered. St. Petersburg and its surrounding region was one of these restricted areas, and by the beginning of the twentieth century the few Jews who won entry to the prestigious St. Petersburg Conservatory were eager to take their places in Russian society and culture and to become the next generation of Russian composers. Forces both within and beyond the Jewish community would intervene, however, and several Jewish composers found their plans radically shifted.

As we have seen, the political emancipation afforded to the Jews of Western Europe led to a Haskalah, an intellectual "enlightenment," and a clamor for educational opportunities that had been heretofore denied them. In certain circles such exposure led some to drift away from traditional Jewish life in efforts to embrace—and be embraced by—secular culture. With their recently bestowed citizenship papers in hand, many Western European Jews sought to participate fully in the commercial, social, and political lives of their new homelands. Unfortunately, those newly minted legal documents were often not enough to overcome centuries of anti-Semitism, and some of the most talented Jewish intellectuals and artists (including those who underwent conversion) often found their energies and interests rebuffed by an in-bred, "pure-blooded" society.[3]

If Western countries that had wholeheartedly (at least on paper) acknowledged the equal rights of all their citizens could reject Jewish participation in the arts and politics, then it should come as no surprise that Eastern Europe, which continued to view the Jews as a "problem" was less than enthusiastic about welcoming them into mainstream cultural life. An infamous solution to the "problem of the Jews" was reached by Czar Alexander II, who sought to exile one-third of the Jews of Russia, forcibly convert one-third, and kill the final third. The privileged few who won coveted berths in Russian universities and conservatories quickly lost any illusions about the majority's feelings toward them. Rejected by the Russian establishment, many utilized their new training in history, anthropology, and other social sciences to create a form of Jewish "nationalism" inspired by similar introspective undercurrents sweeping throughout Europe. This new Jewish movement sought out the roots of Jewish civilization and found them in the music and literature of the people—the "folk."

Early Ethnography

In 1898 historians Saul Ginsburg (1866–1940) and Pesach Marek (1862–1920) placed notices in three widely read Russian-Jewish journals seeking contributions to a definitive collection of Jewish folk songs. Neither possessed any professional interest or training in music, but they recognized that the "history of the Jews in Russia" that they sought to produce would require inclusion of such cultural artifacts. There had been isolated earlier attempts to gather Jewish folk songs,[4] and a variety of Jewish and non-Jewish composers had utilized Jewish folk songs in their work.[5] As long as Jewish life appeared to flourish (if only in the small towns and villages of the Pale), the propagation of the people's music through time-honored oral/aural transmission had been sufficient to guarantee its survival. As the nineteenth century drew to a close, the combination of revived anti-Semitic violence and the migrations that followed brought that survival into question.

In response to this perceived crisis, Ginsburg and Marek's call for artifacts elicited contributions of items from throughout Russia. It is not clear whether they had ever intended to publish the words and music together, but as musical items were received, they were turned over to Joel Engel (1868–1927) for his editing and consideration. By 1901 the pair had brought out their important collection as *Jewish Folksongs in Russia,* containing 30 pages of introductory material by the editors, 320 pages of song texts, and a 14-page bibliography compiled by one S. E. Weiner. Engel published his *First Album of Ten Jewish Folksongs* in 1905.

The three friends previewed their ethnographic work much earlier, however, in a public program presented under the auspices of the music division of the Imperial Society for National Science, Anthropology, and Ethnography. The lecture/concert was presented at the Moscow Polytechnic Museum in November 1900, with Marek presenting the literary aspects of the songs and Engel lecturing on the music. Soprano Fanny S. Vachman of the Moscow Conservatory sang Engel's arrangements of the songs, accompanied by Engel's wife at the piano.

Aside from winning critical praise in the Russian and Yiddish press, the program was important in many ways. The setting provided a dignity and scholarly respect for the Jewish folk song that it would not otherwise have earned. Moreover, its venue attracted an audience that was largely not Jewish. The warm reception and semi-official sanction accorded these songs belied the snobbish disregard this music had heretofore received among the Jewish intelligentsia. It also provided Joel Engel with the inspiration and incentive to pursue his interest in Jewish folk song and to continue speaking on its behalf. Engel, a graduate of the Moscow Conservatory and a well-respected music critic for a leading Moscow newspaper, *Russkaya Vedomosty,* had himself participated in an anthropological expedition into the Jewish backwoods of Russia during the summer of 1897. Now that his interest in transcribing and arranging these obscure Jewish tunes had been validated, he became an eager exponent of the music. In April, 1901 Engel repeated the format of the Moscow program, this time in a small hall at the St. Petersburg Conservatory with Ginsburg sharing the podium and bass-baritone Joachim Tartakov singing the musical illustrations.

The audience in attendance at the St. Petersburg lecture was quite different from that present at its Moscow premiere. The material presented held special interest for a group of Jewish students from the local conservatory, especially Ephraim Skliar (1871–1943). Unlike many of his fellows, Skliar was the son of a cantor and spent his youth singing in synagogue choirs and officiating as cantor in his hometown of Slutzk (Minsk province). At the age of 12 the young singer was enticed to join an itinerant cantor in his travels. By the time his voice changed, Skliar found himself in Warsaw where, eager for more systematic musical training, he prepared himself for entrance into the Warsaw Conservatory. Skliar entered the school in 1890 and promptly switched his major from bass violin (the only instrument that did not require a rental fee) to theory and composition. His teacher Zygmunt Noskowski[6] was better known for his anti-Semitism than for his skills as a composer, but in time, he, too, recognized that Skliar was the star of his class.

In 1894 well-known Russian composer Mily Balakirev[7] arrived in Warsaw to participate in a tribute to Polish composer Frederic Chopin and to inspect some of the local schools. Two of Noskowski's students were invited to show their work to the visiting composer, but Skliar was not among them. Two other students of Noskowski's recognized the injustice done Skliar and took it upon themselves to arrange a private meeting for him with the visiting master. Balakirev was enormously impressed with Skliar's work and urged him to come to St. Petersburg to study there with Rimsky-Korsakov. When Skliar expressed concern about securing the necessary permits to study outside the Pale, Balakirev was momentarily nonplused (having never suspected Skliar's Jewish origins—and not particularly welcoming the knowledge) but instantly recovered and resolved to make the proper arrangements. Several years passed, during which Skliar assumed the entire encounter had been forgotten, but in the end both travel papers and expense money arrived from Balakirev.[8] Skliar quickly became a favorite at the St. Petersburg Conservatory, and his work even came to the notice—and approval—of the much-respected, Moscow-based composer Sergei Taneiev.[9]

Skliar's story is interesting because he neatly interwove an early immersion in Jewish musical and ritual life with his later secular musical studies. The resulting juxtaposition of these two poles produced his lingering interest in Jewish music and, on the heels of Engel's presentation, Skliar's 1902 efforts at the Conservatory to form a Jewish music club known as *Kinor Zion* (Lyre of Zion). In that same year, Skliar arranged a Yiddish song called "*Farn Obsheyd*" (Bidding Farewell) for Rimsky-Korsakov's composition class. The teacher spent an entire session analyzing and praising the work, at the conclusion of which he is said to have turned to his Jewish students and remarked, "Why do you imitate European and Russian composers? The Jews possess tremendous folk treasures. I myself have heard your religious songs, and they have made a deep impression upon me. Think about it. Yes, Jewish music awaits her Jewish Glinka."[10]

Example 5.1 From "Farn Obsheyd"

I must bid you farewell, I cannot speak, it is already time for me
  to leave.
My hope is that there lies ahead, a bright new way for both of us.
The people will one day revere us, as we stride like heroes.
We will soon find happiness in that dear, Holy Land.
Good fortune has bound us together, in our lives there will come
  a time
The wounds of our exile will be forgotten, we will be free from
  bondage.

The Society for Jewish Folk Music

Skliar's graduation from the Conservatory in 1903 postponed the
realization of his dream to create a Jewish nationalist school, but
Engel's repeated visits to St. Petersburg kept the idea alive among the
Jewish students at the Conservatory. In 1906, Skliar (who remained
in St. Petersburg as choral director of the local synagogue) was joined
in his vision by new student Lazare Saminsky (1882–1959), and
plans for a formal organization began to develop. Soon additional
students, including Solomon Rosowsky (1878–1962), Michael
Gniessen (1883–1957), and Alexander M. Zhitomirski (1881–1937),
shared their zeal, as did folklorist Susman Kisselgof (1876–after
1930) and a variety of other professional and avocational musicians
and music enthusiasts.

By 1908, the group decided to apply to General Drachevsky, gov-
ernor of the city, for legalization of an organization they hoped to call
The Society for Jewish Music.[11] Rosowsky, Nesviski-Abileah, and
Tomars were designated to present their case, but the general
received them without sympathy. "What, a society for Jewish music?
Is there such a thing as Jewish music?" he retorted.

Rosowsky had received a law degree from Kiev University before
turning to music and he took it upon himself to make the appeal. He
described the Jewish folk song and pointed to its use by a variety of
respected Jewish and non-Jewish composers, including Glinka and
members of the Russian nationalist school, the *Kutchka*. Thus
prompted, the general reconsidered, recalling that he had "heard a
Jewish melody once in Odessa at a Jewish wedding," and suggested
that the group should call themselves *Die Gesellschaft für Jüdishe*

Volksmusik, The Society for Jewish Folk Music. The petitioners realized that they had perhaps lost a small battle but had indeed won the
war, and The Society for Jewish Folk Music was born.[12]

The Society set itself an ambitious agenda. The members vowed to
continue research on the Jewish folk song (sacred and secular), to create harmonizations of the melodies they uncovered, and to promote
and support composers working in the field. To accomplish these
goals, members of the Society resolved the following: to help publish
compositions and papers on research in Jewish music; to organize
musical meetings, concerts, operatic performances, lectures, and so
forth; to organize a choir and orchestra under its auspices; to establish
a library of Jewish music; to issue a periodical dedicated to Jewish
music; and to sponsor contests (and award prizes) to encourage the
composition of music "of a Jewish character."[13] With permission to
form chapters in cities across Russia (in accordance with local laws),
the Society was eager to spread its work throughout the country.

Two main committees governed the Society's work. An
Administrative Committee was responsible for securing the considerable financial support needed to accomplish all of the Society's
goals. Responsibility for reviewing new compositions and deciding
which would be published and/or performed fell to the Society's
Musical and Arts Committee.

As secretary, Israel Okun successfully solicited grants from the
Baron Guinsbourg family and the Bund;[14] subscriptions to the
Society's musical publications, concerts, and lectures were also sold.
These were of interest to a wide audience that went beyond musi-
cians. Playwright and ethnographer Shlomo Anski, poet Mordecai
Rivesman, Jewish culture enthusiast and later YIVO curator Mendel
Elkin, and the critic Isaiah Knorosovski were all included on the
Society's membership roles. Yiddish poet Y. L. Peretz (1852–1915)
offered encouragement from the sidelines, as did Alexander
Glazunov and Anatole Lyadov (teachers at the St. Petersberg
Conservatory) and *Kutchka* member Cesar Cui.

The group's initial publications were issued in 1909: Ephraim
Skliar's four-part choral settings of the folk song, "Di Gilderne Pave"
(The Golden Peacock) and Imber's poem "Hatikvah" were among
the earliest. Its first concert was held in a small hall at the St.

Petersburg Conservatory. Some 150 concerts followed in the next two years, presented by small ensembles of instrumentalists and vocalists organized by the Society, coached by Society composers, and primarily performing Society members' music in programs presented within and beyond the Pale and as far off as Leipzig, Königsberg, and Budapest. By 1912 the Society had published 33 works and an anthology of collected folk songs and had sponsored five major concerts featuring such renowned artists as violinists Jascha Heifetz and Ephraim Zimbalist, cellist Joseph Press, and vocalist Feodor Chaliapin. In addition, its membership roster boasted 389 members—two-thirds in St. Petersburg and the rest in other Russian cities. By 1913, formal chapters of the Society had been established in Kharkov and Moscow, with an Odessa branch founded the following year (chiefly inspired by the work of Cantor Moshe Rudinow and his wife, Ruth Leviash).

The Moscow chapter of The Society for Jewish Folk Music had a strained relationship with its northern neighbor. While Joel Engel's work had to a large extent ignited the fire that led to the Society's creation, the Moscow chapter in which he played a guiding role remained somewhat in the shadow of the original St. Petersburg group. A certain "creative tension" existed between the two groups, largely a reflection of the temperaments that were said to characterize the conservatories in each city. St. Petersburg was criticized by its detractors as being too "intellectual," while the Moscow Conservatory was described as "overly emotional." Indeed, there appeared to be a real disagreement regarding the "worthiness" of music proposed for publication by the Moscow branch, and the Society's publishing arm never did publish any music by Moscow-based composers.[15]

The seemingly petty bickering between these two important chapters belied a much more fundamental issue: What, indeed, constituted Jewish music? Saminsky and Rosowsky, of St. Petersburg, came to advocate for the cantillation motifs as the cornerstone of a unique Jewish musical oeuvre. Engel and the Moscow school favored the indigenous folk song as a reflection of the people, though without particular regard for the regional provenance and Jewish authenticity of the melodies they uncovered. In truth, none of the composers could be credited with taking an especially careful approach to their collection of Jewish music materials. On summer trips home during conservatory vacation periods, many composers (from both schools) sought out "reliable informants" in the heart of the Pale (yeshivah students, old men and women, itinerant musicians) and notated their melodies, largely without benefit of recording technology. One better-organized (but not necessarily more scientific) expedition headed by Susman Kisselgof was sent into the Vitebsk and Kherson regions. The material recovered was partially included in the Society's *Song Collection for the Jewish School and Home* (1911) and partially turned over to individual composers for their own use.

Creating a New Genre

The resulting use of the material by Society members betrayed the real source of their interest in it: the inspiration it could provide for the creation of secular Jewish art music. The earliest settings of these songs, while faithful to (at least one version of) the original melody, flirted shamelessly with becoming freestanding compositions. Strophic songs (those with a simple, repeating verse), which in their natural habitat would have been rendered either unaccompanied or with the most perfunctory of predictable harmonies, found themselves set in a sort of "theme and variations" treatment that only a trained composer could have envisioned or executed.

Rosowsky's arrangement of "Lomir Zikh Iberbetn" (Let's Make Up) is a good example of the artistic setting of a traditional song. The melody satisfies all the "requirements" of a good folk song: a narrow range to allow for singing by most consumers and sufficient musical simplicity and repetition to make it memorable after a limited number of hearings. The song speaks to a universal situation in which the singer, one of a pair of quarreling lovers, is now eager to resume the relationship. This selection also expresses particularly Jewish content, both by making familiar Jewish references in its original Yiddish text and by utilizing the distinctive *Ahavah Rabbah* scale stereotypical of Eastern European Jewish song both outside and within the synagogue.

Example 5.2 From "Lomir Zikh Iberbetn"

Let us forgive one another, light the samovar.
Let us forgive one another, don't be a fool.
Let us forgive one another, buy a pair of oranges.
Let us forgive one another, let us go dancing.
Let us forgive one another, let us not fight.
Let us forgive one another, we'll enjoy each other.
Let us forgive one another, I will be your groom.
Let us forgive one another, there will be happiness and rejoicing.

The first verse of the song is set quite simply. The piano accompaniment, generally falling on the second half of the beat, is reminiscent of the style of the folk musicians through whose performances the song would have gained its original popularity. The subsequent verses are stylistically more sophisticated, with occasional harmonic variation (especially in the third verse) betraying the composer's involvement. Still, the song never entirely loses its original charming character.

Joseph Achron's (1886–1943) "In a Kleyner Shtibele" takes even more primitive melodic material as its subject. The poem is in the style of a children's nursery rhyme, and the melody is childlike in its simplicity. The "verse" of the song limits its range by outlining just the first four notes (and lower seventh) of the *Ahavah Rabbah* scale. The "chorus" uses an even more limited motive, moving back and forth between just two adjacent notes in a sing-song chant reminiscent of many children's songs.

Example 5.3 From "In a Kleyner Shtibele"

> In a little cottage lives an old woman with her seven children, all of
> them quite strange:
> With such noses, with such eyes, with such ears, with such heads,
> With such hair, with such beards, with such stomachs, with such feet,
> with such hands.
> They eat nothing, they drink nothing, they just dance, jump, and
> sing songs
> About a witch, about a sorceress, about a dragon, about a black
> magician.
> Let us play together, children, let us dance together, children.
> Let us sing together, children. What? A little song!

Unaccompanied, "In a Kleyner Shtibele" is barely worth noticing. Nothing but an anthropological expedition would have brought it to the composer's attention. Once discovered, however, this simple song became raw material for a brief but impressive setting by a talented and creative composer. Achron chose to not alter the original tune, instinctively recognizing that any tampering with the melody would irreparably alter its folk character. Instead, the modest melody is supported by a remarkable piano accompaniment—one divorced both rhythmically and harmonically from the original tune. The resulting work is clearly rooted in the folk tradition and, simultaneously, a major artistic step away from it.

Example 5.4 From an accompanied version of "In a Kleyner Shtibele"

The members of The Society for Jewish Folk Music had only limited interest in existing folk material. After all, they reasoned, a composer is only fully creative when he or she is free to explore uncharted musical waters. At the same time, though, the Society faced a unique problem in setting out to develop a new musical genre: How will the music be clearly Jewish if it is also completely original?

In the case of the earliest art songs, composers were able to rely upon their texts to retain their connections to the Jewish community. Yiddish—and, in the nationalistic spirit of the historical moment, occasional poetry in Hebrew—gave these new works a special appeal for their audiences. When the content of the song, in addition to its language, was also uniquely Jewish, questions regarding its "authenticity" could effectively be laid to rest.

The Compositions of Moses Milner

Moses Milner (1882–1953), the source of a number of such "new Jewish songs," is among the least well known of the Russian-Jewish composers—both because he was one of the few who remained in Eastern Europe and because he eschewed personal publicity. His proclivity for writing music that resonated with Jewish life seems to have been based upon the traditional experiences of his early years.

The young Milner (changed from Melnikoff) was orphaned at the tender age of eight. His fine alto voice brought him to the attention of the famous cantor Nissan Belzer (1824–1906), with whom the boy traveled for two years, apparently acquiring some rudimentary musical knowledge along the way. Milner was later associated with the Brodsky Synagogue in Kiev[16] where he sang under the direction of Abram Dzimitrovsky. Following the loss of his youthful voice, Milner was briefly apprenticed to an engraver, but soon returned to the Brodsky Synagogue, where he was put in charge of the synagogue's music collection. Milner also began studying piano with Dzimitrovsky and ultimately entered the Kiev Conservatory in about 1902. With financial assistance from Baron Vladimir Guinsbourg (whose wife had adopted one of Milner's sisters), Milner entered the St. Petersburg Conservatory in 1907, where he studied piano, harmony, counterpoint, and instrumentation. He completed his studies there in 1914.

Susman Kisselgof encouraged Milner's association with The Society for Jewish Folk Music, which published his setting of *Unsane Tokef* from the High Holy Day liturgy in 1913. Concerts of his works were presented at the St. Petersburg Conservatory in October,

1917 and in November, 1921. Joseph Achron assisted in the June 1922 production of another all-Milner concert that was performed by the State Philharmonic. His opera *The Heavens Aflame* was briefly mounted with the composer as conductor at the State Opera in Leningrad in 1923,[17] and Milner later served as musical director of the Jewish State Theatre in Kharkov from 1926 to 1931. Despite focusing almost exclusively on music for the Jewish community, Milner appears to have remained in favor among the Soviet officials, at least through April 1948, when an article in the now-defunct Yiddish newspaper *Eynikayt* spoke highly of him.

The other works by Milner published by The Society for Jewish Folk Music include some of his original, highly "nationalistic" songs, though these appear to date from the period of his earliest formal studies in Kiev, circa 1902–1906. Among these is his setting of Bialik's "Unter die Grininke Beymelakh"[18] and the much better-known "In Ḥeder" set to Milner's own text. "In Ḥeder" captures the relationship between an aging rebbe and his young student on the latter's first visit to religious school. Such a vignette was familiar to residents of the Pale, as was the ubiquitous *lernsteiger,* the singsong chant of the European yeshivah with which the teacher urged his pupil to "learn Torah."

ko-metz a- lef aw   ko-metz beys baw   ko-metz gi-mel gaw   kaw-metz da-let daw

Example 5.5 From the *lernsteiger:* used in Milner's "In Ḥeder"

By employing this traditional motif, and of course with such a quintessentially Jewish experience as its subject, Milner effectively mutes the critical question of "how can original music be Jewish?" At the same time, the intimate interplay between voice and piano in this largely through-composed[19] song demonstrates that Jewish story-telling can be elevated to the ranks of high musical art.

Jewish Instrumental Music

The first composers to create Jewish instrumental music were not able to rely upon Jewish subjects or even Jewish languages to tell their stories. We should therefore not be surprised that the earliest instrumental works published by the Society rely heavily on pre-existing folk melodies to make their connections to the Jewish community. Alexander Zhitomirski's 1909 arrangement of "Dem Rebben's Nigun" (The Rabbi's Melody) and Lazare Saminsky's "Hasidish" (Hasidic Dance) in the same year are little more than adaptations of folk songs, their lyrics displaced by the violin's voice. By 1912, Joseph Achron completed "Hebräische Viglied" (Hebrew Lullaby) and "Hebräische Tanz" (Hebrew Dance), both of which also relied heavily upon pre-existing folk melodies. However, these works possess a level of sophistication and originality that the earlier works do not reach and so are more deserving of examination.

Achron's "Hebräische Viglied" is inspired by "Unter dem Kind's Vigele" (Under the Child's Cradle), so well known in Eastern Europe that it was the "Rock-a-Bye Baby" of its time.

Example 5.6 From "Unter dem Kind's Vigele"

Under the child's crib stands a little white goat.
The little goat went off to trade in raisins and almonds.
Raisins and almonds are very sweet.
My child will become healthy and strong.

Following a brief, somewhat brooding piano introduction, the violin intones the melody in a sparse rendition faithful to the tradi-

Example 5.7 From the last verse of the "Hebräische Viglied"

tional tune. At the same time, this first articulation is somehow distant from the original folk song—missing the rhythmic variation required by the text and lacking in the warmth that would normally accompany the familiar words. The piano accompaniment retains the dark quality of the introduction, harmonically supportive of the melody, but completely unobtrusive. In sum, what we hear is a kind of raw theme, ripe for variation in subsequent renderings.

While not dramatically different in tone, the second appearance of the melody has the piano and violin engaged in a kind of canon, with the tune played first on the piano and echoed by the violin in a higher register, this time with melodic and rhythmic embellishment. The end result of this "duet" is a feeling of greater passion and movement, leading logically to the next "verse." The third and final version completes the melody's development from humble folk tune to full-fledged art song. Here, Achron, himself a master violinist, joins his expertise as an instrumentalist with his talents as a composer, producing a virtuosic violin solo in which the violin plays a duet with itself (in a range an octave higher than the prior two verses), supported by constantly rippling sixteenth notes in the piano accompaniment. The listener has heard the song through three progressively involved performances, each straying further from its roots, yet never completely divorced from them.

Achron's "Hebräische Tanz" is based upon much more complex raw material. The traditional melody quoted in the first edition by *Die Gesellshaft für Jüdishe Volksmusik* is in three distinct segments:

Example 5.8 From the original source material for "Hebräische Tanz"

In this ambitious composition, Achron remains inspired at all times by some portion of the traditional tune, but he does not feel compelled to quote it sequentially or even literally. The prelude, falsely leading the listener to anticipate a somber composition, is based upon the opening figures of the second and third segments. The piano quotes the first motive in unison octaves; then the violin impressively intones the opening theme of the third segment in octaves and fifths. The piano repeats its opening figure and then echoes the violin's quotation—but with the fuller chords (five voices) of which only the piano is capable. Seemingly embarrassed by its own diversion, the piano returns to its own motive. Then, as if to demonstrate that it will indeed be the predominant instrument in this composition, the violin launches into an elaborate cadenza derived, for the first time, from the second half of the second theme. Only after cascading nonmetrically from its highest register through a sequence of descending figures does the violin, seemingly exhausted by the early burst of passion it has already displayed, give in to the delightful, truly dancelike opening theme.[20]

What follows this deceptive opening is a simple, yet satisfying statement of the first and second themes, articulated in a traditionally symmetrical AABBAA pattern. If this were to be merely an artistic arrangement of a folk song, the recapitulation of the A section would have literally repeated the original material. However, Achron hints that much more is to come by varying the style and complexity of the accompaniment and by moving the violin's statement to a higher octave. After repeating the closing figure of section A several times (either reluctant to let it go or determined to get every bit out of it possible!) the violin surrenders musical primacy to the piano that "sings" the B section and then returns again to section A—all under an impressive, distracting, yet melodically insignificant violin part.

The segments we have so far described set the stage for the composition's second half: The violin steals back our attention in a brief, suddenly slower, minor-tinged variant of the original theme, creating another deceptive "introduction." It then enters the final section of the composition, which is based on the "third" melodic theme introduced in the opening prelude. This segment, once again truly dancelike, is only briefly treated in a folk-style manner. The distinctive opening motive and running sixteenth notes quickly become the inspiration for a series of melodic sequences, cumulatively propelling the pitches higher, the pace quicker, and the solo violin role ever more flamboyant. While the original melody disappears in the race to the finish, it remains a source of melodic and harmonic inspiration, imprinted figuratively, if not literally, on every aspect of the impressive conclusion.

Example 5.9 From "Hebräische Tanz"

Cantillation As Inspiration

However creative and artistic Achron's early compositions may be judged, they are still clearly beholden to the traditional folk material on which they are based. In later works, Achron and his fellow

Society members sometimes divorced themselves from preexisting materials, substituting folklike melodies and themes—newly composed, perhaps, but clearly reminiscent of simple songs from the past. Others found cantillation motives a better, more "authentic" source of inspiration while at the same time allowing for freer interpretive use of traditional material.[21]

Example 5.10 From "Schir Haschirim"

"Schir-Haschirim" (The Song of Songs) by Lazare Saminsky uses the exotic chant of the Georgian Jews as its inspiration and, indeed, its sole melodic component. Quoting the opening verses of King Solomon's love poetry,[22] the song is characterized by a simple chanting of the text, punctuated by a sparse (though harmonically interesting) piano accompaniment. The composer indicates that the song should be sung in a recitative style, and it is notated without meter, retaining the ad libitum quality of traditional chant. The limited range of the melody, covering only five notes (a sixth note, the highest in the piece, is touched in a brief climax toward the end of the song) results in a necessarily repetitive quality to the music, also reminiscent of the recurring patterns of cantillation.

Samuel Alman's[23] (1877–1947) "Haftarah" also takes its inspiration from cantillation, but is much less rigid in its adherence to familiar motifs. Alman's composition, for violoncello and piano, is influenced by the Ashkenazic tradition of intoning prophetic books in a minor mode, but he only rarely quotes directly from recognizable motifs. (The distinctive descending phrase called for by the neume *darga* is the sole exception.) Instead, Alman utilizes the short melodic phrases typical of liturgical chant to recall its spirit. The listener, encouraged by its descriptive title to hear the synagogue chant in this brief composition, is not disappointed.

The extent to which Jewish musicians "should" feel obligated to include traditional Jewish musical materials in their work is a question that we will revisit as later composers grapple with it throughout the twentieth century. Clearly, however, the invention of "Jewish art music" made the concert stage a comfortable home for the Jewish musician. Interestingly, at the same time this new genre was being created, Jewish performers were taking their places on another kind of stage—with musicians of The Society for Jewish Folk Music working behind the scenes and in the orchestra pit. The Jewish theater became a potent force in the Jewish community and, as we shall see, a fertile meeting ground for many players in the Jewish cultural arts.

Example 5.11 From "Haftarah"

6 ~

All the World's a Stage:
The Story of Yiddish Theater

As dramatic as the history of the Jewish people has been, Jews have not been a theatrical people. Biblical writings can at times be quite literary, yet even the most "dramatic" of them—the Book of Job, with rich dialogue among its characters—fails to reach the level of true "theater." The first real "spectator events" were products of Greco-Roman culture that the rabbis uniformly abhorred. Circuses were filled with buffoonery and sacrifices to pagan gods, while sporting events featured naked athletes glorifying the human body. Greek tragedies featured incestuous relationships among humans and their various deities.[1] It is not surprising that the Rabbis of the Talmud specifically forbade Jewish participation in such public displays. Furthermore, Rabbinic condemnation of such fare found its way into contemporaneous midrashim[2] ascribing similar attitudes to biblical figures. One story concerns Joseph during his time in Egypt and depicts a certain Nile festival. During featured theatrical presentations to which the masses flocked, Joseph is described as having returned "to the house to cast up his master's accounts" (Genesis Rabbah 87:7) rather than attend the performances.

Apparently women were particularly forbidden to attend shows of any kind. Another midrash illuminates the dialogue between Naomi and her daughter-in-law Ruth. Ruth is reminded that joining the Jewish people means a significant change in her lifestyle since, as Naomi points out, "it is not the custom of the daughters of Israel to frequent theaters and circuses" (Ruth Rabbah 2:22).[3]

The Maccabean War (167 B.C.E.) appears to have largely wiped out Hellenistic influences on the Jewish community in Palestine.

During the following century, however, Herod reinstituted such forms of entertainment and built various amphitheaters in major cities throughout the country, including Jerusalem. These were clearly gentile institutions, however, and not representative of Jewish culture. By the second century C.E., tragedy passed out of vogue, to be replaced by crude comedies that sometimes ridiculed Jews and their customs. The Rabbis' hostility to such developments led them to prohibit Jewish construction workers from even helping to build the stadiums and theaters where these productions were mounted (Avodah Zarah 16a).

There were apparently some less pious members of the community who rejected the Rabbis' stance. Some fragmentary evidence exists of tragedies based upon biblical themes written by one Ezekiel of Alexandria during the first century B.C.E., perhaps in an attempt to distract Jewish audiences from more overtly pagan productions. Josephus, a Roman-Jewish historian (ca. 38–after 100 C.E.), mentions a first-century Jew known as Alitirus of Rome who was reportedly among Caesar Nero's favorite performers. The sarcophagus of an actress named Faustina found in Roman catacombs of the first or second century features Jewish symbols and the word *shalom* (peace) in Hebrew. More surprisingly, the third-century rabbinical scholar known as Resh Lakish (Simeon ben Lakish) is said to have earned his living as a circus strongman (Bava Metziah 84a, Gittin 47a).

Much later, Jewish actors were apparently popular in court pageants and other dramas staged in Renaissance Italy. Mantua became a center for such performances, and its Jewish community of 2,000 apparently provided and paid for various forms of entertainment (with Friday performances scheduled early so as to end before the Sabbath). By 1525 the participation of Jews in various state performances was considered a given. However, despite such Jewish involvement in foreign productions (and their presumptive presence in the audiences), theatrical performances mounted by Jews, for Jews, did not appear on the horizon until well into the Renaissance. Dramas based upon biblical and apocryphal themes were written by Spanish exiles in Italy and Holland; some isolated Jewish plays were also written in Portuguese. The first Hebrew play to be published was *Asirei Tikvah* (Prisoners of Hope), written by Joseph Pensa de la

Vega in 1673. The Bible figured prominently in the Romantic poetry of Moses Chayim Luzzato (1707–1747), and his followers wrote historical dramas on Marranos as well as biblical themes through the end of the eighteenth century.

The *Purimshpiel*

The only dramatic works to enjoy widespread appeal and rabbinic approval were *purimshpiele,* beginning with unorthodox retellings of the story of Esther in which a foolish king and his evil henchman bent on destroying the Jews are outsmarted by a Jewish queen and her wise uncle. The biblical book is read in the synagogue at the evening and morning services on the joyous festival of Purim, but without the usual decorum expected during religious rituals. Tradition dictates that the name of the villain Haman be "blotted out" by making loud noises every time his name is mentioned,[4] a practice that leads to a rather raucous atmosphere. A festive meal is served on the afternoon of Purim, at which time revelers are also encouraged to drink until they cannot tell the difference between the good Mordechai (Queen Esther's uncle) and the wicked prime minister Haman.[5] This confusion is furthered by the additional custom of masquerading on Purim.[6]

The roots of the *purimshpiel* lie in public celebrations in honor of Purim noted as early as the fifth century.[7] In a region near Antioch, the holiday was observed with rowdy gatherings where participants sang, told jokes, and hanged Haman in effigy before burning "him" in a bonfire. Suspecting that they were rude disguises for a reenactment of the crucifixion, Emperor Theodosius II ordered these festivities stopped in 408, but the Jews apparently ignored the command rather than give up their beloved celebrations. By 415 rumors spread that, in lieu of dummies, Christian children were being burned. Predictably, this led to a pogrom that wiped out much of the local population—and their Purim festivities.

In medieval Europe, the revelry of parading yeshiva students bore clear signs of influence by the local Christian community. Ancient Greek festivities at the same season had celebrated a goatlike divinity, and now headdresses featuring goat horns became associated with

Purim, as well as with the Christian Shrovetide[8] and Mardi Gras. When "formal" Purim plays began, apparently in the sixteenth century, they shared some of the characteristics of Christian mystery plays.

Purim plays reached their fullest flowering in seventeenth- and eighteenth-century Germany, with special resemblance to German Shrovetide plays called *Fastnachtspiele*. Just as Christian mummers, carolers, and *Fastnachtspieler* went through the streets to entertain, *purimshpieler* often burst, unannounced, into their neighbors' homes to make their presentations. In small towns, three or four revelers might perform; in the cities, groups of up to 30 included musicians in their shows. Crowding into the dining rooms of wealthy ghetto residents, the troupes performed for pennies, brandy, and cakes.

The oldest published *purimshpiel* text, printed in Frankfurt-am-Main, dates from 1708 and is, indeed, a retelling of the Purim story. While the Esther drama was an obvious favorite, *purimshpiele* also took their inspiration from other Bible stories. Dramatic episodes like the sacrifice of Isaac, the sale of Joseph, the destruction of Sodom and Gomorrah, Moses' confrontation with Pharaoh, and the encounter between David and Goliath were all sources of inspiration. Occasionally secular plays took the place of biblical dramas: A 1588 comedy called *The Scholar and the Devil* was apparently based on the Faust legend[9] and vignettes featuring a "gypsy wedding" or "the gypsy and the bear" remained popular throughout the nineteenth century. More often, however, such scenes were merely interludes in the telling of biblically based tales, a blending of the sacred and secular that was common in European folk theater. These more elaborate shows would also feature musical interludes—as well as slapstick "fights,"[10] comic sketches, and acrobatic displays with no connection whatever to the principal story but featuring some of the traveling clowns, mimes, and acrobats who entertained villagers in marketplaces throughout medieval Europe.

Contemporaneous European plays made frequent use of "stock characters" who would appear—out of any necessary dramatic context—in virtually every play. Descended from the ancient Roman masks and the Italian commedia dell'arte,[11] such roles as the phony wise man or "quack" doctor (Dottore), the old man attempting to maintain his authority over a younger man or wife (Pantalone), the cowardly soldier masking his fear with false bravery (Capitano), and the servant who outwits his master (Harlequin) became fixtures in European comedy from the Renaissance through the nineteenth century. These characters, portrayed by troupes touring across Germany and Poland, became favorites among Jewish audiences and often appeared in *purimshpiels*. It was not uncommon to see the likes of Goliath depicted as the soldier Capitano, while King Ahasuerus merged into Pantalone. Even the sainted Mordechai was sometimes transformed into Prince Mondrino or Mondrish, the Court Fool (both from the Polish *mondry*, meaning "clever.")

Jewish Wedding Entertainers

While Purim-theater was the only "formal" performance sanctioned, there were other occasions when members of the Jewish community sought distraction from their often-impoverished and generally oppressed daily lives. The positive obligation to rejoice with a bride and groom outweighed the negative injunction to mourn the loss of the Jerusalem Temple, and so wedding celebrations came to require the accompaniment of musical merriment. Itinerant folk musicians, *klezmorim*, entertained the wedding party and their guests. The most fashionable affairs also featured an assortment of clowns engaged to entertain the assembled guests as social commentators, jesters-in-residence, and general masters of the reception ceremonies. The *lets* (an ancient word appearing in the Talmud and related to the modern Hebrew word for clown, *leytsan*) and *narr* (German for "fool") were the silliest of performers, spewing strings of rhyming-but-nonsensical dialogue (I bought a pear, dare, prayer…) while taking farcical pratfalls and drumming each other over the head with the equivalent of rubber chickens. The *marshelik*, dressed in military garb, with a much more serious demeanor, functioned as a kind of emcee, entertaining through talmudic *pilpul*, sophisticated wordplay and elaborate attempts to draw connections between apparently unrelated points of law. The *badh'n* was among the most versatile of performers, able to contrive extemporaneous sermons, often in rhyme, filled with allusions to biblical stories and talmudic law. His specialty was making the bride and her female guests cry with tales of the burdens of married life, only to return the entire assemblage to laughter with improvised commentaries on the reception itself and comical insights into the wedding guests and the relationships between the two newly linked families.

Abraham Goldfaden: Father of the Yiddish Theater

These fragmentary Jewish entertainments came together under the impresario's touch of Abraham Goldfaden (1840–1908). Born Avrum Goldinfodim in Volhynia, Imperialist Russia, Goldfaden had what may be termed an "enlightened" Jewish upbringing. His watchmaker father, Khayim Lipeh, sent him to a czarist public school so that he would not be among the many young Jewish boys conscripted into the Russian army. In 1857 Goldfaden enrolled in a government-endorsed rabbinical seminary in Zhitomir, Ukraine, where he was exposed to Hebrew and Yiddish literature, liturgical chants, and religious folk songs, as well as more traditional Jewish texts.

From childhood, Goldfaden had enjoyed singing and reciting poems and progressed to performing songs and poetry at local weddings. Goldfaden learned to write his own poetry, stories, and songs reflecting Jewish culture while in Zhitomir, and he benefited from exposure to the Russian-Ukrainian, French, and Italian drama being performed in local theaters. When the head of the Zhitomir rabbinical school, Hayim Selig Slonimsky, married a well-educated woman from Warsaw, Goldfaden worked with her on the script of Solomon Ettinger's *Serkele*, [12] which she brought with her to the school. Together, she and Goldfaden arranged a public performance of the work, with Goldfaden playing the title role. [13] This experience had a profound effect on Goldfaden—one that would impact on the rest of his life.

Goldfaden had little musical training, but his reliable memory and wide exposure to a wealth of traditional Jewish melodies stood him in good stead. He began to write for Hebrew and Yiddish journals and published collections of his own poetry in volumes called *Tsitsim U'ferakhim* (Blossoms and Flowers) in 1865 and *Dos Yideleh* (The Little Jew) the following year. Goldfaden set excerpts from one poem, "Dos Pinteleh Yid " (The Essence of Being a Jew), to an old Yiddish tune, and years later it was featured in Jacob Gordin's *Gott, Mensh un Toyfel* (God, Man, and Devil, or the Jewish *Faust*). Another poem, a satirical Sabbath song, parodied Hasidic ideas and became popular among students at other yeshivot before being published as an anonymous folk song.

In 1866 Goldfaden graduated from the seminary and was sent to teach in Simferopol. However, he soon joined his well-to-do uncle in Odessa. While Goldfaden tutored students, performed as a *badḥ'n* at local weddings, and attended many local plays and concerts, his cousins played his tunes on the family piano and notated his many songs and poems. Goldfaden also appeared in private productions of Yiddish plays. In 1869 Goldfaden published his next collection, *Dos Yideneh* (The Little Jewess), which, in addition to more songs, contained the texts of two short plays: *Tsvey Sh'khnos* (Two Female Neighbors) and *De Mumeh Susyeh* (The Aunt, Susyeh). These early publications gained Goldfaden increasing recognition, and his songs began to be taken up by other performers.

In 1875 Goldfaden traveled to Lemberg, in Galicia, intending to study medicine, but he soon returned to performing and writing. After several failed publishing ventures, Goldfaden made his way to Iasi, Romania, in 1876. There he met Yisroel Grodner (1841–1887), a Yiddish entertainer[14] who had been performing Goldfaden's material along with works by the popular *badḥ'n,* Eliakum Zunser (1836–1913). Grodner was skilled in the use of costumes and props and also concluded his performances with a dance (regardless of the tenor of the material). Goldfaden began to collaborate with Grodner, soon adding more music to the productions, as well as a stronger story line with dialogue. Yitschok Joel Linetzky (1839–1916), a friend from his days in Zhitomir, was also in Iasi at the time and encouraged Goldfaden to pursue this work.

Grodner's routines featured a stock character of his own making, *freylikher ḥusid'l* (merry little *ḥasid*) for whom Goldfaden wrote poetry and songs based on his earlier works. Grodner and Goldfaden soon hired Sacher Goldstein (1860–ca. 1911) to play the female roles in their enlarged productions. The growing troupe's early performances, held outside, were curtailed by bad winter weather, so the group traveled to Galatz, another small Romanian town. There, Goldfaden developed a form of vaudeville show that he presented in a small theater improvised in the coffee room of a hotel.

In 1877 the group moved on to Bucharest. War between Russia and Turkey had made Romania an important outpost for the Russian army, and increased activity there caused the community to prosper. Goldfaden's group was the beneficiary of this thriving atmosphere and they acquired their own small theater hall. Goldfaden recruited several members of the local synagogue choir to join his cast,[15] including Zelig Mogilevsky, who came to be known as Sigmund Mogulesko (1858–1914). Mogulesko, who had also performed with the local opera house, initially played secondary roles and female parts. His first starring part featured him in the title role of Goldfaden's *Shmendrig*, based upon a popular Romanian folk sketch. Goldfaden later featured Mogulesko in an early version of *Di Tsvey Kuni-Lemel* (The Two Kuni-Lemels).

The popularity of Yiddish theater spread throughout Eastern Europe, and Goldfaden's work was imitated by many other entertainers. Grodner left Goldfaden (taking Mogulesko with him) and enlisted Joseph Lateiner (1853–1935) and Moshe Horowitz (ca. 1850–1910) to write for them.[16] Meanwhile, Goldfaden returned his troupe to Galatz, where they remained successful until the end of the Russo-Turkish war. In 1879 Goldfaden took an enlarged retinue of actors, musicians, and choristers (and their families) back to Odessa where they performed augmented versions of his *Shmendrig* and *Kuni-Lemel* and, in 1880, a new production called *Di Kishif-makherin* (The Sorceress) about a Yiddish Cinderella.

With this new work, Goldfaden arrived at his ultimate concept of Yiddish theater: a real theater, with stage, scenery, and costumes; a clear plot line with fixed dialogue; musical interludes featuring solos, choruses, and dances; and well-trained male and female actors.[17] More than just excellent entertainment, Goldfaden conceived of his theater as an important form of Jewish education. Ironically, the ancient Greeks, whose work the rabbis had abhorred, were the first to view drama as true education. The rabbis saw theater as idle leisure entertainment from which one could not possibly derive the kind of life lessons they saw in the study of Torah. Goldfaden, however, found a way to reach the people, and he reported in his memoirs that education had always been his goal in creating a Yiddish theater:

> My heart was filled with pain to see my people in a low state of spiritual development. I realized that they were utterly ignorant of the holy spark of their peoplehood. So far, I had tried to infuse it into their hearts by means of my songs. The people needed a school. They needed to understand their own life and that of our people. They needed a means by which to truly understand their traditions. Historic pieces should be given before their eyes, so that they can learn their background, and find out who they really were.[18]

It may be difficult to uncover the "educational" value of some of Goldfaden's earliest work, but from 1879 to 1883, when his troupe enjoyed its greatest success, Goldfaden produced some of his most substantial, and clearly didactic, plays. During that period the company traveled extensively throughout Russia and the Ukraine, presenting a series of new works by Goldfaden: *Shulamis, oder Bas Yerusholayim* (Shulamith, or Daughter of Jerusalem), set in the time of the Second Temple; *Dr. Almosado, oder di Yiden in Palmera* (Dr. Almosado, or the Jews in Palermo), based on true events of the fourteenth century; *Bar Kokhba, oder Suhn fun dem Shtern* (Bar Kokhba, or Son of the Star), describing the leader of the famous Judean revolt against the Roman empire in 132–135; *Keynig Akhashverush, oder Keynigen Esther* (King Ahasuerus or Queen Esther), a complete *purimshpiel,* but missing much of the foolishness normally associated with that earlier genre; *Akedas Yitshok* (Binding of Isaac), based upon the biblical account of Abraham's "sacrifice" of his son (and including other biblical tales); *Dos Tseynteh Gebot, oder Lo Takhmod* (The Tenth Commandment, or Do Not Covet); as well as a version of Goethe's *Faust* and a morality play called *Todros Bloz, oder Der Ligner* (Todros Bloz, or The Liar).

The Story of *Shulamis*

Just because Goldfaden sought a loftier story and a stronger moral than in his earlier works did not mean that his plays would be wholly believable or that their musical content would reach higher ground. Indeed, Goldfaden sought to educate through entertainment, and the latter goal meant that he must keep the interests of his audiences uppermost in his creative mind. The example of *Shulamis,* among Goldfaden's most successful works (and still performed at the beginning of the twenty-first century by Yiddish theater troupes around the world) is illustrative.

As the play opens, Avshalom is traveling through the desert on a pilgrimage to Jerusalem.[19] His journey is interrupted by the cries of a young woman. Following the sound of her voice, Avshalom finds Shulamis trapped in a well and not only rescues her but also immediately falls in love with her. The two vow—by the well that brought them together and by the howling of the distant jackals—that they will reunite, but Avshalom must continue on to Jerusalem. There, forgetting his recent pledge, Avshalom meets and marries the beautiful Avigayil. Their marriage is blessed with two sons, and, in a touching scene, the young mother sings a lullaby to her children.

Goldfaden surely wanted this moment to resonate in the hearts of his audience. Jewish mothers have sung lullabies to their children throughout the generations, and this vignette is certain to strike a familiar chord. However, Goldfaden has a dramatic motive here, too. The audience does not know that tragedy will soon strike this happy family, and, if they identify with the mother and her children, the pain of the coming events will be that much stronger. To guarantee the audience's reaction, Goldfaden "borrows" the lyric from the well-known folk lullaby of his time, "Unter dem Kind's Vigele":

Unter dem kind's vigele	Under the child's crib
Shteyt a klor vais tsigele	Stands a little white goat.
Dos tsigele iz geforn handlen	The little goat went off to trade in
Rozhinkes mit mandlen	Raisins and almonds.
Rozhinkes mit mandlen, zeyr zis	Raisins and almonds are very sweet.
Mein kind vet zain gezint un frish.	My child will become healthy and strong.[20]

Goldfaden is enough of a showman to realize that (notwithstanding the fact that the entire production is in Yiddish, a language unknown in the time of the Second Temple) a first-century Palestinian Jewish mother could not have been singing a song still in vogue among the Jewish mothers of Eastern Europe nearly 1,800 years later. He therefore "reworks" the lyric into a new but equally accessible melody. By setting familiar text, however, he guarantees that the song will be an instant "hit" and well remembered by the audience long after the final curtain. Indeed, Goldfaden's "Rozhinkes mit Mandlen" (Raisins and Almonds) quickly usurped "Unter dem Kind's Vigele" as a favorite lullaby and achieved the ultimate (backhanded) compliment of being widely regarded as a folk song.

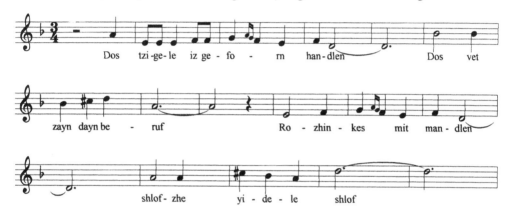

Example 6.1 From "Rozhinkes mit Mandlen"

As the play continues, catastrophe strikes: One of the children is eaten by the jackals, while the other is drowned in a well. Avigayil's grief is compounded by her husband's realization that the reintroduction of jackals and wells into his life cannot be merely a dreadful coincidence. Avshalom confesses his earlier vow and the bereaved parents realize that Shulamis must indeed have been Avshalom's *basherte,* his pre-destined bride.[21]

Throughout the passing years, the beautiful Shulamis has remained faithful to her beloved, lingering by the well that brought them together and feigning insanity to discourage the steady stream of would-be suitors who seek her hand. Avshalom, released by Avigayil, seeks the help of a clan of nomads to find his *basherte,* and the play concludes as they are finally reunited.

Shulamis herself is not a particularly heroic figure. Indeed, one might question her devotion to a cad who could forget his vow to her almost as soon as it had left his lips. Still, this melodramatic romance included scraps of Jewish history, cultural tradition, and morality, and was thus instructive. It was also a favorite entertainment vehicle whose musical score passed into the popular repertoire with great ease.[22]

Unfortunately, at just the point when Goldfaden was reaching his greatest critical success, the 1881 assassination of Nicholas II ushered in a period of great uncertainty for the Jewish community. Alexander III, the new czar, instituted a series of restrictions on Jewish life and did nothing to quell the pogroms that broke out that year with renewed virulence. Jewish leaders pointed with concern to Goldfaden's sometimes satirical views of Jewish life (and to the more comical characters in his plays) and feared that he was subjecting Jews to ridicule at an especially dangerous period. Still, Goldfaden's new productions played to packed houses until February 1883, when Alexander announced a total ban on Yiddish theater throughout his realm. Some speculated that the popularity of *Bar Kokhba* and its story of Jewish revolt struck too close to home for the czar. But whatever the cause, the new edict effectively put an end to Yiddish theater in Russia.

In 1885 Goldfaden responded to the ban by moving his troupe to Warsaw, where they reprised the productions that had been popular in Odessa. This time Goldfaden failed to develop significant new works for his new audiences and, despite the positive reception for *Shulamis,* he never achieved the same measure of success in Poland that he had enjoyed in earlier years. Goldfaden also suffered a spiritual depression during these years because he felt that his educational mission had been particularly important for the Russian Jews whom he could no longer reach. Meanwhile, word spread of the success of Yiddish theater in America and by 1887 Goldfaden decided to see it for himself.

Yiddish Theater in the New World

Boris Thomashefsky (1868–1939) was among the pioneers who brought Yiddish theater to America. As a boy of just 13, he left his home in Ukraine to seek his fortune in America. His first "starring role" was as a singer in a synagogue choir in New York. In 1882 he persuaded one of the synagogue's trustees to sponsor a visit of a theatrical ensemble called the Golubek Troupe, despite the fact that their fame—and fortune—had been exhausted during their stay in London. The troupe's appearance in New York was not met with universal welcome; members of the local German Jewish community[23] tried to dissuade the company from presenting its Yiddish productions, but the clamor among the immigrants for a "taste of home" ultimately launched the Yiddish theater on American shores. In 1882, Thomashefsky made his own theatrical debut as a singer in the company's production of Goldfaden's *Di Kishifmakherin,* and the young man later played several female parts before achieving "matinee idol" status in a variety of swashbuckling, leading man roles.

Thomashefsky's group was not alone in New York for long. The arrival of Sophie Goldstein, her new actor-husband Max Karp (1856–1898), and playwright Joseph Lateiner caused a stir that forced Thomashefsky and company to retreat to stages in Philadelphia and Chicago. Sigmund Mogulesko and Moshe Horowitz soon followed, as did companies featuring David Kessler (1860–1920), Jacob P. Adler (1855–1926), and Keni Liptzin (1856–1918)—all three of whom began their career with Goldfaden's troupes in Europe. These names were to be featured on marquees across New York for decades to come.

Goldfaden was disappointed by his first experience in New York. With so many of his protégés achieving significant careers (and often still performing his works), there was some concern that Goldfaden would interfere in their success. Lateiner and Horowitz, in particular, feared retribution from Goldfaden (or prosecution under rumored, but nonexistent, copyright laws) for their usurpation of his earliest work and conspired to keep him away from any active role in New York's theater scene. Goldfaden retreated to London and later Paris but was unsuccessful at starting new companies there. He returned to Lemberg and spent the closing years of the nineteenth century there, revising some of his earlier works and penning several new, dramatic plays. Celebrations in 1896 marking the twentieth anniversary of the Yiddish theater were followed in 1900 by literary notices marking Goldfaden's sixtieth birthday, but the aging impresario's days in the limelight were over. Returning to New York in 1902, Goldfaden was regarded this time as a beloved relic of an earlier era and supported by pension money provided by Thomashefsky and Adler.

Goldfaden succeeded in convincing a doubting Thomashefsky to mount a production of *Ben-Ami* (Son of My People), Goldfaden's last drama, in 1907. The story is of a European aristocrat removed from his Jewish heritage who makes his way to New York but ultimately makes peace with himself and his identity by moving on to Palestine and working the soil of the Jewish homeland. Conceived as a dramatic work with incidental music, the play was clearly influenced by the birth of Zionism in the waning days of the nineteenth century.[24] Thomashefsky feared his audience's reaction to the heavy subject matter, though, and convinced Goldfaden to add some lighter verses to it. The play opened in December 1907 but achieved its greatest success only after Goldfaden's death on January 9, 1908. The successful six-month run that followed was a fitting tribute, as was the inscription on his tombstone: *Fater fun der Yiddishe teater* (Father of the Yiddish theater).

But as audiences mourned the loss of the father, they reveled in the succession of his children and in the evolution of his mission to "educate the masses." The immigrants stood with feet precariously balancing two worlds: the old world, with its familiar language, traditional values, and overt anti-Semitism; and a strange new world where Jews were more covertly despised but where hard work and mastery of "the rules of the game" could afford anyone an opportunity to prosper. The new arrivals needed to learn those rules—chief among them, how to retain their Jewish identities while conquering a foreign tongue and an odd political invention called "democracy." The theater that Goldfaden created to educate the Jews about their heritage became a key to their cultural identities—and now it helped them become Americans.

From Greenhorn to Yankee

While Goldfaden's operettas and the many plays that his successors fashioned after them continued to draw audiences, American theater burgeoned in several directions. Vaudeville shows captured the spirit of the Yiddish theater's early days, with independent series of acts appearing on stage as jugglers, dancers, singers, and musicians. These newfangled *badhanim* and *klezmorim* took their musical and comedic cues, as usual, from the lives of their audiences—but now those lives were changing in dramatic ways.

Life in America was hard for the immigrants, and the tension between the pull of the Old World and the New found continuing expression on stage. Solomon Shmuelvitz's song "A Brivele der Maman" captured the pain of separated families as the European mother begs her son to send word from America.

A bri - ve - le der ma - men zol - stu - nit far za - men shrayb ge - shvind li - bes kind shenk ir di ne - ho - me

Example 6.2 From "A Brivele der Mamen"

> My child, my comfort, you are going away, be a good son.
> With tears and fear your dear, devoted mother is begging
> Across the seas; and don't forget your mother.
> You're leaving, my child, my only child, across far seas.
> Oh, you should arrive fresh and healthy, and don't forget your mother.
> Hey! Go in health and come with happiness.
> See that you send a letter each week, your mother's heart, my son,
>   delight.
>
> A letter to mother, don't be late in writing.
> Write quickly, dear child, give her this consolation.
> Mama will read your letter and be comforted.
> You ease her pain, her bitter heart, you refresh her spirit.[25]

Meanwhile, the sons and daughters who made their way to America found little time to write home, instead putting in long hours in miserable sweatshops. Songs like "Mayn Rue Platz" (My Resting Place) by Morris Rosenfeld (1862–1923) summarized the feelings of tired workers whose dreams of an American "golden land" had long ago confronted a tarnished reality.

Example 6.3 From "Mayn Rue Platz"

> Don't look for me where myrtles grow, you will not find me there,
>   my love.
> Where lives wither at machines, there is my resting place.

Others sang Rosenfeld's anguished song of missed time with their children, whom they saw only at night after long days toiling in stifling factories.

Example 6.4 From "Mayn Yingele"

> I have a dear little boy, such a good son!
> When I look at him, it seems to me the whole world is mine.
> It's seldom that I see him, my beauty, when he wakes.
> I find him only sleeping, I see him only at night.

Despite the hardships of life in America, some considered the alternatives in Europe and, as in this song by Arnold Perlmutter (1859–1953) and Herman Wohl (1877–1936), found reason to praise Christopher Columbus for having the "good sense" to discover America:

Oy le - bn zol Ko - lom - bus trinkt bri - der - lekh le - ha - yim

Example 6.5 From "Leb'n Zol Columbus"

America is a town, a delight, I swear!
The Divine Presence rests on it, we should live like this,
No wars, no guns, no bloodshed, I don't need these problems,
A governor we don't need, we have no use for a czar.

    Oh, it's good, sing along everyone:
    "Long live Columbus!" Brothers, drink "to life!"
    Long live Columbus, for (discovering) the New World.
    Be happy, don't listen to the grumblers.
    Shout, Jews, "Long live Columbus!"

Some saw the hardships of life in America for what they were but chose to laugh through their tears. Jacob Leiserowitz (1893–1965) and Abe Schwartz (1881–1963) injected humor into the sad lives of their audiences by making fun of more recent immigrants and the disintegration of their energies and dreams.

Tzu mir iz ge-ku-men a ku - zi - ne sheyn vi gold iz zi ge -ven di - gri - ne di

be-ke-lekh vi roy -te po-me - ran - tzn fi -se-lekh vos be-tn zikh tzum tan - tzen tan -tzen

Example 6.6 From "Die Grine Kuzine"

A pretty cousin came to me, beautiful as gold she was, the "green" one.
Cheeks like red oranges, feet just begging to go dancing.

Under her pretty blue eyes, black lines.
The cheeks, the red oranges have already faded in the street...

Today I met my cousin, and I asked her, "How are you, green one?"
She answered me with bitterness, "May the blazes take Columbus's
land!"

Others used their songs to rally their fellow workers. Long before
a tragic fire at the Triangle Shirtwaist Company took the lives of 146
people in 1911 (most of them young Jewish women), Jews had taken
leading roles in the movement to improve working conditions.
David Edelstadt's[26] (1866–1892) songs echoed from the factory
floors to the theater stages, creating momentum that ultimately led
to real changes and the birth of the earliest labor unions—first on
New York's Lower East Side and ultimately across America.
Edelstadt's "Vakht Oyf" (Awake) was sung regularly at workers' ral-
lies and meetings.

Vi   lang o vi lang vet ir blay - bn nokh shkla - fn un tro - gn di shend le - khe keit

Example 6.7 From "Vakht Oyf"

How long, oh how long will you remain still slaves
and wear the shameful chain?
How long will you create splendid riches
for those who steal your bread?

Edelstadt's "In Kamf" (In Struggle) was written in 1889 and soon
became the unofficial hymn of Jewish workers in America and
abroad. It is said that during a massive London demonstration
against the Kishinev Pogrom of 1903, the crowd of thousands spon-
taneously began to sing "In Kamf."

Mir   ve - rn ge - hast un ge - tri -   bn   mir be - rn ge - plogt un far - folgt

Example 6.8 From "In Kamf"

We are hated and chased, we are afflicted and persecuted
for the sole reason that we love this poor languishing people.
We are shot, hanged, they steal our life and our rights
because we demand the truth and freedom for poor slaves.

The impoverishment of life among the immigrants made the hunger for relief from their troubles all the more urgent. Spending money on a ticket to the theater was a luxury few could really afford, but the opportunity to pass a few hours distracted by comedic antics, or empathizing with someone else's (theatrical) troubles generally won out over more practical considerations. Devotees of the most popular singer/actors of the Yiddish stage would argue the merits of their favorite performers like the most ardent sports fans defending the honor of their favorite teams. Shop girls saved their pennies to purchase balcony seats to Wednesday matinees (risking their jobs in the bargain!) just to imagine themselves as marquee headliners fated to "die" in the arms of their favorite stars.

Jacob Gordin: Raising the Bar

If occasional songs of Yiddish vaudeville and comedic or melodramatic plays acted by Boris Thomashefsky, Sigmund Mogulesko, Ludwig Satz, Sophie Karp, and a host of others attracted large, emotional crowds eager to laugh—or cry—along with the performers, serious plays being staged in "art theaters" brought out more sophisticated audiences eager to experience "high culture."

The first significant shift in the tenor of Yiddish plays and performers came at the end of the nineteenth century in works by Jacob Gordin (1853–1909). A Russian-Jewish "radical" of sorts, Gordin made no effort to conceal his distaste for the "folksiness" of plays by Goldfaden and his emulators, writing for the unique American Yiddish theater audiences. Gordin and his fellow Russian intellectuals had little respect for the Yiddish language or for the Jewish masses, besotted with Jewish tradition, who considered it their mother tongue. Gordin and his ilk considered Russian the language of high literature, and while they worked hard to master English, they scorned Yiddish as the language of the uncultured hordes. Gordin railed against the popular Yiddish theater of his time, which he considered low class *shund,* "literary trash," with its wooden actors as caricatures of genuine figures delivering silly dialogue filled with bold, often ad-libbed asides to the audience and speaking in an embarrassing combination of Yiddish and English.

Ironically, Gordin and his intellectual friends shared Goldfaden's drive to educate the masses and finally realized that to do so, they would have to speak to them in their language. Gordin began to write for the radical Yiddish newspapers that appeared on the Lower East Side, and one early vignette was dramatized by another writer as a vehicle for Mogulesko. Yiddish actors were excited by the higher standards of language and realism in this new work and many were suddenly eager to aim higher.

Jewish theater's first forays into more secular art consisted of performances translating great works by recognized playwrights into Yiddish. Plays by Goethe, Moliére, Shakespeare, and Ibsen were among the many produced for Yiddish-speaking audiences in the years from 1890 to 1905. Meanwhile, Jacob Gordin, attending a performance based on his own early vignette, became inspired by the possibility of raising Yiddish theater (and actors) out of the morass of their unenlightened past and into the light of a new era of realistic plays. His first full-scale work, *Siberia,* featured Mogulesko and Jacob P. Adler playing, at first, to a noisy assemblage expecting the same light fare in which these actors usually appeared. Gordin's play struck the audience as dry and humorless. Adler tearfully addressed the crowd prior to the third act, lamenting their inability to appreciate the "masterpiece" by Gordin. Properly chastised, the audience sat attentively until the final curtain—and then wept at the moving climax.

The actors, too, recognized that these meatier, more realistic roles were good for them. Gordin's next play, *The Pogrom in Russia,* was produced at Boris Thomashefsky's theater in 1892, with the playwright not only supervising the costumes, but also taking a bit part for himself—the better to keep an eye on the production. When the actors, still fearful of the audience's reception, begged for musical interludes, Gordin grudgingly agreed to insert traditional Russian folk songs that the characters might realistically have sung. He drew the line, however—and threatened to withdraw the play—when the director tried to sneak in a lightweight couplet typical of more popular plays. Gordin's reputation attracted a new audience to the theater for the play's opening night, one unaccustomed to "traditional" Yiddish theater fare. This audience listened attentively from the start, applauded wildly after each act, and caused a near-riot with its enthusiasm at the play's conclusion.

Gordin's efforts to raise the caliber of Yiddish theater—and of its public—met with only limited success. Following the Kishinev pogroms of 1903, the Lower East Side swelled with a new wave of immigrants accustomed to the *shund* plays of Eastern European folk-life and Abraham Goldfaden. *Gott, Mensch, und Teufel* (God, Man, and Devil) and *Mirele Efros* achieved real success (and were later remade as films), but only because they represented no real departure from the Jewish values the audiences sought. From Gordin's perspective, each of these "realistic" plays railed against the corrupting power of money[27] but the audience saw in them a rebuke against those who would seek to undo well-established traditions of success through hard work, respect for elders, the obligation to take care of those in need, and the importance of keeping a promise.

Gordin was so eager to bring his Jewish audiences into line with the mores and behaviors of the secular world that he failed to genuinely connect with the masses. The next generation of Yiddish writers—on both sides of the Atlantic—realized that quality plays could educate and uplift their audiences without asking them to reject their Jewish heritage.

The Vilna Troupe

Some of the earliest "art theater" flowed from the pens of giants known best for their literary writing. Short stories and novels by Mendele Moykher Sforim (Sholem Yankev Abramovitsh, 1835–1917) were later adapted for performance, but dramatic works by Yitschok Leib Peretz (1852–1915) and Sholom Aleichem (Sholem Rabinowitz, 1859–1916) were conceived for the "living stage." This "first generation" of literary writers for the Yiddish theater—overlapping with, but rarely competing with lighter fare by Goldfaden and his colleagues—established the possibility of high-quality drama in Yiddish. Sholom Asch (1880–1957), David Pinski (1872–1959), H. Leivick (Leyvik Halpern, 1888–1962), Osip Dimov (Joseph Perlman, 1878–1959), and Peretz Hirschbein (1881–1948) built on their foundation and continued the tradition of quality Yiddish theater with conspicuous Jewish content into the twentieth century and the New World as well.

The success of such dramatic work depended upon theater companies able to give them appropriate performances. In 1910 Y. L. Peretz rented Warsaw's Philharmonia Hall for a seminar on Yiddish theater. He urged the establishment of sophisticated troupes to produce great literary works in the tradition of Chekov, Zola, and Ibsen, with realistic actors trained in the lifelike methods of the Stanislavsky group that founded the Moscow Art Theater.[28] His ardent call was heeded at first by a succession of youthful amateurs whose talents rarely matched their passion. Peretz Hirschbein had started such a troupe in Odessa in 1908, however, shortly after the Czar's ban on Yiddish theater was rescinded, and produced his own plays along with those by Sholom Aleichem and Sholom Asch. Young Jacob Ben-Ami (1890–1977), who had been playing bit parts in other companies, joined the group and even began directing. When the troupe disbanded in 1910, Ben-Ami made his way to Vilna, where he joined one of the amateur groups answering Peretz's call—a group at first called the "Organization of Yiddish Arts" but ultimately known simply as "the Vilna Troupe."

The Vilna Troupe prided themselves on their attention to the literary quality of the plays they undertook. They also strove for productions that would emphasize ensemble work, rather than elevating some cast members to star status, despite the high caliber of their work. One of the Troupe's finest innovations was the adoption of a uniform Lithuanian Yiddish pronunciation for all cast members.[29]

The Vilna Troupe received rave notices wherever they performed, and soon came to the attention of Polish actress Esther Rokhl Kaminska (1870–1925), who encouraged the company to bring their tour to Warsaw. The Troupe arrived in 1917 and all of the Yiddish intelligentsia were on hand for their opening night (except Y. L. Peretz himself, who had died two years earlier). Their debut performance of *Yankl Boyle* by Leon Kobrin[30] (1872–1946) was greeted with rave reviews in the Warsaw press and by critics from other cities who had crowded into the theater. The Troupe were feted at a dinner at which it was roundly proclaimed that Yiddish theater had "arrived."

The Vilna Troupe were lauded by Jews and non-Jews alike. Warsaw remained their base, but they toured the provinces (in their own private train) where they were met with brass bands and adoring fans who would carry company members into town on their shoulders. The actors were treated like heroes, but the company regarded itself as an institution. The Vilna Troupe understood that they were introducing many of their audiences to art and literature. In an era when Jews still lived life on the margins of mainstream society and, in the smaller towns under continuing threats to their very existence, the Vilna Troupe represented a vindication of Yiddish identity and culture and a level of artistic and literary accomplishment that even the intelligentsia had scarcely believed possible.

The Dybbuk

Notwithstanding the enormous success of the Vilna Troupe in their early years, the company achieved its greatest acclaim from its 1920 production of *The Dybbuk* by S. Anski (Solomon Zeynwil Rapaport, 1863–1920). The idea for the play was rooted in the ethnological expeditions carried out by Jewish nationalists in the early years of the new century. Between 1911 and 1914, Anski participated in a mission deep into the Ukraine. In addition to collecting poetry and songs, he and his fellow researchers catalogued various folk customs, notating some of the legends and superstitions surrounding them as well. The resulting drama was replete with those images.

In the course of the play we learn some important background about what took place before the action begins: Two young friends were once so devoted to each other that they vowed—long before either of them was of marriageable age—that if one would someday have a son and the other a daughter, those two children would wed. At a time when arranged marriages were the norm, such agreements were typically made between the parents of existing children—even infants. Nevertheless, a bargain is a bargain. Unfortunately, as the years passed, the two friends parted to study in different yeshivot and eventually lost touch.

Early in the play we learn that one of the two, the widower Sendor, has become a successful merchant and provides meals for poor yeshivah students in his home.[31] That is, Sendor pays the bills, but his only child, Leah, serves the students. One of the students, Chanan, falls in love with Leah—so totally in love that he cannot even keep his mind on his studies. Attempting to keep himself pure, he sings of his love by chanting passages from The Song of Songs, and at a too-young age he studies the mystical books of the Kabbalah[32] in hopes of finding eternal truths—and the key to winning Leah. Chanan studies deep into the night, and the circles under his eyes—together with his strange, "obsessed" behavior—further diminish the chances that a poor boy such as he could win the hand of a wealthy man's daughter. Indeed, Sendor soon announces that Leah has been betrothed to a brilliant student from another nearby yeshiva. This news proves too much of a strain on Chanan, who dies as much from a broken heart as from sleepless nights and missed meals.

Chanan's demise is unfortunate but has no effect on Sendor's plans. The entire community is invited to the nuptials—the town beggars arrive first to enjoy the free-flowing food and drink. Shortly after the bridegroom declares Leah his own,[33] though, the bride faints. As her family crowds around her, the voice of the dead Chanan emerges from her lips, claiming her as his bride. The offici-ating rabbi declares that the girl is possessed by a *dybbuk* and the wedding party promptly disperses.

According to folk tradition, each person is put on this earth to accomplish some task, whether large or small. A *dybbuk* is the wan-dering soul of a person who has died before his task can be accom-plished. The local rabbis insist that Chanan leave the girl but he refuses. They threaten and cajole him, urging him at least to reveal the reason for his possession of Leah. Again he refuses. Finally, Sendor takes his daughter to a wonder-working Hasidic rabbi who threatens Chanan with eternal excommunication. Faced with such a punishment, Chanan agrees to depart—but not before revealing that he is the son of Sendor's long-lost friend and that Leah is truly his *basherte*, his destined bride. Sendor has brought this calamity upon himself by neglecting his old promise (and ostensibly by not being there for the comrade of his youth, who could have benefited from the helping hand of his prosperous friend). The *dybbuk* fulfills his promise, and his spirit leaves the young woman's body, but Chanan has captured her soul. Leah dies and her spirit joins Chanan's in death.

The response to *The Dybbuk* was nothing short of astonishing. Director David Herman (1876–1937) reached into his own background as the child of a Hasidic family to create an atmosphere at once authentic and symbolic. The production utilized the ensemble to the fullest, with pantomime, choral speaking, and mass action as important as the individual roles. The Jewish intelligentsia saw in it a confirmation that Jewish folk culture did indeed exist and that the traditions of the Jewish nation were as rich as any other. But the play was equally well received by non-Jewish audiences.

On the strength of the reputation of *The Dybbuk,* the Vilna Troupe toured throughout Europe and won critical praise in Romania, Belgium, Holland, England, Germany, and France. It paved the way for professional Yiddish theater troupes throughout Europe, including Russia, which, after the revolution of 1917, was once again receptive to Jewish culture. Indeed, state-subsidized Yiddish theaters flourished in Moscow and St. Petersburg (now Leningrad), and *Habimah,* a Hebrew-language troupe in Russia, was associated with the Moscow Art Theater. In an interesting juxtaposition of musical and theatrical arts, several of these new companies engaged trained composers to create the incidental music for their plays. In 1918 Joseph Achron wrote incidental music for Sholom Aleichem's *Stempenyu;* for *The Witch,* based on Goldfaden's earlier work; and for productions by Alexander Granovsky's Jewish Chamber Theatre (forerunner of the Moscow Yiddish State Art Theater). *The Dybbuk* was produced by *Habimah* in 1922 in a translation by Chaim Nachman Bialik, with incidental music by Joel Engel.[34]

While quality Yiddish theater was thriving, the Vilna Troupe began to experience internal tensions. The Troupe arrived in New York in 1924 but, despite a warm reception, began to break up. Individual members built new ensembles around themselves and went on tour, each claiming to be "the original Vilna Troupe." The groundwork for the positive reception given these groups in Yiddish-speaking communities across America had been laid a decade earlier.

A Second Golden Era of American Yiddish Theater

As we have seen, between 1890 and 1910 a steady stream of immigrants from Eastern Europe created an eager audience for Yiddish theater. New York's Second Avenue boasted the largest number and widest variety of offerings, but audiences in Philadelphia, Baltimore, Boston, Chicago, Cleveland, Detroit, New Orleans, San Francisco, Newark, Milwaukee, and Montreal were also entertained by professional troupes and amateur theater clubs. The professional groups favored the more populist productions of Goldfaden, Lateiner, Horowitz, and their followers, while many of the amateur clubs attempted more literary plays. The most successful of these groups, the *Folksbienne,* was founded by Jacob Gordin and Joel Entin in 1915 and continued presenting at least one production each season into the twenty-first century. However, uncertainties surrounding funding and even the availability of space kept most of the amateur groups from flourishing,[35] and by the 1920s most of these groups had gone into a decline that reached its nadir by World War II. The lofty, literary ideals of some of these groups found fuller expression in professional art theaters.

In the years during and immediately after the First World War, American theater companies began to catch up with the avant-garde culture of their European counterparts, many of whom toured the United States to widespread acclaim. At the same time, an increasing proportion of American-born (or Americanized) Jewish audiences who could no longer tolerate the antics of *shund* players and second-rate scripts began to seek their entertainment in the English-language theaters of Broadway or the movies. It was clearly time for a change.

Maurice Schwartz's Yiddish Art Theater

In 1918 Maurice Schwartz (1890–1960) took space in the *Jewish Daily Forward* announcing his plan to establish an art theater. Already a veteran of stages in Cleveland, Philadelphia, and New York, Schwartz was a highly regarded actor and passionate about the theater. He believed that literary plays could receive the attention they deserved in an intimate environment, one that could sustain dramatic subtleties. His Irving Place Theater was to be the setting.

Schwartz hired an impressive cast to join him in his new venture. Celia Adler (1889–1979), daughter of Jacob P. Adler and Dina Stettin Feinman, had come to the attention of Jacob Gordin when she began her career playing child roles in productions that featured her parents. She went on to play with David Kessler, Boris Thomashefsky, and Rudolph Schildkraut (1862–1930) but by 1918 she was ready for a new challenge.

So was Jacob Ben-Ami. Since his arrival in the United States in 1912, Ben-Ami had quickly acquired a reputation as a *literatnik*, (a somewhat derogatory Yiddish perversion of *literatur*). He had organized an evening of Peretz's one-act plays in 1916, and the New York intelligentsia was already looking to him to help create a new era in Yiddish theater. Ben-Ami was a natural complement to the ambitious new company.

Lazar Freed (1888–1944), highly regarded for his refined acting, also joined the company. He was Celia Adler's husband (although they divorced soon after) and a friend of Ben-Ami's from their childhood days as choirboys in Minsk and, later, as members of the Hirschbein Troupe.

Ludwig Satz (1891–1944) was a somewhat surprising addition to the group. Although he had appeared in Gordin's *Gott, Mentsch und Teufel,* he had not previously allied himself with the "literary" group. His association with the company was brief. He would spend most of his career playing light comedies and bringing audiences to laughter—or tears—billed as "the man of a thousand faces." However, Satz was a capable and intelligent actor who played real character roles with Schwartz's theater.

Berta Gersten (ca. 1896–1972) also joined the company at the start. She had begun her theater career playing a boy in Gordin's *Mirele Efros* in 1908 but played leading roles with Schwartz. Gerstein appeared often opposite Jacob Ben-Ami and later became his wife.

Despite his lofty pronouncements, Schwartz was not quick to introduce "literary plays" into the repertory, fearing that the new theater would surely lose money. Ben-Ami had insisted on such fare when he signed his contract, however, and one Wednesday (a traditionally slow day in the theater anyway) Schwartz gave permission for the company to present whatever Ben-Ami chose—although he (Schwartz) would have nothing to do with the production.

Ben-Ami chose *Der Farvorfn Vinkel* (The Secluded Nook), a manuscript by his old friend Peretz Hirschbein. With no special announcement preceding the production, the audience was indeed small, but as the curtain came down on act one they applauded wildly. Schwartz, watching from the wings, seized the moment to make an impromptu speech, reiterating many of the points in his *Forward* manifesto and urging the audience to support "his" efforts and the fine cast. Word spread about the production, and the critics rejoiced at the new turn of events. *Der Farvorfn Vinkel* eventually moved to the more profitable weekend nights and played for 14 weeks. Schwartz himself took a role in the production, and the entire company was lauded.

Despite the success of Schwartz's new venture, Jacob Ben-Ami, Celia Adler, and other actors left the company at the end of the season to establish their own *Naye Teater* (New Theater). They were eager to overturn the "star" system (of which Schwartz was still an advocate) giving all performers alphabetical billing, to adopt uniform Yiddish dialect,[36] and to rid the theater of the prompter necessitated when companies undertook too many productions with too little rehearsal (Schwartz's Irving Place Theater presented 35 plays in its first season).

Ben-Ami's new Jewish Art Theater adopted Stanislavskian principles of truthfulness and realism, and engaged directors to create well-conceived productions. They received unanimous critical acclaim, but the company's financial backers were not as committed to new ways for the New Theater as were the actors. The company soon disbanded.

A succession of literary enterprises rose and fell throughout the Jewish community (many involving Jacob Ben-Ami), but the only consistent address for quality theater remained Maurice Schwartz's Yiddish Art Theater. Moving to new quarters on Second Avenue and Twelfth Street, the Yiddish Art Theater presented a wide variety of plays. Schwartz presented classics such as Goldfaden's *The Two Kuni-Lemels* and *The Witch,* Gordin's *Mirele Efros,* and Peretz's *Golden Chain.* In addition, he imported such European productions as *The Dybbuk* and *The Travels of Benjamin III* by Mendele Moykher Sforim. Schwartz also presented newer works by Leivick, Kobrin, Dimov, and Asch.

Like his European counterparts, Schwartz called upon highly regarded composers to create incidental music for some of his productions. Joseph Achron, in New York since 1925, created a new kind of musico-dramatic partnership when he contributed scores for a reworking of Goldfaden's *The Tenth Commandment* and new productions of Asch's *Kiddush Hashem, The Witch of Castillo,* and *Stempenyu.* These early bold steps into a world of (secular) Jewish art music complemented the creation of this new form of (secular) Jewish literature.

As Yiddish art theater dabbled in translations of plays by non-Jewish writers (Ibsen, Shakespeare, Moliére), and as Yiddish actors made the transition to English-language theater (and later films), they brought their audiences with them. The long-playing success of Schwartz's Yiddish Art Theater (and the various other companies that rose and fell) was testimony to the eagerness of Yiddish theater—and its audiences—to grow. Goldfaden had begun the process of "educating the masses," and now a new Yiddish art theater (with strong influences from Europe) was continuing the process of enlightening the Jewish community and, indeed, integrating it into American life. The virtual demise of Yiddish theater in the era following World War II was partly a result of demographic realities as Yiddish-speaking audiences dwindled in number. Its demise was also a result of the success of the Yiddish theater in helping several generations of immigrants find their place in a new cultural world.

7 ~
Synagogue Music in America

Many of the immigrants who filled American Yiddish theaters also spent time in American synagogues that they found upon arrival, or more commonly, that they created to serve their particular demands. While synagogue attendance was based first upon a sense of religious need (or obligation), the musical conduct of the service played a key role in the congregants' affective experience. As we shall see, the development of that music keenly reflected the worshipers' evolving sense of ritual propriety.

The Music of Colonial America

The first American synagogues were established in the Spanish-Portuguese tradition. Twenty-three immigrants from Portuguese religious oppression fled from Recife, Brazil, and arrived in New Amsterdam in 1654 where they founded Shearith Israel synagogue (1655). Those who followed them built Yeshuat Israel in Newport, Rhode Island (1658); Mikveh Israel of Savannah, Georgia (1735); another synagogue called Mikveh Israel in Philadelphia (1747); and Beth Elohim of Charleston, South Carolina (1749). The ritual of these congregations closely followed the London/Amsterdam traditions that evolved in the years following the Spanish expulsion in 1492 and was never significantly influenced by changing styles in the surrounding musical community. The role of *hazzan* was not chiefly a musical position throughout the colonial era. In the absence of rabbis (there were no ordained rabbis in America before the 1840s), *hazzanim* were ritual "jacks of all trades," serving as *shohtim* (ritual slaughters), *mohelim* (circumcisors), and religious school teachers; presiding at marriages and burials; and chanting the service. The synagogue lay leaders maintained a strong hold on all matters—from awarding ritual honors to assigning seating in the sanctuary—and in an era when only one synagogue served an entire, homogeneous population, there was little opportunity (or reason) for musical leadership.

The Arrival of the Germans

The arrival of immigrants from Germany in the period 1840–1860 brought Ashkenazic Jews to American shores and a dramatic change in Jewish communal and musical life. The German Jews brought with them the new reforms that were sweeping through Germany in the post-Emancipation era. They also brought rabbinic leadership to America for the first time. The role of the *ḥazzan* was reduced significantly but his extramusical responsibilities still commanded most of his time. The *nusaḥ* of old had been abrogated by the reforms, and even congregational singing of demure hymns played a subservient role to that of the choir. At first, the (often non-Jewish) choral director and the organist had more influence on the synagogue service than did the *ḥazzan*.

The 1866 appointment of Alois Kaiser (1842–1908) as cantor at Congregation Oheb Shalom in Baltimore, Maryland, however, began to turn the tide in favor of a much more pivotal role for the synagogue *ḥazzan*. Cantor Kaiser served the congregation for 42 years and contributed some of his own compositions to the service. Jacob Schuman (d. 1941), who succeeded him in 1908, followed the example of his predecessor and introduced classical compositions and operatic arias to be used as melodies for the synagogue. The congregation continued singing Protestant-style hymns. Indeed, the first *Union Hymnal* published by the new Union of American Hebrew Congregations (and edited by Kaiser) in 1897 featured hymn tunes by Haydn, Mozart, Brahms, Sir Arthur Sullivan, and a variety of non-Jewish American composers—in addition, to the "traditional" works of Sulzer and Lewandowski.

Kaiser's innovations were paralleled on the West Coast by the activity of Edward Stark (1856–1913) of Temple Emanu-El in San Francisco. Stark conducted most of his service in English and stressed music. He and his congregants expected excellent performances from the non-Jewish singers hired for the choir. He wrote many of his own compositions and supplemented his repertoire with the new work of Solomon Sulzer. He also adapted music of Haydn, Gounod, Schubert, and Mendelssohn, as well as anthems from the Protestant tradition.

The increasing numbers of American Jews broke down the "one community, one synagogue" expectations of the past. In addition to the distinctions between Ashkenazic and Sephardic rites, musical practices like the introduction of the organ were often the "lightning rod" that precipitated a split in the community.[1] With increasing possibilities for American worshipers, the musical choices made by a congregation often determined membership patterns.

Because of the unique musical and liturgical decisions being made in isolated congregations, there is no pattern of innovation that uniformly identifies American Reform musical practice in the nineteenth century. The arrival of unprecedented numbers of Eastern European Jews beginning in 1880 brought greater diversity to the American Jewish landscape, but the implications of new European musical developments they brought with them played an even greater role in the evolution of American synagogue music.

The Golden Age of *Ḥazzanut*

Eastern European Jews arriving on American shores between 1880 and 1920 quickly formed synagogues as extensions of the *landsman-shaften*[2] that determined their identities in the New World as well as their points of origin in the Old. These demographic associations facilitated all sorts of business and fraternal transactions among new immigrants. They also guaranteed a smooth liturgical transition for observant Jews from Europe who wanted to be sure to find a familiar sounding ritual in America.

But while synagogues with names like Bialystocker Shul (Bialystock Synagogue) and Kletzker Society (Society of Kletzk) facilitated communal bonds, the one thing they could not necessarily provide in America was a *ḥazzan* "from the Old Country." European *ḥazzanim* were just coming into their own: the *chor-shuls* of the more enlightened communities were proud of their local cantor-composers, and "star" cantors with great vocal talents were not eager to give up the high regard in which they were held in Europe. Moreover, the most traditional of the *ḥazzanim* approached the New World with some trepidation, unsure of the quality of its Jewish life and certainly unwilling to take on the myriad responsibilities of the earliest American clergy.

The most eager among the new American congregations took matters into their own hands and specifically imported selected *ḥazzanim* from Europe. New York's Anshe Suvalk (People of Suvalk) were the first to go this route: After incurring significant debt from the construction of an impressive edifice, they decided to solve their membership (and financial) problems by engaging a "star" cantor from their native Poland. Their selection, Chaim Weinshel (1834–1901),[3] fulfilled their expectations, attracting a throng of curious worshipers—although he himself was unimpressed by the small-town atmosphere of American Jewish life or the caliber of its leadership.

Notwithstanding Weinshel's disappointment with the American Jewish scene, other congregations began to follow the example of Anshe Suvalk by importing their own "stars." Even when the process yielded a candidate who did not fulfill the community's expectations (long-distance negotiations being what they were), congregational leaders were often loathe to part with their cantors, fearing that they would be unable to find an acceptable replacement.

The practical need to fill an important communal role was thus tinged with an air of "competition" among congregations eager to attract the finest *ḥazzanim* to their midst. Congregations that succeeded in engaging an impressive *ḥazzan* were quick to take out advertisements in the local press announcing the news. In short order, communities that did not need (or could not afford) a year-round cantor would nevertheless enter the fray as the High Holy Days approached.[4]

Throughout the waning years of the nineteenth century, congregations across the United States continued to eagerly import European cantors. As the twentieth century dawned, a new phenomenon contributed to the renown of many European cantors, including those who had never yet set foot on American shores: the recording industry. Zawel Kwartin (1874–1952) and Gershon

Sirota (1874–1943) were among the first to be recorded (as early as 1903), but they were just the beginning of a long line of cantors whose talents were displayed, and careers enhanced, by lucrative recording contracts.

Some controversy over the propriety of the "cantor as entertainer" evolved from the popularity of cantorial recordings, especially as American recording companies like RCA and Columbia entered the marketplace. No expense was spared on these efforts. Most of the recordings featured professional choirs (of men and boys), and many cantors performed with full orchestral accompaniment. Some considered the proliferation of these recordings unseemly—even sacrilegious. Accounts were made of the sounds of sacred texts emerging even from houses of ill repute! These reports were countered, however, by "fan letters" from Jewish soldiers far from home who received spiritual sustenance from such recordings, and the industry flourished.

The proliferation of cantorial recordings only fed the furor over "star cantors" and popularized the "cantorial concert." It was no longer enough for communities to vie for the most favored cantor to officiate in their synagogues or to sell tickets to holiday services. Now these same congregations hosted concerts by their own, or visiting, *ḥazzanim*—complete with choral accompaniment. Some of the best-known "stars" even engaged managers (or acted as their own agents) and appeared in major concert halls, generally performing their own compositions.[5] These concerts were frequently attended by Jews as well as non-Jews—including stars of the stage and opera.

It would seem to have been only a short leap from cantorial concerts in Carnegie Hall and other major venues to concert appearances by cantors on the operatic stage, yet this was a journey that few *ḥazzanim* were prepared to make. The most prolific concertizers and recording artists remained traditional Jews, proud of their liturgical calling and unwilling to compromise their reputations by appearing in such secular venues.[6] One of the greatest of the "star cantors," Yossele Rosenblatt (1882–1933), was reportedly offered $3,000 per performance to appear in the role of Elazar in a Metropolitan Opera production of Halevy's *La Juive*,[7] but he refused. Later, he was supposedly offered an enormous sum to sing *Kol Nidre* in Al Jolson's *The Jazz Singer* and again refused. (He eventually agreed to appear off-camera, uncredited, singing a significantly less important selection—at a much reduced fee.)

The impact of all this cantorial concertizing on synagogue ritual was limited. Some traditional congregations did engage all-male choirs to enhance their services (as well as to appear in concerts) at least on holidays. Conductors like Leo Low (1878–1962), Meyer Machtenburg (1884–1979), Zavel Zilberts (1881–1949), and Oscar Julius (1903–1986) became stars in their own right, composing and arranging much of the music performed in the synagogue and beyond it. Cantorial compositions recorded and performed in concerts, however, were rarely performed in the synagogue. Not only did they frequently repeat text (a practice that was traditionally prohibited in an actual worship setting), but the selections were simply too long! *Ḥazzanim* who unnecessarily elongated the service through vocal displays had been vilified since the ninth century;[8] modern congregations were not going to be held captive by cantorial showpieces.

What did emerge from the popularity of this golden age of *ḥazzanut* (traditional cantorial singing) was a transplantation into American synagogues of a continued reverence for traditional synagogue *nusaḥ*. Reform synagogues in Europe, and now in America, had displaced the time-honored synagogue chants. Traditional synagogues maintained their link to the past and to the continuity of ritual music by retaining *nusaḥ* as an important component of American synagogue life.

Interestingly, though, despite the many regional variations that European Jewry had spawned, *nusaḥ America* emerged as an essentially Lithuanian form, since a preponderance of the "imported" European cantors hailed from that region. The homogeneity of the resulting American tradition helped create a "Jewish melting pot" among immigrants from many lands and in far-flung communities across the United States (especially outside the major population centers). As the Jewish community became increasingly mobile over the course of the twentieth century, this uniform practice helped American Jews relocate beyond their "hometown synagogues" while retaining a sense of comfort and continuity from the presence of familiar melodies.

New Music for the American Synagogue

Traditional synagogues may have been content to maintain the musical customs of the past, but as the twentieth century unfolded, Reform congregations continued to clamor for "modern" fare. Cantors and, to an even larger extent, composers arriving from Europe (and increasingly, those born or educated in America) found communities eager to hear new music. The importance of the position of "synagogue music director" led many musicians to accept employment in the synagogue and to turn at least some of their creative talents to settings of the liturgy. American-born Abraham Wolf Binder (1895–1966)[9] assumed the first of his many positions as choral director at a Brooklyn synagogue in 1911. From that and subsequent appointments, he attempted to reinfuse the synagogue service with some of its ancient Jewish flavor while composing contemporary works—including entire services—with modern sensibilities.

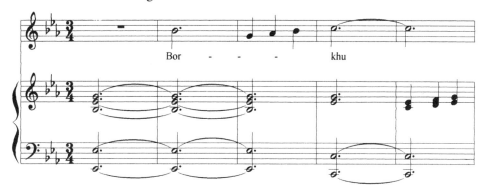

Example 7.1 From *Bor'khu* by Binder

Lazare Saminsky landed at Temple Emanu-El shortly after his arrival in America and played an important role in the shaping of that congregation's services. Lazar Weiner's (1897–1982) tenure at the Central Synagogue in New York City lasted some 30 years and inspired a wide variety of new compositions for the cantor and choir. By the 1930s, Jewish composers fleeing Europe swelled the ranks of America's Jewish composers and saw men like Isadore Freed (1900–1960)[10] and Heinrich Schalit (1886–1976)[11] assuming positions outside New York City, making their marks on cities across America as well as on future generations of cantors and students of Jewish music.

Example 7.2 From *Shaḥar Avakeshkha* by Freed

Most of the aforementioned composers crafted at least one complete Sabbath service as an outgrowth of their ongoing involvement with the music of the synagogue. Other composers of Jewish origin, whose paths did not regularly cross the synagogue *bimah*[12] or choir loft, made their contributions to synagogue music by responding to the challenge of a commission. In either circumstance, these composers sought to elevate the overall musical quality of the service and, in at least some cases, to restore the homogeneity of style lost when traditional *nusaḥ* had been abandoned. While not the earliest such effort, the *Avodat ha-Kodesh (Sacred Service)* of Ernest Bloch is deserving of special attention here.

The Sacred Service by Ernest Bloch

Born and educated in Switzerland, Ernest Bloch (1881–1959) studied music there, in Brussels, and in Germany before returning to his family's watch business in Switzerland. He finally rejected the family profession in favor of his musical aspirations and wrote many compositions with no particular musical agenda at all before embarking on a "Jewish cycle" that lasted for approximately 20 years. On the strength of successful compositions like his *Schelomo* (for Cello and Orchestra) in 1916 and *Ba'al Shem Suite* (for Violin and Piano) in 1923,[13] Bloch was commissioned by Cantor Reuven Rinder of Congregation Emanu-El in San Francisco to compose a setting of the Sabbath morning liturgy. Bloch responded by composing an eloquent, through-composed work in five sections, based largely on four themes of his own construction:[14]

Example 7.3 Four themes from *Avodat ha-Kodesh*

Bloch took great care in his setting of the Hebrew text. Indeed, his service achieves some of the loftiest settings the liturgy has seen. Unfortunately, the service is "larger than life" and not practical for presentation in most synagogues. It calls for a 60-piece orchestra, and, halakhic issues aside, most synagogue sanctuaries simply cannot accommodate such an ensemble. The number of choral voices needed to be heard over such instrumental accompaniment—even with microphones—is substantial, and the parts demand more talents than most amateur synagogue choral societies could hope to possess. That the work is nearly devoid of any traditional synagogue music is less disturbing in this context than it might be had it been commissioned with more "traditional" expectations in mind.[15] However, the absence of any role for the congregation—or the rabbi—in this composition, makes it a work of "performance" and not of "participation."

Notwithstanding the extraordinary proportions of the Bloch *Sacred Service,* most other fully composed services met with similarly limited success. Although some excerpts from these services have taken root in contemporary practice[16] (at least in those synagogues for which they were written), the more common fate of these services has been for them to lapse into disuse. This "failure" was less a function of unappealing musical quality than a result of the congregation's lack of familiarity with the music—along with the elimination of any reasonable role for them in the services. Throughout the 1930s and 1940s, congregations continued, in principle, to welcome the creation of new music. However, the usurpation of the role of the congregation (and even the rabbi) by the cantor and choir became an increasingly serious impediment to the acceptance of new music and even to continued congregational loyalty.[17]

The Role of Congregational Singing

The period following World War II saw major demographic and psychological changes in the American Jewish community. A new wave of immigration brought the remnants of war-ravaged Europe to American shores and closed the chapter on European leadership in Jewish music. Now it became necessary for American Jews to pro-

duce their own musical leaders. The seminaries that had been training rabbis since the late nineteenth century finally established
schools to train cantors as well. Hebrew Union College–Jewish
Institute of Religion opened its School of Sacred Music for cantors
of the Reform movement in 1948; the Jewish Theological Seminary
started training Conservative cantors in its Cantors Institute in
1952; and the Cantorial Training Institute at Yeshiva University
opened its doors to Orthodox cantors in 1954.[18]

The graduates of these schools faced a Jewish community different from what their predecessors had known. Returning soldiers
eager to resume their lives and start families led to the growth of sub-
urbia and the proliferation of synagogues outside major city centers.
These new congregations were started by young people with strong
ideas about their role in the synagogue service and eager to play an
active part in determining their spiritual destinies.

Unfortunately, the transition was not a smooth one. The cantorial
training schools were dominated by faculty who had trained with the
old European models. The 1954 reissuing of 25 volumes known as
the *Out-of-Print Classics of Synagogue Music* reaffirmed the role of
music by Sulzer, Lewandowski, and Naumbourg in the synagogue
and the style of *nusaḥ* promulgated by Gerovitsch and others of the
nineteenth century. The "high church" style of practice continued to
dominate the training of Reform cantors, and the role of the cantor
as not just soloist, but also sole purveyor—and conservator—of synagogue music in Conservative and Orthodox synagogues was pronounced from the ivory towers of the cantorial schools.

But the congregants in the pews wanted to sing, too! A second
generation of Orthodox American Jews had already begun to establish "Young Israel" synagogues, where *sheliḥei tzibbur* taken from
among the many male congregants capable of leading regular
Shabbat and weekday services led their fellow worshipers in song,
thereby replacing increasing numbers of traditionally oriented (and
some felt, domineering) *ḥazzanim*.

In the Conservative and Reform movements, young people
empowered by their affirmative experiences in denominationally
affiliated summer camps rejected the notion of trading their sum-
mertime active participation for docile subservience to a cantor and

choir back at their home synagogues. The Conservative movement was the first to attempt a response. The Cantors Assembly[19] published *Zamru Lo,* a three-volume anthology of "congregational tunes" designed to increase the participation of worshipers in the synagogue service, while still maintaining the traditional *nusaḥ.* Composers also started considering the needs of congregants when writing for the cantor and/or the choir. "Singable refrains" allowed congregants to take an active role in at least part of a composition chiefly scored for cantor and/or choir. Max Wohlberg (1907–1996) was singularly successful at writing cantorial recitatives as well as longer settings that remained faithful to traditional *nusaḥ* while also providing an opportunity for the congregation to sing.[20]

Me - khal - kel ḥa - yim be - ḥe-sed   me-kha - yei mei - tim be - ra - ḥa -mim ra - bim

Example 7.4 From *Mekhalkel Ḥayim be-Ḥesed*

The music of Chicago-based Max Janowski (1917–1991) had a similar effect on the music of Reform synagogues. The Hasidic-style lilt of his largely unison *Yismeḥu* is a favorite of many congregations; the unison refrain of his moving *Sim Shalom* enables the congregation to take an active role in its presentation; and his lyrical, strophic *ve-Shomeru* enables the congregation to sing along with the melody, even as the choir intones its lovely harmonies.

Yis-me-ḥu yis-me-ḥu ve-mal khu-te-kha shom - rey   sha - bat   ve - kor - ei o -neg

Example 7.5 From *Yismeḥu* by Janowski

There were certainly composers who followed Janowski's example. Canadian composers Srul Irving Glick (1939–2002) and Ben Steinberg (b. 1930) were especially successful at writing music that welcomed congregational participation. In addition, composers from Herbert Fromm (1905–1995), to Samuel Adler (b. 1928), to Stephen Richards (b. 1935) have arranged well-known composed melodies and *mi-Sinai* tunes for congregational singing.

Example 7.6 From *Shiru L'Adonai* by Steinberg

Example 7.7 From *Anim Zemirot* by Fromm

Popular Music in the Synagogue

However forthcoming cantors and composers may have become in welcoming new music and group singing into the synagogue, it became clear to some by the late 1960s that the music of the synagogue was not providing the kind of warmth and spiritual nourishment that some congregants wanted. Notwithstanding efforts to bring new music into the synagogue, Jewish liturgical music had not changed substantially in 100 years. The immigrant generation had needed to retain the music of its past—partly out of a false sense that "European" culture represented authenticity[21] and partly as a "security blanket" against the raging and unpredictable winds of changing American popular culture. Unlike the music of virtually every previous generation of Jews, the music of America's Jews had failed to take on the trappings of the majority culture surrounding it. American Jewish music was artificially frozen in a nineteenth century vernacular—and this musical language simply did not speak to the baby-boom generation. Young people who sang spirited folk tunes and neo-Hasidic melodies in summer camps and youth services were not happy in their parents' synagogues, singing their grandparents' songs.[22]

Some cantors and composers noted the generation gap in their sanctuaries and sought remedies amid the popular culture of the missing youth. Charles Davidson (b. 1929), who had earlier invoked Hasidic, Oriental, and jazz idioms in Sabbath services written for his Conservative synagogue, turned to rock music for his *Seliḥot* service, *The Hush of Midnight* (1970).[23] Davidson wisely retained the motives and melodies of the High Holy Day period that are introduced at this service. However, he underlaid those traditional tunes with a rock beat and the accompaniment of piano and electric guitars.

Example 7.8 From *Ashamnu* from *The Hush of Midnight*

Interestingly, despite its somewhat dated musical idiom (Davidson revised the service somewhat in 1986), *The Hush of Midnight* continues to be presented in communities across North America. Part of the welcome for this particular work stems from the familiarity of the traditional material as well as the accessibility of several melodies composed by Davidson and woven throughout the hour-long service. Davidson's score also comes with an extremely important recommendation: that cantors and conductors hold a "teaching session" prior to the service, so that interested congregants may learn the new melodies in advance. Then they, together with the (mostly two-part) chorus, can encourage others to sing along during the service.

Other composers relied only tangentially on pre-existing melodies to "legitimize" their new music. Raymond Smolover, writing for his Reform congregation in a New York suburb, borrowed melodies by Max Helfman,[24] Robert Strassburg,[25] and Ernest Bloch for his 1968 "folk/rock" service, *The Edge of Freedom*. In describing his motivation for writing this new work, Smolover wrote:

> I realized that we had been asking our children to accept our God and the God of our fathers, and what He sounds like. I realized after almost twenty years of teaching them the sound of my God, that I must listen to the sound of theirs. I dared enter their world aware that I may be respectfully tolerated, amusingly indulged, or murmuringly ignored. They welcomed me. It may be that the Folk/Rock Service is not completely their sound nor my own. It may be what happened, when their God met mine."[26]

But as welcomed as Smolover may have felt, his music did not pass the test of time—in part because he was, after all, an interloper in a youth culture not of his making or understanding, but more because the times changed. Even services by young people themselves— Michael Isaacson's (b. 1946) folksy *Avodat Amamit* [*sic*] and Debbie Friedman's (b. 1951) folk/rock *Sing Unto God* (both written in 1972)—quickly became outdated.[27] Creative responses to the musical/spiritual yearnings of America's Jewish youth were better answered by two very different sources: Shlomo Carlebach and the Hasidic Song Festival.

Reinventing Hasidic Music

Shlomo Carlebach (1925–1994) was among the most unorthodox Orthodox rabbis of the twentieth century. With a unique personality reflecting the full fervor of his adopted Hasidic background[28] as well as a genuine love for his fellow Jew, Carlebach traveled North America telling stories, reaching out to Jews of all persuasions (including those with no affiliation), and using his talents to craft melodies that touched his listeners and became instant staples in *havurot*[29] and *minyanim* across the denominational spectrum. His setting of "Esa Einai" (Psalm 121), one of his earliest hits, was not originally intended for use in regular worship;[30] however, the melody has been borrowed for use in conjunction with other texts, including the Sabbath Hymn of Glory *(Anim Zemirot)*.

E - sa ei -nai el - he - ha - rim mei-a - yin mei - a - yin ya - vo - ez - ri

Example 7.9 From "Esa Einai" by Carlebach

A - nim ze - mi - rot ve - shi - rim e - rog ki - ey - le - kha - naf - shi - ta - a - rog

Example 7.10 From *Anim Zemirot* adapted to a folklorized version of "Esa Einai"

Some of the other Carlebach melodies that became regular parts of worship services were written for entry into Israel's annual Hasidic Song Festival. In 1968 a small-budget Israeli play called *Ish Ḥasid Haya* (Once There Was a Hasid) brought traditional Hasidic songs and stories to the generally nonobservant masses who filled its audiences. The success of this material inspired enthusiasts to revitalize Hasidic music by soliciting songs—in an ostensibly Hasidic style—to be presented in an annual Israeli festival, starting in 1969. The fascination with most things Israeli on the part of many American Jews after the 1967 Six-Day War[31] led Israeli promoters to bring a version of the Hasidic Song Festival to North American audiences.

The only things "Hasidic" about most of these songs were their relatively short melodies and traditional lyrics. Still, the presence of catchy new tunes for brief liturgical texts encouraged the use of many of these songs in the prayers of American Jews looking for easy-to-learn melodies and more congregational singing—even by congregants who were not fluent in Hebrew. Carlebach's *ve-Ha'er Einenu* quickly jumped back into the morning services from which its lyrics were taken, and Nurit Hirsh's (b. 1942) *Oseh Shalom* not only launched her subsequent career (limited almost exclusively to secular songs), but also became a staple of weekday and Sabbath services in countless synagogues across the continent.

Ve - ha - er ei-nei-nu be -to - ra-te-kha ve - da - bek li - bei - nu be -mitz-vo-te - kha

Example 7.11 From *ve-Ha'er Einenu* by Carlebach

Varied Voices in the Modern Era

While the popularity of the Hasidic Song Festivals gradually waned,[32] the border between popular song literature and the music of worship was effectively breached. A succession of popular American artists began (or, like Debbie Friedman and a more musically sophisticated Michael Isaacson, continued) to contribute music that was just as successful in the synagogue on Saturday morning as it was in concert on Saturday night. Not surprisingly, the Reform movement led the way in this more liberal musical style. The guitars that dominated American folk and popular music were welcome in many Reform synagogues and even replaced the organ as the instrument of choice in congregations moving away from the decorous classical style of Sulzer and Lewandowski to a more inviting and participatory "warm Reform" service.

The Orthodox movement continued to eschew instrumental accompaniment, but many congregations were equally active in adopting some more contemporary sounds into their services. The

Orthodox also borrowed tunes that had been written originally for non-liturgical presentation but that inexorably crept into synagogal use. The common preference among Orthodox synagogues to utilize lay *sheliḥei tzibbur* (as opposed to seminary-trained *ḥazzanim*) also contributed to the random utilization of contrafacted melodies from among popular Israeli and American songs.

E - rev shel sho - sha-nim   nei - tze na el ha- bu -stan

Example 7.12 From "Erev Shel Shoshanim,"original tune by Yosef Hadar

Mi - me- ko - mo   hu   yi -fen be -ra -ha-mim

Example 7.13 From *Mimekomo* adapted to "Erev Shel Shoshanim"

The Conservative movement lagged somewhat behind the popular tendency to insert contemporary songs and styles into the liturgy. The sanctuaries where adults worshiped tended to hold fast to a traditional body of music taught to cantorial students at the movement's Jewish Theological Seminary and/or gathered in *Zamru Lo*. Members of the movement's United Synagogue Youth groups and campers and staff at Conservative Ramah Camps eagerly adopted popular tunes into their own youth services, but the hegemony of the Conservative cantorate rejected these innovations as "camp songs." Moreover, the music of Israel was embraced in settings throughout the Conservative community: Ramah summer camps, Solomon Schechter Day Schools, adult education programs, and beyond. That broad and seemingly never-ending font of new material was largely a distraction from and a disincentive to the creation of new music from within the movement's ranks.

Implied pressure placed on Conservative cantors by the popularity of "alternative" music being utilized among youth groups and in *havurot* (often breakaways from the more traditional services conducted in Conservative synagogues) led to a gradual willingness of

Conservative cantors and their congregations to experiment with the music of the synagogue. Some Conservative synagogues installed organs in their sanctuaries and occasionally used other instruments as well. The ordination of female cantors in 1987 [33] brought dramatically new voices to the Conservative synagogue, and many of these women, whose presence itself represented a major change, were more inclined to welcome innovation into the service.

The real watershed in congregational singing came, though, with the success of one Conservative synagogue on New York's Upper West Side. B'nai Jeshurun, or "BJ" as it is affectionately known to its members (and derogatorily scorned by its detractors), gained widespread popular appeal during the tenure of Rabbi Michael Meyer (1985–1993) and continues now under the leadership of Rabbi Marcelo Bronstein, Rabbi J. Rolando Matalon, and Hazzan Ari Priven. It attracted hundreds of worshipers to regular services when it began adopting a family-friendly attitude and a repertoire of reverent but upbeat, new melodies (as well as "refurbished" versions of older tunes) that welcomed and embraced the Sabbath with fervent singing. The contrast between the numbers of BJ attendees overflowing onto Manhattan's sidewalks and the number of empty pews in most other "mainstream" Conservative synagogues was directly attributed to B'nai Jeshurun's music.[34] Demand from within and outside the congregation inspired the synagogue's leadership to record its melodies as teaching tools and as models for others to follow.[35]

Future Thoughts

As the twenty-first century dawns, the future course of American synagogue music is not clear. Some traditionalists may decry the continuing preference for community singing—of any kind of music—over the preservation of *nusaḥ* as the final "nail in the coffin" of Jewish musical continuity. For many, the "usurpation" of the role of cantor/*ḥazzan* by bar mitzvah celebrants and lay precentors[36] appears to signal an ironic return to the anarchy of the early nineteenth century and a tragic surrendering of musical and professional ritual standards.

Others may applaud the enfranchisement of the congregation as an appropriate response to every Jew's search for an active, participatory role in the synagogue. They may see the decline in choral singing as a victory for the community and herald the embrace of contemporary music as an inevitable and historically consistent response to a new era and the cultural heritage of its majority.

Yet the "return to spirituality" that has also come with the turn of the millennium will likely preclude a complete abrogation of Jewish musical tradition. The *mi-Sinai* melody used to chant the opening sections of the Sabbath *Amidah* may need to be adapted to new texts as congregations invoke the mothers of Israel as well as the fathers,[37] but few communities have completely rejected the traditional tune. Many of the newer melodies are sung with a spiritual fervor comparable to that of the Hasidim—whose earliest music borrowed secular styles and "rescued" pre-existing melodies so that the masses might serve God with all their hearts.

One of the most interesting examples of "new/old" music was written by Ami Aloni[38] (1928–1999) in 1986. In his setting of *Ahavat Olam* for cantor, choir, and accompaniment, Aloni appears to be harkening back to the *chor-shul* tradition of old—a style that many congregations rejected as paternalistic and indulgent on the part of professional musicians and an affront to congregants eager to take an active role in the service. On the other hand, Aloni is writing a selection for use on the High Holy Days, an occasion when the congregation is willing to accept choral singing and cantorial solos as part of a large repertoire of musical styles that enhance a special liturgical moment (and a somewhat longer service). Moreover, Aloni has adapted a musical theme familiar to the entire community—the *mi-Sinai* melody that infuses the *Ma'ariv* service—and so the congregation is not only satisfied by hearing familiar music but implicitly is encouraged to sing along with the cantor and choir. The melody may not be immediately obvious during the earliest moments of the setting; in fact, the selection opens with a countermelody to the familiar tune, only hinting at the traditional material in the accompaniment. However, as the passage draws to a close, the concluding text and the final blessing triumphantly (and traditionally) intone the time-honored melody and practically beg the worshipers to join in the familiar refrain.

Example 7.14 From the concluding blessing from *Ahavat Olam* by Aloni

In many ways, Aloni's setting of *Ahavat Olam* summarizes all the possible permutations of American synagogue music and offers "something for everyone." The cantor and choir lead, but the congregation sings along; the treatment is fresh and contemporary; but the "tune" is as traditional, universal, and accessible as any in the Ashkenazic liturgy. In this regard, it also summarizes much of Western synagogue music history and thus may serve as a model for composers and congregations of the future.

8 ~
Jewish Music on the Concert Stage

America's Jews may have rejected the notion of "performing" choirs in their synagogues, but they were certainly not opposed to the idea of Jewish music on the concert stage. As we have already seen, Jewish audiences had been enjoying cantorial concerts of Jewish music as well as theatrical presentations throughout the twentieth century. In addition, many of those who had become accustomed to the new idea of Jewish art music during programs presented by The Society for Jewish Folk Music were now part of the American listening public and eager to participate in the development of this still-emerging genre. Some of the Society members themselves were also among the new Americans, and their influence as writers and as teachers of another generation of Jewish musicians led to a slow-but-steady development of Jewish art music in America.

The latest music written by The Society for Jewish Folk Music (and those influenced by it) had made the transition from compositions based upon pre-existing Jewish tunes to original works "in the style of " traditional Jewish songs. This blurring of the line between "real" Jewish music and music "of interest to Jews" was an important development in its time. It enabled American Jewish composers who were writing alternately for the synagogue, for the theater, and for the serious concert hall to avoid making a distinction between "Jewish" and "general" music. Indeed, these modern composers were not formally concerned with writing music for Jewish audiences. Rather, they wrote music that satisfied their own muses. As Jews became more integrated into American life, and as Jewish culture became more familiar to non-Jewish audiences, the question that the

Society had implicitly posed in its earliest discussions was raised once again: What constitutes "Jewish art music"? The answers offered by America's Jewish composers were many and varied.

The Life and Music of Lazar Weiner

More than any other composer, Lazar Weiner (1897–1982) seems to have most directly inherited the mantle of The Society for Jewish Folk Music. Weiner was born in Cherkassy, a small town near Kiev in the southern part of the Ukraine and received a limited Jewish education as a young boy, but, as a singer in Abram Dzimitrovsky's choir at the Brodsky Synagogue in Kiev, he became familiar with the Western European synagogue literature of composers like Sulzer, Lewandowski, and Nowakowsky. He also sang in the children's chorus at the local opera house and began studying piano with Dzimitrovsky, progressing to the point of winning a partial scholarship to the Kiev Conservatory. There he continued his piano studies and added classes in harmony. Weiner's first compositions imitated the keyboard studies of Bach and Chopin, offering little hint of the music that was to come.

As we have noted, the living situation for Jews in Russia had never been favorable. It deteriorated further, however, when a neighbor of the Weiner family, Mendel Beilis, was imprisoned on charges of having murdered a Christian child to use his blood for ritual purposes.[1] The Weiner family's decision to leave Russia in the wake of this incident (and over the young musician's strong objections) cut short Lazar's formal music education, but his arrival in New York in 1914 afforded him new opportunities.

After a difficult transition to American life (during which he even protested against the notion of never returning to Russia by resisting learning English), Weiner found his first job in 1917 as accompanist to a voice teacher. By playing in a Carnegie Hall studio for 20 lessons a day, Weiner quickly became familiar with the classical and operatic vocal repertoire. In addition, he accompanied cantorial concerts by Yossele Rosenblatt, David Roitman, Gershon Sirota, Zavel Kwartin, and Berele Chagy and concert performances by opera star Rosa Raisa.[2]

The busy young man also acted as librarian for the Little

Symphony Amateur Orchestra and eventually became its conductor—despite his complete lack of any conducting background. Weiner flourished in the role, but the group disbanded after two years, leaving him with valuable experience—and a close friendship with Nahum Baruch Minkoff (1893–1958). Minkoff had been a nondistinguished violinist with the erstwhile ensemble but is remembered far better as a Yiddish poet. Weiner was an ardent reader of Russian literature, but at the time, his knowledge of Yiddish was almost nonexistent. As he was drawn into Minkoff's circle, he became acquainted with the poet Yehoash (né Yehoash Solomon Bloomgarden, 1872–1927) and playwrights David Pinski and Peretz Hirschbein.[3] Weiner quickly developed an abiding love for the Yiddish language and became fascinated with the avant-garde poetry his new friends were writing.

By 1922, Weiner had set a number of Yiddish poems to music. In an interesting twist of fate that was to have lasting repercussions for the young musician, Weiner decided to send his work to the only composer he knew of who might understand the Yiddish texts and give him an honest critique of his work: Joel Engel.[4] Engel, whose early ethnographic lectures had ultimately inspired the formation of The Society for Jewish Music, examined "Tzela-Tzeldi" (the name of a gypsy girl in a poem by Jacob Glatstein), "Shtile Tener" (Soft Voice), and "In Feld" (In the Field) and pronounced them full of promise. He wrote back to Weiner and encouraged him to pursue his composing—but urged him to contribute to his own people by imbuing his work with a Jewish flavor.

Weiner not only took Engel's advice to heart,[5] but also devoted his entire life to Jewish music. He taught himself traditional *nusaḥ* and cantillation. Weiner also became interested in the activities of The Society for Jewish Folk Music and the music it had produced. Society members Lazare Saminsky, Joseph Achron, and Solomon Rosowsky had arrived in America and became his friends, teaching him much about Jewish music and influencing his style.[6]

Weiner's interest in Yiddish was not limited to the writing of art songs. In 1923 he organized the New York Freiheit Gesangs Verein (Freedom Singing Society), an amateur chorus of several hundred Jewish shop workers. With little repertoire available in Yiddish, Weiner translated works of Felix Mendelssohn and Robert

Schumann into Yiddish, arranged Yiddish folk songs for chorus, and urged his friends (who now included Vladimir Heifetz [1893–1970] and Reuven Kosakoff [1898–1987]) to write for the Yiddish chorus. Weiner's eagerness to upgrade and popularize the Yiddish repertory drove him to organize additional choirs, including the Folk University Chorus, the Yiddish Culture Chorus, and the International Ladies' Garment Workers' Union (ILGWU) Chorus.[7]

Weiner's greatest successes as a choral conductor came, however, when he assumed the directorship of the Workmen's Circle Chorus in 1930—a post he held until 1965. Throughout those years, Weiner honed the amateur group into a professional-sounding ensemble.[8] During his 35 years with the Chorus, Weiner performed such works as Schubert's *Miriam's Song of Triumph,* Mendelssohn's *Walpurgis Nacht,* and other works by Mozart, Beethoven, and Rossini—all in Yiddish translations by the most prominent contemporary Yiddish poets. The Workmen's Circle Chorus also served as a forum for Weiner's presentation of his own works: *A Mol in a Tsayt* (Legend of Toil, 1933), *Mentsh in der Velt* (Man in the World, 1939), *Hirsh Lekert* (Fight for Freedom, 1943), and *Tsu Dir, Amerike* (To Thee, America, 1944). These works were premiered with such ensembles as the New York Symphony, the New York Philharmonic, and the NBC Orchestra in annual concerts in New York City's Carnegie and Town Halls.

In 1930 Weiner also became the music director of Central Synagogue. That position brought him his first real exposure to synagogue music literature since his early experiences as a choir boy. His first responsibility in that prestigious Reform synagogue was to replace a repertoire of music largely by non-Jewish composers—over the strong objections of the congregation, which held fast to its familiar "tradition." To overcome the community's resistance, Weiner commissioned works by a variety of composers, including his friends Joseph Achron, Jacob Weinberg (1879–1956), and Reuven Kosakoff. Weiner directed the New York premiere of Ernest Bloch's *Avodat ha-Kodesh* and of Darius Milhaud's *Sacred Service* (see below). Weiner's own liturgical compositions, ranging from short selections to complete services, also helped to infuse the Central Synagogue congregants with a devotion to high-quality Jewish music. In 1935, when Central Synagogue and radio station WABC jointly sponsored a weekly program of Jewish liturgical music, Weiner became its director and had the opportunity to teach all of New York what he had taught the Central Synagogue community.

In his later years, Weiner appeared less frequently as a pianist and began to relinquish his various conducting positions, but he remained active as a teacher at Hebrew Union College and as a vocal coach. He also continued to present short series of lectures on Jewish music and art songs, which he had begun offering at the Juilliard School of Music in 1948 and at New York's 92nd Street "Y."[9] Weiner composed music virtually to the end of his long and active life in 1982.

Lazar Weiner and the Yiddish Art Song

In the lengthy list of Weiner's accomplishments, his greatest contributions, however, came through his composition of Yiddish art songs—the genre pioneered in St. Petersburg that realized its fullest flowering throughout Lazar Weiner's life.

The heart of Weiner's Yiddish art songs lies in his commitment to his texts. Albert Weisser observed that the composer's "sensitivity to the sound and structure of Yiddish is unmatched among modern composers."[10] It is primarily the texts Weiner chooses and the innate Jewish consciousness of the poetry that provides Weiner's music with its "Jewish" feeling. In the more secular poetry, devoid of ethnic or religious connotations, Weiner's music is appropriately universal.

Some of Weiner's earliest works are illustrative of the many sides of his music and its interrelatedness with the text. In "Tzela-Tzelda" (1922), the motivating element is not Jewish but rather Russian folk material. Tzela-Tzelda is a gypsy, and the staccato piano and fiery parallel thirds and fourths of the following introduction arouse the passionate nymph:

Example 8.1 Introduction from "Tzela-Tzelda"

Glatstein's poem is set in two worlds: one, that of the youthful girl of the past; the second, the old woman of the present who can no longer dance. As Glatstein turns to the somber mood of old age, Weiner abruptly changes key, and his rhythm is a more reserved one based on slow quarter notes, rather than excited eighth notes.

Example 8.2 From "andante" of "Tzela-Tzelda"

Tzela-Tzeldi, light-footed nymph,
With the crash of cymbals
Your graceful doe-like dancing feet
Become as quick as a rabbit's.

Tzela-Tzeldi,
Your chestnut head has turned gray,
Your blue eyes do not see,
Your days are slowly fading.
Deep sorrow, mute within you
Is like the silence of an autumn sky.
But Tzela-Tzeldi, when the cymbals crash
You're up again with dancing feet!
Oooh, up! Tzela-Tzeldi!

Tzela-Tzeldi,
Hold back the sighs of your nights,
Have no fear of the hand of death.
Still, I wonder,
Say, what mountain of earth can keep you buried
If, when the cymbals crash
You're up with dancing feet,
Graceful nymph!

Ooh, up! Tzela-Tzeldi!

Weiner's seemingly disjunct music in this setting simply reflects an almost stream-of-consciousness poem, and the two moods of youthful joy and aging sadness are portrayed plainly and consistently.

Weiner was not so far removed from the folk tradition that he had trouble setting a strophic poem. Aaron Nissenson's "Volt Mayn Tate Raykh Geven" (Were My Father a Rich Man) calls for a simple setting and, melodically, that is just what Weiner gave it. While the melody here is easily singable, Weiner's accompaniment goes far to add insight into the simple verse. The agitated opening bars (set in parallel fourths) and the chromatic thirds of the second phrase are expressive first of the frustrations of the poor speaker, and then of his eager dreams of what he would do with his wealth.

Example 8.3 Opening bar of "Volt Mayn Tate Raykh Geven"

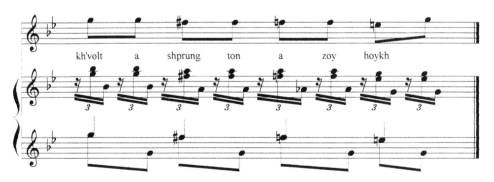

Example 8.4 Next phrase of "Volt Mayn Tate Raykh Geven"

If my father were rich I would not look for bargains.
I would buy a horse who could spring into the heavens.
I would leap up so high I could touch the sun
And return to the earth with the sun in my grasp.
From all over the world forty beauties would appear.
They would each give their hearts to me, their hero.
Among the beauties of the world you would also come.
From among the beauties of the world I would choose you.
I would hang the sun again where she had been hanging,
And let the horse go free, and go walking with you.

One of the simplest and, at the same time, most moving of
Weiner's early songs is "A Gebet" (A Prayer). Jacob Rolnick's verses
are increasingly imploring pleas to God for rest, alongside a quiet
expression of growing desperation. Weiner's 1923 setting, composed
shortly after Engel advised him to take up more Jewish themes, is
reservedly poignant, capturing without display the subtlety of the
poet's emotion.

Example 8.5 Opening excerpt from "A Gebet"

Master of the Universe, dear God of my father, hear my heartfelt prayer.
Make whole the torn fragments of my soul, and send me a little bit
of peace.
Master of the Universe, God of my father, hear my heartfelt prayer.
Destroy the remaining shreds of my heart, and send me a little bit
of rest.

Weiner's early music thus establishes many of the tensions that characterize his work: melodic simplicity versus tonal and structural complexity; and universal themes as opposed to those intrinsically Jewish. In his middle years, Weiner was to concentrate more and more on Jewish themes.

Weiner's almost Schubertian treatment of Leivick's strophic "ode" to Siberia, "Ergets Vayt" (Somewhere Distant, 1936) is, ironically, beautiful. The vocal line and its accompaniment are almost exactly the same for each verse, beginning in a slow minor mode that alternates regularly between duple and triple meters.

Example 8.6 From the opening of "Ergetz Vayt"

Somewhere distant, somewhere distant lies the land, the
forbidden land,
The hills glow silver, not trodden by anyone.
Somewhere deep, somewhere deep in the unkneaded earth
Are treasures without end, are buried treasures.
Somewhere distant, somewhere distant a captive lies alone.
On his head dies the shadow of the setting sun.

Somewhere someone wanders deep in piles of snow
And loses his way to the forbidden land.

Interestingly, despite the irony of the poetry and the sophistication
of the setting, this song was folklorized, made popular by an immigrant generation that was physically far removed from the *farbotenem
land* (forbidden land), but not from the horror of exile in Siberia.

Weiner's "A Bord" (A Beard), written in 1945 to a brief poem by
Aaron Lutzky, is one of his most obviously Jewish compositions.[11]
Certainly the melodic line, outlining as it does a combination of the
learning and haftarah modes, could only be explained as the result
of a Jewish mind inspired by the vision of an old man with a long
white beard.

Example 8.7 Excerpt from "A Bord" compared with haftarah chant

A white beard wants to run away from an old man
And, waving like a banner, flutters like a fan in the wind.
As he holds his hat on his head with the fingers of his left hand
The beard chokes with laughter as it flies past his right ear.

Lutzky's poem is colorful, if somewhat irreverent, and with humor
and grace Weiner captures the impudent wind in fluid, incessant
arpeggios on the piano.

A song that many regard as among Weiner's greatest was written
to a text by L. Magister.[12] The composer's first contact with the text
inspired him to create a choral composition in 1936—almost a short
cantata—to *Di Reyd Funem Novi* (The Speech of the Prophet).
Despite the success of that setting, Weiner's friends suggested that he

reexamine the text from the point of view of the solo song, and, in so doing, Weiner totally recreated the poem.

Following a regal opening that prepares us for a grandiose statement, the singer chants the initial words in an unexpected recitative: "These are the words of the prophet to his folk, and to all people." A series of disjunct modulations keeps us waiting for the first real melodic theme to appear. When it finally does, it is a lovely pastorale, setting Isaiah's well-known expression of solace, "Comfort, oh comfort My people" (Isa. 40:1).[13] The lyric moment is brief, though; the breadth and emotion of the poet's/prophet's words defy rhythmic or melodic continuity, and so with only an alternating triplet-eighth-eighth figure to link the section together, Weiner allows his melody to wander chromatically with the prophet.

Example 8.8 "Comfort, oh comfort My people"

These are the words of the prophet to his folk and to all the people.
The heavens declare his words, the earth pays heed to their meaning.
"Comfort, oh comfort My people!"
A light will arise, from the desert born, and bring to light forgotten
    forms from their deep slumber.
The sun will shed light giving radiance o'er the trees in the forest,
O'er the fruits in the vineyards, o'er the blossoms that grow in
    the fields.
And one man in greeting another will say unto him,
"Peace and goodwill unto you."
And the other will answer him,
"Blessings, may you be blessed with peace and comfort."

And enemies will meet as friends, and friends will meet as comrades,
And comrades as brothers and sisters.
These tales will we tell to our children.
Many years ago, poverty roamed the face of the earth,
And the hungry begged for naught but a morsel of bread.
The weary passed away before their time and the blood of the
    innocent flowed as a stream over the earth.
Horrible tales will we tell them, but no one will ever believe them.
Thus shall we mold us a monument—a token to remember forever
    more and forever more.

A standard theoretical analysis of this piece serves little purpose. Weiner's interest here is in the color—the emotion of his text. In this case, the enormous grandeur of the sentiment defied containment by the composer in any standard harmonic progression or rhythmic schema. The recitative (both where marked and where merely approximated) served the composer best—and indeed seemed more suited to this text than might any more-lyric line. It is not by coincidence that the vocal line is strongly reminiscent of the ancient chant in which the prophecy is historically recited. Steeped in respect for the tradition and overwhelmed by the utopian sentiment of the verse, there was little Weiner could or would do other than to punctuate these lines with bits of color. A composer's passion need not always adhere to harmonic convention.

Weiner's more easily "contained" passion, and yet the one that motivates his work and overwhelms his reason is his great love for the Yiddish language. His identification with Jacob Segal's poem "Yiddish" (set in 1946) gives us a hint at the regard in which Weiner holds "the wealth of his treasure"—but the almost melancholy imploring of the music needs more than theoretical analysis.

The vocal and piano parts to this music are disjunct from the outset. While the singer caresses the words—his devotion to the Yiddish language—the piano's incessant chromatically descending line is sadly ominous.

Example 8.9 From "Yiddish"

> Yiddish, my dear heritage, from you the Ba'al Shem Tov has drunk,
> The holy Modzhitzer preacher, the Bratzlaver, the Berditchever,
>   and so many simple, working people
> While journeying through lands and over the world's countless
>   roadways
> Where reality and legend are melded together.
> Yiddish, the wealth of my treasure.

As the singer tells the tale, the memory of old, long-gone rabbis and poor Jews who also held Yiddish close to them is evoked, and the singer pauses to punctuate these recollections. The wandering of the Jews is remembered passionately, the music building—and then the opening, melancholy accompaniment to the poet's and the composer's love for Yiddish returns to conclude the setting.

In 1946 Weiner began to fear that Yiddish was a dying language. Having just witnessed the murder of two-thirds of the world's Yiddish-speaking population, his fear in the late forties was very real. Many of his friends felt that Weiner himself would be a more universally known figure if he had not chosen to devote himself to Yiddish. (Weiner himself agreed.) In the song he wrote, the voice sings lovingly of Yiddish, while, in the piano, life goes on beyond it. Weiner's musical life went on, too—but the language he loved moved with it.

Weiner's life was not limited to the performer's stage or to the composer's desk. He was always sincerely interested in all forms of music (but especially Jewish music) and went beyond the roles of performer and creator in his efforts to further their development.

From 1937 to 1939, as an active member of the MAILAMM Society[14] (from the first letters of *Makhon Aretz Israeli La-Mada'ey ha-Musika* [Israel Institute for the Musical Sciences]), he devoted himself to the cause of advancing Jewish music in the United States and what was then Palestine. In 1939 he helped to found the Jewish Music Forum, specifically for the advancement of Jewish scholarship and the performance of Jewish music.[15] Weiner was also involved in the 1944 founding of the Jewish Music Council of the Jewish Welfare Board, as well as the Jewish Liturgical Music Society of America.[16]

Lazar Weiner received numerous awards and citations for his pioneering work in the field of Yiddish music. In many ways he was, indeed, a pivotal figure in American Jewish musical life. Joel Engel's faith in his promise was more than realized.

The Jewish Music of Ernest Bloch

At the same time that Lazar Weiner was affirming the place of the Yiddish art song on the musical map of the twentieth century, Ernest Bloch (1881–1959) was making his transition from "composer" to "Jewish composer"[17] and creating a place for "Jewish music" in the concert halls of America and Europe. The Swiss-born and -educated musician had several secular compositions to his credit, but in the wake of the mixed reactions they received, he was beginning to despair of any real success in his musical career. While in this frame of mind, Bloch was drawn to the pessimistic texts of the biblical Ecclesiastes (attributed by tradition to the elderly King Solomon), but felt strongly that they could only be set in their original Hebrew, a language with which he did not feel comfortable. As he struggled with how to treat these verses, he happened to attend a cello recital and was struck anew by the expressive, almost "vocal" qualities of that instrument. Recognizing the answer to his dilemma, Bloch composed *Schelomo, Rhapsody for Cello and Orchestra,* completed in 1916.

It is important for the listener to appreciate the "textual" origins of this composition, because no overt musical references identify it as a Jewish work. For that matter, none of Bloch's compositions ever quoted preexisting Jewish musical materials.[18] So what made them Jewish?

Bloch, himself, maintained that in these works he was writing from the depths of his Jewish soul and that his Jewish passions would certainly be apparent to the listener. He wrote:

> It is not my purpose, not my desire, to attempt a "reconstruction" of Jewish music, or to base my work on melodies more or less authentic. I am not an archaeologist. I hold it of first importance to write good, genuine music. It is the Jewish soul that interests me, the complex, glowing, agitated soul, that I feel vibrating throughout the Bible; ... the freshness and naiveté of the Patriarchs; the violence of the Prophetic Books; the Jew's savage love of justice; the despair of Ecclesiastes; the sorrow and the immensity of the Book of Job; the sensuality of [T]he Song of Songs. All this is in us, all this is in me, and it is the better part of me. It is all this that I endeavor to hear within myself, and to transcribe in my music: the time-honored emotional urge of the race that slumbers deep down in my soul.[19]

But if Bloch is writing from his own personal sense of what is "Jewish," how is an audience to relate to his music? Can a non-Jewish listener appreciate his music? What about Jews who are more, or less, traditional or knowledgeable about the Bible and Jewish culture?

Some musicologists and historians maintain that all music can be divided into two types: "absolute" music and "program" music. "Absolute" music is absolutely—and only—music. It does not exist to teach, to refer the listener to a certain event, or even to evoke particular emotions. It wants only to be a pleasing coincidence of pitches that the listener will enjoy. Most instrumental music falls into this category and the titles of such compositions are merely descriptive: Symphony in D Major, Sonata for Violin and Piano, or Variations on a Theme are typical appellations.

"Program" music has an agenda—literally, a program. Whether through words or only through music, it intends to tell a story. Vocal music is always programmatic, since the music must be assumed to reflect the composer's ideas about the text, but a composition does not need to set text in order to tell a story. The tone poems and other romantic works of the late nineteenth century tell entire stories through music, with titles like *The Merry Pranks of Till Eulenspiegel* (Strauss), *The Sorcerer's Apprentice* (Dukas), *Pictures at an Exhibition*

(Mussorgsky), *Scheherezade* (Rimsky-Korsakov), and *La Mer* (Debussy). Even Beethoven's Sixth Symphony ("Pastoral") evokes a setting, and titles like that of the final movement ("Prayer of Thanksgiving after the Rainstorm") speak volumes about the composer's intent, without requiring another word of explanation.

But if titles are the key to program music, they can also be the key to "Jewish music." At the very least, "Jewish" music intends to evoke in the listener some identification with something in his or her experience that is somehow "Jewish." If we know that "Schelomo" is the Hebrew name of King Solomon, we may hear something that evokes biblical imagery or the ancient Near East, but we are certainly waiting for something more particular than a "work for solo cello and orchestra." Granted, the initiated listener will hear much more, but the title will already tell us what to listen for and hint at what we may be missing.

Bloch intended his work to be at once universal and particular. In his experience, the Bible was among the great creations of human civilization and certainly well known to the educated Western concertgoer. As such, the ancient Israelite who was often at the center of Bloch's inspiration would have been a familiar figure. In some instances, Bloch's own lack of intimacy with the Hebrew language and his ambivalence about religious texts drove him to create his own variants of Jewish traditions. These would unintentionally, but pointedly, be much easier for non-Jewish listeners to digest. In the final movement of his *Israel Symphony* female singers chant this unusual text of Bloch's own making:

Adonai, my *Elohim*
O my *Elohim*!
Allelouyah![20] O my *Elohim*!

Hear Thou my voice, my *Elohim*,
Hear my prayer.

O I implore Thee, O my *Elohim*,
Thou art my refuge.
I implore Thee,

In Thee I trust,
I am steadfast, O my *Elohim*!

Allelouyah![21]

On the other hand, works like *Ba'al Shem Suite* for violin and piano present a much greater challenge to the uninitiated listener (Jewish or not). To appreciate Bloch's "program" the listener must first know that the Ba'al Shem [sic] was the founder of Hasidism and something about Hasidic philosophy. Then the listener should understand the titles to the work's three movements. "Vidui," the title of the first movement, is not just "Contrition"; it is a particular Jewish confession of sins recited on Yom Kippur, when Jews atone for transgressions against God.[22] "Improvisation" is a poor English translation for "Nigun," the name of the suite's second movement and the wordless melody that played such an important role in Hasidic life. The last movement is called "Simḥat Torah." While "Rejoicing with the Law" is a technically accurate translation, it does not adequately capture the joyous fervor with which Hasidim (and other traditional Jews) complete the yearlong reading of the Torah and immediately begin it over again.

"Program notes" may explain a great deal, providing background critical for a complete understanding of a composition such as the *Ba'al Shem Suite*. However, one would have to be quite insensitive to miss the emotional content of this music[23]—and totally unfamiliar with standards of Western art to miss the superior skill and artistry exhibited by Bloch in this work.

Bloch turned much of his attention over the next twenty years to creating works with a Jewish theme, beginning his personal Jewish musical journey with a setting of Psalm 114 for soprano and orchestra. Later, in addition to *Schelomo* (1916) and *Ba'al Shem Suite* (also known as *Three Pictures of Hasidic Life,* 1923), Bloch composed *Trois Poemes Juifs* (Three Jewish Poems, with movements entitled "Danse," "Rite," and "Cortege Funebre," written to memorialize his father in 1913), *Israel Symphony* (begun in 1912, set aside in favor of *Schelomo,* then completed in 1916), settings of Psalm 22 for baritone and orchestra and Psalm 137 for soprano and orchestra, *Meditation*

Hebraique (1924), *From Jewish Life* (with movements called "Prayer," "Supplication," and "Jewish Song," 1924), and *Abodah: Meditation for Yom Kippur* (1929). His epic *Avodat ha-Kodesh* (Sacred Service) was completed in 1933 but, while intended for use in the synagogue, soon made the transition to the concert stage, where it found far greater acceptance. Much later, Bloch wrote *Six Preludes for Organ* (1949) and *Four Wedding Marches* (1950), which have found their way into the synagogue although not intended specifically for such use. *Suite Hebraique* ("Rhapsody," "Processional," and "Affirmation," 1951) was his last Jewish-themed work. Bloch continued teaching and composing through 1958 and died on July 15, 1959.

Like the composer himself, Bloch's champions decline to paint him into a narrow corner labeled "Jewish composer." However, even they must acknowledge the sheer number of Jewish-themed works he produced and note, as well, that he was writing at a time when Jewish culture was not as well recognized or received as it became at the close of the century. Bloch's work helped set the stage for similarly oriented works by other composers of Jewish origin. Some of those musicians ultimately exceeded Bloch's renown, but none produced a comparable volume of "Jewish" material.

Aaron Copland, Jewish Composer?

Long before he had achieved his reputation as the quintessential American composer of such favorites as *Appalachian Spring, Billy the Kid,* and *Rodeo,* Aaron Copland (1900–1990) was a young student studying in Paris with the legendary Nadia Boulanger.[24] He happened to attend a performance of Anski's *The Dybbuk,* and was captivated by the production's opening overture composed by Joel Engel and based upon an old Hasidic melody.[25]

Example 8.10 Traditional Hasidic melody

The melody haunted Copland until it finally came to rest as the inspiration for his trio for piano, violin, and cello. Copland named his composition *Vitebsk,* after the region in which the melody was discovered by Jewish ethnographers seeking their cultural roots.

Copland's *Vitebsk* was as close as the composer ever really came to his own roots, and ironically, the work is nothing like either the engaging overture that inspired it or the many melodious compositions Copland went on to write. Indeed, one might seriously question whether Copland was consciously trying to compose a "Jewish" work or simply exploiting a melody that happened to have a Jewish provenance. Since it was Copland's only gesture toward his own heritage, it is easy to assume that the work was an isolated experiment.[26]

Copland's dalliance with Jewish music may have been fleeting, but others of his era went on to write significant works containing real Jewish musical content. Arnold Schoenberg, Darius Milhaud, and Mario Castelnuovo-Tedesco, all European émigrés to America, spent time in California, both teaching and writing. Despite coming into contact with each other through their various activities, each wrote in his own style. On the other hand, in a period when many composers of Jewish origin were successfully ignoring their cultural heritage, it is noteworthy that all three were personally and musically involved with their Jewish roots.

Arnold Schoenberg: Jewish Musician in 12 Tones

Arnold Schoenberg (1874–1951) played an important role in the development of twentieth century music. Born in Vienna and educated there and in Berlin at a time when musicians were fighting an ideological battle over the primacy (and preferability) of Brahms over Wagner,[27] Schoenberg, who was musically almost completely self-taught, aligned himself with the Wagnerites because of his fascination with the composer's progressive musical ideas.[28] Schoenberg's repudiation of prevailing tonal and harmonic practices in favor of his eventual evolution of 12-tone tonality and the serial technique challenged the established musical traditions of his era.[29]

Schoenberg's provocative and controversial musical positions paralleled his unconventional relationship to his Judaism. As a youth, Schoenberg repudiated his Jewish heritage, but this rejection did not keep him from working on compositions with biblical themes. Following the groundbreaking success of his *Pierrot Lunaire* (Moonstruck Pierrot) [30] in 1912, Schoenberg began sketches for a cantata to be called *Die Jakobsleiter* (The Jacob's Ladder). Later, he spent time between 1925 and 1930 working on an opera, *Moses und Aron* (Moses and Aaron). Although neither work was ever completed,[31] they set the stage for other biblically inspired works he wrote later.

When Adolf Hitler came to power in 1933, Schoenberg's renouncement of his Judaism was outweighed by his Jewish birth, and he lost his position as director of the Prussian Academy of Arts in Berlin. Schoenberg responded by fleeing to France and returning to the Jewish faith (in a private ceremony witnessed by artist Marc Chagall). A month later, Schoenberg emigrated to America where he spent time in Boston and New York before settling in California. There he taught first at the University of Southern California and then at the University of California at Los Angeles. Schoenberg's American period was quite fertile, generating four theoretical books and some important compositions.

In his last years, as a clear response to his newfound Judaism, Schoenberg also produced several important works with Jewish themes. *Kol Nidre* (1939) was written for speaker-rabbi, mixed chorus, and small orchestra, with text in English based on the traditional passage from the Yom Kippur evening liturgy. His 1945 *Prologue to the Book of Genesis* for orchestra and chorus returned his attention to biblical ideas, and his final works included settings of several psalms for mixed chorus, a capella, completed in 1950.

One of Schoenberg's most interesting (and accessible) works is *A Survivor from Warsaw*, written in just two weeks in 1947. The composition, scored for male chorus and chamber orchestra, is dominated by the "testimony" of a speaker who recounts his experiences as one of the last inhabitants of the notorious ghetto.[32] Through most of the piece, the music seems to be almost incidental to the text, setting the mood and reflecting the speaker's story in much the same way that the score for a film affects the viewer's experience. The work's most sustained, coherent musical moments come at its conclusion with the appearance of the all-male chorus, singing the *Shema* and *ve-Ahavta*.[33]

Example 8.11 *Shema* from "Survivor"

Schoenberg's *Survivor* utilized the 12-tone technique that he had pioneered years earlier, and thus one would not expect to find any traditional Jewish musical motives in this work. However, some have noted the similarity (in shape, if not actual pitches) between Schoenberg's *Shema* and the ubiquitous version by Solomon Sulzer.

Example 8.12 Sulzer and Schoenberg versions of *Shema*

Given the composer's estrangement from traditional Jewish materials and his rejection of conventional tonal materials of all types, the listener might well conclude that these superficial similarities were merely coincidental. The larger question, however, is whether Schoenberg intended this work as an especially Jewish statement or, rather, as a universal comment on a horrific chapter in human history with particular relevance for Jewish listeners. The composer did not supply an answer. Unlike Copland's isolated contribution, however, *A Survivor from Warsaw* is part of a significant (if unconventional) body of work by a composer with an enigmatic outlook on his Jewish heritage.

Darius Milhaud: Frenchman and Jew

Unlike Arnold Schoenberg, with whom he studied briefly, Darius Milhaud (1892–1974) had no ambivalence about his Judaism. Milhaud opens his autobiography, *Notes without Music,* by stating unequivocally, "I am a Frenchman from Provence, and by religion a Jew."[34] There may have been some ambiguity regarding Milhaud's nationality: He fled France in 1940 with his wife and son and enjoyed a long teaching career in the United States before finally returning to his birthland late in life. There was no question, however, regarding either his Jewish identity or the role it played in his music.

Milhaud displayed musical ability as a young child and began his formal studies at the age of seven. A highly regarded violin player, he completed his basic schooling in Provence, then went to Paris to continue his music education. There he began composing a long list of vocal works, compositions for piano and organ, selections for string and wind instruments (solo and ensemble), and orchestral works including ballets, cantatas, and operas. Jewish musical themes began to appear in his work as early as 1925, when he composed a two-act opera, *Esther de Carpentras,* which incorporated not just the biblical story, but Purim customs, folklore from Carpentras, and unique Jewish musical motives from his native region. (The work received its first public performance at Paris's Opera Comique in 1938.) Milhaud went on to compose settings of Zionist folk songs in the 1930s[35] and accepted a 1947 commission from Reuven Rinder (of San Francisco's Temple Emanu-El) to write a Sabbath service. Milhaud's *Service Sacre* for baritone (cantor), mixed chorus, and organ (or orchestra) is a melodious work based in large part on *nusaḥ* from his own Provencal tradition.[36] Milhaud's first trip to Israel in 1952 featured the premiere of his *Candelabre a Sept Branches* (Seven-Branched Candelabra) for piano. That same year he composed a cantata, *Les Miracles de la Foi* (The Miracles of Faith), and an opera, *David,* which was premiered in Jerusalem in 1954 and performed at La Scala in Milan the following year. In 1961 Milhaud was commissioned to write a cantata for the 13th birthday of the Jewish State; his *Bar Mitzvah* utilized the haftarah portion (and chant) recited by Milhaud at his own coming of age. One of Milhaud's final compositions was another cantata, *Ani Ma'amin,* set to a libretto in English written by Elie Wiesel.

Mario Castelnuovo-Tedesco: Son of Italy

Another composer whose proud Jewish consciousness reflected in his music was Mario Castelnuovo-Tedesco (1895–1968). Born in Italy, he studied music with a series of private instructors (beginning with his mother) before going on to study at the Cherubini Institute of Music in Florence. The death of a grandfather drew him closer to his religious heritage: His 1925 discovery of settings of Hebrew prayers among his grandfather's papers tied his Jewish and musical identities together. Castelnuovo-Tedesco's first "Jewish" work, a piano selection titled *Le Danze del Rè David* (The Dances of King David) was based on his grandfather's jottings. In 1926 he followed these with three choral works based on Hebrew melodies. Motives from Jewish tradition infused several other of the composer's works: a 1925 piano suite; a vocal work, *Three Hebrew Chants;* and a vocalise for solo voice, commissioned by the Paris Conservatory of Music in 1928. This last composition was later adapted for stringed instruments and, as *Chant Hebraique,* became a staple in the concert repertoire.

In 1931, famed violinist Jascha Heifetz (1901–1978), who had earlier performed Castelnuovo-Tedesco's *Concerto Italiano,* commissioned the composer to write another violin work for him. At a time when anti-Semitic movements were stirring (again) in Europe, Castelnuovo-Tedesco resolved to respond by infusing this work with a Jewish identity. He later wrote:

> I felt proud of belonging to a race so unjustly persecuted. I wanted to express this pride in some large work glorifying the splendor of the past days and the burning inspiration in which inflamed the envoys of God, the Prophets. The violin seemed to me particularly adapted to personify, as a protagonist, the free and vivid eloquence of the Prophets; the orchestra in the multiform aspects of the symphonic texture could evoke all the voices of the surrounding world, voices of people, voices of nature, voice of God.[37]

The composer was eager to use more "authentic" melodies than the folk materials he had incorporated into his earlier works and based this concerto on the Italian Jewish traditions notated by violinist Federico Consolo.[38]

After emigrating to America in 1939, Castelnuovo-Tedesco taught and composed in the Los Angeles area. Among his later works of Jewish inspiration were *Sacred Service for Sabbath Even* for cantor, mixed choir, and organ; some additional organ selections for Jewish weddings (for the Conservative Cantors Assembly in 1951); and *Naomi and Ruth,* an oratorio based on the biblical story.

The pride that the American Jewish community might have expressed in the Jewish musical contributions of these three adopted sons was muted by the relative unfamiliarity of their milieu: Schoenberg's atonal music was simply foreign to the ears of most Jewish listeners, and the exotic Jewish traditions of Milhaud and Castelnuovo-Tedesco did not resonate with listeners of Eastern European background. One must also acknowledge the unhappy reality that American audiences of the twentieth century were largely disinterested in contemporary music, no matter how accessible or ethnically oriented it might have been. It took the panache and considerable musical accomplishments of a native-born *wunderkind* to bring American Jewish audiences to a proper appreciation of Jewish music on the concert stage.

Leonard Bernstein: Jewish America's Favorite (Musical) Son

American audiences of all backgrounds swelled with pride as Leonard Bernstein (1918–1990) became the first native son to overcome the European hegemony over conducting positions with ranking world orchestras. Bernstein was only 26 when he captured America's heart—and respect—by stepping into the breach created by an ailing Bruno Walter and leading the New York Philharmonic Orchestra in a critically acclaimed concert. The previously anonymous, young assistant conductor was catapulted by that success into a career unprecedented in the history of Western music of any sort. Excelling in every venue he touched, Bernstein won praise as a conductor, pianist, teacher, and composer of a wide variety of musical forms.[39]

Bernstein's musical successes were as much a personal victory for him as they were a source of vicarious accomplishment for America. Bernstein had pursued his musical education over the strong objections of his father, who had urged him toward more conservative pursuits.[40] Interestingly, despite (initially) frustrating his parents with his career choice, he did observe one important family tradition: The Jewish heritage that had been inculcated in him from his youth remained an important aspect of his personal and musical identity.[41]

A year before his 1943 conducting debut, Bernstein completed his first symphony,[42] though the work did not receive its premiere until 1944. At the conclusion of that season, the New York critics awarded Bernstein's Symphony No. 1 their highest accolade, pronouncing it the most impressive new work of the year. One wonders how the critics might have received the work if they had also appreciated its considerable Jewish musical content.

Bernstein subtitled his symphony "Jeremiah," signaling his intent to tell the story of the prophet who had led Israel in the sixth century B.C.E. Jeremiah's testimony is recorded in the biblical Book of Jeremiah, and in Lamentations, a series of five poetic odes written by Jeremiah as witness to the horrible destruction of the First Temple and the exile of the Jewish people into Babylonian slavery.[43] The symphony's three movements are labeled, not with the customary Italian titles announcing form or speed, but with the names of the three "chapters" in Jeremiah's life: "Prophecy" (his own), "Profanation" (as the people rejected his message), and "Lamentation" (as the prophet's warnings came true). The didactic intent of this symphony could have been satisfied with these programmatic titles, but Bernstein endowed each movement with unique Jewish musical significance as well.

The theme of the first movement is based upon a juxtaposition of two unrelated excerpts from traditional Ashkenazic *nusaḥ:* the concluding motive of the *Amidah* mode used for the distinctive "amen" cadence that defines segments of the festival morning service, and a lesser-known idea from the *Kerovah* mode. While creating a technically correct, if somewhat esoteric, "Jewish" idea, the resulting primary theme of the movement is fittingly imbued with passion and pathos.

Example 8.13 "Jeremiah" first movement theme

Regular synagogue attendees are accustomed to hearing passages from the Book of Jeremiah (and other prophetic books) chanted as part of the haftarah that follows the weekly Sabbath Torah reading. Indeed, since the rite of passage for virtually every child becoming a bar mitzvah[44] includes the recitation of at least part of the prophetic portion, the haftarah chant is not only well known to many Jewish listeners, but also part of many worshipers' personal musical experience.

ma-pah   pash-ta   mu-nach   ka-ton   mer-kha   tip-ha   etnahta

Example 8.14 Haftarah chant according to Idelsohn

For Leonard Bernstein, that chant represented the "sound" of Jeremiah. When he arrived at the second movement of his "Jeremiah" Symphony, though, he intended to represent the prophet through the eyes—and voices—of the people who rejected his insistent entreaties that they mend their evil ways. The people mocked Jeremiah, throwing his words back at him with sarcasm and disdain. Bernstein used the traditional chant as the theme of his second movement, "Profanation," but in depicting the people's rejection of Jeremiah and his message, he gave it the jagged edges and jazzy rhythms that would later become a defining characteristic of much of his music.

Vivace con brio

Example 8.15 Second movement theme from "Jeremiah" Symphony

As unusual as it is for symphonic works to have programmatic content, it is even rarer for themes from one movement to reappear in subsequent movements. Nevertheless, Bernstein brings back the opening first movement theme near the end of the second movement. It is a moment of high tension, both musically and programmatically. The people have not only rebuffed Jeremiah's prophecy, but have been energized by their rejection of him and are now caught in an orgy of mockery and spiritual abandon. Rather than renouncing his people and leaving them to sow the seeds of their own destruction, Jeremiah tries desperately to be heard. As the orchestra reaches a frenzied crescendo, a lone French horn blasts Jeremiah's message. In the end, however, it is too late. The people are exhausted by their own debauchery, and Jeremiah is overwhelmed by his failure.

Jeremiah's Lamentations is a book of infinite sorrow. The once-glorious Temple has been destroyed, and the city itself lies "abandoned, like a widow" (Lam. 1:1). Jewish tradition proscribes even the most perfunctory synagogue *nusah* on the Ninth of Av, when the loss of the Temple is mourned. Only the recitation of Lamentations itself carries pitch, and this special Ashkenazic chant that evolved for the reading is a repetitive, mournful tune:

Example 8.16 Opening line of traditional *Eykha*

Bernstein's "Lamentation" goes beyond the implied program of the symphony's first two movements and quotes directly from the text of Jeremiah's elegy. The composer chose to let the time-honored chant stand almost untouched by his own creative urges, and the orchestra provides only sparse accompaniment to the excerpted passages. In a decidedly nontraditional move, Bernstein also chose to utilize a female vocalist to sing Jeremiah's laments. The decision highlighted Bernstein's insight into Jewish philosophy and his belief in a "feminine" side of God that nurtures and protects even while its stereotypical "masculine" side judges and rebukes.[45]

Example 8.17 Opening line of "Lamentation" from "Jeremiah" Symphony, third movement

Shortly after the premiere of the "Jeremiah" Symphony, Bernstein accepted a commission from the Park Avenue Synagogue to compose a setting of liturgy for the Sabbath service. His "Hashkivenu" for cantor, mixed chorus, and organ was completed in 1945. An impressive work—at times melodious and haunting, at other times dramatic and demanding—it is Bernstein's only work "for the synagogue." Since its premiere, its rare performances have been primarily on the concert stage. "Hashkivenu" was also the last "Jewish" work Bernstein wrote for many years.[46] Then, in 1961, Bernstein began work on his third symphony, another programmatic work[47] that he subtitled "Kaddish."

In Jewish tradition, the *Kaddish* is a doxology that praises God. A continuous refrain that glorifies God as the prayer proceeds, it functions as a sort of liturgical divider between one section of a service and another. The *Kaddish* appears in a variety of forms, depending upon its position in the service and/or the occasion on which it is recited,[48] but its best known form is as a "mourner's" prayer. Those who have lost a loved one are susceptible to doubts and questions about God's wisdom and goodness. The *Mourner's Kaddish* calls upon the recently bereaved to declare publicly (the *Kaddish* can only be recited with a prayer quorum of ten adults) their continuing belief in a "magnified, sanctified, and exalted" deity. It is also believed that the appearance of the deceased's child in the synagogue to recite the *Kaddish* during the period following a death is testimony to the parent's success in raising a respectful and devout child and will assure the decedent's swift passage into the world to come.

The *Kaddish* Symphony is scored for speaker (again a female), soprano solo, adult mixed choir, boys choir, and orchestra. Bernstein wrote the speaker's text himself and envisioned an era in which humankind was distanced from God and on the verge of self-destruction.[49] The speaker decides to recite *Kaddish,* her own *Kaddish,* fearing that there will be no one left alive to say it after her. She chides God for having promised never to destroy the world only to allow His children to do it for Him. God is alternately her father and her paramour (just as the rabbis understood a "masculine" God as the romantic partner of the "feminine" people of Israel). And she is all of humankind—a disobedient child and an angry lover. She calls God to a *Din-Torah* (a Torah judgment) for breaking Divine promises, but ultimately reconciles herself to Him and allows herself to again speak His praise.

Bernstein's "libretto" is as replete with Jewish tradition as any text could be. Although all of the imagery derives from the Bible (and is thus accessible to all, albeit in its "Old Testament" form), the speaker's identity and passions are driven by Jewish history and philosophy, and the *Kaddish* itself is a uniquely Jewish text. Yet there is not a note of "Jewish" music anywhere in the symphony. Indeed, in this composition, Bernstein made his only forays into an exploration of the possibilities of 12-tone music, a major leap outside the boundaries of accustomed Western practice and Jewish tradition.

Bernstein's next major composition had a similarly enigmatic identity. The work, *Chichester Psalms,* written in 1963, takes excerpts from the Book of Psalms and sets them in their original Hebrew. In fact, the settings are so driven by the internal rhythm of the texts that Bernstein included instructions in the copyright notice prohibiting the performance of the work in any language other than Hebrew.

The texts that Bernstein utilized are diverse. The first section of the work sets Psalm 108:2 ("Awake psaltery and harp! I will rouse the dawn!") in a kind of dramatic introduction before proceeding to set Psalm 100 in its entirety. This segment is in an irregular but uplifting 7/4 rhythm, the tempo is full of gusto, and the melody skips from peak to peak in short bursts of unbridled joy.

Example 8.18 From "Hari'u l'Adonai kol ha'aretz"

Raise a shout for the LORD, all the earth,
Serve the LORD with gladness; Come into His presence with
    shouts of joy.
Acknowledge that the LORD is God; He made us, and we are His,
His people, the flock He tends.
Enter His gates with praise, His courts with acclamation.
Praise Him! Bless His Name!
For the LORD is good; His steadfast love is eternal;
His faithfulness is for all generations.

The second section opens with an achingly beautiful solo for boy alto and women's chorus. The child's innocent voice declaiming text from Psalm 23 is supported by an accompaniment from the women's voices. Only a subtle chromatic turn in the repetition of the initial statement of "Adonai Ro'i," (The Lord Is My Shepherd) hints at what is to come.

The surprise that follows brings in the men's voices with text from the much less familiar Psalm 2. The male chorus asks "Why do nations assemble..."and they proceed to rage through this lusty, tongue-twisting assault on God's plans for the world:

Example 8.19 From "Adonai Ro'i"

Example 8.20 From "Lama Rageshu"

Why do nations assemble, and peoples plot vain things;
Kings of the earth take their stand, and regents intrigue together
Against the LORD and against His anointed?
"Let us break the cords of their yoke, shake off their ropes from us!"
He who is enthroned in heaven laughs: the LORD mocks at them.

In the midst of the men's impassioned outrage, the women return with their original melody—apparently oblivious to the agitation stirring in the lower voices. The men's section fades away and the women reprise their opening. Confidence in the providential powers of God appears to have held the day, with only a quietly bubbling instrumental coda warning of the turmoil that continues to lie just below the surface.

The concluding section begins with a lengthy instrumental preamble, with melodic hints deriving from themes heard in the first movement's opening introduction. This segment seems literally and figuratively to be the aftermath of the "battle" just waged between the men's and women's voices. The instrumental section appears to be searching frantically for its own melody and, as the prelude churns through several keys, for its own sense of harmony. That "harmony," in both the musical and metaphysical sense, arrives with the reentry of the choir. The singers—women and men united once more—find the psalmist's answer to the strife in the world in a beautifully understated, unaccompanied chorale setting of the familiar text from Psalm 133:1: "How good and how pleasant it is that brothers dwell together…. Amen."

Chichester Psalms was commissioned for an annual gathering of liturgical choirs from the English abbeys of Westminster, Salisbury, and Chichester and has been a popular part of the choral-orchestral repertoire since its premiere. It is short, varied, and accessible. Somewhat demanding, it can be successfully performed by a well-disciplined amateur ensemble. Although it is in a "Jewish" language, it speaks to universal human questions and emotions.

Bernstein's 1971 *Mass* appears to be as far from "Jewish" music as a composer could get. The unorthodox work, commissioned for the opening of the Kennedy Center in Washington, D.C., was vilified for its theological irreverence and, ironically, was criticized for being too obviously in the consistent musical style of Leonard Bernstein. The composer described the work as "a theater piece for singers, players, and dancers" and scored it for soloist (celebrant), mixed chorus, boys chorus, orchestra, marching band, and electric guitar. In addition to the musicians and dancers who appeared on stage, the work opened with a prerecorded tape of mixed choral singers and percussion played over loudspeakers positioned among the members of the audience.

Example 8.21 "Hiney mah tov" from Chichester Psalms

With so many forces and art forms at work, this "blasphemous" work was clearly confusing to traditional Catholics and had many Jews wondering what "their Lenny" was trying to prove.

At least one point Bernstein wanted to prove was that the Catholic liturgy had clear antecedents in Jewish tradition. The *Sanctus* section of the Mass has the boys choir singing "Holy, Holy, Holy is the Lord of Hosts"—in Hebrew. *Barukh haba be-shem Adonai* (Blessed is He who comes in the Name of the Lord) takes on a very different meaning in the context of Catholic worship, but Bernstein accomplished an important educational mission by juxtaposing the two traditions.

Bernstein realized a long-held dream with his 1974 ballet suite,

Dybbuk. For years he had toyed with the idea of writing a composition based upon Anski's play. He had also been eager to work again with choreographer Jerome Robbins, with whom he had collaborated on *West Side Story.* By the time he approached the project he added another ingredient to the mix, one that derived from the premise of the story itself and that Bernstein later claimed infused every note of the music—Kabbalah.

> Bernstein drew a diagram of a cabalistic [*sic*] tree representing the emanations of the Godhead and called *sephirot,* or numbers. The diagram embraces such spiritual and physical qualities as understanding, strength, grace, endurance, and glory. He noted that ten numbers plus 22 letters of the Hebrew alphabet creates 32 channels of connection by which upper aspects of the tree could be connected with the lower. The name of *The Dybbuk's* heroine, Leah, consists of letters that add up to 36, which is also the number of unknown, just men—saints put on the earth to do good deeds. 36 is also twice 18, and 18 is the sum of letters for the word *ḥai,* meaning life. Life times, two equals Leah's and the suitor's life—an indication that the forbidden marriage must take place. The composer then worked at achieving 36's and 18's within the octave range, a scale with nine notes—a multiple factor of 18 or 36.[50]

It is impossible for the listener to hear Bernstein's kabbalistic and arithmetic machinations in the music. What one does hear is a remarkable work, at once contemporary and original, yet infused with the folk spirit of Eastern Europe. Its movements honor the protagonists in Anski's play, but they also pay tribute to Bernstein's forebears and to his strong sense of connectedness to his Jewish heritage.

The workaholic Bernstein was often criticized for not focusing on one musical pursuit. Many felt that he would have achieved even greater success had he focused exclusively on either conducting or composing (and excluded the teaching and piano performance that remained an important and fulfilling part of his life).[51] Bernstein's admirers recognized the multiple interests that drove the man throughout his life and the unique combination of talents that enabled him to succeed in so many venues. The Jewish community benefited as much as any segment of the music world. In particular,

Bernstein made an important contribution to the concert repertoire, demonstrating convincingly that music can have a decidedly "Jewish" agenda while retaining its "universal" appeal.

Steve Reich and *"Minimal"* Jewish Music

As the twentieth century drew to a close, increasing numbers of composers who previously considered themselves citizens of the global village returned to their own unique ethnic roots for musical inspiration. Just as it had been earlier in the century, it became fashionable once again for composers to create contemporary arrangements of popular folk songs or new compositions heavily influenced by traditional melodies. Still, such borrowings generally represented a Western view of Jewish culture, one missing any sense of ancient heritage or Eastern authenticity. When Steve Reich (b. 1936) decided to confront his history, he tried to get as close as he could to "the source."

Reich did his homework. He learned that the Temple service had featured the singing of psalms but that the ancient tradition of psalm singing had been lost in the West. (It has been maintained among Yemenite Jews). He discovered that the Temple orchestra had featured stringed instruments with some winds and percussion but, again, that the actual tunes could not be traced. Freed from any pre-existing notion of what Jewish music "should" sound like, he set out to write a work based on the spirit of the Temple service and driven by the meaning and rhythms of its Hebrew texts. The result was *Tehillim* (Psalms, 1981).

Steve Reich's *Tehillim* sets excerpts of the Hebrew psalms for four female vocalists and chamber orchestra. It is within the mold of his earlier, minimalist compositions[52] yet builds on a wider base of musical material, again based upon Reich's musical intuition regarding the needs of the texts. The first two segments are conjoined, as are segments three and four; only a brief interval (typical of more conventional, multi-movement works) separates parts two and three. The themes of each of the movements are treated canonically or in variations, and a rhythmic ostinato undergirds most of the music. The effect when the rhythm track stops is quite startling.

Example 8.22 From *Tehillim*[53]

While the individual settings of each psalm excerpt are fairly melodious, the work does suffer somewhat from being "too much of a good thing," and is not to every audience's taste. Indeed, absent an understanding of Reich's motivation in scoring the work, one might be hard-pressed to find any Jewish content (except in its texts). However, in some respects, Reich's cerebral, historic approach to his (re-)creation of Jewish music is just as legitimate as any other.

The composers and works highlighted here are those whose contributions to the development of Jewish music on the concert stage have been numerically and/or qualitatively significant. This is not to negate the work of a host of other musicians who have composed isolated works with Jewish themes. Fortunately, their numbers are too great to mention—and growing annually. The legitimacy of the genre called "Jewish art music" seems now to be well established. The question of "how Jewish" these works really are, or were intended by their composers to be, is one that will need to be examined on a case-by-case basis—and will likely not inspire uniform answers. As the character of "Jewish" life and identification continues to evolve, and especially as the definition of what constitutes "Jewish music" even in the synagogue continues to be debated, the nature of Jewish music on the formal concert stage will continue to unfold.

9 ~
Building the Jewish State

We have seen a variety of ways in which negative events in Europe at the end of the nineteenth century had unintended positive repercussions leading to the development of new forms of artistic expression. Doors to Russian culture and patriotism remained closed to Jews but gave rise to Jewish nationalism, a renewed interest in traditional forms of ethnic Jewish life, and the creation of new Jewish literature, theater, and music. Anti-Semitism led many Jews to leave their native lands for new lives in the West, where educational opportunities and religious freedom allowed Jewish life and culture to flourish in the synagogue and in otherwise secular arenas.

The First Aliyah (1882–1903)

But a small number of Jews fleeing European prejudice turned their sights not to the American "Golden Land" but to the east, to a land once "flowing with milk and honey" and eager to see her children return. The first modern pioneers who set out for the Land of Israel in response to government-agitated pogroms in 1881 called themselves *BILU'im,* an acronym from the Hebrew words, *Beit Yaakov, Lekhu Ve-nelkha,* meaning "O House of Jacob! Come, let us walk" (Isa. 2:5). Their Zionism appropriated the language of the Bible and of the liturgy in which generations had prayed for a time when the Jewish homeland would be restored. Many of their songs used modern Hebrew poetry as lyrics but borrowed the style (and even the actual melodies) of Russian folk tunes to encourage their fellow Jews to return with them to the land of their ancestors.

One of the early rallying songs of the first wave of new immigrants was "Di Sokhe" (The Plow) written by Eliakum Zunser, a well-known Lithuanian *badḥan*.[1] The pioneers were eager to work the land, rebuilding the Jewish homeland with the sweat of their own labor.

Example 9.1 From "Di Sokhe"

In the plow lies the good luck, the luck of life, for nothing will I want.
The morning arrives and I don't need to borrow [any money].
I don't need to worry about money (to pay all my bills, for they will
    be paid).
It is prepared for the winter, a satisfied and healthy one.
I sow and reap quite happily in God's free world.

One of the first songs created by the pioneers themselves was "Ya-Ḥa-Li-Li," a poem by Noach Shapira (1866–1931) set to Middle Eastern melody heard in Israel by the new immigrants. Shapira helped settle Zichron Yaakov in 1890 and wrote the simple text in 1895.

Example 9.2 From "Ya-Ḥai-Li-Li"

[Chorus]Ya-ḥai-li-li worker!

Wake up, my brothers, don't sleep, rise up to your work. [Chorus]

The world stands on work, rejoice, sing with a thankful voice! [Chorus]

Only work will deliver us from all trouble all our lives. [Chorus]

In her (work) we will find riches and success and it will bring us blessing. [Chorus]

The poem "Birkat Am" (The Blessing of the People, 1894) by Chaim Nachman Bialik[2] (1873–1934) transforms the builders of Israel into priests with a holy mission. The verses anonymously set to music encourage support for the efforts of the brave pioneers who are refreshing the soil of the Holy Land with their tears and their sweat.[3]

Te'ḥe - zak-na ye-dei kol a -ḥei - nu ba - meḥo - ne - nim

Example 9.3 From "Birkat Am"

Strengthen the hands of all our brothers
Who foster the soil of our land—wherever they are.
Don't leave your spirit, happy and joyous,
Come united as one to help our nation.

The author of "Ḥushu, Aḥim, Ḥushu" (Hurry, Brothers, Hurry), Yehiel Michael Pines (1843–1913), was a leading religious Zionist. He led an offshoot movement of pioneers who were unsuited to life in the early agricultural settlement of Mikveh Israel. This group, known as Shahav (*Shivat Haḥarash Ve-hamasger,* "The Settlement of the Plow and the Locksmith") settled in Jerusalem and built the land with a different sort of labor described in his poem set to a Russian folk song:

Ḥu-shu a-ḥim ḥu-shu na - ri -ma pe - a -mei - nu   ru-shu a-ḥim ru-shu le - e-retz a- vo-tei - nu

Example 9.4 From "Ḥushu, Aḥim, Ḥushu"

Hurry, brothers, hurry, let us lift our steps,
Fly, brothers, fly, to the land of our ancestors.

Rest is not for us, relaxation is not for us.
In this land of malaria, from the authority of the arm.

My friends will mock me,
"What is this land of inheritance to you?"
There the jackals will howl.
"Find yourself a new land!"

The earliest years of the new settlement also saw the birth of the song known as "Hatikvah," Israel's unofficial national anthem.[4] Naftali Herz Imber (1856–1909) apparently began the poem in Iasi, Romania, in 1878, but added verses during his 1882 visits to early settlements in Rishon le-Tziyon, Reḥovot, Hadera, and Zikhron Ya'akov. The complete text of the poem that he called "Tikvatenu" (Our Hope) was first published in Jerusalem in 1886. In popular usage, the first verse quickly became a recurring chorus, and the second verse took the place of the first. The other significant textual emendation came at the hands of Dr. Yehudah Leib Metman-Cohen (1869–1939), who established the first Hebrew high school in Jaffa. Dr. Metman-Cohen substituted *Hatikvah bat shnot alpayim, lih'yot am ḥofshi be-artzeynu eretz tziyon virushalayim* (The 2,000-year-old hope, to live as a free people in our land, the land of Zion and Jerusalem) for Imber's original text *Hatikvah hanoshanah lashuv le-eretz avoteynu le-ir bah David ḥanah* (The old hope to return to the land of our forefathers, to the city in which David dwelt). Other modest changes were effected through popular usage.

The more lasting question revolves around the origin of the tune with which "Hatikvah" is customarily sung. In an atmosphere in which immigrants from European countries were regularly importing songs from their native lands and either translating their lyrics into Hebrew or substituting entirely new ones, few people were seriously concerned with the origin of a tune being sung (or even its appropriateness for use with its new text). Although A. Z. Idelsohn[5] (1882–1938) has observed the use of melodies similar to that of "Hatikvah" in Jewish and non-Jewish cultures around the world, the similarity between the popular tune to which Imber's poem is sung and a familiar Romanian folk song cannot be ignored. Indeed, music critic Menashe Ravina and amateur Israeli musicologist Eliahu Hacohen have traced the origins of the tune to one Samuel Cohen, a Moldavian immigrant to Rishon le-Tzion in 1878. Cohen began singing Imber's poem to a Moldavian-Romanian folk song he knew as "Carul çu Boi" (Cart and Oxen) shortly after Imber's visit to his settlement and the tune, with its new lyrics, became widely—and anonymously—accepted.[6]

Notwithstanding enduring questions about the musical origins of "Hatikvah," the song gained acceptance very quickly and was adopted by the nascent Zionist movement after other attempts to write an "anthem" did not produce a viable alternative. The popularity of "Hatikvah" and its power to move singers from a variety of Jewish backgrounds has continued unabated since its emergence in the new settlements of Israel more than a century ago.

Kol od ba-le-vav pe-ni-ma ne-fesh Ye-hu-di ho-mi-ya

Example 9.5 From "Hatikvah"

> As long as a Jewish heart beats,
> And facing East casts an eye towards Zion
> Our hope is not lost.
> The hope which is two thousand years old,
> To be free in our land,
> The land of Zion and Jerusalem.

The Second Aliyah (1904–1914)

Despite the lofty language and noble spirit of their poetry, most of the earliest pioneers did not seek to fulfill a religious dream or to lead lives of increased devotion. They were primarily assimilated, secular Jews who chose to embrace Jewish culture only in reaction to their exclusion from Russian society. By 1905, however, when another wave of pogroms[7] mobilized a second wave of immigration to Palestine, many of those who emigrated did so out of a genuine sense of religious calling. The arduous trip to the Jewish homeland became known as an aliyah,[8] a metaphysical as well as a physical journey to a place—and a condition—of elevated spirituality and holiness. The songs these pioneers brought with them reflected their greater commitment to a traditional way of life and their hope that the Jewish homeland would be rebuilt in the tradition of the Torah.

Ve ta - her li- be- nu ve- ta - her li-be-nu ve - ta - her li-be - nu le - ov -de - kha be -e- met

Example 9.6 From "ve-Taher Libenu"

(From the *Festival Amidah*)
Purify our heart to serve You sincerely.

Songs of unknown origin but great popularity combined a commitment to working the land with personal spiritual development and took several forms. "Anu Banu Artzah" ("We Have Come to Our Land to Build and Be Rebuilt in Her") and "Im Ein Ani Li" (If I Am Not for Myself, attributed to Hillel in *Pirkei Avot* [Ethics of the Fathers] 1:14) were popular rallying cries to encourage further aliyah. "El Yivneh Hagalil" (God Will Build the Galilee) evidenced the pioneers' conviction that God would be behind their efforts.

El yiv - neh ha - ga - lil   El yiv -neh ha - ga - lil   El yiv -neh ha - ga - lil

ba - ruch yiv - neh ha - ga - lil   El yiv -neh ha - ga - lil   El yiv -neh ha -ga - lil

Example 9.7 From "El Yivne Hagalil"

God will build the Galilee. Blessed is He who builds the Galilee.

In 1912, the principal of the Herzlia Gymnasium school in Jaffa asked his Hebrew and music teachers to collaborate on a marching song to galvanize their students on a coming hike through the country's southern region. Music teacher Hanina Karczewski (1873–1926), who had arrived in Israel just four years earlier, chose to utilize an existing Yiddish song by Herman Tzvi Erlich. Hebrew teacher Yisrael Dushman (1884–1947), who had immigrated with his family in 1895, wrote his own lyrics to suit the tune. The song was immediately taught to the students, who sang "Po Be-eretz Ḥemdat Avot" (Here in the Land [that is the] Delight of the Forefathers) enthusiastically on their ten-day trip from Jaffa to Metulla, spreading it to whomever they passed. The song quickly spread throughout the Diaspora, changed to "*There* in the Land of the Forefathers."

Example 9.8 From "Po be-Eretz Ḥemdat Avot"

Here in the land which is the delight of the forefathers all our hopes
   will be fulfilled.
Here we will live and here we will create lives of brightness, lives
   of liberty.
Here the Divine presence dwells, here the language of the Torah
   will blossom.

   Plow a trough, sing a song, rejoice joyfully, the buds have already
      blossomed.
   Plow a trough, sing a song, rejoice joyfully, the seeds will yet arrive.

Of course, not all of the immigration of this period was driven by religious fervor. The collective agricultural settlements known as kibbutzim were established by the pioneers of this era, and they were motivated purely by socialist aspirations and a desire to build a totally egalitarian community.[9] A song with lyrics by Saul Tchernichowsky[10] (1875–1943) gave expression to the pioneers' belief in the abilities of man and was extremely popular in their circles.

Sah - ki sah - ki   al ha -ha -lo - mot   zu a - ni   ha - ho - lem   sah

sah - ki ki   ba - a - dam a - min   ki o - de - ni ma - a - min   bakh

Example 9.9 From "Ani Ma'amin"

Laugh, laugh at the dreams, thus I, the dreamer say.
Laugh, because I believe in man, because I still believe in you.

Because my soul still longs for freedom I will not sell it to a
   golden calf.
Because I still believe in man, also in his spirit, a strong spirit.

I will also believe in the future, even though the day is distant.
But it will come, and it will carry peace and blessing to another
   nation.

Then my people will return and blossom, and in the land a generation
   will arise.
They will cast off their iron chains, eyes will see the light.

Then a poet will sing a new song, his heart will be awakened to
   beauty.
For him, the young one, they will gather flowers from my grave to
   make a wreath.

Interestingly, side-by-side with such "heretical" sentiments as
those of "Ani Ma'amin" (I Believe), the religiously oriented songs
became part of the rich corpus of favorite songs from the pre-state
era and attained great popularity even outside the observant community.

The Third Aliyah (1919–1923)

The international turmoil of the First World War reduced immigration to Palestine to a mere trickle in the years 1914–1917. The population dislocations created in the war's wake, the upheaval caused by the Russian Revolution of 1917, and the optimism with which the Balfour Declaration[11] was greeted later that same year inspired a new stream of Eastern European pioneers—some 35,000 in all. Nearly one-third of these would-be settlers ultimately left, disillusioned by the hardship of life in a still-unblossoming land and the mounting resistance of the local Arab population to continuing Jewish settlement. Those who remained, however, were an ideological "hard core" committed to the Zionist dream and willing to endure any hardship to realize their vision.

The songs of this period expressed much the same sentiment as those of the earliest pioneers: We will build the land. Some of the songs were extremely simple. "Anu Nihyeh ha-Rishonim"[12] (We Will Be the First) used direct language with a European-inflected Ashkenazic accent and an old Russian folk tune. Although neither it nor its singers were "the first," the song spoke well to its generation and remained in favor for years after.

Example 9.10 From *"Anu Nihyeh ha-Rishonim"*

We will be the first, thus we said, one brother to the other.
We will be among the builders, level the string, level the line.

We go, we come, there is work without end.
We will plant trees among the rocks, also on the mountains and in
the valleys.

We will pave the roads, we will chisel rocks into chalk stones.
"Hurrah" the hammers will answer as we sing our song.

"Ha-Ma'apilim" (The Daring Ones) was actually inspired by a mountain-climbing expedition in 1915. Members of a Jerusalem settlement called Maccabee[13] attempted an ambitious journey, but in the end only three of their members were able to reach the summit. Levin Kipnis (1894–1990) was one of them and he was asked[14] to write about the trip as a political statement. His poem was later set to music by Hanina Karczewski and, popularly known as "El Rosh ha-Har" (To the Mountaintop), became an anthem for the pioneers' struggles.

Example 9.11 From "El Rosh ha-Har"

To the mountain top, to the mountain top, who will block the road to
    the redeemed ones?
From over the mountain the glorious land already calls to us.
    [Chorus] Climb up! Climb up, to the top of the mountain, climb up!

Brothers, climb! Brothers, climb! Whose heart is cowardly and afraid
    of obstacles?
Take a step, you'll see, we will double our strength. [Chorus]

The Life and Death of Yosef Trumpeldor

Among the defining moments of this brief era was the tragic episode at Tel Hai and the death of Yosef Trumpeldor. Trumpeldor (1880–1920) had been the only Jewish officer in the Russian army, elevated to that status after his service in the Russo-Japanese war and lionized for his gallantry in the battle that cost him his left arm. He spent time as a Japanese prisoner of war, and worked assiduously for the welfare of his fellow prisoners. Trumpeldor took special interest in his fellow Jewish soldiers and, influenced by Tolstoy's vision of collective communes, organized Zionist groups among those whose aim was to settle in Palestine.

After the war Trumpeldor devoted himself to organizing groups of Jewish soldiers intent on the colonization and defense of the fledgling settlements. Trumpeldor went to Palestine and worked for a time at Kibbutz Deganyah, participating in the defense of the settlements of the Lower Galilee. During World War I he led a British brigade of Jewish soldiers, then returned to Russia, where he created the "he-Halutz" (The Pioneer) movement, preparing young Jews for immigration to their ancestral land.

Trumpeldor himself returned to Palestine in 1919 and was asked to organize the defense of the Upper Galilee settlements following some isolated skirmishes between local French authorities and Arab rebels. Trumpeldor and five of his comrades died from injuries sustained in a battle that broke out during negotiations with the Arab forces. The last words attributed to him, "Never mind, it is good to die for our country," capped the myth of a man whose activities had taken on legendary qualities even during his lifetime. The youth movement, Berit Trumpeldor (Betar) was founded to promulgate the military and nationalist aspects of his philosophy and activities, and his death was memorialized in stories, poems, and songs that are still recalled in annual commemorations at Tel Hai.

Ba Ga - lil   be - Tel Ḥai   Trum - pel - dor na - fal

Example 9.12 From "Shir al Trumpeldor"

At Tel Hai, in the Galilee, Trumpeldor fell;
For our people and for our land, the hero Joseph fell.
Through the mountains and hills he ran to redeem the name of
    Tel Hai
Saying to his brothers there: "Follow in my footsteps."

In every place, and at each moment, remember me,
Because I fought and fell for my birthland.
All day I plowed, and at night I held the barrel of my gun until the
last moment."[15]

The Fourth Aliyah (1924–1928)

The brief period of the Fourth Aliyah brought with it large numbers of Polish small businessmen fleeing anti-Semitism. Despite the sometimes less-than-altruistic motivation for their immigration (about one-third of the 68,000 new settlers of this period also eventually left the country), these well-educated Europeans helped establish the early values that give today's Israel its unique characteristics. Notwithstanding the contributions of some earlier musicians, this era also saw the arrival of many of Israel's first popular composers (and poets) and the supplanting of imported folk melodies by songs written in the Jewish homeland.

One of the most important musical figures to arrive during this fourth wave was none other than Joel Engel. During his brief time in Palestine (he died in 1927), he was largely occupied writing music for the Ohel Theater and teaching kindergarten. Several of the children's songs he composed during this period had lyrics by Yehiel Heilperin (1880–1942), a pioneer of teaching Hebrew in the Diaspora, founder of a Jewish kindergarten, and a professor of pedagogy in Warsaw prior to his arrival in Israel in 1920. Their collaboration produced many great favorites. The lullaby, "Numi, Numi Yaldati" (Sleep, Sleep My Little Girl) is still beloved.[16]

Example 9.13 From "Numi, Numi Yaldati"

[Chorus] Sleep, sleep my little girl, sleep, sleep.
Sleep, sleep my small one, sleep, sleep.

Father went to work, father went.
He will return with the appearance of the moon and bring you a
    present! [Chorus]
Father went to the vineyard, father went.
He will return with the appearance of the stars and bring you grapes.
    [Chorus]

Mordechai Zeira (1905–1968), considered one of the "fathers of Israeli song" arrived in Israel from his native Russia in 1924.[17] His very first song, "le-Moladeti" (To My Birthland), also known as "Pakad Adonai" (God Remembered), captured the undulating rhythms of the ship bringing the immigrants to their adopted homeland. The text by Hillel Avichanan[18] (1897–1978) describes an unusual love between an eager traveler and the ship bringing him to the Promised Land. Meanwhile, the refrain invokes a sense of religious imagery, acknowledging that this is the land that God chose and hinting at the famous line from Psalm 133: "How good, and how pleasant it is that brothers dwell together."

Le - mo - la - de - ti   he - vet   o - ti   be - yam ga - lim va - ke - tzef

Example 9.14 From "le-Moladeti"

To my birthland you brought me, on a sea of waves and foam.
I will kiss your mast, my boat, I will never forget you.

God remembered this forsaken corner of Zion,
Oh, how pleasant for brothers to dwell together.

Zeira's "Havu Levenim" (Give Us Bricks) evokes an entirely different spirit—an eagerness to build the new land. Lyrics by poet Alexander Penn (1906–1972) capture the enthusiasm of the builders, singing as they work.

Example 9.15 From "Havu Levenim"

Give us bricks, there is no free time to stand [still] for even a minute,
The builders build without fear or weariness.
We will raise up wall upon wall to meet any obstacle or disturbance.
We will all sing an anthem of building our land.
In place of yesterday we have tomorrow.
And for each wall, with the momentum of our building,
The future of our nation is our reward.
Give us bricks, village, settlement, and town,
Sing the song of the builders, sing of building and revolution!

Penn also wrote lyrics for a traditional Bedouin song he learned shortly after his 1927 arrival in Israel.

Example 9.16 From "Sa'enu"

[Chorus] Carry us, carry us, to the desert, carry us.

Don't, please don't [sound] the drum and flute, because the
shepherds slumber.
At night the stars twinkle on the paths. [Chorus]

To the desert carry us on the humps of camels.
On their necks small bells ring. [Chorus]

Penn's adoption of a traditional Middle Eastern melody heralded
an important moment in the development of Israeli music. While
Ashkenazic immigrants fleeing European anti-Semitism constituted
the largest number of new arrivals, the native Bedouins and Jews
from Arab lands had been a constant presence in Israel. The Eastern
cast of their songs represented an excitingly different sound to
Western ears and offered composers and lyricists alike new rhythms
and melodic colors to explore and exploit.

This "Eastern" orientation was certainly not lost on native-born
Israeli composers. Yaffo-born David Zahavi (1910–1975) wrote his
first song at the age of 17 and, while setting verses from Ya'akov
Fichman's[19] (1881–1958) song of the desert, borrowed the sounds he
had learned from the people of the desert themselves. The resulting
melody derives its irregular meter from the natural, internal rhythms
of the Sephardic Hebrew spoken by the Oriental Jews.

Example 9.17 From "Orḥah ba-Midbar"

To the right and to the left, just sand and more sand,
The desert glows golden without a path.
The caravan passes in pleasant silence, like the image of a wonderful
dream.
A sound rises and falls rhythmically, camels pass on the sad landscape.
Din-don, din-don, this is the song of the wanderer,
Quiet and dignified, quiet and plodding.

Yedidyah Admon (1894–1985) was born in Russia but arrived in Israel at the age of 12. He was a member of the first graduating class at the Jerusalem Teacher's Seminary (1913) and, during his studies there, was much influenced by his teacher A. Z. Idelsohn and by the Arab and Bedouin songs he heard around him. "Shedemati" (My Fields), written in 1927, was inspired by their earthy, guttural text by Yitzchak Shenhar (1902–1957).[20] Despite the song's rhythmic and melodic irregularity, it became extremely popular.

Example 9.18 From "Shedemati"

My field
At dawn I seeded it with tears,
The prayer of the farmer was heard.
My field has been saturated with dew.
Drunken from sunlight,
In front of the harvester
The wheat bends.
With a big step the shining scythe will be swung upwards.

The Fifth Aliyah (1929–1939)

The 1930s was a period of increasing tensions in Europe and great urgency in Palestine, as escalating numbers of would-be immigrants resorted to illegal tactics to escape the Nazi regime. Urgent, clandestine efforts by the Jewish Agency[21] and leaders of the unofficial settlers' government to increase the Jewish population of the *yishuv* (Jewish Mandatory Palestine) were met by an intractable British resolve to enforce ever-tightening quotas on Jewish immigration. Many of the songs of this era were called *shirei ha-apalah,* "songs of daring,"[22] and like "Olim" (Immigrants)[23] capture the quiet desperation of those seeking refuge in the not-yet-declared Jewish state.

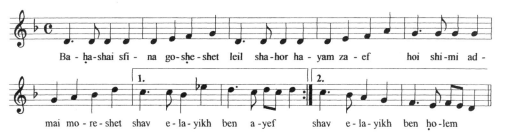

Example 9.19 From "Olim"

> In the stillness the ship runs aground, a dark night, the sea is angry.
> O, listen, land of inheritance, your tired son returns to you.
> In the stillness the ship runs aground, the heart beats there with hope.
> O listen, land of inheritance, your dreaming son returns to you.
> In the stillness my brothers go up to the land of their inheritance,
> And in their ears she whispers a secret: This way for life! This way
>   for life!

One of the ways the Jewish authorities sought to increase sympathy for the plight of these would-be immigrants was by painting an impressive and inviting picture of the homeland for Jewish communities around the world. The Jewish Agency had an extremely active division of public relations, sponsoring the publication of books of Palestinian song[24] and the creation of films depicting beautiful landscapes, idyllic pioneers toiling in the fields, and the eternity of the Jewish traditions reaffirmed by the return of the scattered masses to sacred soil. Avigdor Hameiri (1890–1970) wrote lyrics to a Yiddish folk song for use in one of the productions at his avant-garde theater "ha-Kumkum" (The Coffeepot). The Jewish Agency's appropriation of the song for its own purposes[25] made it famous throughout the world:

Me - al pis-gat har ha-tzo-fim esh - ta - ha-ve lakh a - pa-yim

Example 9.20 From "Yerushalayim"

From the peak of Mt. Scopus I bow deep to you.
From the peak of Mt. Scopus, greetings to you, Jerusalem.
One hundred generations I dreamed about you,
To be privileged to see the light of your face.
Jerusalem, Jerusalem, shine your face on your children.
Jerusalem, Jerusalem, from your ruins I will build.

From the peak of Mt. Scopus, greetings to you, Jerusalem.
Thousands of exiles from the ends of the world lift their eyes to you.
With thousands of blessings may you be blessed, shrine of the king,
   royal city!
Jerusalem, Jerusalem, I will not move from here,
Jerusalem, Jerusalem, the Messiah will come, he will come.

The film *le-Ḥayim Ḥadashim* (To New Life) was produced in 1934 for distribution by the Keren Hayesod (Jewish National Fund), a fund-raising arm of the Jewish Agency. At the time, its lyricist Natan Alterman (1910–1970) was already a published poet.[26] Its composer Daniel Sambursky (1909–1975) had only arrived in Palestine the previous year, but he quickly became one of the leading composers there, writing songs for adults and children, and leading the public "community singing" that was so popular in Israel. "Shir ha-Emek" (Song of the [Jezreel] Valley) became a well-known anthem in the country and around the world.

Ma ma lai-lah mi - leil dema - mah be - yiz - re - el
nu-mah e - mek e-retz tif-e-ret a-nu le-kha mish - me - ret

Example 9.21 From "Shir ha-Emek"

Rest comes to the weary, and calm to the worker,
A pale night spreads over the fields of the Jezreel Valley.
Dew below and moon above, from Beit Alfa to Nahalal.

Oh, what a night, silence in the Jezreel [Valley]
Sleep, valley, glorious land, we will guard you.

The Birth of Israeli Art Music

While songs of this era were reflective and (it was hoped) manip-ulative of international political concerns, the arrival of certain immigrants had an unanticipated internal impact. Among the refugees who arrived in the 1930s was a cadre of mature composers. Their encounter with some of the unique sounds of the Middle East led to the creation of Israel's first art music, a distinctive blending of East and West.

The first such immigrant to work toward creating a new national-ist Israeli school was Paul Ben-Haim (1897–1982). Born Paul Frankenburger, he was educated in Munich, Germany, and studied conducting and composition. He served as assistant to Bruno Walter and conductor of the Augsburg Opera and Symphony Orchestra but left Germany in response to Hitler's seizure of power in 1933. Frankenburger changed his name to Ben-Haim upon his arrival in Palestine and began teaching in conservatories in Jerusalem and Tel Aviv. Despite its Middle Eastern locale, Israel has always been enthu-siastically involved in the performance of traditional classical music. Ben-Haim might have continued to pursue a traditional career in Western music had not a fortuitous introduction to Bracha Zefira led to a dramatic change in Ben-Haim's activities and, as a result, the future of serious music in Israel.

The Role of Bracha Zefira

Bracha Zefira (1911–1990), born in Palestine to Yemenite parents, was orphaned at a tender age. She was raised in Jerusalem in a suc-cession of orphanages and foster homes in neighborhoods filled with immigrants from a variety of Eastern communities. The sensitive child was surrounded by music and thrived in the polyglot environment. Zefira's own gifts were recognized when she was still a teenager and she was sent to Germany to study music. There, for the first time, she realized that Western music was typically accompanied in some way and that audiences expected harmonic support for a melody line—no matter how lovely that solo line might be.

Upon her return to Palestine in 1930, Zefira resolved to make the melodies of her childhood accessible to a wider (Western) public by performing them with accompaniment. Her husband Nahum Nardi (1901–1977) was a talented pianist and composer who set many of her recollected Oriental songs to Western-style arrangements. The words to some of the songs, however, represented a problem: In some cases, Zefira simply did not remember the complete texts. In others, she felt that the original, liturgical passages were not appropriate for concert performance. Interestingly, in casting about for substitute lyrics for several songs, she settled on verses by Chaim Nachman Bialik. His Ashkenazically accented poetry would not have seemed an obvious choice to suit her florid Oriental melodies, yet the collaboration between Nardi and Zefira made their settings of "Yesh Li Gan" (I Have a Garden) and other Bialik poems quite popular.

Example 9.22 From "Yesh Li Gan"

I have a garden and a well, on the well there hangs a bucket.
Every Sabbath my beloved comes, pure water he drinks from
    my pitcher.

All the world is asleep, hush, apple and pear are sleeping.
My mother sleeps and so does my father, only I and my heart are awake.

The bucket, like my heart, is awake, dripping gold into the mouth of
    the well,
Dripping gold and dripping crystal my beloved goes, my beloved goes…

The marriage of Zefira and Nardi did not last long,[27] and by 1939 she was eager to find other composers with whom to work. Her introduction to Ben-Haim led him to discover the world of Oriental music. This, in turn, led to further arrangements for Zefira to perform—and for a time he also served as her accompanist. But it also dramatically changed Ben-Haim's outlook on music in Palestine.

The Eastern Mediterranean School

Paul Ben-Haim was fascinated by the Oriental melodies he discovered. The notion of melody-driven music had been out-of-vogue in Western circles for more than a thousand years, but represented uncharted territory for the ambitious composer. The twentieth-century lifting of any preexisting conventions regarding harmony left Ben-Haim free to indulge the distinctive Eastern melodies as he saw fit. Borrowing from their natural environment (and discontinuing the custom of busy, Western-style accompaniments created by Nardi), Ben-Haim focused on the melodies themselves. He sometimes layered parallel melodic lines with horizontal harmonies, or composed vertical harmonies of open chords or chords built on the interval of the fourth so that an airy, "pastoral" feeling would infuse the music.

Ben-Haim was joined by colleagues who also arrived from Europe in the late 1930s: Alexander Uriah Boskovitch (1907–1964), who arrived in 1938[28]; Marc Lavry (1903–1967), who arrived from Germany in 1935; and Hungarian composer Oedoen Partos (1907–1977). Boskovitch was the first to give a name to the Eastern

Mediterranean school (also known as the Oriental-Pastoral-Mediterranean school), but they were all equally attracted to this unique musical approach.

Like the members of The Society for Jewish Folk Music before them, these founders of a new school began their experiments with arrangements of existing folk songs. In addition to working directly with Zefira, these composers created a variety of instrumental and choral settings of Sephardic and Oriental material. They quickly moved on, however, to using preexisting materials merely for inspiration and, finally, to creating their own "Eastern-style" melodies.[29] In addition to capturing the melodic contours of the Eastern communities, these composers also attempted to imbue their music with a unique character that they considered appropriate for the music of the reborn nation. They wanted their music to represent the landscape of Israel, the rhythms of the Hebrew language and of the indigenous Eastern communities, and the eternal (if ephemeral) spirit of the Torah—not so much as a religious text, but as testimony to the ancient history of Israel and the values of her people.

Just as sports enthusiasts can argue the merits of their favorite teams without reaching any consensus as to which players are "the best," it would be difficult to suggest that any one of the composers of the Eastern School made a greater contribution than the others. In light of Ben-Haim's earliest arrival in the Middle East and the long and varied list of his works, we will examine some of his most important compositions, considering them representative of the efforts of his colleagues as well.

The Music of Paul Ben-Haim

As we have already noted, Ben-Haim's earliest works upon settling in Palestine were his arrangements for Bracha Zefira.[30] The Middle Eastern flavor that would infuse so many of his later works was already beginning to be felt in his 1937 String Quartet, and Ben-Haim developed an especially warm and intimate style in his chamber works, including the Piano Trio of 1939.

Ben-Haim's monumental symphonies are deserving of special mention. His First Symphony (1939–1940) was also the first symphony to be completed by any composer in the land of Israel and was premiered by Palestine's own symphony orchestra.[31] In it, a quiet, lyrical, middle movement is sandwiched between dramatic opening and concluding sections. The Second Symphony (1943–1945) bears the mark of the full-blown Middle Eastern school. Pastoral throughout, it is strongly influenced by folkloristic themes and representations of the country's landscape and natural beauties. Ben-Haim's Concerto for Strings (1947) and Piano Concerto (1948) followed in the style of the Second Symphony. The titles of the piano work ("Visions," "Voices in the Night," and "Dance") reveal the composer's burgeoning interest in lyrical, representative forms.

Some of Ben-Haim's compositions of the 1950s achieved great popular renown. *Fanfare to Israel* (1950) for full orchestra or symphonic band is frequently performed. The 1951 suite *From Israel* most overtly displays the stereotypical features of the Eastern Mediterranean school in its five movements: a sprightly "Introduction," a lyrical movement inspired by The Song of Songs, a setting of a "Yemenite Melody," a slow intermezzo called "Siesta," and a bright finale depicting a festive "Celebration."

Commissioned by the Koussevitsky Foundation in 1953 and completed that same year, the work earned Ben-Haim the prestigious Israel Prize in 1957. Meanwhile, in 1956, Ben-Haim composed *Pastorale Variée* (Pastoral Variations) for clarinet solo and chamber orchestra. This flowing work also embodies the Mediterranean school, with long, meandering, melodic lines, irregular rhythms, and subtle harmonies.[32]

The list of Ben-Haim's Palestine-based compositions for solo voice was dominated by the arrangements and songs he wrote for Bracha Zefira in the 1940s. Reminiscences of those early works can be heard in the song cycle *Melodies from the East*, one of the composer's last works, written in 1970. Ben-Haim's other works for vocal soloist also include *Kokhav Nafal* (A Star Fell Down, 1969–1970), written to settings of poetry by Matti Katz,[33] and *Myrtle Blossoms from Eden* (1965–1966), five songs for soprano (or tenor), contralto (or baritone), and piano (or orchestra).

Ben-Haim also left an impressive list of choral compositions. In the 1950s he set a group of Ladino songs for a capella choir and produced several choral settings of Hebrew songs based upon Sephardic melodies. His *Liturgical Cantata* (1950) and *Kabbalat Shabbat* (1966–1967) were written for the Union of American Hebrew Congregations. Ben-Haim had already written *Shabbat Mitzion* in response to a 1962 commission from The Temple on the Heights of Cleveland, Ohio (with the Conservative Cantors Assembly). In that "liturgical period" he also composed *Three Psalms* (1962) for soloists, choir, and orchestra (or organ), and *Hymn from the Desert* (1962–1963).

The setting of a biblical passage by an Israeli composer raises a question regarding the role of Jewish identity and values in the art music of Israel. Given the general conservatism of ritual practices in Israel, composers there did not write music intended for use in the synagogue. At the same time, we have already noted the proclivity of European and American Jewish composers to write programmatic music reflective of their ethnic interests and religious heritage. Should not Israeli composers, surrounded by constant reminders of Israel's ancient biblical heritage, have been no less inspired?

Like other composers of Jewish art music, Israeli writers were less interested in producing music reflecting any "religious" orientation than they were drawn to the historical and expressive content of sacred Jewish literature. For these composers (as for many modern Israelis), their personal involvement in ritual activity (and any potential reflection of it in their music) was less important than their feeling of "oneness" with the Jewish people and their pride in its ancient writings.

Israeli composers were also, however, motivated by the Bible and liturgical texts. The Western world's general familiarity with the Bible provides a frame of reference and (potentially) a near-universal appeal to musical settings of it. The expressiveness of the Bible's authors[34] provides literary images that inspire musical interpretation. And the unique internal rhythms of the Hebrew language itself (in the Sephardic accent adopted in the modern era) offer the music of Israel a distinctiveness that sets it apart from the national music of any other country. Ben-Haim was among the first to exploit biblical passages for their many simultaneous layers of opportunity.

Visions of a Prophet: Roni Akarah

Ben-Haim's impressive *Roni Akarah* (1956–57) embodies all of these aspects of Jewish/Israeli consciousness. Its text, from Isa. 54:1–5, is familiar, recited twice a year as part of the weekly haftarah portion. The enigmatic text promises renewal and countless progeny to the seemingly desolate and barren.[35] The real ingathering of the Jewish people into their homeland spoke to contemporary Israel as a fulfillment of the biblical prophecy and a genuine cause for rejoicing.

Roni Akarah is set in four brief movements, each with its own character and musical content. The first takes literal inspiration from the title, rejoicing in the sound of the Hebrew language itself as much as in the promise of the prophet. Much of this introductory section is in unison (or two parts), allowing the text to be clearly heard.

Example 9.23 From *Roni Akarah*

> Shout, O barren one, you who bore no child,
> Shout aloud for joy, you who did not travail!
> For the children of the wife forlorn shall outnumber those of
>   the espoused
> —said the LORD.

The second segment is in some ways a throwback to a much earlier period. Ben-Haim labeled the movement a passacaglia,[36] a form that originated in Spain during the early Baroque era and utilizes a repeating musical pattern in the bass line.[37] Ben-Haim also derives structural inspiration by adopting the Renaissance preference for "word painting," taking literally the text of this movement: "Enlarge the site of your tent, extend the size of your dwelling,…" (Isa. 54:2). At the same time that the prophet urges the "wife forlorn" to enlarge her capacity, Ben-Haim "enlarges" the composition by adding, first the tenor, then the alto, and finally the soprano voices to the pattern established earlier by the basses.

Example 9.24 From "Harḥivi"

The third line of Isaiah's vision promises that the children will spread throughout the world: "For you shall spread out the right and the left; your offspring shall dispossess nations, and shall people the desolate towns." The first destination for the Israelite nation following the destruction of the Temple in 586 B.C.E. and their expulsion from Jerusalem was Babylonia (Iraq). To set Isaiah's promise, Ben-Haim borrowed from the Babylonian Jewish repertoire, choosing the simple chant with which the Iraqi Jews intone one of Judaism's most sacred texts. This chant became the raw material for the theme of *Roni Akarah*'s third movement.

Example 9.25 Babylonian *Shema* and Ben-Haim's treatment as "Ki Yamin u'Semol"

The prophecy remains oblique and unsubstantiated until its fifth verse.

> For He who made you will espouse you—His name is "LORD of Hosts." The holy One of Israel will redeem you—He is called "God of all the Earth."

If God is the widow's "husband" then the veracity of His promise cannot be doubted. For the text's only invocation of God, Ben-Haim remains in an Eastern mode, calling on solo voices in a modal passage very much reminiscent of Gregorian chant.[38] The slow-moving solo alto voice (joined later by solo male voices singing in the organum-style harmony built on fourths and fifths that characterized early Christian chant) is a striking contrast to the frenzy of the previous movement and seems well suited to speaking, even allegorically, of the One God who will redeem His promises—and His people.

Example 9.26 From "Ki Vo'alayikh Osayikh"

The short reference to God is enough to give new meaning to the prophecy and to swathe it in a sense of authenticity worthy of repetition. The last movement concludes with a reiteration of the opening text and a recapitulation of the original musical idea. Just as the prophetic vision is endowed with credibility, Ben-Haim endows the composition with symmetry and balance. *Roni Akarah* achieves a two-fold mission: It offers a musical midrash on the contemporary fulfillment of a biblical prophecy; and it establishes Paul Ben-Haim as a composer who can simultaneously take his place on the world stage among outstanding twentieth-century musicians and sire a unique school of modern Israeli art music.

The list of both immigrant and native-born Israeli composers in the generations of and following Ben-Haim and his colleagues is substantial. It would have been unrealistic, however, to expect the Eastern Mediterranean School to have attracted, much less maintained, the interests of all of them during the more than sixty years that have elapsed since the first blending of East and West. In particular, the continuing evolution of Western music has given rise to various forms and sounds that have occupied the attention of composers around the world, including Israel. It is of great interest to note, however, that Israeli composers of many schools and generations have continued to be drawn to the sounds of the Orient and inspired by the landscapes, history, and literature of Israel. Compositions with programmatic titles and/or utilizing the folk melodies (or the spirit of melodies) of Israel abound in disproportionate numbers. A few examples of composers and their compositions will represent the wide range of works produced during the modern Israeli era.

Ben-Zion Orgad: The Second Generation

Ben-Zion Orgad (né Ben-Zion Buschel) was born in Germany in 1926 but arrived in pre-state Israel with his family in 1933. His first language was German, but by being educated from an early age in an atmosphere where Hebrew was the language of formal instruction (as well as common parlance), Orgad was among the first composers of his generation to develop an intimate knowledge of the modern Israeli language. His appreciation of Hebrew can be felt even in his instrumental compositions such as his early *Ballad for Violin* of 1949. In that same year he also composed *Hatzvi Israel,* a two-movement symphonic work for baritone and orchestra based on David's lament upon the death of his beloved friend, Jonathan (II Sam. 1:19–27).[39] Familiar as he was with Hebrew texts, Orgad's earliest compositions were dominated by vocal works, including a setting of Psalm 8 for male voices (1952) and two cantatas based upon biblical passages, *The Story of the Spies* (Sipur ha-meraglim) (1952), and *The Vision of Isaiah* (Ḥazon Yeshayahu) (1953).

During this early period, Orgad did experiment with purely orchestral writing and produced *Movements* (1947), a programmatically oriented work with a prelude entitled "Steps in the Night," a middle section in rondo form[40] titled "Awakening," and a concluding passacaglia called "Prayer in the Rain."

In addition, some of Orgad's most successful compositions were written for solo instruments or for small ensembles.[41] Still, his settings of texts remain among his most expressive and diverse works. *Mizmorim* (Songs of Thanksgiving and Praise) (1966–1968) for solo voices and chamber orchestra contains three movements based on psalm verses, as well as a prologue and epilogue. In each section a soloist/precentor dominates, with the remaining voices representing the community at prayer. In 1970, *The Old Decrees* (ha-Gezeirot ha-yeshanot) for soloists, choir, and orchestra was composed based on five stories of atrocities committed against Jews by crusaders in 1096. *A Tale of a Pipe* (Sipuro shel ḥalil) (1971) for vocal solos, female choir, and chamber orchestra, is based on a religiously inspired story by Shmuel Yosef (Shai) Agnon.[42] *Sufferings for Redemption* (Yisurei ge'ula) (1974) is a cantata for solo voices and orchestra based on eight poems expressing messianic hopes.[43]

Mark Kopytman: A Late Arrival from Russia

Mark Kopytman (b. 1929) was a physician and accomplished composer in his native Russia, and taught in various Soviet music academies prior to his arrival in Israel in 1972 at the age of 43. Like the immigrant composers of the 1930s, Kopytman was intrigued by the music of the Eastern communities and reflected them in many of the works he composed in his adopted homeland. Writing upon completion of his composition "*...this is a gate without a wall...*" Kopytman noted that his later works "try...to employ as germs of composition the micro-intonations of Jewish folklore, mostly those originating in the Yemen region, the peculiar thematic motifs of which seem best adaptable to my creative purposes. This tendency is also linked with the use of heterophony as practiced by the performers of traditional music in the region...."[44]

While in Israel, Kopytman has composed music for various solo instruments, including flute, trombone, piano, percussion, and harpsichord. His most remarkable works, however, are those that utilize the distinctively traditional sounds with which he was first captivated—including *About an Old Tune* for chamber ensemble (1977), which Kopytman described as "influenced by the high poetic and musical quality of Yemenite folklore."[45] He also wrote a series of compositions entitled *Cantus* (1979–1990), all of which attempt to utilize melodic elements from Jewish folklore, synagogue cantillation, and/or the microtonal sounds of the Near East.[46]

Kopytman also used a well-known Yemenite song to dramatic and melodic advantage in his *Memory,* for symphony orchestra and voice (1981). This exotic work opens with a nondescript "hum" of sounds, roughly representative of the earliest moments of a dream. Then, as the "dream" comes into focus, a Yemenite singer walks silently to center stage and chants her traditional melody, without accompaniment.

Mi ni - shi - ka - ni mi ne - shi - kot a - ha - va

Example 9.27 From "Mi Nishikani"

Who will kiss me with the kisses of love?

As the vocalist walks off stage, still trailing the final notes of her song, the orchestra resumes playing, snatching seemingly random phrases and generic inspiration from the traditional tune. The "memory" appears to blur, though, as the singer's performance grows more distant, and Kopytman's composition does not attempt to recreate the song in any meaningful way. Still, the traditional tune is reprised near the conclusion of the work, providing a helpful reminder of the inspiration behind the work, and a welcome symmetry to the composition.

Andre Hajdu: Scholar/Composer

Another "late" immigrant to Israel is Andre Hajdu (b. 1932). Born in Hungary, Hajdu had collected gypsy tunes there and was awarded a prize for his *Gypsy Cantata* (1955). After spending time in France and Tunis, Hajdu settled in Israel in 1966 and began to study Hasidic music, making a significant contribution to ethnomusicological research on that community. His music is eclectic, ranging from two piano concertos to choral settings of unusual Jewish texts from which the composer draws literal inspiration.

Hajdu's brief *Arba Midot* is a good example of some of his vocal work. Taken from *Pirkei Avot* (Ethics of the Fathers) 5:13 (and excerpted from a collection of 56 song for various vocal combinations entitled *The Mishna* [Migdal ha-poreah ba-avir] composed 1972–1974), Hajdu writes a musical midrash depicting the four types of person of whom the rabbis speak and attempts to capture the moods inspired by each:

The passage begins with this simple introductory statement: "There are four types of people in the world," and goes on to enumerate them. The first is, "He who says 'What is mine is mine, and what is yours is yours.'" The text admits that this represents a sort of middle ground, but also quotes others who say that this was the attitude of the evil people who inhabited Sodom. The clipped pronunciation of "S'dom" (Sodom) and the open chord with which this word is sung reveal the implied critique of this position.

The second individual says, "What is mine is yours, and what is yours is mine." The rabbis claim that this person is an ignoramus,[47] and the music mocks this position as well. The third type of individual generously says, "What is mine is yours and what is yours is yours." Not surprisingly, the rabbis regard this person as a *ḥasid*, a righteous one, and the lush chord that intones this word is filled with shimmering praise. The last person claims, "What is mine is mine and what is yours in mine." He is certainly an evil person, chastised for his selfishness in a loud, open chord.

The opening statement returns to complete this short work, as if to say, "There are four kinds of people in this world—and that's just the way it is." While Hajdu's word painting represents the literal meaning of the text, it does not attempt to comment on it. The composer's selection of enigmatic texts (some of his other choral works have set legalistic passages from the Talmud) betray his interest in, and familiarity with, a body of traditional literature that goes well beyond typical biblical and prayer book excerpts. In setting these, Hajdu makes an unusual connection to his Jewish roots and exposes audiences to texts that they might not otherwise confront. Without proselytizing, Hajdu expands the range and reach of Jewish musical expression.

Noam Sherrif: Native Son

Among these last composers, both within Israel and outside of it, none has achieved as much renown as Noam Sherrif. One of the first native composers (b. Tel Aviv, 1935), Sherrif is a highly regarded composer and conductor. He came to the attention of the Israeli musical establishment as a young man of 22 when *Akdamut Le'Moed*, his first orchestral composition, was chosen to inaugurate the opening concert of the newly built Frederic R. Mann Auditorium in Tel Aviv. (Interestingly, his teacher Paul Ben-Haim was part of the jury that selected the winning composition, but the music was submitted anonymously and Ben-Haim did not recognize the work of his beginner student.) Sherrif described the work, written during an extended stay in Jerusalem, as emerging under the influence of "the special, incomparable atmosphere [that] awakened unique sensations in me as I wrote. I felt that the music was being written by itself, that I had no special control over it." Based on the interval of the descending fourth, the solemn opening and closing sections of *Akdamut Le'Moed* appear reminiscent of psalm intonation, while the lively middle section is more folklike. Years later, Sherrif described the piece as representative of the music of Israel in its time, "pioneering and optimistic, perhaps a bit cut off from the larger world but full of the promise of the charm in its golden sands and its blue skies."[48]

Sherrif also won popular acclaim for his beautifully orchestrated *Israel Suite* (1965). The six short movements are arrangements of familiar melodies representing different aspects of Israel's musical heritage: "Omrim Yeshna Eretz," a setting of a poem by Saul Tchernichowsky written by Joel Engel while he was still in Russia; "Geshem, Geshem," a beloved children's song about the rain, also by Engel, written during his final years in Palestine; "Kirya Yefefiyah," a traditional Sephardic setting of the text by Spanish poet and philosopher Yehudah ha-Levi (before 1075–1141); "Ein Zeh Pele," a popular horah; "Numi, Numi Yaldati," the ubiquitous lullaby by Engel; and "Nigun Bialik," a well-known Hasidic tune.

Sherrif's other original works are often influenced by the liturgical melodies and cantillation of the Oriental communities, and by attempts to represent the sounds of the Near East with unusual combinations of Western instruments. Sherrif's *Music for Woodwind, Trombone, Piano, and Bass* (1961) borrows the melody and irregular meter of a traditional Yemenite tune. His *Chaconne for Orchestra* (1968) and *Sonata for Chamber Orchestra* (1973) continued in a similar vein, as did the programmatic symphonic work, *A Vision of David* (1986), written to commemorate the one hundredth anniversary of the birth of Israel's first prime minister, David Ben-Gurion, and featuring both a narrator and a tape of Ben-Gurion's voice.

Example 9.28 Yemenite tune that inspired *Music for Woodwind, Trombone, Piano, and Double Bass*

We will ascend to our land with singing, and joy and happiness.

Sherrif was also chosen to compose a work for the festive concert commemorating the five hundredth anniversary of the expulsion of the Jews from Spain. The resulting work, premiered in May 1992 in a performance by the Israel Philharmonic Orchestra[49] in Toledo, Spain, was *Pasion Sefardi,* eight movements for soprano, mezzo-soprano, two tenors, bass, choir, and orchestra. Following an instrumental introduction, the work proceeds to set traditional Hebrew and Ladino texts, borrowing some of the beloved Sephardic melodies that united the exiled Jewish communities of Spain throughout their 500-year dispersion.

Israel's art music has continued to evolve during the last 30 years as many of the "veteran" composers discussed here continue to write. New voices are also being heard, including those of native-born Israelis and recent arrivals from abroad. Some of these composers see themselves as citizens of the global village who happen to live in Israel and, with no specific "Israeli agenda," look for acceptance among the international community of twenty-first century musicians. Others, though, are still drawn to the unique texts, languages, and traditions that make up Jewish/Israeli culture. New immigrants, in particular, seem much more likely to recreate the experiences of their forebears, bridging their former lives with their current environment.

As the ethnic histories of these new Israelis mingle with the distinctive sounds of the Middle Eastern milieu (which continue to be heard among the polyglot voices in the Jewish state), there will be new mergers of East and West and new contributions to the art of Israel—and the world.

10 ~

Popular Music of the New State

The unfolding of Israel's new styles of art music had little impact on the development of her popular music. Occasional Eastern melodies crept into the popular consciousness, as did a continuing spate of Eastern-style popular tunes by decidedly Western composers.[1] However, despite the engagement of its serious composers with Eastern melodies and notwithstanding the massive immigration of Oriental immigrants[2] following the establishment of the state, Israel continued to turn toward the West for its popular musical models. Russian songs and styles continued to be appropriated (especially during the War of Independence), the meandering French ballads made their impression on some of the more romantic songs, and even the music of America eventually influenced Israeli composers. In the early years of the state, however, song contents continued to be inspired by internal historical events—and in the beginning, that meant a state of war.

Songs of the War of Independence

The declaration of the State of Israel on May 14, 1948, was greeted immediately by attacks from Israel's Arab neighbors on all sides. Every able-bodied person was mobilized,[3] and as the war stretched into months, even the popular music of the day reflected the realities of a nation at war. Rather than rallying the people with militaristic patriotism, however, Israel's songs promised reunions between separated loved ones, celebrated the friendships that were born of shared hardships, and paid tribute to the fallen defenders of the new state.

"Ha'amini Yom Yavo" (Believe Me, the Day Will Come) by Raphael Klatshkin (1904–1987) and Menashe Baharav[4] was among the most popular songs of the period. Tellingly, in the "letter" written by the soldier at the front to the girl he left behind, he does not report on his misery or even on his glorious performance in battle. He promises, instead, to return to her and help her forget all their troubles and urges her to set his place at the table.

Example 10.1 From "Ha'amini Yom Yavo"

Today the war is my sister, thus I am far from you,
You can celebrate our encounter in our little kitchen.
At my chosen place set an overflowing cup of wine,
Imagine that it is me there, sitting with you as always.

> Believe me, the day will come, it will be good, I promise you.
> I will come to hug you, and to help you forget everything.

Upon his induction into Israel's army, Haim Hefer (b. 1925) organized the Chizbatron, Israel's first performing army ensemble.[5] Hefer had composed the lyrics to "ha-Finjan" (The Coffeepot) in 1947 (before the outbreak of the war) and set them to a simple Armenian folk tune. Heard and popularized by soldiers singing around their own campfires, it remains a favorite.

Example 10.2 From "ha-Finjan"

A cool breeze blows, let's add another twig to the fire,
In the reddish arms of the flame the sacrifice will be offered.
The fire is flickering, a song is blossoming,
The coffeepot goes around and around.

The approach to Jerusalem from Tel Aviv passes through a region dominated on one side by steep hills and on the other by sharp drops off a winding road. In November 1947, from the moment the United Nations voted to partition Palestine into Arab and Jewish states, Arab snipers at a small village called Bab-El-Wad (in Hebrew, Sha'ar ha-Gai, the Gate of the Valley) prevented travelers from reaching their destination in Jerusalem—effectively cutting off the city. Shortages of food and water became extreme, and, while caravans of supply trucks made valiant attempts to reach the hungry city, one truck after another was attacked. Finally, in April 1948, the Palmaḥ (Israel's then-illegal military forces) organized a massive caravan accompanied by 1,500 soldiers in a bold attempt to finally break the blockade. Armed with new weapons just (secretly) imported from sympathetic forces outside the country, the soldiers accompanied 175 trucks into Jerusalem, turning the tide of the blockade. These efforts continued for the next several weeks until an alternate route to Jerusalem, known as the Burma Road,[6] could be completed. While the success of this operation galvanized the Israelis and saved Jerusalem, the price in lives lost was high. To this day, the wreckage of burnt-out trucks remains by the side of the road as a memorial to those who gave their lives there, and the song that tells their story, "Bab El Wad," by Haim Guri[7] (b. 1923) and Shmuel Pershko, remains a part of Israel's Memorial Day observances.

Bab el Wad la- ne-tzaḥ zkhor na   et sh'mo-te - nu sha -ya- rot par -tzu ba -de-rekh el ha-ir

Example 10.3 From "Bab El Wad"

Here I pass by, standing by the side of the stone,
A black asphalt road, with rocks and cracks.
Evening slowly comes, a wind blows from the ocean,
The light of the first star shines from over Beit Maḥsir.

[Chorus]
  Bab El Wad, please remember our names forever.
  Convoys burst out on the way into the city.
  On the sides of the road lie our dead.
  The iron skeletons are silent like my dead friend.
  Bab El Wad, please remember our names forever,
  Bab El Wad, on the way to the city.

The War of Independence was not fought for military glory or aggrandizement of national borders. Rather, it was a war fought by farmers and dreamers with no choice but to survive. They longed for an end to the fighting and the beginning of their lives in a secure and independent state, and yearned to grow old treasuring friendships forged in the heat of battle. The song "Hayu Zemanim" (There Were Times) that Haim Hefer and Moshe Wilensky[8] (b. 1910) wrote for the Chizbatron captured the soldiers' fondest hopes. Now that the hair of the soldiers in the song really has turned gray, the European-style ballad of another era is indeed sung with that very nostalgia that the song promised would come one day.

Example 10.4 From "Hayu Zemanim"

  The day will come and you'll sit by the fireplace,
  Your back will also be stooped like a hump.
  You'll remember your days in the Palmaḥ,
  And you'll tell the stories while smoking your pipe.
  And all around the children will sit,
  And your wife will also be advanced in years.
  She will shed a tear and wipe her nose,

And she will sigh, there were times, there were times…

> There were times that we sat in the post,
> There were times we fought and we loved,
> But now there's nothing to recognize,
> On that old post sits a city,
> Perhaps thanks to those times.

The Fifties

Israel's first years were occupied with building the new state and building homes for the thousands of new immigrants who streamed into it. The earliest pioneers had conquered the swamps of Israel's northern region; attention turned now to irrigating the desert.

Israel's army took a leading role in creating new settlements; entertainment troupes representing these Naḥal units (an acronym for Noar Ḥalutz Loḥem, young fighting pioneers) were established in 1951. In addition to launching the careers of some of Israel's most famous performers—Yossi Banai, Chaim Topol, Arik Einstein, Yehoram Gaon, Shalom Hanoch, Miri Aloni, and Nechama Hendel, to name just a few—the troupes galvanized the new nation with their activities and their songs. They performed throughout the country and were widely heard on government-sponsored radio. "Horah Mamterah" by Yehiel Mohar[9] (1921–1969) and Moshe Wilensky, while first sung by the Naḥal Troupe, was popularized by Yemenite songstress Shoshana Damari.

So - vi so - vi mam - te - rah le - fa - zer pe - nei - or - rah so - vi ve - ha - tey - zi ma - yim

Example 10.5 From "Horah Mamterah"

> The flow of water sings in the pipe, water pipes are the veins
>   of the desert.
> This is the way of the song, from the faucet to the clod,
> The deep water would rise, the pump says "Bread!"

Desert, desert, what has been changed? Negev, sprinklers came upon you.

> Turn, turn sprinkler, turn and scatter pearls of light.
> Turn, sprinkle water along the road, the land will give its fruit.
> Since there is no rain from the skies.

Haim Hefer collaborated with Sasha Argov[10] (b. 1914) to produce "la-Midbar" that Hefer's Chizbatron ensemble performed in the aftermath of the War of Independence. The "wilderness" captured the imagination of the young, as did the song, later popularized by a duo known as The Parvarim.[11]

La -mid bar e - retz lo ma - yim ho at ad -ma- ti shav-nu ei - la -yikh

Example 10.6 From "la-Midbar"

> Go, go to the desert, the paths will carry you,
> Evening is quickly approaching. Go, my brother, to the desert.
> Again we will return, the cliffs will shout,
> The large bright sun will yet shine on us.
> To the desert, land without water.
> You are my land, we have returned to you.
> Land of salt, wind and fury, the fighters have returned like a storm,
> To the desert, land without water,
> You are my land, we have returned to you.

The exultation that greeted the establishment of the state and the rapid achievements of its early years infused many with a sense that "anything is possible." One dream that loomed especially large in the late afternoons, as the setting sun cast its shadows on distant mountains, was the notion of bringing back some of the glimmering clay from the "red rocks" of Petra in nearby Jordan. In 1954, five young men set out on such an expedition but were captured on the way and killed by hostile Jordanian forces. Haim Hefer and new immigrant Yochanan Zarai (b. 1929)[12] wrote a song about the tragic episode, which was recorded by actor and sometime singer Arik Lavie and gained great popularity. Unfortunately, the song also had the unin-

tended result of encouraging other young people to attempt the perilous journey and was therefore banned from radio play for many
years. Even without public performances, the song remained an
"underground" hit, illustrative of the still-tense atmosphere surrounding Israel's relations with her neighbors.

Example 10.7 From "ha-Sela ha-Adom"

Behind the mountains and the desert the legends say there is a place
From which no man has returned alive; and it is called "the red rock."

Three set out at sunset; in front of them burned the mountains
        of Edom.
An old dream, a map and a canteen they took with them to
        the red rock.

The first went as a scout, raised his face, looked at the stars above,
But the sight that his eyes saw was that of the red rock.

In the wadi, as they rested between the stones, he spoke as if hit by
        a dream,
"I see her face is white." His friends answered, "The red rock."

The circle of the sun smote their heads, and they inhaled the dust
        and heat of the desert,
And suddenly as if their blood froze in them, they saw the red rock.

The burst of the shooting was short; one groaned "I'm shot" and he
        was silent.
His friends answered with mouths full of dirt, "We have arrived at
        the red rock."

The Sinai Campaign

The War of Independence had been halted by brokered armistice, not by any real peace. Continuing hostilities by Arab forces intensified with the 1955 deployment of Egyptian *fedayeen* (infiltrators) squads who committed murder and sabotage inside Israel and caused 1,300 Israeli civilian casualties between 1949 and 1956. By the end of 1955, an agreement between Egypt and Czechoslovakia provided Egypt with Soviet-made artillery and escalated the Middle East arms race. The passage of Israeli shipping through the Suez Canal was blocked when Egypt nationalized the canal. Later in 1956, Egypt blocked Israeli access to shipping through the Red Sea port of Eilat as well. "Operation Kadesh" (as the Sinai campaign was known) was launched in late October 1956 with three objectives: destroy the *fedayeen* bases in the Gaza Strip and the Egyptian border; prevent an Egyptian attack on Israel by destroying airfields in the Sinai; and open the Gulf of Eilat to Israeli shipping.

The Sinai Campaign of October 29–November 5, 1956, accomplished all of its military objectives.[13] It also inspired Yehiel Mohar and Moshe Wilensky to compose *"Mul Har Sinai"* (In Front of Mount Sinai) for performance by the Naḥal Troupe during that brief campaign and the tense days that followed. The only song to be definitively linked with this action, and the only one to retain its place in the national repertoire, it was also the only popular song to overtly juxtapose biblical history with contemporary imagery. Certainly, many songs had borrowed, or totally appropriated biblical verses. Prophetic images of water returning to the wilderness were especially popular during this period of irrigating the desert, with songs like "Mayim, Mayim"[14] (You Shall Draw Forth Water) from Isaiah 12:3 and the anonymous folk song "Yesusum Midbar" (The Wilderness Is Blossoming) from Isaiah 35:1 on most lips. Images from Deuteronomy 26:15 of "Eretz Zavat Ḥalav U'devash" (A Land Flowing with Milk and Honey)[15] and the evocation of King Uziyahu's engineering exploits in II Chronicles 26:9[16] were also favorites during these early years of the state. But *"Mul Har Sinai"* encapsulated the relationship between modern Israel and its biblical heritage:

Example 10.8 From *"Mul Har Sinai"*

It is not a legend, my friend, and not a passing dream.
Here, in front of Mt. Sinai, the bush is burning.
And it is glowing in song in the mouths of regiments of young men,
And the gates of the city are in the hands of the Samsonites.

> [Chorus]
> Ho, the flame of God in the boys' eyes.
> Ho, the flame of God in the roar of engines.
> This day will be recounted, my brothers,
> When the nation returned to stand at Sinai.

My friends, it is not a dream, and not a [prophetic] vision being
envisioned.
From then until today the bush burns.
It burns with a song of strength in these hearts
Of the young men of Zion and the chariot of Israel.
[Chorus]

The 1956 campaign marked the first return of the Jewish people
to Sinai since Joshua had led Israel into Canaan. Jewish national history begins at Mt. Sinai: There God appeared to Moses in the form
of a burning bush and instructed him to return to Egypt to redeem
his enslaved people. There, at Mt. Sinai, the children of Israel
became Jews when they accepted the Torah. During forty years of
wandering through the desert, the slave generation that could not
imagine or accept freedom (and its responsibilities) died out, making
way for an energetic and committed new nation to emerge and to

take its rightful homeland. Now, 3,000 years later, the Jews have returned to the foot of Mt. Sinai. The bush is still burning: God is still a presence in the life of Israel. But now that same flame is burning in the eyes of the young men and women who are the defenders of Israel. Now the chariots flying through the desert are not Pharaoh's chariots on a mission to collect the slaves and return them to Egypt; now the mighty chariots of a strong and powerful Israel roar through the desert—once again to reject Egyptian enslavement.

The linkages in Mohar's poetry are clear, and Wilensky's song is up to the challenge. While Israel's songs of war are mostly songs of peace, this song is full of pride. There is no false bravado or unnecessary militarism here. Instead, the strong melody confidently negotiating a wide range, and the blaring trumpets, in accompaniment, symbolize the conviction and determination of this nation to defend itself against any and all aggressors.

The Sixties

The early 1960s was an era of relative peace for Israel. Although military tensions with her neighbors continued, the country and its music worked hard to create an illusion of calm. Pastoral melodies filled the airwaves, and a gentle song of descending evening by Oded Avisar (1918–1976) and Aryeh Levanon[17] (b. 1932) won the first-ever Festival of Israeli Song, held at the end of Independence Day celebrations in 1960.

Example 10.9 From "Erev Ba"

Again the herd flocks at the gates of the village,
And dust is rising from the earthen roads,
And far away a pair of bells accompanies the lengthening of
    the shadows.
Evening comes, evening comes.

The Six-Day War

The Six-Day War of 1967 effected a dramatic change in Israel and in her music. The little nation that had tried to live quietly among mighty, hostile neighbors was forced to defend herself yet again.[18] To the great surprise of the world, Israel defeated her attackers in a stunning display of strategy and strength. Capping the victory was the reunification of Jerusalem, whole and under Jewish rule for the first time in nearly 2,000 years.

The initial emotion was unbridled euphoria and there was more than a bit of braggadocio in the songs written in the immediate aftermath of the war. A borrowed folk melody taunted Egyptian officials in "Nasser Meḥakeh le-Rabin" ([Egyptian President Gamal Abdul] Nasser Waits for [Israeli Army Commander Yitzchak] Rabin). An irreverent Shmuel Kraus[19] (b. 1932) penned "Pegisha ba-Milu'im" (Appointment with the Reserves), a sarcastic description of life in the reserves with nothing to do (because the war was over before they got there). "Maḥar" (Tomorrow), written by Naomi Shemer in 1964, gained new popularity as some of its lyrics promising that everything is possible took on new meaning in the wake of Israel's remarkable victory.[20]

One other song Naomi Shemer had written before the war took on new meaning as well. Just weeks earlier, Shemer had been commissioned to write a song for the annual Independence Day Song Festival. Jerusalem's Mayor Teddy Kollek had specifically requested that she write about Jerusalem, and Shemer complied, borrowing verses from Jeremiah's Lamentations to express her own sorrow over the tragedy of the continuing inaccessibility of the Old City and its holy places. The audience in the hall was noticeably moved by the music and immediately asked singer Shuli Nathan to repeat the song so that they might join in singing its powerful refrain.

And then came the war and the unexpected reunification of the city. Shemer's "Yerushalayim Shel Zahav" (Jerusalem of Gold) was on the lips of every soldier fighting to reclaim the Old City, in the heart of every dancer rejoicing in the streets of Jerusalem following its capture, and rising from every corner of the nation as the celebratory shofar was blown once more on the Temple Mount. Shemer's song galvanized and unified the people as no song ever had before—or since. But it was immediately apparent that the song needed to be revised as soon as possible, since it had been written when the Temple Mount stood quiet and the markets were empty. Shemer quickly added a final verse to reflect the new life pulsing through the streets of the Old City and the new version was eagerly sung throughout Israel—and beyond.[21]

In the weeks, months, and even years that followed, Jerusalem continued to figure prominently in the music of Israel. The Hasidic Song Festival,[22] launched in 1969, offered "Sisu et Yerushalayim" (Rejoice in Jerusalem) and "Yevarekhekha" (May you be blessed [from Zion]). Popular songs like "Lakh Yerushalayim" (To You, Jerusalem), "Zot Yerushalayim" (This Is Jerusalem), and "Yerushalayim Shel Az" (Jerusalem of Then) filled the airwaves.

But the price for reunifying Jerusalem was a heavy one. More than 500 soldiers fell in the fighting, much of it hand-to-hand combat in the narrow streets of the Old City. The joy that greeted the liberation of Jerusalem was heavily tinged with sadness at the price paid, and for some, like those in the song by poet Dan Almagor (b. 1935) and composer Nurit Hirsh (b. 1942),[23] Jerusalem would never be the same again:

A - mar ha - ro - khel mi - maz - ke -ret Mo-she Ye - ru - sha - la-yim she - li

Example 10.10 From "Yerushalayim Sheli"

Said the peddler from Mazkeret Moshe, "My Jerusalem:
It is Maḥane Yehudah on holiday eve
And the hummus of Rahmo and the scent of fish,
Sabbath of *popitas* [an Oriental food], the curses of drivers

Laundry on the road and a shower from a bucket,
My Jerusalem, my Jerusalem."

Said the shoemaker from the neighborhood of Katamon,
    "My Jerusalem
Is seven years of rains on the shed,
A neighborhood without a store, a bus[ride] without charge,
The early show on Shabbat at the Orion [theater],
Also, [the neighborhood of] Katamon Gimel is for me
My Jerusalem, my Jerusalem."

Said the bath attendant from Me'ah She'arim, "My Jerusalem
Is a black *shtreimel* [Hasid's hat] and grey books and 'A daughter of
    Israel does not walk in shorts.' *
It is whispered prayers for other days, not here, because up above
    she is winking to me,
My Jerusalem, my Jerusalem."

Said the young man there next to the Nablus Gate, "My Jerusalem
Is a cross on a store and police at midnight, a sister who informs, and
    a ditch with bombs,
An Independence Day parade and clenched hands, 'Yes sir! What,
    kebab or *shishlik* [ground beef on a skewer]?'
My Jerusalem, my Jerusalem."

Said the soldier from Ashdot Yaakov, "My Jerusalem,
I was there once on a morning of bereavement:
Alleys and a sniper in the tower on the left,
Since then I haven't returned, I simply can't. Avner and Gadi, for me,
    they are
My Jerusalem, my Jerusalem."

---

* a sign in the neighborhood warning against immodest dress

The War of Attrition

As the initial euphoria over the 1967 victory faded, Israel was forced to confront many hard truths. Hundreds were dead and more died each day in the continuing war of attrition. One of the favorite songs of this era was Naomi Shemer's "Anaḥnu Shnenu Me'oto Hakfar" (We Were Two from the Same Village), about inseparable childhood friends separated by death in a six-day war that showed no signs of really ending. The 1969 Song Festival was won by a song called "Ballada Lakhovesh" (The Ballad of the Medic),[24] the graphic story of a soldier who gave his own life to save a wounded comrade.

The realization of the heavy toll taken by the six days of intense fighting in 1967 and the daily reports of more casualties brought continuing pain to a nation that had replaced its initial rejoicing in the early flush of victory with a lingering sense of sorrow. A young poet named Rachel Shapira (b. 1945) touched hearts across the country with her image of the ministering angel who was able to give her young charge every gift but one. Composer Yair Rosenblum (1944–1996) captured all of the irony and pathos of "Mah Avarekh" (With What Shall I Bless?) in his moving song, recorded and sung across Israel by the Navy Performing Ensemble.[25]

Example 10.11 From "Mah Avarekh"

"With what shall I bless him, with what shall he be blessed,
   this boy?" asked the angel.

And he blessed him with a smile that was like a light,
And he blessed him with eyes, great and perceptive,
To catch every flower and living creature and bird,
And a heart with which to feel all the sights.

"With what shall I bless him, with what shall he be blessed,
    this youth?" asked the angel.

And he blessed him with feet to dance endlessly,
And a soul to remember all the melodies,
And hands that collect shells on the shore,
And ears attuned to adults and children.

"With what shall I bless him, with what shall he be blessed,
    this young man?" asked the angel.

And he blessed his hands that were trained with flowers,
They were also successful in acquiring the strength of steel,
And his feet dance to the beat of the trail,
And his lips sing the rhythms of commands.

"How shall I bless him, with what shall he be blessed, this man?"
    asked the angel.

I gave him whatever was possible to give:
A song and a smile and legs to dance,
And a gentle hand and a sensitive heart,
And with what else shall I bless you?

"How shall I bless him, with what shall he be blessed, this boy,
    this young man, this delicate one?"

This youth—he is now an angel,
No more will he be blessed, no more will he bless.
Oh God! If only You had blessed him with life.

The continuing tensions were a source of fear to some and frustration to others. The same young people who had fought the war, and whose friends and brothers and fathers were still dying in its aftermath, began to rally. Yaakov Rotblit[26] (b. 1945) was their spokesperson, angering the religious establishment and the government alike with his irreverent lyrics;[27] Yair Rosenblum borrowed the international vocabulary of "rock and roll" to sound their urgent "Shir le-Shalom" (Song for Peace).

Example 10.12 From "Shir le-Shalom"

Let the sun rise and give the morning light.
The purest prayer will not bring us back
He whose candle was snuffed out and was buried in the dust.
A bitter cry won't wake him, won't bring him back.

Nobody will return us from the dead dark pit,
Here, neither the victory cheer nor songs of praise will help.

> [Chorus]
> So sing only a song for peace, do not whisper a prayer,
> Better sing a song for peace with a big shout.

Let the sun penetrate through the flowers,
Don't look backward, leave those who departed.
Lift your eyes with hope, not through the rifle sights.
Sing a song for love and not for wars.

Don't say "the day will come"—bring the day, because it is not
    a dream,
And within all the city's squares cheer only peace.
[Chorus]

The Yom Kippur War

Despite continuing tensions surrounding the "unfinished business" of 1967, the war that began on Yom Kippur in October 1973 caught Israel by surprise. As the military struggled to respond, the prayers that had been interrupted on the holiest day on the Jewish calendar became songs to support the soldiers at the front and their loved ones left at home. Moshe Wilensky, whose music had sustained Israel through each prior period of combat, stepped forward again. As *sheliah tzibbur* to a nation in crisis, Wilensky asked God to hold open the gates for those final prayers left unsaid:[28]

Example 10.13 From "Petah Lanu Sha'ar"

> Open the gates at the time of the closing of the gates, for the day
>   is waning. . . .

Israel was tired. The Six-Day War, six years of a war of attrition, and the final insult of having their enemies intervene in the decision of "who shall live and who shall die"[29] made Israelis yearn for peace in ways that had never been articulated before. Desperate for an end to the fighting that had consumed so much national energy—and so many of her youth—a battle-weary nation was eager to accept the notion that this really would be "ha-Milhamah ha-Aharonah" (The Last War). Haim Hefer's graphic lyrics brought home the realities of war; the juxtaposition of those harsh words with Dov Seltzer's[30] (b. 1932) wistful melody only emphasized the need to fulfill this song's promise:

Example 10.14 From "ha-Milhamah ha-Aharonah"

I promise you, my little girl, that this will be the last war.
In the name of the tank commanders with their dusty faces, who went
    through fire and mortar,
In the name of sailors who raided ports, their eyes stinging from
    the salt of the waves,
I promise you, my little girl, that this will be the last war.
In the name of the pilots who burst into furious battle and were
    consumed in the fire of missiles and anti-aircraft artillery,
In the name of the paratroopers, who, between the lead and the smoke
    saw you like an angel over their heads,
I promise you, my little girl, that this will be the last war.
In the name of gunners, who, among the splintering of shells,
    endured a column of fire along the front,
In the name of doctors and medics who, with their body and soul
Returned spirit and life, infused blood,
I promise you, my little girl, that this will be the last war.
In the name of the signalers whose voices tore through the night.
In the name, in the name of all the units.
In the name of all the fathers who marched out to terrible battle
And who want to come home to you,
I promise you, my little girl, that this will be the last war.

Songs of Peace and Prayer

Israel's recovery from the Yom Kippur War was painful. The political fallout from the country's lack of preparedness[31] was another wound in the nation's already-damaged psyche. Israelis did not want to sing any more songs of war and loss.

Anwar Sadat's trip to Jerusalem in 1978 held out the possibility that the promise of Hefer's verses might come true. Slowly overcoming years of enmity, Israel made peace with one of her most formidable opponents and rejoiced with Uzi Hitman's[32] (b. 1952) song of friendship and hope.

A -ni no-la-de-ti   el ha-man-gi-not   ve - el ha-shi-rim shel kol ha-me-di-not

Example 10.15 From "Noladeti le-Shalom"

I was born to the melodies, and to the songs of all the nations.
I was born to the language, and to the place, to the few, to the many
Who would extend hands in peace.

[Chorus]
I was born for peace, it should only arrive.
I was born for peace that should only come.
I was born for the peace which will appear.
I want, I only want to be a part of it!

I was born to a nation two thousand years old,
A land reserved for her, with a portion in heaven.
And she sees, expects—here, the day rises,
And the hour is beautiful—it is an hour of peace.
[Chorus]

Peace with Egypt came with a steep price: the return of the Sinai Peninsula. Cities that had been planted in the desert since 1967 were uprooted and demolished, but not without intense national debate. Many argued that no piece of land was worth the price of peace; others decried the return of any territory.

While the debate over the price of peace continued, life in Israel began to acquire an air of calm as the recurring cycles of war that had afflicted the country's early years finally appeared to be past. Israel's participation in the annual Eurovision Festival seemed a metaphor for her membership in the family of nations: Almost simultaneous with the signing of the treaty with Egypt, Israel became a regular participant[33] in the exciting international music event that pitted the winners of several national festivals (including Israel's Independence Day programs) against each other in an internationally televised competition. Israel won the competition in 1978 with "A-Ba-Ni-Bi," a rock-influenced song of the joys of love (spoken in a children's secret nonsense language), and repeated her victory the following year with "Halleluyah," a celebration of singing. These early entries represented a retreat from some of the more uniquely Israeli songs (and subjects) of past competitions, partly reflecting the improved national mood, but perhaps also an attempt to capture wider audience appeal in the international forum. Israel's 1983 entry by lyricist Ehud Manor (b. 1941) and singer/songwriter Avi Toledano[34] (b. ca. 1950), though, carried the sense of national pride that had characterized songs of other eras. Although it did not capture first place,[35] it most assuredly captured the attention of the world with the confident assertion of its lyric: Israel is alive!

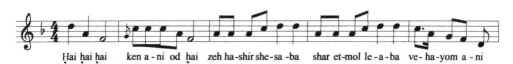

Ḥai ḥai ḥai   ken a - ni od ḥai   zeh ha-shir she-sa -ba   shar et-mol le -a -ba   ve- ha-yom a - ni

Example 10.16 From "Ḥai"

Listen, my brothers, I'm still alive, and my eyes are still raised up
    to the light,
My thorns are many, but so are my flowers,
And ahead of me there are many years to count.

I ask and I pray, it's good that the hope was not yet lost.
A psalm is passing from generation to generation
Like a fountain from long ago 'til eternity

I ask and pray, it's good that the hope was not yet lost:

    Alive, alive, alive, yes I'm still alive,
    This is the song which grandfather sang yesterday to father
    And today [it's] me.
    I'm still alive, alive, alive, the nation of Israel is alive.
    This is the song which grandfather sang yesterday to father, and
        today [it's] me. (Literal translation)

The 1980s was also an era of nostalgia. Jewish tradition allows that one acquires "understanding" at the age of forty (*Pirkei Avot* 5:24), and as Israel approached that age, her popular music appeared to reflect a growing maturity as well. Many of her newest performers were from Oriental families. The Ashkenazic hegemony that in the 1950s had attempted to assimilate all Eastern immigrants into Western patterns had relaxed its hold on culture. Ofra Haza (1959–2000), born to Yemenite parents, was discovered in a theater workshop for disadvantaged children in a Tel Aviv neighborhood optimistically named Hatikvah (the hope). It was her performance of "Ḥai" that carried the song and her career to international fame, but in between appearances in Europe and Asia, Haza recorded three albums of *shirei moledet,* (songs of the birthland) from Israel's early years. Her reprisals of shepherd songs and romantic ballads (many of them songs by Western composers imitating the Eastern style) were part of a movement to bring back a simpler time in Israel's past—and a time when everyone seemed to be united by the common goal of building a state. As the state approached its important milestone, new songs also yearned for "the days of yesteryear" when a simple horah brought disparate people shoulder-to-shoulder to dance through the night. A year before "Ḥai," Avi Toledano had performed his own "Horah" (with lyrics by Yoram Tohar-Lev) in Israel's annual song festival, now called the Pre-Eurovision Festival.

od maz - hiv ha - sa -deh she - a - zav - nu az od ha - a - retz no - seit ye - vu-

lah ve - od ya- fim hem ha -lei - lot bikh -na - an te -rem ha -she -mesh o - lah

Example 10.17 From "Horah"

The field we left is still golden; the land is still bearing its harvest,
And the nights are still beautiful in Canaan before the sun rises.
Trains still cross the green citrus grove, a stork gently hovers above,
And a mist still hangs over the valley, between the sunrise and the dew.

And also the horah, with its "hey,"
The sound still rises, it is not silent.
And that horah, with its "hey," its song will always fill my heart.

In 1984, Tohar-Lev and Nurit Hirsh collaborated on a song for the annual Children's Song Festival. With fond references to songs and dances of the past, they helped instill in the next generation a nostalgia for an era it had never known but from which it could certainly learn much.

Shu - vi har - mo - ni - ka   shu - vi   ha - ho - rah   ha - ma - pu - hit   ve - he - ha - lil

ya - had nir - ko - da ve - ya - had nah - zo - rah   el ha - "El yiv - ne   ha - ga - lil"

Example 10.18 From "Shuvi Harmonikah"

Hey, hey, put out your feet and join hands as one person.
Hey, hey, we'll dance like we used to, a dance with a taste that has
  not passed.
Return "Harmonika," return "Horah," the harmonica and the flute.
Together we'll dance and together we'll return to the "El Yivne
  ha-Galil."

> From evening to morning, from morning to evening we have
>   strength for more and more.
> From morning to evening, from evening to morning, we'll
>   continue to dance.

The Bad, the Ugly—and the Good

Not everything about Israel—past or present—was wonderful, and Israel's songs did not only paint pretty pictures. At the same time that Israel's security became less of a concern, the fading of that old "pioneer spirit" created a climate in which the children of immigrants became emigrants themselves.

Israel's twenty-year administration of a large and hostile Arab community in territory recovered during the 1967 war was another source of great tension. The five-year *intifada* (uprising) that began in 1988 brought clashes between Israeli soldiers and young Palestinians, negative headlines in newspapers around the world, and great stress to many who still remembered Golda Meir's lament of the 1960s: When asked her feelings about sending Israeli boys to war, the then prime minister (and surrogate mother) of the nation explained that she could "forgive the Arabs for killing us—but would never forgive them for making killers out of us."

Chava Alberstein, who began her career singing Yiddish songs of her parents' generation, and whose performance of now-classic Hebrew songs had captured the hearts of Israel years earlier, found her own voice in the wake of the *intifada*. Echoing Meir's pain, Alberstein turned to the final song of the Passover haggadah. The long poem, with no apparent connection to the Passover story, is written as an allegory; the many nations who beat each other—and ultimately the Jews—are struck down by the angel of death who, in turn, is destroyed by The Holy One, Blessed is He, who has always been the champion of Israel. In Alberstein's song, however, much has changed, as the identities of the victim and the aggressor are unclear.

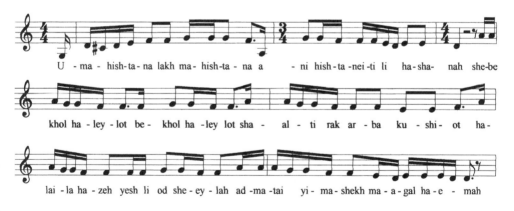

Example 10.19 From "Ḥad Gadya"

That father bought with two coins, one little kid, one little kid.
Our father bought a goat with two coins, thus says the haggadah…

…And came the angel of death and killed the slaughterer that
    slaughtered the ox
That drank the water that quenched the fire that burned the stick that
    hit the dog
That bit the cat that devoured the goat that our father brought…
And suddenly you sing "one little kid."
Spring has not yet arrived and Passover hasn't come.
And what will be different for you, what is different,
I have changed this year.
Because on every night, on each night I asked only four questions.
This night I have another question: How long will the circle of
    terror continue?
And persecutor and the persecuted, the beater and the beaten,
When will this madness be finished?

And what changed for you, what changed, I changed this year.

I was once a lamb and a tranquil little goat, today I am a tiger
    and a devouring wolf.
I was already a dove, I was a deer, today I don't know who I am.

That father bought with two coins, a little kid, a little kid
Our father bought a goat for two coins, again we begin from
    the beginning…

These songs of introspection and self-criticism, while finding
audiences—especially among Israel's fringes (left and right!)—were
by no means the dominant force in Israel's cultural life. Instead,
Israeli music benefited from exchanges with the global village of
which Israel was now a full member. Ofra Haza sang traditional
songs of her Yemenite youth which landed on the pop charts of
Europe, and her MTV video debut was even featured on the influential *Today* television show in America.[36] Meanwhile, Israel, which
had flirted with the music of the world during the 1970s, now
embraced the music of Russia, Bosnia, and Africa brought by new
waves of immigration. The Jewish nation once again brought home
its children—native and adopted—from all over the world.

Not all of these new immigrants were equally welcomed (the controversy about "how Jewish" some of the immigrants were or were not continues to contribute to political and religious tensions in Israeli society), but it eagerly accepted their exotic musical traditions. The creation of the Sheba Choir by Israeli musician Shlomo Gronich[37] (b. 1949) was one of the first attempts to blend the unique Ethiopian style with conventional Western practices. His evocation of their dangerous journey, with poignant lyrics by native Ethiopian writer Haim Idisis, captured the multiple facets of their experience as travelers and as immigrants:

Ha -ya -re-aḥ mash-gi-aḥ me -al al ga- vi sak ha -o -ḥel ha -dal ha -mid -bar mi -taḥ -tai ein so -fo le -fa- nim ve -i - mi mav -ti -ḥaḥ le -a - ḥai hak -ta - nim od me -at od ktzat le -ha - rim rag-la - yim ma-a- matz a-ḥa-ron lif-ney Ye - ru -sha -la - yim

Example 10.20 From "ha-Masa le-Eretz Yisrael"

The moon oversees above, on my back, a poor sack of food,
The desert is beneath me, there is no end to it before me.
And my mother promises my little brothers:

> A bit more, a short while to lift your feet, one last effort before Jerusalem.

The light of the moon takes a strong stance, our sack of food is lost,
The desert does not end, the howling of jackals,
And my mother encourages my little brothers:

A bit more, a short while, we will soon be redeemed,
We won't stop going to the land of Israel.

And in the night there are suddenly robbers, with a knife and
a sharp sword.
In the desert, the blood of my mother, the moon is my witness,
And I promise my little brothers:

A bit more, a little while, the dream will be fulfilled, a bit more,
We will arrive in the land of Israel.

In the moon is the image of my mother looking at me. Mother,
don't leave.
If you were by my side you would be able to convince them
that I am a Jew.

A bit more, a short while, soon we will be redeemed,
We won't stop going to the land of Israel.

A bit more, a short while, to lift eyes, one last effort before
Jerusalem.

The collaboration between Shlomo Gronich and Ehud Manor
that produced "Shir Yisraeli" (Israeli Song) conjures a wonderful
image of the "salad bowl" that is the Israeli experience—both human
and musical. It speaks volumes about the potential of people to join
together from disparate geographic regions and cultural traditions
and to blend their histories and values to produce a unique end
result—in this case, the infinite variety of Israeli song.

Example 10.21 From "Shir Yisraeli"

Your snow and my rain, your wadi and my river
Finally meet on an Israeli shore,

> [Bridge]
> With all the dreams and yearnings,
> With the good and bad memories,
> In a new-old song that repairs the tears,
> How good it is, how good and how pleasant.

> [Chorus]
> In a Greek rhythm with a Polish accent,
> In a Yemenite pronunciation with a Romanian violin:
> Who am I, who am I, yes, me,
> My God, my God, an Israeli song.

Your valley and my mountain, your forest and my desert
Finally meet, in an Israeli landscape
[Bridge and Chorus]

My *lamed* and your *ḥet,* my *ayin* and your *resh*
Meet, finally, with an Israeli drum.
[Bridge and Chorus]
(Literal translation)

11~
Popular Music in America

As we have seen, the massive immigration of European Jews to America at the beginning of the twentieth century brought with it a variety of musical forms. The theater became the focus of American Jewish popular music, presenting folk and composed melodies written in Europe and providing the catalyst for the creation of new music uniquely reflective of American life. However, most of the music written in America continued to bear the imprimatur of the European experience. It was not until many years later that American Jews began to express themselves musically as Jews, but now in the style and language of the New World. Ironically, an important impetus for the creation of a uniquely American popular Jewish repertoire was once again an event on the other side of the Atlantic Ocean— but this time it was the Six-Day War in Israel.

From Hesitant Zionism to Jewish Pride

Much of the American Jewish community had been slow to embrace modern Zionism. The Jewish Agency did a brisk business spreading the new music of the pre-state era throughout Europe, but that same music received only a lukewarm reception in America. To be sure, there were pockets of American interest in the rebuilding of Israel,[1] but Jews in the United States had much to risk from outwardly identifying with a Jewish state. Although America appeared to be a land of opportunity for all comers, pockets of anti-Semitism continued to exist: Jewish admissions to the most prestigious universities were subject to limiting quotas; Jews were routinely excluded from membership at tony country clubs; Jewish home buyers were not welcome in all the new suburbs; and, at least in the South, "no vacancy" signs regularly greeted Jewish tourists seeking hotel rooms. Moreover, while the "golden land" appeared to welcome newcomers with open arms, quotas for Jewish immigrants were strictly enforced, even during the dark days of World War II. Jews were by no means the only ethnic group to suffer from these kinds of prejudices and protectionism, but the long history of Jewish persecution had taught American Jews to keep a "low profile."[2] During the late 1940s and into the 1950s, when the young Middle Eastern nation seemed strongly tinged with a socialist cast, American society was fragmented by Senator Joseph McCarthy's hysterical anticommunism, leading some would-be supporters of the Jewish state to fear the charge of "dual loyalty." It was easier for most American Jews to simply take no position regarding Israel.

In 1967, more than two decades after the revelations of the Holocaust, latent fears (some called it "survivor syndrome") were brought to the fore when Israel's survival appeared threatened. Happily, any reservations concerning Israel's future were soundly demolished by her stunning victory in the Six-Day War.

The profound emotional catharsis for American (and indeed all of Diaspora) Jewry was deepened by the fact that America itself was undergoing a profound societal shift. The struggle for civil rights for African Americans, the feminist movement, and popular rejection of American involvement in Vietnam were all under way and rapidly changing the face of America. Jewish students were disproportionately represented on American college campuses and, both there and in the general society, were among the activists in each of these movements. Many, but not all, of these activists were estranged from their Jewish identity.

As major battles in these arenas began to be won, some Jewish activists used the training they had received to focus back on the Jewish community. Jewish members of countercultural communes created *havurot*[3] and feminist activism led to the creation of the Jewish women's movement.[4] Social activists and leaders of the antiwar movement eventually turned to critiquing the American Jewish establishment, attacking Jewish Federations and seeking a voice there.[5] "African studies" and "women's studies" courses, and then departments, were established at many universities across the country. And in this atmosphere of more public ethnic identity, "Jewish studies" also took *its* place amid the ivory towers of academe.[6]

It was inevitable that a people finally enfranchised to openly investigate its own past would begin to contribute to its present as well. On college campuses across America, young people with little previous knowledge of or identification with Jewish life and ritual practices publicly began to wear symbols that identified them with Judaism and the Jewish community: the *kippah* (yarmulke/skullcap) replaced the fedora and the baseball cap, while necklaces with six-pointed stars and *chai* (the Hebrew word for "life") charms appeared on young women and men. Jewish foods from bagels to chicken soup entered the national culinary cuisine, and Jewish neuroses—real and caricatured—were portrayed in feature films, television, and theater. All that was missing from American Jewish life was the music.

From Ritual to *Ruaḥ*

But not for long. Even before the Six-Day War, the earliest American Jewish musical creations began emerging from the Orthodox camp. Baruch Chait and Michael Zheutlin, The Rabbis' Sons, accompanied liturgical texts to the strum of acoustic guitars—not to enhance prayer but to create a "secular" connection between Jewish living and the folk-rock sounds of America's youth. In doing so, they created a new genre in American Jewish life and, after a hiatus of nearly 100 years, resumed the traditional Jewish practice of adapting to the surrounding culture by adopting it.

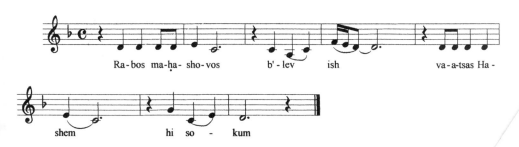

Example 11.1 From "Rabos Maḥashovos" by Baruch Chait

Many designs are in man's heart, but the counsel of the LORD—
only it will prevail.
The counsel of the LORD will endure forever, the designs of His heart
throughout the generations.

The modern Orthodox community, which had long sought to straddle the line between traditional Jewish ritual practice and active participation in the secular world, was quick to embrace this new musical style. "*Ruaḥ*" (spirit) bands were formed to play at weddings, bar mitzvahs, and youth conferences. One group, which actually called itself Ruach attained great popularity with its own original songs, but was also among the first to "borrow" a well-known American song to which it adapted Jewishly oriented lyrics.

To the tune of "Puff, the Magic Dragon" :[7]

Puff, the kosher dragon lived in Palestine,
and frolicked in the synagogue and drank Schapiro's wine.
Little Rabbi Goldberg loved that kosher Puff,
and fed him lox and matzah balls and other kosher stuff....

The right-wing Orthodox camp also produced performers and ensembles to sing liturgical texts in nonliturgical settings. These groups were certainly not motivated by a desire to assimilate the musical vocabulary of America. Rather, the Hasidic community sought refuge from modern popular music—and in particular, from its lyrics—by creating new tunes in the old European style of the Ba'al Shem Tov and his followers. Most popular were the boy choirs assembled into performing ensembles under the aegis of Pirchei Agudas Yisroel (literally, the "blossoms of the society of Israel"). What the first of these groups lacked in vocal polish they made up for through their enthusiastic renditions of catchy tunes with sophisticated arrangements and impressive instrumental accompaniment. Melodies like "Urah Kevodi," by Moshe Greiniman, quickly jumped over the lines separating the Hasidim from the modern Orthodox, and from there it was a short leap to the religiously oriented summer camps, schools, and youth movements with diverse political and theological orientations.

Example 11.2 From "Urah Kevodi"

Awake, O my soul! Awake, O harp and lyre!
I will wake the dawn.

As noted in Chapter Seven, Shlomo Carlebach was among the first singer-songwriters from the Orthodox camp. Carlebach used his music to reach out to Jews of all backgrounds. The limited texts and purposely repetitive Hasidic-style songs he wrote and sang (interspersed with his own stories and inspirational religious messages) were the key to his outreach efforts and enabled Jewishly uneducated members of his audiences to become a part of the music-making. For many, it was also among their most powerful Jewish experiences—encounters they would not have sought within the confines of the synagogue setting but to which they gravitated eagerly on college campuses in California, in the coffee houses of New York's Greenwich Village, and in hundreds of formal and informal gatherings in between. Interestingly, Carlebach's participation in the Hasidic Song Festivals enhanced his popularity for some who thought of his music as "Israeli" rather than Jewish.

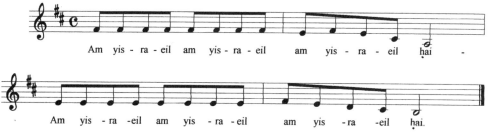

Example 11.3 From "Am Yisrael Ḥai"

The people of Israel lives!

For other performing groups, it was the music of Israel, rather than the sounds and texts of the synagogue, that provided a point of musical departure. One of the first full-fledged American Jewish "rock" groups called itself Tayku.[8] The five Orthodox members created innovative arrangements of Israeli popular songs by David Zahavi, Nurit Hirsh, and Shmuel Kraus and composed their own original songs blending then-current rock and roll styles with lyrics in modern Hebrew. True cosmopolitans, the ensemble also reached into its Jewish heritage, creating a '50s-style arrangement of the familiar "I Have a Little Dreydl" by Mikhl Gelbart (1889–1962), as well as a hybrid, "American" adaptation of a traditional Sabbath table song sung by the Sephardic communities of Jerusalem.

Example 11.4 From "Yah Ribon" traditional Sabbath table song

> O Creator, Master of this world and all worlds. You are the King who
> reigns over kings—
> Your powerful and wondrous deeds it is beautiful to declare before You.

Jewish Music on the Liberal Agenda

After the Orthodox, the Reform community took a leading role in the creation of American Jewish music for recreational use. The National Federation of Temple Youth (NFTY) and summer camps under Reform movement auspices encouraged the guitar-strumming song leaders in their midst to channel their creative talents into new music. Friendly "competitions" whose "winning" entries were recorded helped to disseminate new tunes throughout the movement, building a diverse but uniformly acknowledged repertoire.[9] They also helped launch the careers of some of the leading figures in contemporary American Jewish music on both sides of the syna-gogue/secular divide: Michael Isaacson, Debbie Friedman, and Jeff Klepper[10] (b. 1952) are all products of this pragmatic, nurturing environment.

Or za-ru-a   la-tza-dik   ule-yish-re lev sim-ha

Example 11.5 From "Or Zaru'a" by Klepper

Light is sown for the righteous; and for the upright of heart, gladness.

Leaders of liberal Judaism were also among the first to consciously use music to advance their educational agenda. Recognizing the ability of music to convey text and values, entire curricula were built around Jewish educational themes. Once it decided to formally assert its support for the Jewish state, the Union of American Hebrew Congregations produced a collection of upbeat, eclectic songs by Steve Reuben (b. 1949) to teach about leading figures in modern Zionist history (including David Ben-Gurion, Chaim Weitzman, and Golda Meir) and some of the unique institutions of Israel ("A kibbutz is not the last car on a railroad train…").[11] Collections of *Especially Jewish Symbols* and *Especially Wonderful Days* were produced by the publishing house Alternatives in Religious Education to teach very young children about the significance of some Jewish practices and holidays. Tinged with humor as well as representing some liberal educational positions, the songs proved popular among the youngsters for whom they were created, as well as indulgent older audiences who had "technically" outgrown the music but who appreciated the subtle value concepts in the lyrics.

I wear a ki-pah on my head to re-mind me that God is a-bove. Wear-ing a ki-pah is one of the ways we show our re-spect and our love.

Example 11.6 From "Kippah" by Klepper

Conserving Tradition in the Popular Arena

Mirroring its somewhat absent role in the creation of synagogue music, the Conservative movement has continued to lag behind the Orthodox and Reform communities in creating a body of Jewish music that speaks to its own clearly identifiable preferences in musical style or communal values. The warm and enthusiastic embrace of the music of Israel in movement day schools and summer camps (for whom spoken Hebrew is a high priority) precluded a need for a uniquely American repertoire with which to express Jewish texts and ideas. On the other hand, there have been some singer-songwriters who have emerged from within the Conservative movement and/or whose personal identification with Conservative institutions has created a special empathy and familiarity with them among Conservative Jews.

Craig Taubman (b. 1957), a former music director at Camp Ramah in California, writes and sings Jewish music for listeners at various stages of personal and Jewish development when he is not pursuing his career as a prominent producer and performer of children's music for the Disney Channel. Taubman's Hebrew lyrics usually excerpt familiar liturgical texts but are obviously not intended for ritual use. In fact, by setting some of the tradition's best-known passages, Taubman forces the listener/singer to look at the texts in a different way. These musical midrashim are useful from an educational perspective but intended for personal entertainment, rather than classroom consumption. On the other hand, Taubman does not resist the chance to teach through his music. Frequently creating texts that combine Hebrew and English, Taubman often grounds his English lyrics with parallel (or complementary) passages in Hebrew, attributing to his songs both the more "authentic" Hebrew/Jewish voice and the opportunity/obligation to educate through the generally more familiar English language.

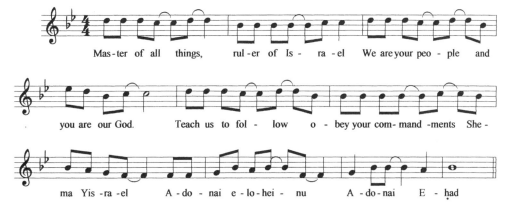

Example 11.7 From "Master of All Things" by Taubman

One of the longest-lived and farthest-reaching bands to make its mark on the American Jewish musical scene is Safam.[12] Their first album, recorded in 1974, featured several popular Israeli songs, along with some American Jewish "classics" and some of the group's own creations. Over the years, their repertoire has included a much greater proportion of original material, mostly by members Robbie Solomon (b. 1946) and Joel Sussman (b. 1950). Safam was a pioneer in the adoption of nontraditional musical styles for some of its most popular and innovative selections: "Tzur Yisrael" boldly appropriated contemporaneous rock music, while "Mah Navu" borrowed Haitian reggae.

The group also excelled at pairing sounds from the Jewish musical past in unlikely partnerships: their eclectic *Hallel* service (not intended for liturgical use) begins with an opening blessing that is at once contemporary, yet strongly resembles traditional *nusaḥ*. The setting of Psalm 112 continues with a clear debt to the jazz idiom then lapses briefly into a segment reminiscent of the traditional European *chor-schul.* Later in the "service" the music reaches again into the European past, this time revealing its love of Hasidic song and klezmer nuance. The final passage from Psalm 118 brings the work to a movingly reverent but original conclusion.

Example 11.8 "Ana Adoshem" by Robbie Solomon

O LORD, deliver us! O LORD, let us prosper!

Elsewhere, Safam reincarnates historic Jewish music and liturgical practices. The group's lively "Anim Z'mirot" borrows both from Hasidic music and the European synagogue. "Lekha Dodi," while superficially resembling a marching band more than a liturgical hymn, was inspired by the mystical practice of the kabbalists of Safed who physically accompanied the Sabbath "bride" from the outskirts of their communities into their synagogues and homes with lively singing.

Example 11.9 From "Lekha Dodi" by Robbie Solomon

Come my Beloved to greet the bride—
The Sabbath presence, let us welcome!

English As a Jewish Language

Safam was also in the vanguard of a practice that would once again stretch the definition of what constitutes "Jewish music:" the creation of popular Jewish music whose lyrics were in English.[13] It was inevitable that American Jewish music would come to this point. By the 1960s and 1970s, English was not just the primary language but the only language of most American Jews. Yiddish was spoken in limited circles, chiefly by the parents and grandparents of America's youth. But for most American Jews, Hebrew, while increasingly popular as the vernacular of Israel and the language of Israeli song, remained a language solely of prayer—not of public discourse. American Jews discussed their Jewish identities in English; it was natural for them to sing at least some of their Jewish songs in English as well.

We have discussed the fact that in previous eras, the folk music of many Jewish communities did not necessarily contain Jewish content. Neither Ladino songs of love and the castles of Barcelona nor Yiddish songs of work and courtship had anything at all to do with specifically Jewish rituals, customs, or beliefs. Those songs were in uniquely Jewish languages, however, and so spoke exclusively to the Jewish community. English, of course, has never been a uniquely

Jewish language, and so demands on the music—and even more, the lyrics—of American Jewish song are much more pronounced.

Safam set the standard for popular English-language Jewish music with its "World of Our Fathers," recorded in 1980. Its lyric tells the story of the American Jewish experience, from the immigrant generation, to the assimilated children who followed, to the grandchildren who sought to return to their ethnic heritage. The popular American folk-song style of its verses contrasts dramatically with the klezmer-style refrain, ironically linking traditional Jewish practices and identification to a musical style of the past while telling its story in a modern and "foreign" musical style. However, it succeeds in much the same way that Moses Milner's "In Ḥeder" charted a new course for Yiddish art song by telling a quintessentially Jewish story and borrowing the musical vocabulary of the religious school. "World of Our Fathers" makes the transition into English by telling its own Jewish story and borrowing the music of the Jewish past.

Came to A-mer-i-ca in nine-teen hun-dred four I was flee-ing per-se-cu-tion and the ar-my of the czar Reached El-lis Is-land a-lone and half in-sane and I left there with a dif-'rent name

Example 11.10 From "World of Our Fathers"

> Came to America in 1904, I was fleeing persecution and the army of the czar,
> Reached Ellis Island alone and half insane, and I left there with a different name.
> If it wasn't for my people I don't know what I'd do, and I thanked the Lord above me that I was born a Jew.
> They sheltered me and fed me 'til I got on my feet, and my father's words came back to me,

"Just don't forget where you came from my son, and the world of
   your fathers you'll soon leave behind,
Just keep the faith of your people wherever you go, there a friend
   you will find."

I was just another greenhorn looking for a job, I prevailed upon a
   *landsman** to finally take me on.
Worked as a peddler ten hours every day, in the evening I brought
   home my pay.
Scrimped and I saved 'til I put enough aside, and I sent it to my father,
   his passage for to buy.
Money for the steerage and money for the bribes, it was four years
   since my mother died.
      I won't forget where I came from, my mother, each day in the
         synagogue I pray for you
      I've built a life for us here in America, how proud you would be
         if you knew.
      [Chorus] Ai dai dai in America…

We worked to bring my sisters and my baby brother, too,
Then we moved up to New England near some people that we knew.
I made a bit of money in Boston's old North End which we gradually
   learned how to spend.
A bunch of little citizens I brought into this world,
But most of them were no-goods who squandered while I toiled.
Sophisticate Americans they very soon became, of their father they
   would grow ashamed.
      Just don't forget where we came from, my children,
      The world of our fathers is what made us strong.
      Don't sell your souls for the thrills of America, what price must
         you pay to belong?
      [Chorus]

It's been so many years, my grandchildren are grown,
And the one who is a doctor even keeps me in his home.
He says to me, "*Mein Zeyde* [my grandfather], when the children learn
   to speak
A bissele Yiddish [little bit of Yiddish] you should teach them."

---

*One from the same European home town

There are times, so many times, when I feared that all was lost,
We had come so far so fast that I wondered what the cost.
But now I see my father's world begin to rise in my great-grand-
    children's eyes!
[Chorus]

Safam's songs in English cover a wide range of topics, reflective of Jewish history ("Peace by Piece"), social action agenda ("Amnesty"), the plight of Soviet Jewry ("Leaving Mother Russia," "Grandfather's Train"), the Holocaust ("Reminiscence: A Photo Album"), and much more. Whether attempting to capture the sounds of Israel ("Home to Jerusalem," "Yamit") or using driving rhythms to draw youthful listeners to Bible stories ("Brother on Brother"), Safam is unequivocal in its passionate embrace of Jewish values. Its adoption of varied musical styles with no connection to prior Jewish musical practice neither weakens the impact of the songs nor dampens the welcome reception accorded them by audiences across North America for more than a quarter century.

English became a dominant voice in those circles of all denominations and political persuasions that did not see either liturgical texts or Israeli songs as the sole entrée on the American Jewish musical menu. The Orthodox community quickly co-opted English as the vehicle in which to do its outreach work.[14] As half of a duo called Megama and later as a solo artist, Moshe Yess (b. 1944) sang cynical songs about non-observant Jews who prayed to materialistic idols ("Jack Schwartz"), poignant ballads about Holocaust victims who retained their faith in the face of unspeakable horror ("Yosef, My Son" and "The Ballad of Chaim Chilkowsky"), and overt rallying cries encouraging his listeners to get a Jewish education ("I've Got the 'What Page Are We On in the Prayer Book' Blues") and marry traditional Jewish partners ("*Frum* Wives").

Example 11.11 From "I've Got the 'What Page Are We On in the Prayer Book' Blues"

I've got the "what page are we on in the prayer book" blues,
"Am I supposed to sit or stand in the synagogue" blues.
Well, my folks sent me to *ḥeder* when I was just a child,
But instead of learning *aleph-beis* [Hebrew alphabet] I was out there
    running wild.

I've got the "what page are we on in the prayerbook" blues,
And the guy right next to me is takin' a snooze.
I don't know what I'm reading, I don't know what to speak,
God spoke to us in Hebrew, but to me the thing is Greek.

I've got "my kid knows less than me in the prayer book" blues,
And "it's not too nice to see in the synagogue" blues,
So it's *ḥeder* for you young man, and learn your *aleph-beis*.
Don't you dare take after me with egg all on your face.

I've got the "what page are we on in the prayer book" blues,
"Am I supposed to sit or stand in the synagogue" blues,
Well I guess I'll see you later, 'cause I'm going back to *ḥeder*.
I've got the "what page are we on in the prayerbook" blues.

Lenny Solomon (b. 1961), his team of gifted writers, and a band called Shlock Rock turned parody into an art form, appropriating the music (and rhyme schemes from the original lyrics) of rock songs and Emmy-award-winning Disney tunes for their own Jewish purposes,[15] from "Help Me, Rambam" ("Help me Rhonda" by the Beach Boys) and "You've Got that *Shabbos* Feeling" ("You've Lost That Loving Feeling" by the Righteous Brothers) to "Into the Sea" ("Under the Sea" by Howard Ashman and Alan Menkin).

"Into the Sea"
You see, we don't want to be here, there's so much that we can't take.
Our people have been mistreated, and that was a big mistake.
The world that you see around you, soon it will be no more,
So now I have come to warn you, we want to go out the door...

Into the sea, into the sea,
Go through the sand and into the land of milk and honey.
In Egypt they work us night and day, so in their land we cannot stay,
We're letting you know, our people must go now, into the sea...

Into the sea, into the sea,
When Naḥshon jumps in we won't have to swim, just walk rapidly.
Tell Miriam to lead the band, we're going to the Holy Land.
Each little tribe a path will divide here into the sea.

When we get through here we'll sing *Az Yashir** into the sea.
No time for baking, matzah we're taking, we'll think banana when we
    eat the mannah.
Don't follow us here, you will get stuck here, into the sea!

Women in Popular Music

Since the mid-1970s, women have played an increasingly important role in the world of popular Jewish music. Debbie Friedman has unquestionably taken center stage among female Jewish performers—indeed, among all Jewish performers. Friedman's first ventures into Jewish music were in synagogue music, albeit in a popular vernacular (see Chapter 7) followed by educational materials setting

---

*The opening words of Moses' Song of the Sea

vocabulary from Behrman House's *Hebrew and Heritage* curriculum to music for elementary school audiences.[16] Friedman quickly enlarged the range of her material, drawing on the images of biblical women for some of her most popular songs. "Lekhi Lakh" was one of her first "hits," though making only oblique reference to Sarah's partnership in Abraham's journey.[17] "Miriam's Song," included with "Lekhi Lakh" on Friedman's 1989 recording *And You Shall Be a Blessing*, glorifies Miriam by focusing on her role in leading the women's celebration of the Red Sea crossing.[18]

And the wo - men dan - cing with their tim - brels fol - lowed Mir - iam as she sang her song Sing a song to the One whom we've ex - al - ted Mir - iam and the wo-men danced and danced the whole night long

Example 11.12 From "Miriam's Song"

[Chorus]
And the women dancing with their timbrels
Followed Miriam as she sang her song.
Sing a song to the One whom we've exalted.
Miriam and the women danced and danced the whole night long.

And Miriam was a weaver of unique variety.
The tapestry she wove was one which sang our history.
With every thread and every strand she crafted her delight.
A woman touched with spirit she dances toward the light.
[Chorus]

As Miriam stood upon the shores and gazed across the sea,
The wonder of this miracle she soon came to believe.
Whoever thought the sea would part with an outstretched hand,

And we would pass to freedom, and march to the promised land.
[Chorus]

And Miriam the Prophet took her timbrel in her hand,
And all the women followed her just as she had planned.
And Miriam raised her voice in song.
She sang with praise and might,
We've just lived through a miracle, we're going to dance tonight.
[Chorus]

Linda Hirschhorn (b. 1947) followed a similar path, first setting well-known biblical and liturgical texts for synagogue as well as popular use. Her 1987 song "Sarah and Hagar" focuses on the two biblical women, attempting to frame the roots of contemporary political differences between Jews and Arabs as an outgrowth of the tension between the mothers of Abraham's two sons, Isaac and Ishmael.

Example 11.13 From "Sarah and Hagar"

I am calling you, O Sarah, this is your sister, Hagar
Calling through the centuries to reach you from afar.
Here is my son, Ishmael, your sister's son alive.
We share the sons of Abraham, two peoples, one tribe. . . .

Some of Hirschhorn's greatest successes as a singer and songwriter have come through her work with Vocolot, an ensemble of six female vocalists whose tight harmonies and earthy rhythms have charted new courses for popular Jewish music. Others have gained popularity singing songs reflective of women's experiences in biblical and later history, as well as endowing ancient lyrics and roles with a uniquely feminine perspective. While the texts of many of these songs—as well as the singers themselves—reflect a distinctly liberal cast,[19] the late twentieth century also saw the creation of women's singing groups from within the more traditional community. Right-wing Orthodox women, prohibited from singing in mixed groups by the rigid interpretation of the Talmudic assumption that "*kol be-ishah erva*" (the voice of a woman is a provocation, Berakhot 24a), have formed groups who sing exclusively for other women. These women are expressing their spirituality and devotion to God within the still-segregated framework of their tradition, but in a more public forum than they would previously have sought.[20]

New Jewish Music: Pop Art

There are new sounds on the Jewish concert stage that straddle the line between the popular genres and their more sophisticated counterparts. Best described as a kind of "pop art," this music places traditional Jewish texts in settings that combine the appeal of lyrical melodic lines with the polish of often-complex vocal harmonies. Some of the music of Vocolot fits this description, but the genre was established much earlier by others.

The seven-voiced vocal group known as Beged Kefet was an early entry into the realm of American Jewish popular music but was actually conceived in Israel. The original members of the group[21] were all students together in 1982 in the one-year program in Israel sponsored by Hebrew Union College and formed their ensemble in response to the school's requirement that all students perform some type of community service. Happening upon Yad le-Kashish (Lifeline for the Aged), Myriam Mendilow's senior citizen center/crafts workshop, the group returned several times to sing for the elderly citizens of Jerusalem who spent their time there. Upon their return to the United States, they continued singing,[22] devoting all profits from their performances (and later recordings) to Yad le-Kashish. Their eclectic repertoire began with then-popular Israeli folk and popular songs, and was enhanced by adaptations of songs in English previously made famous by the trio Peter, Paul and Mary (including "There Is a Man" and "If I Had My Way," with biblically based lyrics about Moses and Samson, respectively, as well as the secular "Music Speaks Louder than Words"). Members of the group also composed and performed songs with familiar Hebrew texts. Benjie Ellen Schiller's "Halleluhu," with text from Psalm 150; "Adonai, Adonai" from the Festival Torah service and the Sabbath table song "Yah Ribon Olam" set by Leon Sher; and Billy Dreskin's memorable setting of "Elu D'varim" with text in Hebrew and English from Mishna Pe'ah (recited as part of the daily morning service) are among the most popular. They also created some selections in English relating specifically to the needs of the elderly.

The uniqueness of the ensemble's original music stems from its integration of melody and harmony. Just as Western art music exists with harmony as a critical component of the total work, so much of Beged Kefet's music weaves its special sounds from the interrelationship of intricate vocal harmonies with accessible, but sophisticated, melodies. The end result is aurally pleasing but difficult for a single singer to recreate and less than satisfying in the absence of harmony. The eagerness of community choral ensembles to acquire Beged Kefet's arrangements attests to their "art-worthiness" while the hesitance of most to attempt to "folklorize" these selections down to their single-voiced, melodic essences confirms the sophistication of this music.

The Jewish choral music of David Burger (b. 1950) falls into a similar category. The New York native, who spent the early part of his career writing for Richie Havens,[23] spent much of his avocational energy immersed in Jewish music. This son of a cantor was exposed early to the sounds of the synagogue and imbibed more sophisticated Jewish musical experiences as a member of the Zamir Chorale,[24] whose repertoire spanned the spectrum of Jewish choral music from Rossi through the composers of modern Israel. As a member of Tayku, Burger joined his interests in contemporary American pop and rock music with the Hebrew/Israeli texts of his Jewish experience. It was not long before he began to merge his interests into a gen-

Example 11.14 From "Adonai, Adonai" by Sher

uinely choral medium, with a series of compositions composed for the Zamir Chorale. The first, "T'filah Lishlom Medinat Yisrael" set text from the Prayer for the Welfare of the State of Israel penned in the days following the 1948 establishment of the state. It was soon added to the liturgy of many American congregations. Burger's choral setting, accompanied by guitars, piano, and drums, was premiered in 1975 at the Zamir Chorale's annual concert in celebration of Israel's independence held in New York's Carnegie Hall and sung by the Chorale later that summer in concerts it performed across Israel. "T'filah" was greeted warmly by audiences in both countries and became an anthem of sorts for Zamir.[25] It inspired Burger to create other works premiered by Zamir, including "Shema Kolenu" (1976), "Songs to Jerusalem" (1977),[26] "Shalom Rav" (1978), "Hatikvah" (1979, a setting of the original text by Imber), and "Megillat ha-Atzma'ut" (1998, text from Israel's Declaration of Independence), commissioned in celebration of Israel's 50th anniversary. As these works were shared among the growing network of

Jewish choirs, Burger received additional commissions for Jewish, as well as secular, works.[27]

Burger's works for Zamir and similar ensembles are marked by the integration of popular musical vernacular with the formal conventions of choral art. Burger has a special gift for writing memorable melodies that are often presented as solo (or unison) lines in his music. The development of those melodies through harmonization and/or juxtaposition with other musical ideas results in a multi-layered composition that cannot easily be reduced to its component parts for truly "popular" performance. Nevertheless, the works as a whole have been embraced by the Jewish masses and contribute much to the evolution of the notion of "Jewish music" in twentieth-century America.[28]

A - vi - nu she-ba-sha-ma - yim   tsur yis-ra - el ve -go -a - lo   ba -

rekh et me-di-nat yis-ra - el   rei-sheet tsmi -ḥat   ge - u - la-tei   nu.

Example 11.15 From "T'filah Lishlom Medinat Yisrael"

A Blast from the Past: Klezmer Music

Among the most exciting "new" developments in modern Jewish music has been the late twentieth-century rediscovery of klezmer, folk music of the itinerant European Jewish musicians that traveled with them on their journey to the New World. As with Yiddish theater and other aspects of Ashkenazic culture dependent upon links to the "old country," klezmer's popularity faded with the cessation of massive immigration from Eastern Europe and the increasing socialization—and assimilation—of America's Jews. By the late 1960s, klezmer had become a distant memory, a relic of another era, stored on 78 RPM recordings in attics and basements of Jewish homes but replaced at weddings and other communal functions by the music of Israel and popular American repertoire. The children of the aging *klezmorim* turned to American dance bands, classical music or, iron-ically, the folk repertory of America's other ethnic communities. Young Jews flocked to Irish music, jazz, and American folk song.

But in 1973, while exploring the string band music of Appalachia, Henry Sapoznik was asked whether Jews had their own music. With this simple question, this son of a European-born cantor, a deliber-ate refugee from the Jewish music of his Lubavitch yeshivah and the Catskill hotels where his family spent Passover vacations, now turned back to his own traditions. Beginning with a cache of old records at New York's YIVO Institute for Jewish Research,[29] Sapoznik unearthed the vestiges of European klezmer music, already reinter-preted and transformed by American recording technology. Sapoznik's enthusiasm for his own music, which he saw now with different eyes, led him to additional research into klezmer music, funded by U.S. government grants.[30] He met elderly Jews who had played in the klezmer ensembles of the 1920s and on some of the first klezmer recordings by companies like Columbia and RCA Victor.[31] By 1979, Sapoznik had formed Kapelye to play a concert in Providence, Rhode Island. In 1981 the group, enhanced by clar-inetist Andy Statman, Sapoznik's own cantor father, and others, formed Der Yiddisher Caravan, a national touring show that per-formed cantorial selections, Yiddish theater songs, and klezmer music in concert venues across the United States.

Coincidentally, others had also begun to delve into klezmer music. Clarinetist Giora Feidman, formerly of the Israel Philharmonic Orchestra, popularized klezmer in Israel and in appearances in America. Andy Statman and ethnomusicologist Zev Feldman had staged a retrospective of the work of veteran European-American klezmer musician Dave Tarras (1897–1989) in 1978. Hankus Netsky, a jazz music instructor at the New England Conservatory of Music, had rediscovered the klezmer music of his trumpeter uncle Sol Katz in a Philadelphia basement. Netsky enthu-siastically recreated the big band sound of the early American klezmer recordings with his students and colleagues, forming the Klezmer Conservatory Band.

The rebirth of klezmer continued on an upward trajectory of iso-lated but increasingly important events involving Henry Sapoznik and his growing network of colleagues. Sapoznik's research resulted in Folkways Music's retrospective reissue of some classic 78 RPM recordings, *Klezmer Music: 1910–1942.* In 1982, Sapoznik became the director of the Max and Frieda Weinstein Archives of Sound Recording at YIVO. That summer, his band Kapelye appeared in the Hollywood version of Chaim Potok's *The Chosen*[32] and issued their first album. In 1983 Sapoznik and Andy Statman were joined by Pete Sokolow and other top New York Jewish and jazz musicians, performing their show *Klezmer Meets Jazz* at New York's Jewish Museum and at Joseph Papp's Public Theater. Pete Sokolow used the arrangements he wrote for that show to form his Original Klezmer Jazz Band, which issued its first recording in 1984, the same year in which a group calling itself The Klezmorim played Carnegie Hall and the Klezmer Conservatory Band scored a huge success appearing on Garrison Keillor's *A Prairie Home Companion,* broadcast on National Public Radio stations across the country.

Kapelye became the first klezmer band to tour Europe, appearing in Britain, France, Switzerland, Belgium, and Germany (playing one of its best-received concerts in a Berlin mansion that had been used as a Gestapo headquarters during the Second World War). Klezmer had returned to its roots, completing a cycle and launching a rebirth whose popularity in Europe continues unabated—though largely among non-Jewish audiences and with newly formed bands including or entirely comprised of non-Jewish players.

Meanwhile, across America, klezmer bands flourished wherever there were Jews: in Chicago and Philadelphia and San Francisco; but also in Boulder, Colorado; Montpelier, Vermont; and New Orleans, Louisiana. Klezmer appealed to a wide cross-section of audiences: gray-haired grandparents who remembered the klezmer bands of

Example 11.16 From "A Nakht in Gan Eydn" (traditional)

their distant youth; their grandchildren for whom Yiddish culture had no special appeal; and the friends of those grandchildren who came from the ethnic communities in whose music the Jewish musicians of the 1960s had once sought refuge, and who now welcomed a reborn tradition into their midst.

Pushing the Envelope: New Faces of Jewish Music

From its inception in Europe, klezmer had always reflected a unique amalgamation of the music of the Jewish community with the music of the surrounding culture. *Klezmorim* playing at Jewish celebrations and at non-Jewish festivities alike had contributed to a cross-pollination between Jewish and gentile cultures, enriching both. Like the Hasidic community, which eagerly embraced the potential of any melody to bring greater glory to the Creator, klezmer musicians adapted a wide variety of tunes to serve their purposes. This exchange continued in America, with Jewish musicians borrowing jazz and other styles, and crossing over, adapting Jewish tunes to the diverse marketplace of American cultural ideas. Ziggy Elman[33] (né Henry Finkleman, 1914–1968) turned the "Odessa Bulgar" into the swing era's "The Angels Sing," while "Bei Mir Bist Du Schoen" by Sholom Secunda (1894–1974) was equally successful (on both sides of the Atlantic) as a Yiddish-language favorite and as an American pop success sung by the Andrews Sisters (albeit with English lyrics).

The rebirth of klezmer and its obvious appeal to a wide range of audiences predictably inspired a similar fusion of Jewish and other musical forms. Among the first and most seemingly obvious "foreign" interpreters of this newborn klezmer music was Don Byron, an African American clarinetist who was among the original members of the Klezmer Conservatory Band. Even after leaving the Band, Byron kept klezmer in his act, achieving a measure of notoriety that helped launch his solo career. At the same time, he promoted Jewish music in a community unfamiliar with (but ultimately appreciative of) the improvisatory aspects of klezmer and its affinity to both blues and jazz styles. Classical violinist Itzhak Perlman's infatuation with klezmer and the subsequent PBS broadcasts and recordings of his appearances with a variety of ensembles brought another new audience to this Old World music. Just as artistic renderings by members of The Society for Jewish Music brought the European intelligentsia to a new appreciation of Jewish folk songs, so Perlman's "endorsement" enabled music lovers accustomed to more classical concerts to embrace klezmer as a lively and legitimate art form.

Others capitalized on klezmer's historic ability to assimilate musical sounds of the surrounding culture and began to expand the parameters of "traditional" Jewish music. In America, groups like the Klezmatics have begun to push the envelope while clearly evidencing a love for the culture of klezmer. Their music combines the traditional, celebratory aspects of klezmer with original sounds and an almost confrontational style that demands attention from the non-Jewish community. Addressing anti-Semitic stereotypes in America and in Europe (where fans of klezmer from outside the Jewish communities there clamor for tickets to Klezmatics concerts), the clever title of one of their best selling albums was *Jews with Horns*. Klezmer scholar Sapoznik has described the Klezmatics as "the group most responsible for creating a bridge between traditional forms and contemporary esthetics,"[34] combining the diverse musical backgrounds of the band's members (jazz, rock, bluegrass, and rap) with the traditional sounds and instrumentation of the historic klezmer repertory.

Others have perceived klezmer as an all-purpose catchall, able and willing to incorporate as many musical innovations as their creativity can conceive. A 1995 exploration of the klezmer phenomenon by Joel Lewis[35] described a haughty "in-your-face" style of ostensibly Jewish music that believed itself to be a legitimate inheritor of the klezmer tradition but that has troubled even the most open-minded fans of contemporary klezmer. Henry Sapoznik registered his concerns, noting that some musicians who claim to be playing klezmer are actually "obscuring the difference between Jewish music and music played by Jews."[36] In a series of recordings on his new label, Tzadik, John Zorn's *Masada* has drawn on his backgrounds in soul, jazz, and even classical music. Concerts at New York's Knitting Factory, an avant-garde performance venue, have featured the saxophone-playing Zorn and other performers in so-called "Radical Jewish Music Festivals." The titles of the songs are in Hebrew and the performers themselves often appear with dangling tzitzit;[37] but the "Jewish" pedigree of their music is called into serious question by traditionalists who prefer to find a sense of musical continuity in music that purports to represent Jewish culture.

But if some styles and would-be stylists of Jewish music have appeared to go too far in claiming a relationship between their art and Jewish tradition, others have found a way to push the envelope without ripping its seams. Mirroring the higher profile of spirituality in modern society (Jewish and non-Jewish) and the frequent return to Jewish tradition by successful entrepreneurs whose previous association with Jewish life was tangential at best, Jewish musicians from all backgrounds have returned to try to reclaim their Jewish musical roots.

In 1992, jazz musician Ben Sidran (b. 1943) attempted to explore his Jewish heritage through *Life's a Lesson,* a collection of melodies ostensibly representing the High Holy Day liturgy.[38]Bruce Burger's[39] 1995 *RebbeSoul: Fringe of Blue* offered instrumental versions[40] of several popular selections, including the Yiddish "Tum Balalaika," folk versions of the Sabbath table song "Deror Yikrah," the ubiquitous "Hine Mah Tov," the familiar High Holy Day chant *Avinu Malkenu* (in acoustic and electric versions), and well-known Hebrew songs by Naomi Shemer ("Yerushalayim Shel Zahav") and Baruch Chait ("Kol ha-Olam Kulo"). This collection won rave reviews from such disparate publications as *Playboy Magazine,* the *LA Weekly, Billboard Magazine,* and New York's *The Jewish Week.*[41] Burger's collection feels the more familiar of the two, with an almost Hasidic adaptation of world-beat rhythms accompanying the traditional balalaika and mandolin (as well as keyboards, guitars, and occasional electronic devices). Sidran's saxophone seems less grounded in "authentic" Jewish musical sounds and harmonic vocabularies.

In 1996, television actor and Broadway entertainer Mandy Patinkin weighed in with *Mamaloshen,* a collection of richly orchestrated Yiddish songs from the folk tradition and the theater repertoire sung endearingly by Patinkin in a well-studied Yiddish (tutored by Henry Sapoznik). Patinkin's recording features translations of the Yiddish texts; he does not assume that his listeners will be familiar with this material, although audiences at his live performances of these songs have been filled with immigrant grandparents as well as their American-born grandchildren.

Yet despite the accolades that have greeted the work of Sidran,

Burger, and Patinkin, each has also stepped into "controversial" territory. For Sidran and Burger it is their treatment of the most "classic"—and emotion-laden—selections that raises eyebrows and lowers the comfort level of even the most open-minded listeners. Some feel that Sidran's rhapsody on *Ani Ma'amin* (I Believe), the anthem sung by Holocaust victims with their last breath, does not resonate as "fresh" or "contemporary" as much as it offends with its lack of reverence for the history and pathos of the simple melody. Others think that Burger's treatment of "Hatikvah," the Zionist hymn that has become the anthem of the Jewish state, is similarly lacking in historical background or respect.

Patinkin commits the greatest "sin," though, by mixing authentic Yiddish musical memorabilia with tunes written by American Jews but with absolutely no pretense of Jewish identification. Irving Berlin was certainly among the best-loved American composers of popular song, but neither the civil religion of "God Bless America" nor the secular commercialism of "White Christmas" could possibly be mistaken for Jewish music, any more than "Take Me Out to the Ball Game" could be transformed into Jewish culture by being sung in Yiddish—no matter how many Jews enjoy the American national pastime.

Completing the Cycle: New/Old Music for a New Age

Other recent revisitations of the Yiddish experience have been more successful and, indeed, have brought the Ashkenazic musical experience full circle. A 1998 collaboration between the Klezmatics and Israeli singer Chava Alberstein produced *The Well*, a collection designed to rescue Yiddish poetry written in the era after the Holocaust from an extinction caused consciously or subconsciously by a conspiracy between the Hebrew vernacular of the Jewish state and the English language of America—the alternate haven of the refugees from Yiddish-speaking Europe. Chava Alberstein began her career singing the Yiddish songs of her parents' generation. Despite adopting the Hebrew language (and becoming one of Israeli song's best-known exponents), Alberstein retained a deep love for her *mamaloshen* (mother tongue), to which she eagerly returned.

The Klezmatics's embrace of klezmer music brought its members into the world—and aura—of Yiddish music. Their performances are alternately lauded for the continuity of their "true klezmer spirit" and the audacity of their incorporations of rock, jazz, and new age sounds into a supposedly "traditional" folk genre. The band's lead violinist, Alicia Svigals (b. 1963), has admitted that there is tension between the two poles of their music, but concludes that their "authenticity" (and that of most other modern klezmer bands) lies in their ultimate rejection of the American experience: "Coming from generations that tried and tried to assimilate, we realized that we're pretty happy that we're still sort of unassimilated. We've got something that is not quite American. It's its own thing."[42]

Klezmer music, whether in Europe or in America, at the turn of the twentieth century or the twenty-first or the eighteenth, has done what Jewish music has done since it was born in the Middle East at the beginning of recorded time: It has adapted the music of the larger, surrounding culture. What it has never done, however, is assimilate completely. Rather, klezmer music in particular, and Jewish music as a whole (as the Jews who created it), consciously and subconsciously borrowed liberally but never sacrificed its Jewish sensibility. Jewish values, the internal rhythms of Jewish languages, the musical motives of the synagogue and the schoolhouse, have all enabled Jewish music to retain a unique cast that separates it from that of the surrounding community. The contemporary era, with its technological immediacy and the shrinking of the global village, has created challenges that Jewish musical tradition never faced in previous generations. Moreover, the availability of musical notation and easy recording techniques have made possible the exchange of melodies between unlikely partners—and the near-instant incorporation of these tunes into otherwise "traditional" settings. Witnesses who know the source of such "borrowed" materials often rail at the encroachment of these foreign influences, and the conservators of Jewish music traditions (Oriental, Sephardic, and Ashkenazic) author long discourses on the deterioration of their heritage and the unhappy cultural future awaiting the next generation.

But while the challenges awaiting that next generation may be unprecedented, the very factors that have precipitated this twenty-first century crisis of identity have also made possible the preservation of important aspects of Jewish musical history. Ethnomusicologists have studied the sounds of Jewish musical communities around the world. Books of this music and recordings of these songs have created a permanent record of the sounds of Jewish musical tradition. As long as there are people who call themselves "Jews" there will continue to be Jewish music. While it will continue to evolve and emerge as something not quite like its past legacy, those who respect the continuity of the Jewish cultural heritage, in all its diversity, will no doubt find a way to keep it within the sounds of Jewish memory and practice—as Jews have always done. ～

Notes

Preface

1. In his 1957 opening lecture to the First International Congress of Jewish Music, quoted by Bathja Bayer in the entry "Music" in *Encyclopaedia Judaica*, Volume 12, p. 555.

2. All translations of biblical text are drawn from the *JPS Hebrew-English TANAKH* (Philadelphia, Jewish Publication Society, 1999).

All translations of liturgical text (unless otherwise noted) are taken from *The Complete ArtScroll Siddur for Weekday/Sabbath/Festival,* translated by Rabbi Nosson Scherman (Brooklyn, NY, Mesorah Publication, 1985).

All other translations (unless noted) are by the author, with help from Nili Rabinowitz (Hebrew) and Gitl Schaechter-Viswanath (Yiddish).

Hebrew transliterations in the body of the text follow the JPS style format. Yiddish transliterations follow the YIVO style format. Names of individuals are spelled according to their most commonly accepted spelling. Titles of published works are provided in their published form. Prayer titles appear in italics; song titles appear in roman type, in quotation marks.

Transliterations underlying musical examples do not necessarily conform to the above-mentioned style formats but are indicated for ease of articulation while singing.

Chapter 1

1. In the American Jewish community, a series of concerts often takes place on this occasion in acknowledgment of "Jewish Music Season." The Jewish Welfare Board (JWB) "invented" this period as a month-long celebration, often geared toward a theme also chosen by JWB. Later the period was extended to a full season, beginning with Shabbat Shirah and concluding with Yom ha-Atzma'ut. In recent years, with the decline in visibility of the JWB, the "Season" has lost its popularity, but it is still common for communities to enhance the musical attributes of their services on Shabbat Shirah and/or to present special concerts outside the liturgical realm.

2. While Moses led the men in song, the women of Israel rejoiced by dancing to the accompaniment of drums, with Moses' sister Miriam as their leader. This separation of men and women into segregated "musical" units would become a hallmark of Jewish liturgical—and cultural—practice until well into the modern era.

3. Many scholars have asserted that women participated in the sacred rituals, at least during the time of the First Temple. In his *Music in Ancient Israel*, Alfred Sendry cites Augustin Calmet (1672–1757), who claimed that female musicians participated in Temple rituals along with men. Calmet quotes I Chronicles 25:5, which notes that Heman had 3 daughters in addition to his 12 sons, all of whom were skilled in music. Francis William Galpin (1858–1945) goes so far as to suggest that a special school for women musicians existed in ancient Israel. Sendry depends upon various references to "singing women" in the Book of Ezra to support his belief that women of the Levitical clan participated in sacred rituals, although Rashi and most other commentators assumed that these women were secular singers. Indeed, women singers play an important part in conjunction with life-cycle rituals of the Oriental Jewish communities (see further in Chapter 2), but this singing retains an essentially secular role. Sendry claims that fear of competition from female musicians forced them out of their accustomed role during the time of the Second Temple. He further suggests that an anti-female bias among later redactors of the biblical books and the Rabbis of the talmudic period erased clear references to women musicians in the Temple. Despite Sendry's strong convictions, evidence to support his beliefs remains equivocal at best.

4. The psalms remain a distinctive element in our modern liturgy, based largely upon Temple rituals, which are thus recalled in our times. In the morning service, the introduction to the "psalm of the day" *(shir shel yom)*, for example, directly references the Levitical custom of chanting a different psalm each day of the week: "Today is the _____ day of the week, on which the Levites in the Temple used to recite . . . ." The inclusion of Psalm 100 *(Mizmor le-Todah,* "a psalm for praise") is a remnant of ceremonies surrounding the "thanks offerings" that used to be brought to the Temple during morning services.

5. The Dead Sea Scrolls, discovered in 1956, contain references to Psalms 151–155, apparently revered by the Essenes of Qumran (and others) as integral chapters of the Book of Psalms. Psalms 152 and 153 remain lost, but the beautiful texts of Psalms 151 (A Halleluyah of David, the son of Jesse), 154, and 155 have been recovered, although they have not been added to the biblical canon.

6. By Christian Hebraist Alexander Maclaren in his *The Book of Psalms* Vol. 1 (New York: Eaton and Mains, 1893).

7. It is customary to bury old prayer books and manuscripts bearing God's name when they become torn and unusable. Often special places are set aside to store these

items until a large enough collection is gathered to warrant the effort of burial. This place is known as the *beit genizah* (derived from the Hebrew term for "treasury"), a "house of storage," which came to be known colloquially as simply a *genizah*. In some places the act of storing these documents came to supersede the practice of burial. This seems to be the case in Egypt, where a huge *genizah* was uncovered in the ancient synagogue of Fostat, a few miles south of Cairo.

The so-called Cairo Genizah was brought to the attention of the West by travelers who visited in the mid–eighteenth century. Cyrus Adler visited Egypt in 1891 and was able to purchase a number of documents that had been removed from this *genizah* by local antiquities dealers. His purchases were ultimately bequeathed to Dropsie College in Philadelphia. Oxford's Bodleian Library and the library of the Jewish Theological Seminary of America acquired their significant collections of *genizah* fragments in a similar manner. As the fame of the Cairo Genizah became known, scholars in England sought to acquire additional treasures from it.

In 1896 Solomon Schechter was dispatched to Cairo and was able to secure permission to take practically all of the *genizah* documents back with him to Cambridge. Since then, documents from as early as the tenth century have been studied and published; the original *genizah* documents are now housed in public and private libraries throughout Europe and the United States.

8. The text is written in the form of a eulogy for Moses, delivered by God, authored by Amr Ibn Sahal, a *paytan* (religious poet) of the twelfth century. This particular *piyyut* is one of several for which musical notation is also extant—the only such finds in the Cairo Genizah and constituting the earliest known written examples of Jewish chant. The melodies were apparently notated by one Ovadia, a priest who learned the relatively new art of musical notation prior to leaving the priesthood and converting to Judaism.

9. Translation by Rabbi Nosson Scherman as found in *The Complete Artscroll Machzor for Rosh Hashanah*, p. 479.

10. Some believe these psalms were specifically designated to be chanted by pilgrims "going up to Jerusalem" to offer sacrifices on Pesaḥ, Shavuot, and Sukkot.

11. Ancient Babylonia, which produced the Babylonian Talmud, early prayer configurations, and a host of other important texts and laws, is the region known today as Iraq.

12. According to tradition, there were those among the Israelites who were so completely assimilated that there was no hope for their eventual return to the Jewish people. These people died during the ninth plague, but their deaths went unwitnessed by the Egyptians who were enveloped by a darkness so dense that they were unable to move.

Chapter 2

1. In the Babylonian Talmud B.Gittin 7a, a question is asked regarding the origin of the ban on music. Mar Uqba answers that it is because of the verse in Hos. 9:1 "Rejoice not, O Israel, as other peoples exult."

2. Only the shofar, with a signaling, rather than a musical function, would retain its unique role in Jewish ritual. The shofar is thus the only instrument to remain in continuous use among all communities throughout Jewish history, to this day.

3. One of the reasons offered by rabbinic tradition for the loss of the Temple in 586 B.C.E. was that the people were not observing the laws of the Torah. This was not surprising, since no one was actively teaching those laws—and, of course, people could not turn to their home libraries to read the Torah on their own.

4. This economic and ritual division of the calendar allowed the rabbis to invoke the de facto ruling that one should not go more than three days without hearing words of Torah.

5. This process was completed by Aaron ben Moses Ben-Asher of Tiberias between 900 and 930 C.E. His final, authoritative system was adopted by all Jews, and systems developed earlier in Palestine and Babylonia fell into disuse.

6. *Kohanim* and *Levi'im* retained their status through preferred access to Torah honors and their respective roles in blessing the congregation.

7. The term *nusaḥ* is a problematic one, since it refers both to musical practices and liturgical ones. In the latter case, the term is used to apply to the differentiation of liturgies themselves. Sometimes the variation involves only certain words or phrases, while in other cases whole prayers are inserted or deleted, depending upon the local tradition. In more common parlance, however, *nusaḥ* refers to the musical tradition for rendering liturgical texts, and it is in this context that the term will be used throughout this book.

8. A motif (or motive) is a fragment of a musical idea, often just a few notes. For a fuller treatment of this concept, see Chapter 3.

9. In ancient times, all Jews were obligated to make the journey to Jerusalem to offer sacrifices on the festivals of Pesaḥ, Shavuot, and Sukkot. These three holidays thus became known as the *Shalosh Regalim* (from the Hebrew word for "foot"), popularly translated as "pilgrimages."

10. The Torah reading coinciding with the first portion of the Book of Deuteronomy is always read on the Sabbath preceding the Ninth of Av. With the exception of the first and last sentences of that prophetic portion (from the Book of

Jeremiah), which uses the regular chant, that haftarah is read using the chant for the Book of Lamentations. The haftarah recited on the morning of the Ninth of Av is also read using the chant for Lamentations.

11. The tempered scales used in Western music are based on systems of whole tones and semitones. In fact, however, pitch may be measured in much smaller units, as in the Oriental practice of using quarter-tones.

12. The position of the *Dhimmi* extended to all non-Muslims, including Christians. Unfortunately, with the deterioration of relations between Christians and Muslims following the Crusades, much of the benevolence with which the *Dhimmi* had been accepted also dissipated. This had deleterious effects for the position of the Jewish community as well, and by the twelfth century, Jews were, in fact, subjected to various persecutions and even forced conversions. The legal inferiority of the Jews in Muslim lands continued into the nineteenth century—and even later in some countries. Jews in Yemen did not gain full equality until 1948. Ironically, the establishment of the State of Israel later that year led to renewed tensions between Jews and Muslims, this time with political overtones that again affected the quality of Jewish life in those countries. In most cases, however, the situation for the Jewish *Dhimmi* in Arab lands remained superior to that of Jews subjected to Christian persecutions.

13. The Inquisition was an instrument of the Catholic Church designed to expose and purge the "unfaithful" from among the Catholic population. While Jews were clearly regarded as inferior, only those Jews who publicly converted to Catholicism in hopes of achieving higher degrees of assimilation and/or personal achievement (while simultaneously maintaining their Jewish practices in secret) were targeted as infidels. Beginning as early as 1391 there were also (relatively) isolated instances in which Jews were forcibly converted to Catholicism by Christian zealots. The Church finally convinced King Ferdinand and Queen Isabella to expel the Jewish community in 1492 to rid the Catholic world of their influence—and to make it that much more difficult for those who had already converted publicly to Catholicism (referred to as *conversos* by the Spanish, but called *marranos* [pigs] by the Jews) to maintain their secret Jewish lives.

14. From the Hebrew term *"Sepharad,"* meaning "Spain," the adjective "Sephardic" refers to aspects of religious practice and cultural heritage common to Jews whose ancestors once lived in Spain and neighboring areas including Portugal, northern Italy, and southern France.

15. Ladino, also known as Judeo-Español or Judezmo, is a combination of fifteenth-century Castillian Spanish and some Hebrew, reserved primarily for words of Jewish ritual, functional, or value content. It was a dialect unique to the Sephardic Jewish community and continues as the mother tongue of Jews who trace their ancestry to the Iberian Peninsula.

16. Although neither melody was notated until centuries later, we know that the melody must have been used first for the secular Ladino song and then contrafacted onto the older *piyyut* text. The concept of *ma'alin bakodesh,* literally "raising up in holiness," encourages the elevating of a secular melody to a higher status through its juxtaposition with a holier text. It would be considered irreverent to defile a tune associated with liturgical, or even quasi-liturgical text by using it for nonreligious songs.

17. Somewhat later, the story of Doña Gracia Nasi (ca. 1510–1569) provides a noteworthy example of a Spanish woman who, following the death of her husband, not only assumed his position as head of the family business, but also used her wealth in a variety of charitable causes. In more than one case, Doña Gracia's money ransomed Jews who had been incarcerated in debtor's prison or simply taken captive in a random exercise of prejudice against Jews. Her savvy, political skills, and generosity became legendary, and she was regarded as a force to be reckoned with by the local nobility as well as the (male) leadership of the Jewish community.

18. When Ladino was occasionally written during the Middle Ages, it was primarily used for Jewish legal writing (including Torah commentaries) or other Jewish literary works. Then, Hebrew characters were utilized. In the contemporary era, Ladino is written in roman characters, just as Spanish.

19. *Burmuelos* are taco-like foods fried in oil and, therefore, are a fitting accompaniment to the Hanukkah celebration recalling the one-day supply of oil that miraculously burned for eight days.

20. Most people are familiar with the saints whose activities are associated with particular celebrations popularized on even secular calendars (St. Nicholas, St. Patrick, St. Valentine), as well as those who have given their names to various Catholic hospitals, universities, and local churches. Many people do not realize, however, that the proliferation of beatified Catholics has made every day Saint "Somebody" day.

21. "Eḥad Mi Yode'a" (Who Knows One) is one of several folk songs added at the conclusion of the Passover Seder. Its text gives traditional Jewish significance to each number from 1 to 13 (One God in the Heavens, . . . Five Books of the Torah, . . . Eight days for a ritual circumcision, . . . all the way up to Thirteen Traditional Attributes of God). Sung in Ladino as *Quen Su Piense,* the Sephardic version substitutes *Moshe y Aron* (Moses and Aaron) for the *shney luḥot habrit* (two tablets of the Ten Commandments) that are part of the Ashkenazic Hebrew text.

22. During the time that this song was written, the now popular supernatural story of the birth of Jesus was beginning to be circulated as belated proof that this young Jew from Nazareth was the god his followers claimed him to be. The mainstream Jewish tradition could not accept this assertion and countered with a tale of its own "superhero," whom we meet in Genesis as a grown, married man, and whose early history has been the subject of many Rabbinic conjectures.

23 "Shalom Aleikhem" is a *piyyut* by the kabbalist Shlomo Alkabetz (1505–1584). It is based upon the talmudic passage (Shabbat 119b) in which a "good" and a "bad" angel accompany each worshiper home from the synagogue on Friday evening. If the home is properly prepared to receive the Sabbath, the "good" angel prays, "Thus may it be each Sabbath," to which the "bad" angel is forced to respond, "Amen." If the home is not prepared for the Sabbath, the "bad" angel says, "Thus may it be each Sabbath," to which the "good" angel must add his sad "Amen."

24. Jews followed the Dutch explorers into the New World and by the middle of the seventeenth century had established a small community in Brazil. When Brazil was taken by Portugal, the Jews began to fear the same treatment that had exiled them in 1497. A small boatload of 23 Jewish immigrants from Recife, Brazil, made its way to the shores of New Amsterdam (now New York City) in 1654. They received a less-than-enthusiastic welcome from Mayor Peter Stuyvesant, who sought permission from his Dutch patrons to expel the newcomers. Unbeknownst to Stuyvesant, the Jews of Amsterdam had succeeded so well in their new home that several leaders of the Jewish community had achieved seats on the Board of the Dutch West India Corporation that managed Dutch holdings in the Americas. They sent word to Stuyvesant that the new arrivals should be welcomed, and assured him that the Corporation (and the Jews of Amsterdam) would provide any support necessary if the immigrants could not fend for themselves. These Sephardim thus represented the first significant settlement of Jews in North America and provided roots for those who would later follow from England. The Levys, Gratzes, and Cardozos who established many of the first Jewish communal institutions in North America (and who provided significant economic support of colonial efforts during the American Revolution) were descendants of the Sephardic Jews who had taken the northern route out of Spain nearly 300 years earlier.

25. The Yiddish term comes from the Hebrew *klei zemer,* literally, the "tools of song." The musicians themselves soon became identified with the instruments they played. There was no prohibition against one performing routinely as a musician outside the Jewish community. However, lacking opportunities for formal musical training, these wandering musicians relied upon well-developed listening skills to learn and perform popular music of the day. They were much in demand, since they could literally play anything; they were also not prone to the drunkenness and irresponsibility of other musicians of their time. Despite legislative efforts to curtail their activities— including special taxes levied against them, and limitations on where and in what instrumental combinations they could perform—the *klezmorim* flourished.

26. Shabbatai Zevi was born in Smyrna (Ismir) in the year 1626. The son of a wealthy merchant, he was given a traditional education, and his intellectual gifts were recognized early. He was designated a *hakham,* a member of the rabbinic elite, at the age of 18, and was heavily influenced by the spirit and study of Lurianic Kabbalah emanating from Safed at the time.

Zevi was prone to asceticism and seemingly the victim of a manic-depressive illness that left him alternately in melancholy seclusion and in euphoric states of "illumination" during which he committed various acts forbidden by Jewish law, including publicly pronouncing the Ineffable Name of God, the Tetragrammaton. This behavior led the authorities in his home town and several other locales to which he subsequently traveled to banish him. He finally made his way to Jerusalem in 1662. While his spells of erratic behavior continued, during periods free of manic illness Zevi attained a level of respect and renown for his rabbinic and kabbalistic scholarship.

News of an apparent "man of God" with remarkable power to touch people drew Zevi to a meeting with Nathan of Gaza in April 1665. Nathan had already had a "vision" of Shabbatai Zevi as Messiah (no doubt influenced by tales circulating of Zevi's behavior in Jerusalem) and he convinced Zevi to declare himself the Messiah on May 31, 1665. Zevi's charisma and intellect helped convince much of the rabbinic leadership to accept his claims, and news of him and his exploits (enhanced by fanciful exaggeration) made its way throughout the Middle East and across Europe. The European Jewish masses, hungry for deliverance from the oppression of their generally impoverished lives and the tyranny of anti-Semitic governments, were eager to accept news of an impending Messianic deliverance. Zevi's call for repentance was fervently heeded, prompting a new embrace of religious sentiment and even a rash of asceticism.

When Shabbatai Zevi arrived in Constantinople, announcing that he would supplant the sultan of Turkey, he was imprisoned and ultimately offered the choice of accepting Islam or death. In September 1666, Zevi chose Islam. His apostasy shocked his followers, but it took the better part of a year for the Messianic fervor surrounding him to fade. He lived out the remainder of his life with a pension from the sultan, outwardly espousing Islam but maintaining many Jewish practices. Zevi died suddenly on Yom Kippur 1672.

27. Israel ben Eliezer was a popular healer who worked with magic spells and amulets. His philosophy was one of anti-asceticism, characterized by fervent, ecstatic prayer. His followers considered him a *tzaddik,* one of 36 righteous individuals (known and unknown) who are said to exist at any one time, and in whose name the world is said to continue to exist. Rabbi Israel died in 1760, but his disciples carried on his teachings and spread Hasidism throughout Eastern Europe.

28. Known as the Vilna Gaon (literally, the Genius of Vilna), Elijah ben Solomon Zalman (1720–1797) was renowned for his intellect. Born to a well-known rabbinic family in Selets, Grodno province, Elijah eventually settled in Vilna, and while he held no public office there, the community voluntarily paid him a weekly stipend (higher than that of the local chief rabbi!) as a token of its esteem. Elijah eschewed the yeshivot and even the local synagogue, preferring to study and pray in solitude, lest he be tempted into idle talk. Despite such seclusion, his intellectual and spiritual influence continued to grow. Although he, like the Ba'al Shem Tov, was a student of Kabbalah, Elijah became a violent opponent of the Hasidim, rejecting their emphasis on prayer over study, and fearing that their innovations would cause a split in the community.

Under his leadership, Vilna became the center of the *Mitnaggedim* (literally "opposers") and enjoined his followers to burn the writings of the Ba'al Shem Tov. His influence had profound impact upon the development of Lithuanian Jewry, and prominent yeshivot in Mir and Volzhin bore the imprint of his philosophy.

29. From the Hebrew word *"ḥasid"* meaning "righteous" or "pious," the Hasidim are devoted followers of their charismatic and learned leaders. The disciples of Israel ben Eliezer fanned out across Europe and established "courts" to espouse his philosophy—and their own. Sects bearing the names of towns where they were founded— Lubavitch, Satmar (Satu-Mare), Gur, Modhitz, Brazlov, and Belz, among others—continue to flourish under the leadership of an acknowledged *rebbe* (Yiddish for "my teacher") who guides the spiritual and personal lives of his flock. Today, the sects are distinguished by differences in approach to everything from minute interpretations of Jewish law to attitudes on the place and value of secular learning. In some Hasidic circles the traditional emphasis on prayer has faded in favor of study of Torah. In all circles, however, the Hasidim remain faithful to their views of "tradition" and to the leadership of their *rebbe*.

Chapter 3

1. The Western evolution of what we today call harmony is a largely undocumented process, but presumed to be associated with performances of Gregorian chant. Some theories link the development of early harmony to the natural distinctions and distances between human voices. The higher soprano and tenor voices are separated from their lower alto and bass counterparts by intervals of approximately four or five musical steps. Simultaneous chanting by two voices, each seeking its natural level, would thus yield the form of harmony known as "organum" that distinguished early church singing by the ninth century. Interestingly, this natural distinction between human vocal types is ignored in some Eastern communities. Among Yemenites, for instance, there is no effort by groups of singers to match pitch with the song leader. In place of the unison preferred in the West (in which everyone sings a single tone, producing monophony or harmony), Yemenite communities produce a cacophonous style known as heterophony.

2. Giovanni Pierluigi da Palestrina (ca. 1525–1594) was among the foremost Italian composers of his day, famous for his mastery of the polyphonic contrapuntal style popular at the time. Claudio Monteverdi (1567–1643) is considered the most important of the composers who participated in the revolution of Italian music at the end of the sixteenth century.

3. This ensemble was highly regarded, and was sometimes "loaned" to neighboring courts. In 1612 Alessandro, the duke of Mirandola, invited "the Jew Salamon [*sic*] and his company" to entertain at his court.

4. Jewish dancers and musicians (both instrumentalists and vocalists) were well known in Italy from at least the middle of the sixteenth century. Rossi was apparently an accomplished performer by the time he entered the duke's service. Rossi claimed to have been taught everything he knew about composition by the salaried musicians with whom he came in contact in Vicenzo's court. These latter probably included one Ingegneri, a church composer who was also Monteverdi's teacher.

5. Popular during the Baroque era (ca. 1680–1750), the trio sonata is written for two high melody instruments (typically violins) and continuo (bass melody instrument, such as cello, plus a harmony instrument, such as the harpsichord). The genre's texture of one low and two high melody instruments yielded its name. After Rossi, the trio sonata became a favorite vehicle for such composers as Arcangelo Corello, George Frideric Handel, and Antonio Vivaldi. Johann Sebastian Bach later adapted the genre for performance by solo organ.

6. Published by Pietro and Lorenzo Bragadini in Venice, the work's Hebrew title is a play on the opening verse of The Song of Songs, *Shir ha-shirim asher li-Shelomo,* in which authorship of the book is attributed to King Solomon.

7. Leon Modena (1571–1648) was an infant prodigy, reading prophetic portions publicly at the age of two-and-a-half and translating the Pentateuch into Italian by age three. His early education included Hebrew and Rabbinic studies as well as Italian and Latin. Reverses in his father's business forced him to begin offering private lessons in 1589 and to take a job as an elementary teacher and preacher in Venice in 1593 (a position not highly regarded at the time). His autobiography, *Hayyei Yehudah,* lists 26 occupations to which he resorted from time to time, including brokerage, translating, arranging marriages, and ghost writing everything from letters and poetry to sermons for others to deliver! He was well regarded as a speaker by Jews and Christians alike and his expert rabbinical decisions were highly respected—despite their liberal views and the inconsistency of his personal observances.

Modena's defense of choral music was not inspired solely by his friendship with Rossi. He had some musical ability of his own that he utilized to organize a six-to-eight-voice choir (that he conducted "according to the relation of voices to each other, based on that science" [*Encyclopaedia Judaica,* s.v. "choirs"]) for the synagogue in Ferrara at about the same time his responsum was issued. Moderna also served as choral director at the musical academy established in the Venetian ghetto in 1632.

8. Despite the Rabbinic ban on instrumental and vocal music invoked after the destruction of the Second Temple, forms of choral singing were not unknown in the synagogue. It became customary early in Diaspora history for the *sheliah tzibbur* (precenter) to be accompanied by two assistants called *tomekhim* and *mesayye'im;* these may have established the precedent for the later custom of accompanying Ashkenazic *hazzanim* with two singers, typically a bass and a boy soprano. Nathan ha-Bavli (Nathan "the Babylonian," a mid–second century rabbinic leader) describes a Sabbath

service conducted by a *ḥazzan* and male choir consisting of young men with sweet voices. Hai Gaon (*dayyan* [legal authority] of Baghdad, and head of the academy at Pumbedita, 890–898) states that the ban applied only to the singing of Arabian love songs. Maimonides is interpreted by some as permitting a choir at all religious feasts (cf. Yad, *Ta'aniyyot* 5:14). However, Leon Modena is the first to specifically address choral singing for the purpose of glorifying God as permissible on all occasions.

9. From the time that harmony came into use, evolving (but always strict) rules of counterpoint governed acceptable compositional practices. (During the Middle Ages composers could be excommunicated by the church for combining the wrong pitches!) It was not until the end of the nineteenth century, when musical innovations by Richard Wagner in Germany and the Impressionist school in France abrogated existing harmonic conventions, that composers could freely merge Eastern motives with Western musical forms and practices. Rossi was the first, but not the last, Jewish composer to be stymied by the limitations of available musical vocabulary.

10. In "A Possible Influence of Traditional Chant on a Synagogue Motet of Salomone Rossi" (*Musica Judaica* Volume X No. 1, pp. 52–58), Dr. Joshua R. Jacobson argues that Rossi's setting of Psalm 80, *Elohim Hashivenu* may be based upon a traditional melody of Rossi's day. Elsewhere Jacobson suggests that the choral responses in Rossi's setting of the *Kedushah* text, *Keter*, are designed to be interpolated around the *ḥazzan's* traditional solo lines (see below). Even accepting these two exceptions, in most cases Rossi's music seems to bear little resemblance to traditional Italian Jewish custom.

11. On weekdays that do not coincide with a public or private festival, some recite Psalm 137 prior to Grace after Meals. The opening lines of the psalm are more widely recognized as a dirge chanted on the Ninth of Av, the anniversary of the destruction of both the First and Second Temples. Singer Don Maclean popularized these lines with his rendition in English translation, "By the Waters of Babylon," in the 1970s. Rossi likely set this text to accommodate a certain kabbalistic fraternity known as the Shomrim la-Boker (Morning Watchmen), who included Psalm 137 in their daily morning prayers. (See more on this group in note 21.)

12. In fact, many argue that none of Rossi's "Jewish" works reach the level of his secular compositions, perhaps because of his greater sensitivity here to the needs of synagogal texts and/or to the novelty of choral music in the synagogue, or possibly due to his desire to "understate" his musical case.

13. In the morning service *Barekhu* is preceded by two rather lengthy sections of prayers, the *Birkhot ha-Shaḥar* (Morning Blessings) and *Pesukei de-Zimrah* (Verses of Song). The former blessings were originally recited by the worshiper at home upon arising. They were gradually added to the service as an aid to those who were unable to say them properly at home. The *Pesukei de-Zimrah* function as a spiritual "warm-up" to allow the worshiper to get into the proper frame of mind before beginning the *mat-*

be'ah shel tefillah, the core of prayer, consisting of the blessings before and after the *Shema,* and the *Amidah.*

14. Melismatic phrases also allowed the composer room to indulge another popular Renaissance convention, "word painting." Composers took trite advantage of the literal meanings of their texts, so that "he went up" would elicit an ascending vocal line; "she laughed" would usually conjure dotted rhythms; "they fell" would see the vocal line plunge. Rossi painted a somewhat more sophisticated example of this practice in the opening line of Psalm 137 when he set the word *naharot* (rivers) to an undulating musical line, conjuring up the usual passage of moving water.

15. "Semi-autonomous" because, although each line has its own existence, the composer ordains the pitches in such a way that the simultaneous coincidences of pitch will also be harmonically pleasing.

16. It has already been well established that the Rabbis' primary focus was on text, and that music was allowed in the synagogue only as a means to recall and articulate that text. Modena's foreword in *Hashirim asher lish'lomo* included the directive that the words be clearly pronounced. Not surprisingly, the church shared that interest in text and eventually rebelled against the musical and textual excesses occasioned by Renaissance styles. One "legendary" explanation for the distinctly conservative style of *Missa Papae Marcelli,* written by Palestrina in 1567, is that, in the wake of such musical excesses, the church threatened to forbid musical performances of the mass. Palestrina is supposed to have "saved the day" with his demonstration that the mass could be musically beautiful as well as textually articulate; in fact, Palestrina was simply experimenting with the more understated Baroque style that was to follow.

17. In his edition of *Keter,* Professor Joshua R. Jacobson inserts congregational passages from the traditional Italian rite into these "breaches," producing an effective and convincing representation of what the actual performance practice might have been.

18. The larger question regarding the actual use of these *Shirim* in liturgical settings at all remains unanswered. There is an assumption, however, that the *Shirim* were at least tried out in the liberal musical atmosphere of the private synagogue of banker Moses Sullam, who financed the publication. (See also Don Harran, *Salamone Rossi: Jewish Musician in Late Renaissance Mantua,* pp. 212–218.)

19. As a court musician, Rossi was in a political position in which he might have forsaken—or at the very least, not highlighted—his Jewish identity. Indeed, he received an exemption from wearing the identifying orange badge that most Mantua Jews were required to affix to their hats and coats. The publication of *Hashirim asher lish'lomo* affirms his ongoing commitment to the Jewish community and the aesthetic development of its musical rituals.

20. A vacationing member of the wealthy French Rothschild family discovered some music manuscripts with Hebrew lettering in an Italian book store. He acquired the scores and took them to the cantor of his home congregation. Samuel Naumbourg, of the Great Synagogue in Paris, edited the music and published his version of Rossi's work (with Vincent D'Indy) in 1877.

21. Due to the less tolerant atmosphere prevailing at the time, as well as more strict enforcement of rules that had existed even during Rossi's time, but had been ignored at the whim of the presiding authorities, there was apparently no one in the Jewish community with the musical skills necessary to compose such a work.

22. Hoshana Rabbah coincides with the last day of the autumn festival of Sukkot held early in the new Jewish year. During Sukkot, leaves from the myrtle and willow trees are bound to a palm branch to form the *lulav*, which symbolizes the human form and is waved in all directions to acknowledge God's omnipresence. On this last day of the holiday, the willow leaves are removed and ceremonially dashed to the ground in symbolic rejection of the last remaining sins of the year just concluded. The mystical imagery surrounding much of the liturgy and ceremony for the day would have had special appeal for the members of the *Shomrim la-Boker* who chose this day to consecrate their fraternity.

23. *Zerizim*, in Hebrew, are "hurriers," those who hasten to perform good deeds.

Chapter 4

1. The history of Saladin's *Canticum Hebraicum* mentioned in Chapter 3 serves as an interesting example. It was commissioned by an (anonymous) expectant father hoping for the birth of a male heir. The subsequent celebration of his son's arrival was apparently a gala affair witnessed by visitors to the region who noted in a diary of their travels the elaborate performance complete with soloists, chorus, and instrumental ensemble. Some years later, another group of travelers wrote about a similar performance at yet another circumcision celebration at which they were chance guests. Whether this was a subsequent birth in the same family or the sharing of an existing composition by the original father and/or the composer is unknown. However, the folklorized adoption of excerpts from the music as part of the normative ritual in the region testifies to its performance with some degree of regularity.

2. The *kehillah* was a political structure through which Jews enjoyed the illusion of autonomy. In fact, the secular government used the *kehillah* as a means of imposing its will—collecting taxes, legislating permitted regions of domicile, etc.—while allowing rabbinic authorities and other communal leadership to govern religious practices, oversee education, and impose internal taxes for the upkeep of local religious institutions.

A 1791 conference on the status of the Jews of France determined that Jews, as individuals, would have complete freedom as French citizens, but that the Jews, as a community, would be entitled to no special privileges. This attitude was adopted throughout Western Europe.

3. The opening phrase is borrowed from a well-known Christian hymn known as "Old Hundredth" that appeared in the *Genevan Psalter* in 1543.

4. Sulzer did not plan on a career in the synagogue. However, after 12-year-old Solomon was rescued following a swimming accident, his mother saw to it that he would ever after serve the God who had saved him from disaster.

5. Franz Peter Schubert (1797–1828) was a gifted and prolific composer. Despite his early death, his work included 9 symphonies (the 8th was left unfinished), 22 piano sonatas, a large number of compositions for piano (two and four hands) and chamber ensembles, 6 masses, 17 operatic works, and more than 600 songs (German *lieder*), for which he is best remembered.

The Hungarian-born Franz Liszt (1811–1886) had a brilliant career that spanned the Romantic Era. A piano prodigy who studied in Vienna with Carl Czerny and began performing publicly at the age of 11, he spent most of his early career in Paris. From 1848 to 1861 he was court musician at Weimar, where he conducted several important new works, including Wagner's *Lohengrin*. He lived in Rome from 1861 to 1870, then divided the remainder of his life among Rome, Weimar, and Budapest. Liszt was considered one of the foremost composers of Romantic program music (see further below, page 163). His work included 13 symphonic poems, sacred choral music, music for the organ, 2 piano concertos, and virtuosic transcriptions for piano of a wide variety of vocal and orchestral works by Bach, Schubert, Berlioz, Beethoven, and Wagner.

6. See Franz Liszt, *The Gipsy in Music,* translated by Edwin Evans, pp. 52–54.

7. Literally a "little singer," a child who appeared as featured soloist or in duets with the *ḥazzan.*

8. Moses Mendelssohn was a brilliant Jewish philosopher of the eighteenth century. His grandson Felix Mendelssohn (1809–1847) was converted to Christianity at the age of seven and achieved great renown as a composer and conductor.

9. Many have attempted to attach Felix Mendelssohn to the Jewish community—whether to excoriate him for his "Jewish blood" or to provide evidence that the Jews have indeed produced quality music and musicians. Mendelssohn's conversion at a young age appears to have erased any connection he may have felt to the religion of his grandfather.

10. A clef appears at the beginning of each staff and assigns a particular identity to the notes on the staff. The use of different clefs makes it possible for most notes in the vocal (or instrumental) range to appear on the staff, rather than above or below it. The G or treble clef used for women's voices, and the F or bass clef used for men's voices are most familiar.

11. Reported by Eric Werner in his *A Voice Still Heard,* p. 226.

12. Abraham Geiger (1810–1874) was one of the leaders of the Reform movement in Germany. Born in Frankfurt, Geiger moved to Berlin in 1870 and remained in that city until his death.

13. Maier Kohn (1802–1875) was a cantor and teacher. In 1832 he was a member of a committee that organized a choir to improve the standard of the service. His book of choral selections (by himself and others) for three and four voices, published in 1839, was the first modern collection of synagogue melodies and traditional songs. His work was utilized by Idelsohn as source material for Volume 7 of his *Thesaurus,* devoted to South German song.

14. Jacques Fromenthal Halevy (1799–1862) is best remembered for his opera, *La Juive,* an understated example of the French grand opera tradition that remains in the repertory of many of today's best-known opera companies.

15. Jacob Liebmann (Lippmann) Beer (1791–1864), later known as Giacomo Meyerbeer (Meyer was the name of his maternal grandfather) was born near Berlin and died in Paris. He was raised in the traditional Jewish home of his parents and grandparents and his first works had biblical themes—an 1811 cantata entitled *Gott und die Natur,* and his first opera, *The Vow of Jeptha.* His greatest acclaim came, however, from the secular operas he wrote for the Paris Opera, especially *Huegenots* (1836).

16. Bezalel Schulsinger (1790–1860) and Yeruham (Hakaton) Blindman (1798–1891) were considered to be among the primary exponents of the "classical" school of eastern Ashkenazic ḥazzanut. These early cantors did not indulge in the excessive coloraturas and vocal tricks of later generations of virtuoso cantors.

17. Governed variously by Romania and Russia, Bessarabia was a border region off the Black Sea. Kishinev, cite of the famous pogrom, was its central and largest district.

18. "Bel canto" means literally "beautiful singing." An innovation of the late Renaissance, the style stands in contradistinction to the elaborately embellished, operatic singing that became popular on concert stages and in synagogues during the nineteenth century.

19. Minkowsky authored numerous articles and essays in Hebrew, Yiddish, and German as well as two important works: *Die Entwicklung der synagogalen Liturgie bis nach der Reformation des 19. Jahrhunderts* (The Development of Synagogue Liturgy until after the Reformation of the Nineteenth Century, 1902) and *Moderne Liturgie in underzere Sinagogn in Rusland* (Modern Liturgy in Our Synagogues in Russia, 2 vols., 1910).

Chapter 5

1. The extent of Jewish involvement in musical activity in the late modern period is discussed by Ezra Mendelssohn in his essay "On the Jewish Presence in Nineteenth-Century European Musical Life" in *Modern Jews and Their Musical Agendas*, pp. 3–16. It is clear that the Emancipation and Enlightenment of the Jewish community led to the involvement of increasing numbers of Jews in modern musical activity, but all of it was as composers, performers, and concertgoers involved with secular performances. Such activity was not universally welcomed and the work of composers of Jewish origin (even those no longer formally members of the Jewish faith) was regularly reviled by anti-Semites. Interestingly, though, this is only further testimony to the increasing—and numerically disproportionate—involvement of Jews in general music-making.

2. In 1772 certain formerly Polish provinces came under Russian rule. By 1791 a decision was made to deal with the "Jewish problem" caused by this transfer of territory and population by limiting the areas in which Jews could live. With subsequent annexations of Polish and other territories through the early part of the nineteenth century, a total of more than 386,000 square miles and nearly five million Jews thus became subject to Russian domination. This constituted 94 percent of the total Jewish population of Russia, and more than 11 percent of the total population of the region. Kiev and Odessa were included in this region, thus accounting for large Jewish populations—and relatively modern innovations in Jewish life—in these areas. Ironically, this unnatural concentration of large numbers of Jews in a limited region also contributed to a consequence entirely unintended by Russian authorities—the general flourishing of Jewish life and culture in the region.

Policies restricting Jewish freedom of movement were designed both to encourage colonization of certain outlying areas and to exclude Jews from the inner provinces of Russia and its major cities, including Moscow and St. Petersburg, thus protecting local merchants from additional competition. Under Czar Alexander II some limited regions were excluded from the Pale, and hope was kindled that a general loosening of restrictions on Jewish travel and residence would cease. This hope was extinguished by the "May Laws" of 1881 that re-instituted previous restrictions, and even permitted various localities to expel those Jews already living (with permission) within their borders. The Russian government was compelled to relax these restrictions in August 1915, when thousands of Jewish refugees from World War I battle zones sought new residences, but unfettered access to the major cities was not permitted until following the revolution of February 1917.

3. The extent to which certain composers identified Jewishly has long been a matter of debate. We have already mentioned Felix Mendelssohn in this regard, but Gustav Mahler (1860–1911), who did not join the Catholic faith until his 35th year, is another whose cultural identity (and its effect on his music) is questioned by both his fans and his detractors. Other composers, including Giacomo Meyerbeer, Jacques Fromenthal Halevy, Jacques Offenbach (1819–1880), and Arnold Schoenberg (1874–1951), retained a technical commitment to their Jewish birth (though to widely varying extents) but exhibited only limited ongoing connection to the Jewish people through their work. Still, all of these—and many others—suffered the denigration of their music simply because they were born to Jewish parents.

4. In Warsaw, Yiddish writer Y. L. Peretz (1852–1915) transcribed the words to some 50 songs sung to him by Jewish youths and servant girls, but the collection was never published.

5. Anton Rubinstein (1829–1894), Mily Balakirev (1837–1910), Modest Mussorgsky (1839–1881), Nikolai Rimsky-Korsakov (1848–1908), and Maurice Ravel (1875–1937) utilized Jewish (and other) folk tunes for their artistic purposes.

6. Zygmunt Noskowski (1846–1909) was a Polish composer, conductor, and writer on music. Though few of the hundreds of works he composed remain extant, he is credited as composer of the first Polish symphonic poem *(Step)* and is considered one of the foremost representatives of late–nineteenth century symphonic music in Poland. He was also an eminent teacher and contributed much to the education of a generation of Polish composers.

7. Mily Balakirev (1837–1910) was the impetus behind the creation of a Russian nationalist school known as *moguchay kuchka,* "the mighty handful." Best-trained of his group, which included Alexander Borodin, Cesar Cui, Modest Mussorgsky, and Nikolai Rimsky-Korsakov, Balakirev made integral use of Russian folk songs in his work; others in his group were inspired by their spirit, even when folk melodies were not directly quoted. This practice would later resonate with the Jewish students in St. Petersburg and inspire their own similar activity on behalf of Jewish music.

8. Balakirev continued to support Skliar upon his arrival in St. Petersburg, as did Baron David Guinsbourg, a wealthy Jewish patron of the arts.

9. Sergei Ivanovich Taneiev (1856–1915) was a highly regarded pianist and composer. He studied at the Moscow Conservatory under Tchaikovsky and Nicholas Rubinstein and later taught at the school as well. He has four symphonies, an overture, six string quartets, and other chamber music to his credit, as well as an operatic trilogy, choral works, and songs.

10. Reported by Solomon Rosowky in conversation with Albert Weisser on January 2, 1950, and recorded in Weisser's *The Modern Renaissance of Jewish Music,* p. 44. Mikhail Glinka (1804–1857) was universally recognized as the first to utilize the flavor of Russian national music in his patriotic opera *A Life for the Tsar* in 1836.

11. Then, as throughout much of the twentieth century, only those groups that had official permission to convene were sanctioned by Russian law.

12. The details of this story are recalled by Solomon Rosowsky in his "The Society for Jewish Folk Music: Personal Reminiscences" and reported in Weisser's *The Modern Renaissance of Jewish Music,* p. 45. This episode took place on November 30, 1908, and while official permission for the organization to commence its operations was not formalized for another year, this date is generally accepted as the beginning of the Society's activities.

13. These goals are outlined in the Society's constitution, as reported by M. Braunzaft in *Haskulah Ha-muziklith Ha-yehudith* and noted by Weisser, p. 46.

14. An abbreviation for *Algemeyner Yidisher Arbeter Bund in Lite, Poyln un Rusland* (General Jewish Workers' Union in Lithuania, Poland, and Russia), a Jewish socialist party founded in Russia in 1897. Along with its other ideological preferences, the Bund became known as a proponent of secular Jewish nationalism.

15. The Moscow branch did some independent publishing of works by its stars, including Engel, Alexander Krein, and Jacob Weinberg. Works by the Moscow composers were also issued by Jurgenson, a secular publishing house.

16. Due to the sketchiness of Milner's biography, the circumstances under which this transfer took place are unclear. The assertion by some that the young singer was "stolen" by the Kiev synagogue cannot be completely discounted.

17. The opera, also known as *Ashmodei* and *Der Ketz,* dealt with the nineteenth-century struggle between the Hasidim and *Mitnaggedim.* It was apparently given only two performances before being banned forever by the Politrosviet because of its "mystic quality." This information was conveyed in a 1924 letter from Milner to Dzimitrovsky, as described by Moshe Rudinow to Albert Weisser, and reported by Weisser in his *The Modern Renaissance of Jewish Music,* p. 95.

18. Milner later set Bialik's Hebrew poem, "El Hatzipor" (To the Bird), published in 1922.

19. That is, composed virtually all the way through, avoiding most repetition.

20. It is not at all unusual for composers to resort to such elaborate subterfuge before finding the "true voice" of their thematic material. The "recitative and aria" for-

mula of the opera (later incorporated into popular theater as well) similarly "sets the scene," both in terms of the story and its music; the introduction to Beethoven's Symphony No. 1 in C Major demonstrates the same technique in a much more elaborate instrumental composition.

21. While the general flavor of the cantillation motives is certainly influenced by local musical styles, the particular practice of chanting the sacred books according to predetermined neumes is a uniquely Jewish ritual. Individual cantillation motives are generally quite short and appear in a variety of combinations. Some of the motives are distinctive enough that their use, even in isolation, is sufficient to infuse a composition with a familiar "Jewish" identity.

22. The Rabbis admitted the book into the canon by accepting Rabbi Akiva's interpretation of the text as an allegory describing the love between God and Israel, rather than its literal appearance as erotic love poetry. As noted in Chapter 2, The Song of Songs is traditionally chanted in the synagogue on Passover, the festival that recalls the birth of that relationship in Israel's redemption from Egypt. The covenant between God and Israel is also a significant theme in the Sabbath liturgy; the Sabbath itself is often referred to as a "bride" and so The Song of Songs is often read privately on the Sabbath as well, though without the distinctive chant that characterizes its public reading on Passover.

23. Samuel Alman was born in Podolia, Russia, and received his earliest musical training at the Odessa Conservatory. Following a four-year stint in the Russian army, continuing pogroms in his native region inspired him to emigrate to London in 1905, where he continued his musical studies at the Royal College of Music. Alman was a choir master in several London synagogues and the community-based Halevi Choral Society, and is credited with introducing the musical styles of the Eastern European synagogue into English practice. Although obviously not an active participant in the activities of The Society for Jewish Folk Music, Alman was certainly aware of developments emanating from it, including the evolution of the new art music. His compositions included a 1912 opera, *Melekh Eḥad* (One King), several instrumental works, choral selections, and songs on religious texts, as well as three volumes of liturgical music.

Chapter 6

1. Greek mythology and drama are full of such relationships. Sophocles' *Oedipus Rex,* in which a son unknowingly kills his father and marries his mother, is typical of this sort of fare and anathema to the rabbis with their strict moral standards.

2. A midrash is a rabbinic legend intended to comment on biblical passages or "fill in the gaps" in biblical records. A variety of midrashim relating to Abraham's youth, for example, attempt to supply information about the Jewish patriarch that is totally absent from the Bible.

3. An interesting dissenting opinion comes from Rabbi Nathan who permitted Jewish men to attend gladiatorial contests because the opinions of the audience could often save the lives of losing combatants (Avodah Zarah 18b). In a worst-case scenario, the presence of a Jewish witness to the death of a losing Jewish contestant could provide testimony that would free the decedent's widow to remarry. (Jewish law prohibits presumptive declarations of death. Without such confirmation, the wife would be an *agunah,* a "chained woman" never permitted to remarry.)

4. In reality, the noise is made *following* the reading of Haman's name, since it is a requirement that every word of the text be heard by all. Men and women are equally obligated in this regard.

5. In modern times celebrants are discouraged from indulging to the point of drunkenness, although that state was a regular part of the festival in some circles in the past.

6. This custom emerges from the Purim story itself. Esther hides her Jewish identity until the climactic moment when she reveals Haman's plot to destroy her people. God also remains hidden in this unusual biblical book: Although the rabbis comment on seeing the hand of God in several plot turns that could not possibly have occurred coincidentally, there is no overt mention of God in the narrative.

7. The author is indebted to Nahma Sandrow for her research on the history of the Purim play, reflected in her encyclopedic *Vagabond Stars: A World History of Yiddish Theater* (New York, Harper and Row, 1977).

8. "Shrove Tuesday" precedes Ash Wednesday, the beginning of the Lenten season in the Catholic Church. ("Shrove" derives from "shrive," the confession of sins that typically preceded Lent.) Although the day was obviously one with solemn liturgical rituals, various other customs became associated with the occasion, from the eating of pancakes (whose ingredients, including fat and eggs, were forbidden during the Lenten fast) to light dramatic presentations.

9. The Faust legend exists in many versions, all revolving around an individual who sells his soul to the devil in return for knowledge and power. There was a real Faust, a German necromancer and astrologer who died in about 1540. His contemporaries disregarded his supposed magical feats as fraudulent tricks, but he was taken seriously by the Lutheran Church. An anonymous *Faustbuch* published in 1587 kept the legend alive by retelling this story and collecting other tales of ancient wizards, including Merlin. The legend was recast as a play by Christopher Marlowe in 1604. By the nineteenth century, Goethe had attributed humane and lofty motives to the protagonist and has him ultimately purified and saved at the conclusion of the two-part work (1808 and 1832). Although the 1859 opera, *Faust,* by Charles Gounod, was based

upon the first part of Goethe's version, subsequent literary treatments of the story, by Heine and others, did not adopt such positive conclusions.

10. Silly battles in which someone is knocked down—even killed—and then bounces back to life parodied more serious vignettes from contemporaneous non-Jewish theater. In some, pagan actors brought on spring to banish the winter; elsewhere Christian passion plays featured the crucifixion of Jesus and his subsequent resurrection.

11. Commedia dell'arte flourished between the sixteenth and eighteenth centuries. It was based upon improvised performances of stock characters whom the actors always portrayed. These characters were identified by immediately recognizable costumes and/or masks, but individual actors defined the interpretations of "their" characters through the use of mime, juggling, dancing, and acrobatics.

12. Solomon (Shloyme) Ettinger (1803–1856) was a Polish-Jewish doctor and part of a well-educated circle familiar with plays in Russian, Polish, German, and French. His play, *Serkele,* tells the story of a strong-willed villainess who takes custody of her brother's daughter during his extended business trip. Six years later, David Goodheart returns to discover that his sister, Serkele, has declared him dead, usurped his fortune, and treated his daughter as a servant. Goodheart ultimately sets all to right, extracting his sister's repentance, arranging suitable matches for his niece and several others (and providing dowries for them all), and urging his brother-in-law to keep a tighter reign on his wife. As a wealthy, benevolent, and wise figure, David Goodheart is a typical character of the bourgeois drama that emerged in Europe at the time. *Serkele* was passed in manuscript form among friends in a variety of Eastern European cities, and became a favorite among the *maskilim,* the "enlightened ones," who took advantage of political freedoms to discover previously forbidden secular learning. Efforts by dabblers like Ettinger helped move the Jewish community beyond the folk Purim theater.

13. Note that as late as the mid–nineteenth century it was still considered unseemly for women to appear in theatrical (or any other public) roles. The use of men to portray women was a time-honored convention that audiences across Europe had long accepted. Actors were often considered low-class, traveling often and lodging in less than private quarters where it would have been inappropriate for men and women to remain together.

14. Grodner was one of the better known of several ensembles of musicians all called the Broder Singers, itinerant minstrels generally from among the ranks of the *maskilim* (the enlightened ones). The first of the Broder Singers came from the eastern Polish city of Brod (or Brody). In the politically emancipated and open-minded atmosphere of the Austro-Hungarian empire, growing numbers of Jewish patrons frequented cafes where such musicians would entertain, and these singers helped set the stage for the secular performer as entertainer.

15. The music of Solomon Sulzer had become popular in Bucharest, but choristers there did not necessarily have the musical skills to read the composer's scores. They relied, instead, upon excellent memories that enabled them to master the complicated music. Goldfaden knew these talents would advance his own theatrical works.

16. Lateiner and Horowitz ultimately immigrated to America where they were active on the Yiddish theater scene in New York City. Grodner made his way to London, where he died in 1887. Mogulesko became a popular singer, actor, and dancer. He traveled first to London, and later to New York City, where he achieved great success. Throughout his career he continued to portray and to create his own materials based upon characters first introduced by Goldfaden.

17. There are several contenders for the title of "first Yiddish actress," but a stage-struck Sara Segal was certainly the first to join Goldfaden's troupe. Fearing for her reputation—and that of his company—Goldfaden arranged her marriage to Sacher Goldstein as a condition of her joining the company. The 16-year-old ingenue changed her name to the "more sophisticated" Sophie Goldstein and went on to a formidable career on the stage.

18. From a Yiddish pamphlet, *Abraham Goldfaden,* by Nakhman Meisel, in Irene Heskes, "Yiddish Musical Theater: Its Origins in Europe," *Passport to Jewish Music: Its History, Traditions and Culture,* p. 134.

19. During the time of the Second Temple, all Israelite males were obliged to offer sacrifices on the festivals of Pesaḥ, Shavuot, and Sukkot.

20. This folk tune, "Unter dem Kind's Vigele," is the same melody that Joseph Achron used for his *Hebräische Viglied* (Hebrew Lullaby), discussed earlier, in Chapter 5.

21. Much Jewish literature is devoted to the question of how brides and grooms meet. One rabbinic midrash contends that, since finishing Creation, God has been concerned with making matches. No matter how it happens, the notion that marriage partners are destined for each other prevails.

22. We have already discussed the origins and popularity of "Rozhinkes mit Mandlen." Shulamis's "Shabbes, Yontif" (Sabbath, Holiday), sung as she waits patiently for Avshalom to return to her, is among the better known of Goldfaden's arias. "Flakher, Flakher," the "Song of the Fire" sung by the nomads whom Avshalom meets in the desert, achieved new life beyond the theatrical stage as the tune for a popular Purim song, "Haint is Purim, Brider" (Today Is Purim, Brother, translated into Hebrew as "Zeh Hayom Yom Purim").

23. The German Jews arrived in America during a wave of immigration that lasted from 1840 to 1860. By the late nineteenth century, when masses of their East European co-religionists began to follow them to the New World, the Germans had already achieved a measure of economic success and, with it, a fairly secure foothold in American life. The Germans were generally more enlightened—and assimilated—than most of the new immigrants. While accepting the traditional Jewish sense of responsibility for the new arrivals, they were not much able to hide their disdain for these less-educated cousins. The Yiddish language, always viewed as "lowbrow" to the German intelligentsia (they even referred to it as "jargon" rather than a language), now seemed a "throwback" to antiquated European ways. The Yiddish theater, with its stock characters, wooden acting, and melodramatic stories, represented the least appealing aspect of Jewish culture. The German Jews not only stayed away from the earliest Yiddish theater productions, but according to many stories, also tried to dissuade the Eastern Europeans from frequenting the theaters. To the extent that many of the immigrants were dependent upon charitable support from their German benefactors, the Germans had some success in this effort, but ultimately could not stop the encroachment of the Yiddish theater. In later years, as the productions improved, at least some members of the German Jewish community could be found among the eager theatergoers.

24. Theodore Herzl (1860–1904) convened the first Zionist Congress in Basle in 1897, harnessing nascent feelings of religious and political Zionism that had begun to stir in European Jewry since the pogroms of 1881 and the Dreyfus Affair of 1894. Most American Jews were not yet eager to embrace the Zionist cause.

25. As the song progresses, it appears that the son never does write those letters to his mother. In the final verse, he receives one last letter himself, informing him of his brokenhearted mother's demise.

26. David Edelstadt came to America after witnessing the Kiev pogroms of 1881 and contracted tuberculosis while working in a sweatshop. His writing dealt with the struggle of the immigrants against their "slavery." His poetry and song-texts were often published in *Di Varhayt,* an anarchist newspaper, and he quickly became the most widely acclaimed of the labor poets.

27. In *Gott, Mentsch und Teufel* a violin-playing peddler sells his soul to the devil in return for a winning lottery ticket. In *Mirele Efros* a young bride takes over the family business from her charitable mother-in-law (Mirele Efros herself) and comes to value the dollar more for its own sake than as a means to help others.

28. Konstantin Stanislavsky (1863–1938) founded the Moscow Art Theater in 1898 and, as actor, director, and producer, promoted a theory of acting known as "the method." His "method" involved ensemble work among cast members and the subordination of individual actors' styles to the demands of the playwright.

29. With performers coming from a wide geographic area, it was not surprising that each brought his or her own regional pronunciation with them. Other companies were not bothered by such irregularities, and audiences were so used to "suspending their disbelief" regarding the implausibility of some of the early plots that they never noticed that actors playing family members sounded as if they had been raised in different countries.

30. Leon Kobrin (1872–1946) was among the generation of more serious Yiddish writers that included David Pinski, Sholom Asch, and I. J. Singer. At the time of the Vilna Troupe's performance of his play, Kobrin had already emigrated to the United States, but his work was still popular in Europe.

31. Yeshivah students often came from distant villages to study with a particular rabbi. Since they spent all day studying, they had no means of supporting themselves, and, unless they came from extremely wealthy families, they depended upon the generosity of local townspeople to provide them with meals. It was considered an honor to support a yeshivah student (the entire community is said to benefit when some of its members study Torah), but in many impoverished towns there were not enough meals to go around. Students without obvious brilliance or other attractive characteristics would often go hungry a good part of the time.

32. The Kabbalah deals, among other things, with the world to come and the various mystical spheres inhabited by the Creator. Such "other-worldly" knowledge is considered too dangerous for the young. Traditionally, only men over the age of 40 (the age at which it is said that "one has acquired understanding") were permitted to engage in such study. By then, it is assumed that they have raised families and thus been sufficiently immersed in the earthly world that they can attempt the perilous "journey to the world beyond."

33. At a Jewish wedding, the couple is formally wed once the groom places a ring on his bride's finger and recites a traditional formula in the presence of two witnesses: Behold, you are consecrated unto me with this ring, according to the laws of Moses and Israel.

34. *Habimah* also produced a well-received performance of *The Golem* by H. Leivick and several other productions. The company played successfully across Russia, and even toured Europe and America before most of its members relocated to Tel Aviv in 1931. Engel's foray into the world of the theater was not limited to his music for *The Dybbuk*. Some of his final (unpublished) compositions were written for plays by Peretz produced by the Ohel Studio in Tel Aviv in 1926.

35. The *Folksbienne* suffered many of these same problems, but achieved some stability by associating with the Workmen's Circle, though uninvolved with the group's political and other activities.

36. They chose a northern Ukranian dialect common on American stages because it was a midway point between the extremes of the Lithuanian and Polish accents and thus comprehensible to all audiences.

Chapter 7

1. The first organ installed in an American synagogue was introduced at New York City's Temple Emanu-El in 1851. That congregation had also formed the first regularly performing choir (i.e., not simply for the High Holy Days or other special occasions) in 1845. The choir began as an all-male enclave (boys also performed in the group) but women were admitted to its ranks before 1849.

2. *Landsmanshaften* were organizations tied to cities of European origin. New immigrants who hailed from the same home town could be guaranteed a place to worship (and eventually to be buried) as well as introductions to earlier arrivals and leads for employment and housing—all on the strength of their common roots.

3. Grandfather of the famous radio commentator Walter Winchell.

4. Even "synagogues" that were not really synagogues joined the holiday competition. Boris Thomashefsky recognized that some of his theater-going audience might not frequent the synagogue on a regular basis, but even the most lapsed among the East Side Jews could be expected to seek a *minyan* (prayer quorum) on the High Holy Days. Since the theaters would be dark on such important Jewish festivals, Thomashefsky engaged a "star" cantor of his own, and announced that traditional services would be held in the comfortable atmosphere of his People's Theater—complete with professional choral accompaniment.

5. While an exhaustive list of all such performers cannot be assembled here, it is worth noting the names of some of those who achieved great popularity during this period and whose recordings are still treasured examples of the era: coloratura tenor Berele Chagy (1892–1954); Leib Glantz (1898–1964), noted for his fine musicianship; tenor Mordecai Hershman (1888–1940); tenor Ben-Zion Kapav-Kagan (1899–1953); bass Alter Yechiel Karniol (1855–1928), known for his improvisatory skills; baritone Adolph Katchko (1886–1958), whose coloratura was the envy of many tenors, and whose compositions became a model for students of traditional *nusaḥ;* tenors David Koussevitsky (1891–1965) and his brother, Moshe (1899–1966); high tenor Pierre Pinchik (1900–1971), who incorporated Hasidic melodies into his compositions; lyric tenor David Roitman (1884–1943), highly regarded for his authentic use of *nusaḥ;* and tenor Leibele Waldman (1907–1969), noted for his exceptional falsetto technique.

6. The few cantors who crossed over as performers became immediately suspect by the traditional community. Moyshe Oysher (1907–1958), for example, began his

career in the synagogue but then became a popular performer on the stage and in films. When, at the end of his career, Oysher was engaged by a Brooklyn synagogue to officiate for the High Holy Days, he was called before a *beit din* (rabbinical court) to prove his sincerity. (He passed the examination.) Jan Peerce (1904–1984) was the only prominent cantor who succeeded in splitting his career between the sanctuary and the opera stage, but he was never regarded as much a cantor as a performer.

7. The role was considered appropriate because the hero of Halevy's opera, Elazar, was a proud Jew—and because Rosenblatt would not even be required to shave his beard for the part! Rosenblatt was obviously unimpressed.

8. Nahshon bar Zadok, Gaon of Sura from 871–79 declared that "a *hazzan* who knows *piyyut* shall not be admitted to the synagogue" (B. M. Lewin, *Ozar ha-Geonim*, 1 [1928] 70), apparently fearing that such *hazzanim* would unnecessarily prolong the service. Ironically, this pronouncement also appears to be the first use of the term *hazzan* to designate a purely musical functionary, as opposed to the "synagogue assistant" whose responsibility it was during ancient times to help supervise the ceremonies of public worship.

9. Binder's career spanned a wide range of activities. He was active in the formation and leadership of Jewish music societies including the Jewish Music Forum and the Jewish Music Council, and was one of the first instructors of liturgical music at the Reform movement seminary, Hebrew Union College–Jewish Institute of Religion. In addition to composing a wide range of choral and instrumental works, Binder was also a prolific writer, contributing to many journals and encyclopedias. His *Biblical Chant* (1959) continues to be among the best-known books on Ashkenazic cantillation (according to the German tradition).

10. The Russian-born Freed was brought to the United States as an infant and studied music in the United States with Ernest Bloch and in Paris with Vincent D'Indy. He returned to the United States in 1934 and was appointed chairman of the music department of the Hartt College of Music at the University of Connecticut at Hartford in 1944, a position he held until his death. Freed wrote symphonic work on American themes as well as compositions for the synagogue. His *Harmonizing the Jewish Modes* (1958) is still regarded as among the most important works on the subject.

11. Heinrich Schalit was born and educated in Vienna, but settled in Munich, where he worked as a music teacher and as organist of the Great Synagogue. He left Germany in 1933 and was appointed organist of the Great Synagogue in Rome. He later emigrated to the United States, where he served as organist of congregations in Providence, Rhode Island, and Denver, Colorado. In addition to his music for the synagogue, Schalit wrote orchestral, chamber, piano music, and songs.

12. A raised area from which the *ḥazzan* officiates. In Reform and Conservative synagogues the sanctuary is usually constructed with the *bimah* in the front, a sort of "stage" on which both the rabbi and cantor lead the service. The ark containing the Torah scrolls is also on this raised area, and ascending the *bimah* to take part in the service is perceived as "going up" in holiness. Synagogue lay leaders often receive seats of honor on the *bimah* in return for their volunteer services to the community. (In traditional synagogues of Eastern Europe, the rabbi, learned members of the community, and lay volunteers would be honored with seats along the eastern wall of the sanctuary—that is, the wall closest to Jerusalem, toward which traditional Jewish worshipers face during their prayers.)

13. These and other works by Bloch will be discussed in Chapter 8.

14. These themes were first noted by Albert Weisser in his doctoral dissertation "Jewish Music in Twentieth-Century United States: Four Representative Figures."

15. The sole example of "traditional" synagogue music in this work comes with the setting of *Tzur Yisroel* at the conclusion of the first movement. It is believed that Cantor Rinder requested that some traditional music be included in at least one segment of the work and that Rinder supplied Bloch with his own version of the chant in its traditional *Ahavah Rabbah* mode as a sample. Bloch was reportedly so taken with the melody that he left it virtually as Rinder had submitted it, with only the most sparse accompaniment to integrate the passage into the larger work.

16. The brief a capella meditation for *Yih'yu le-Ratzon* ("May the words of my mouth and the meditation of my heart be acceptable. . .") at the beginning of the third movement of Bloch's work is quite popular.

17. There were isolated instances in which congregations continued to solicit new music. Cantor David Putterman (1901–1979), at Conservative Park Avenue Synagogue in New York City, initiated commissions of individual liturgical selections by well-known composers, including many whose involvement with Jewish music had heretofore been extremely limited. Leonard Bernstein (1918–1990), David Diamond (b. 1915), Lukas Foss (b. 1932), Roy Harris (1898–1979), and Kurt Weill (1900–1950) were among the many who responded to Putterman's invitations between 1943 and 1978. The Temple, a Reform congregation in Cleveland, Ohio, had a similar practice of regular commissions. Not surprisingly, though, the compositions that resulted generally continued to languish unperformed—except, occasionally on the concert stage—after their initial premieres.

18. The Reconstructionist movement, which began training rabbis at its Rabbinical College in 1969, only began to acknowledge a need for trained cantors for its congre-

gations in the late 1990s. While most of its affiliated congregations still rely largely on lay precentors (or cantors trained by other movements), the Reconstructionist Rabbinical College, located in Wyncote, Pennsylvania, developed a track for the training of Reconstructionist-oriented cantors in partnership with the Master of Arts in Jewish Music program at nearby (nondenominational) Gratz College. That joint program produced its first "Reconstructionist cantor" in Spring 2000.

19. The professional organization of Conservative cantors, established in 1947. It led the way for the later establishment of the Reform movement's American Conference of Cantors in 1953 and the Orthodox Cantorial Council of America in 1960.

20. As one of the founders of the Cantors Institute at the Jewish Theological Seminary of America and its primary instructor in *nusaḥ* for 40 years, Wohlberg had an opportunity to share his views—and his music—with an entire generation of Conservative cantors. The ubiquity of some of his melodies—most notably, his setting of *Mekhalkel Ḥayim Beḥesed*—is attributable to this influence, as well, of course, as to the accessibility of the melody itself.

21. America's Jewish community was by no means the only one to retain a preference for the cultural heritage of Europe, nor has this problem been completely overcome. Programmers for modern symphony orchestras and choral societies are still trying to find a way to convince audiences that American composers (and musicians) have something to offer.

22. This is not to suggest that the estrangement of young people—as well as some older congregants—from the synagogue was entirely a musical problem. There were obviously demographic and sociological issues in play that went well beyond music criticism. By the same token, however, it was easy for congregational lay leaders and clergy alike to focus on music precisely because it did have so much potential power to actively involve worshipers.

23. *Selichot* are a body of prayers that beg forgiveness for wrongdoings against God. They are recited for a minimum of three days prior to Rosh Hashanah, beginning on the Sunday before the holiday. (If Rosh Hashanah falls prior to Thursday of the coming week, the *Seliḥot* are begun a full week earlier.) *Seliḥot* are typically added to the morning service, but to demonstrate an eagerness to begin the process of repentance, the first of the *Seliḥot* are recited as early on Sunday morning as possible—traditionally at or near midnight on Saturday.

24. Max Helfman (1901–1963) was a composer, conductor, lecturer on Jewish music, and music educator. He led many secular musical ensembles, as well as choirs at synagogues in California and New Jersey. During his years as director of music at the Brandeis Arts Institute (later known as the Brandeis-Bardin Institute) in California, Helfman had a strong impact on the education of many young adults whose prior

exposure to Jewish tradition had been limited, and whom he helped to affect Jewishly, though music.

25. Robert Strassburg (b. 1915) is a conductor, teacher, and composer. He taught at the University of Judaism in Los Angeles and joined the faculty of California State College in 1966. Strassburg wrote several works on Jewish themes, as well as a biographical monograph entitled *Ernest Bloch: Voice in the Wilderness* (Los Angeles, California State University, 1977).

26. Raymond Smolover, on the record jacket for the recording of *The Edge of Freedom*.

27. Although they first flashed onto the Jewish music screen by writing alternative music for the synagogue, both Isaacson and Friedman have written nonliturgical music as well, and will be discussed further in Chapter 10.

28. Carlebach came from German-Jewish stock and was educated in mainstream yeshivot before immersing himself in the Hasidic world.

29. *Havurot,* literally, "friendship" groups, were established in the 1960s as an alternative to synagogues that were perceived to be unnecessarily formal and often unfriendly. *Havurot* were purposefully kept small to allow their members to know one another well and to enjoy meaningful interactions. In addition to holding egalitarian services in which men and women participated equally without need of trained clergy, members of *havurot* celebrated holidays and life-cycle events together. Some established residential communities reminiscent of (but more acceptable than) the "hippie" communes that emerged in America at the same time.

30. The particular text of Psalm 121 is not part of the regular liturgy. However, Carlebach generally did not write with liturgical usages in mind, but rather intended his songs for use in concerts as part of the "popular Jewish music scene" that blossomed outside the synagogue in the late 1960s. This genre will be discussed more fully in Chapter 11.

31. The impact of Israel's popular music on American Jewish culture will also be discussed in Chapter 11.

32. As the years passed, the songs moved further away from the roots of their neo-Hasidic origins. At the same time, the infatuation with Hasidic-style music faded (partly as a result of increasing tensions between Hasidic and non-observant Jews in Israel). The Hasidic Song Festival itself was discontinued after 1986.

33. Women have been ordained as Conservative rabbis since 1985. The Reform movement began ordaining female rabbis in 1975 and cantors in 1976.

34. Charismatic rabbinic leadership, relaxed standards of decorum, an orientation toward social-action programming outside the synagogue, and acceptance of casual clothing worn by worshipers also played a role in the congregation's appeal, but the dramatic differences in the synagogue's musical repertoire were most immediately identifiable to visitors and prospective new members.

35. Two Philadelphia community leaders were so taken with what they saw at B'nai Jeshurun that they helped to fund the creation of "Friday Night Alive," which encouraged participants at experimental services that traveled throughout the region to dance and sing their Sabbath welcomes. Synagogues reported astronomical increases in attendance on those evenings when "Friday Night Alive" came to town (600–800 worshipers filled sanctuaries where barely 40 people had previously attended services). Although few of the synagogues maintained all of the alternatives that "Friday Night Alive" had brought, the impact of singing on the congregation made a lasting impression that promises to continue.

36. A growing number of synagogues are also employing "cantorial soloists." In some cases, congregations feel they need someone with a beautiful voice and some musical background to sing key portions of the service, but cannot afford (or do not think they need) someone with more training to teach in their schools or perform other clerical duties. In other cases, synagogues are forced to accept individuals with limited Judaic backgrounds (some communities even engage non-Jews) because they are unable to secure the services of a better-trained *ḥazzan*. Despite increasing interest in spiritual pursuits by many congregants, many individuals who might be well-suited to the cantorate are foregoing the synagogue in favor of more lucrative (and often less stressful) positions in other fields. Notwithstanding increasing participation by lay people, this dearth of American cantors is becoming an increasingly difficult problem for all movements.

37. The first paragraph of the statutory prayer that takes the place of the ancient sacrifices is historically known as *Avot* or "fathers" since it blesses the "God of Abraham, God of Isaac and God of Jacob." The non-Orthodox movements have recently accepted alternative versions of this text that acknowledge the four mothers of Israel: Sarah, Rebecca, Rachel, and Leah. The additions come in one of two forms: either a consecutive listing of the "mothers" following the "fathers," or a listing of the "parents" as married partners, "Abraham and Sarah," "Isaac and Rebecca," "Jacob, Rachel, and Leah." Some congregations have adopted one version of the text for one service and another version for a different service. Synagogues that do not have a regular cantor sometimes leave the decision in the hands of the presiding *sheliaḥ tzibbur*. Any departure from the original language of the text requires some musical adaptation.

38. Aminadav Aloni was born in Israel, and studied piano at the Haifa Institute of Music. Upon his arrival in the United States, he attended New York University and the

Juilliard School. After spending his early career composing secular music, he began to write Jewish music in 1970 and thereafter divided his career between writing for Hollywood and composing for the synagogue. The author learned of Aloni's death on August 10, 1999, only moments before writing this passage.

Chapter 8

1. Charges that Jews used Christian blood for ritual purposes (most often for baking Passover matzah) had been lodged intermittently throughout the Middle Ages. The accusations against Beilis were startling in the modern era and became known well beyond Kiev. The matter was well documented in its time, and became the subject of the highly regarded book, *The Fixer* by Bernard Malamud, and the inspiration for a film of the same name.

2. Rosa Raisa (1893–1963) was born Rose Burschstein in Bialystok but fled to Naples at age 14 to escape anti-Semitic persecution. There she began studying opera. One of the outstanding dramatic sopranos of her day, she excelled in the Italian repertoire. Raisa debuted in 1913 as Leonora in Verdi's *Oberto, Conte di San Ponifacio* and later (1926) created the title role in Puccini's *Turandot*. She and her husband, baritone Giacomo Rimini, founded a singing school in Chicago in 1937. Raisa died in Los Angeles in 1963.

3. Hirschbein also became part of Weiner's extended family after introducing the young composer to his wife's sister Naomi. The couple were devoted to each other throughout their marriage, ended only by Lazar's death in 1982.

4. Engel was living in Berlin at that time and had started a Jewish music publishing house, *Yuval,* which issued many compositions (most by Engel himself).

5. In conversations with this author in 1975, Weiner maintained that at the time he was "almost an *apikorus*" (a heretic) but the remark from Engel "opened his eyes" and encouraged him to reacquaint himself with his Jewish musical heritage.

6. It is interesting to note, though, that only Weiner was devoted to Yiddish, while the others wrote in Hebrew. (Of course, Weiner also wrote some works in Hebrew, chiefly liturgical compositions, and his colleagues also did some limited writing of Yiddish songs.)

7. The ILGWU Chorus was the most successful of Weiner's early experiences. His six-year association with them was highlighted by a 1941 performance with the NBC Symphony Orchestra at the inauguration of President Franklin D. Roosevelt's third term.

8. Weiner insisted upon having a year to rehearse the group before they would perform. He demanded disciplined singing and one uniform dialect in their pronunciation of Yiddish, a practice adopted years earlier by Weiner's friends in the Yiddish theater. Rather than discouraging his singers, Weiner's perfectionism invigorated them and the group doubled in size even before it had presented its first concert.

9. The YM-YWHA at 92nd Street and Lexington Avenue on New York's Upper East Side for years has been active in the presentation of classes, lectures, and concerts of significant Jewish content.

10. Albert Weisser, "Lazar Weiner: A Tribute," *Congress Bi-Weekly*, p.16.

11. In conversation with this author, Weiner proudly insisted that "only a Jew could have written it."

12. Pen name of Leybush Lehrer, a psychologist by profession, a prominent Jewish educator, and a poet.

13. These words from Isaiah 40:1 open the haftarah recited on Shabbat Naḥamu, the "sabbath of consolation" immediately following Tish'a be-Av observances.

14. Founded by Joseph Achron, Abraham Wolf Binder, Solomon Rosowsky, Lazare Saminsky, Joseph Yasser, and Miriam Zunser in 1932, with chapters in New York City, Los Angeles, and Perth Amboy, New Jersey. In 1932 MAILAMM became affiliated with the Hebrew University in Jerusalem. In addition to creating musical ties between Israel and the Diaspora, MAILAMM established a department at Hebrew University to study biblical cantillation, to organize a library, and to record sacred chants and folk music. In the United States, the society encouraged Jewish creativity in music and presented concerts and lectures by leading composers. MAILAMM disbanded in 1939 but was succeeded by the Jewish Music Forum.

15. The Jewish Music Forum's program consisted of readings of scholarly papers and original works by contemporaneous Jewish composers and general discussions on problems related to the field of Jewish music. Synopses of the papers and programs were published in yearly bulletins; the final one was Volume 9, covering the period 1949–1955. This organization disbanded in 1962.

16. The Jewish Liturgical Music Society dissolved in 1974 but was succeeded by the American Society for Jewish Music.

17. In the listing of Bloch's nearly 80 compositions, his "non-Jewish" works far outnumber his "Jewish" ones. His greatest champions point to his opera, *Macbeth*, five string quartets, and many other chamber and symphonic works written throughout his

life as testimony to his universal appeal. However, Bloch's "Jewish" works have generally achieved greater fame and more frequent performances.

18. The sole exception comes in "Simchas Torah," the final movement of the *Ba'al Shem Suite*, for violin and piano. In that segment, Bloch clearly quotes "Di Mezinke," a popular tune by Eastern European composer Mark Warshawsky. Bloch never acknowledged the quotation, though, and may have utilized the melody unknowingly. While it is quite lively, the song speaks about celebrating the marriage of a youngest child and has no direct connection to the festival of Simḥat Torah or to the Hasidic community that the Ba'al Shem Tov founded.

19. *Program Book of the Boston Symphony Orchestra*, March 23, 1917, pp. 1132–1134. Originally in a letter (in French) to Phillip Hale, 1916. Reproduced, quoted, and occasionally amended by others, this citation comes from Albert Weisser, "Jewish Music in Twentieth-Century United States: Four Representative Figures [Ernest Bloch, Lazare Saminsky, Aaron Copland, and Hugo Weisgall]," p. 40.

20. Interestingly, Bloch's transliteration seems more like the Latin *Allelouyah* than the Hebrew *Halleluyah*.

21. In this case, Bloch is said to have been more interested in specific vocal sounds than in particular words. Bloch apparently wrote vowel sounds into this score (the open "ah" bears a different sound quality and color than the more closed "ooh") and later fashioned his unusual text around those predetermined vowels.

22. *Vidui* is also recited by traditional brides and grooms on their wedding day: The couple fasts, creating their own symbolic Yom Kippur, attempting to "wipe the slate clean" as they stand on the precipice separating one stage of life from another. A traditional Jew on the verge of death recites *Vidui* as well.

23. To test this hypothesis, the author has repeatedly carried out a simple experiment: playing excerpts from Bloch's Second Sonata for violin and piano (1924) and excepts from the *Ba'al Shem Suite* (1923) to students unfamiliar with Bloch's music. The students (with some background in Hasidic philosophy but not necessarily any particular music background) are routinely given the titles of the two works and told to decide which title goes with which composition. No matter which work is played first, or in which order the titles are announced, no group of students has failed to make the correct assignment.

24. French conductor and composer Nadia Boulanger (1887–1979) was herself a student of Gabriel Fauré (1845–1924). After the 1918 death of her sister Lili (also a composer), Boulanger stopped composing, and she is remembered best as an influential teacher. She taught privately, at the Paris Conservatoire, at the Ecole Normale de

Musique in Paris, and at the American Conservatory in Fontainebleau. In addition to Copland, her students included American composers Marc Blitzstein, Elliott Carter, David Diamond, Roy Harris, Walter Piston, Roger Sessions, and Virgil Thomson.

25. Chanted by one of the characters as the overture blends seamlessly into the action, the melody has come to be known as "Mipney Mah," based upon the opening text of the Hebrew language version of Anski's play. That same melody has become familiar to American audiences as a children's song, "Let's Be Friends," which encourages youngsters to approach Yom Kippur by apologizing to people with whom they may have argued in the recent past.

26. Unlike many other composers who happened to be Jewish, Copland never openly associated himself with Jewish causes (although he certainly never tried to hide or deny his Jewishness). Some point to Copland's 1947 choral setting of the creation story, *In the Beginning*, as another assertion of his Jewish identity. However, if the composer meant the work in this way, he not only failed to identify it as such but also failed to understand the fundamental Jewishness of the "story": In Copland's piece, the climax of the music comes with the creation of man; in the Jewish view, the culmination of Creation is the Sabbath.

27. Johannes Brahms (1833–1897) followed in the romantic tradition of Beethoven. Richard Wagner (1813–1883), a champion of German opera, challenged the prevailing ideas of harmony with his use of chromaticism.

28. The composer's rabid anti-Semitic views were another matter entirely.

29. Traditional Western music is based upon an 8-note scale in a combination of whole and half steps with implied tonal centers. The 12-tone scale creates an equal relationship among the pitches, eliminating established tonal and harmonic conventions. The serial technique assigns an arbitrary order to the 12 tones, requiring that each pitch be sounded in its turn (or in combination with others in its immediate sequence).

30. A cycle of 21 songs for soprano and ensemble of five instruments, based on texts from a larger cycle by Belgian poet Albert Giraud.

31. Schoenberg had begun the libretto for the concluding third act of *Moses und Aron* but never set it to music. Acts 1 and 2 are well regarded, though, and often performed—despite missing their finale.

32. During World War II the Nazis herded Warsaw's Jews into a small, walled ghetto. Despite intolerable crowding; shortages of food, clothing, and medicines; and impossibly oppressive rules, the ghetto pulsed with life. Its inhabitants defied their persecutors by establishing and maintaining schools, synagogues, and all manner of cultural life. Following months during which its thousands of residents were decimated by

disease and transferred to extermination camps, the Nazis planned to dissolve the ghetto entirely but were met with surprising resistance by its last remaining occupants. Armed with Molotov cocktails and smuggled arms, the ghetto fighters held off a German army battalion for weeks before succumbing.

33. The Jewish "credo," these verses are traditionally recited by Jews in their final moments.

34. Darius Milhaud, *Notes Without Music: An Autobiography,* p. 1.

35. During this period the Jewish Agency commissioned a number of these settings by well-regarded composers of the time, including Ernest Toch (1887–1964) and Kurt Weill (1900–1950).

36. The work received its premiere performance at Temple Emanu-El in 1949 but, like the service by Ernest Bloch commissioned years earlier, it has been performed mostly in concert.

37. From a 1948 letter to Gdal Saleski, quoted in "Bloch, Milhaud and Castelnuovo-Tedesco," by Irene Heskes, *Passport to Jewish Music,* p. 289.

38. Consolo's *Libro dei Canti D'Israel: Antichi Canti Liturgici del Rito degli Ebrei Spagnoli* (Books of the Chants of Israel: Antique Liturgical Chants from Spanish Jewish Rite) (Florence: Bratti, 1892) included his own arrangements of synagogue music from northern Italy.

39. After years as guest conductor for orchestras around the world, Bernstein was named music director of the New York Philharmonic Orchestra in 1958. Bernstein's teaching career included guest lectures at Harvard, his alma mater, and at Brandeis University, and an unofficial position as America's primary teacher of music appreciation in a series of televised *Omnibus* lectures and "Young Persons Concerts" broadcast by CBS Television between 1958 and 1970. Bernstein wrote *The Joy of Music* and *The Infinite Variety of Music*—both aimed at the nonmusician.

40. Bernstein studied music privately as a child, and continued his education at Harvard University and at the Curtis Institute of Music in Philadelphia, where he studied piano and conducting. Bernstein's father, Sam, was the son of a rabbi and entertained early hopes that his oldest son would follow in his grandfather's path. Sam Bernstein equated all musicians with itinerant (and generally impoverished) *klezmorim.* He encouraged his son to join in his hair supply business and refused to support his musical aspirations, either psychically or financially.

41. One of Bernstein's earliest mentors, renowned conductor Serge Koussevitsky of the Boston Philharmonic, had converted from Judaism to Christianity in order to fur-

ther his own career. Recognizing that Bernstein was not prepared to take such a dramatic step away from his own heritage, he nevertheless encouraged the younger musician to adopt a less "ethnic" surname, "Burns." Bernstein resolved to "make it" as Bernstein or not at all.

Leonard Bernstein, who lent his name to a variety of sometimes controversial political causes, was also an early and devoted friend of the State of Israel. His first visit, in April 1947 (before the United Nations' Partition vote in November of that year), was followed by repeated concert trips during his tenure as "music advisor" to the Israel Philharmonic Orchestra in the early, war-ravaged months of the state—gestures that earned Bernstein "hero" status in Israel. Bernstein returned to preside over the opening concert at Tel Aviv's Mann Music Center in 1957 (with soloists Isaac Stern and Arthur Rubinstein) and to conduct the first concert in the newly recaptured amphitheater on Mt. Scopus following the Six-Day War in 1967.

42. One of the movements was built upon sketches he had begun while studying at Harvard.

43. Ironically, and unbeknownst to the composer, at the same time that Bernstein was completing his symphony, the Nazi war machine was gearing up for an even more terrible assault on the Jewish people. Bernstein, like most of the rest of the world, was unaware of this activity at the time. Toward the end of his life he expressed regret that he had never had the time to realize his dream of composing an opera based on the Holocaust.

44. In contemporary times most young girls preparing for bat mitzvah also learn the chant.

45. While recognizing the folly of anthropomorphizing God, Jewish philosophy and a gendered Hebrew language have openly attributed "male" and "female" qualities to the Creator of the Universe. The Hebrew words that describe God as "judge" and "ruler" are masculine, while those that describe a "nurturing" and "protecting" God are feminine.

46. During the 1950s Bernstein was busy with his conducting career and with compositions for the stage, including *Wonderful Town* (1953), *Candide* (1956), and *West Side Story* (1957).

47. Bernstein's Second Symphony was inspired by a poem by W. H. Auden called "Age of Anxiety."

48. For example, it is customary to recite *Kaddish de-Rabbanan,* a prayer for the welfare of teachers (and their students), after studying the passages of Torah that are part of the daily service.

49. The Cuban Missile Crisis of 1962 took place midway through the composer's work on this symphony and dramatized the tension in a world dominated by cold war.

50. Robert Jacobson, in liner notes for the Columbia recording, *Dybbuk*.

51. In fact, despite his great successes, Bernstein was subjected to constant carping from his detractors. Some challenged his "gymnastic" physicality and eclectic programming choices as a conductor. Others suggested that he should choose between composing popular music or serious music for the concert stage. In fact, though, in addition to the many prestigious positions he occupied, Bernstein also won much recognition for his accomplishments—including Emmy, Tony, Oscar, and Grammy awards.

52. The simplest example of a minimalist composition is a canon. In a canon, a relatively short composition, consisting of several phrases, creates harmony with itself. The canon can typically entertain varying numbers of entering voices. (For example, "Row, Row, Row Your Boat," among the shortest and best-known canons, can accommodate two, three, or four voices.) Reich's earlier works were by no means in strictly canonic form, nor were they necessarily brief, but they did employ a minimum of musical material.

53. Reich's care to root himself in a traditional text and an authentic musical milieu did not extend to his treatment of the words. The original score contains transliteration errors that have been corrected in this brief excerpt, but that also affect the singers' pronunciation on the premiere recording whose production he supervised.

Chapter 9

1. Eliakum Zunser was one of the first *badḥanim* to have a real knowledge of music, and his strong musical background and exceptional personal qualities raised the dignity of his profession. His contact with the Hovvei Zion (lovers of Zion) movement in his native Vilna influenced him strongly, and many of his songs preached Jewish nationalism and Zionism.

2. Chaim Nachman Bialik is considered the father of modern Hebrew poetry. After the death of his father when he was six, Bialik was raised by a stern grandfather who saw to his religious education. However, Bialik was a voracious reader of medieval theology and Haskalah literature, which stimulated his interest in secular knowledge. He was especially influenced by the writings of Ahad Ha-am, whose essays espoused a spiritual Zionism. Bialik ultimately left behind a traditional lifestyle but remained sympathetic to observant Jews and continued to use biblical imagery in his poetry. Bialik moved from Russia and settled in Tel Aviv in 1924.

3. In later years the song was adopted as an anthem of the left-wing Mapai (Labor) party.

4. Acts of the Knesset (Israel's parliament) in 1948 determined that the national flag would include a blue, six-pointed star and two horizontal blue stripes on a field of white, and that the seven-branched menorah (candelabra) would serve as the symbol of the new nation. No such decision was ever reached regarding the use of "Hatikvah" or any other song as Israel's national anthem. Throughout its first 50 years, there was general consensus that "Hatikvah" should serve in that role, although the popularity of "Yerushalayim Shel Zahav" (Jerusalem of Gold) in 1967 caused it to be seriously considered as an alternative. Toward the end of the twentieth century some liberal voices pointed to the fact that "Hatikvah" speaks only of Jewish hopes and therefore implicitly disenfranchises other populations that live within Israel's borders. In the meanwhile, no serious challenge to "Hatikvah" has been offered, and it continues to be used and acknowledged as Israel's national anthem by Jews and by secular governments around the world.

5. Abraham Zevi Idelsohn was the first and foremost musicologist of Jewish music. After training as a cantor in Europe and studying at the Conservatory in Leipzig, he held positions, first in Bavaria and then in Johannesburg, South Africa. There, Idelsohn was inspired by the Zionist ideal and emigrated to Jerusalem in 1906. He organized the Institute for Jewish Music (1910) and the Jewish Music School (1919), all the while conducting research among the various ethnic communities who made Palestine their home. After delivering lectures in Europe and the United States, he was appointed professor of Hebrew, liturgy, and Jewish music at Hebrew Union College in Cincinnati. Idelsohn's monumental *Thesaurus of Hebrew Oriental Melodies* (10 volumes, 1914–1933) was the first serious study in Jewish musicology and remains the most far-reaching work of its kind.

6. By the time of Idelsohn's study of the tune (*Thesaurus*, Volume 4, 1923), this incarnation appeared to be just another version of the many "migratory melodies" he documented. Some similar migration may well have occurred between the Romanian tune and the Czech folk song used as the theme for *The Moldau* by Bedrich Smetana (1824–1884), but the assumption that "Hatikvah" simply appropriated the tune from *The Moldau* is unfounded.

7. The ferociousness of the Kishinev pogrom of 1903 had shocked the entire civilized world. After the failed revolution of 1905, further persecutions led many Jews to fear yet another attack.

8. In the synagogue, one who receives an aliyah is called to the *bimah,* a raised reading platform, and comes into contact with the Torah, the teachings of Jewish history, law, and tradition that, through their study and observance, bring an individual to an elevated spiritual condition. In ancient Israel, pilgrims were obligated to make three

trips to Jerusalem each year to offer sacrifices on Passover, Shavuot, and Sukkot. The city, in the physical heights of the Judean hills, achieved a heightened sense of holiness due to its special role as the site of the Temple. Modern visitors to Israel, and especially those who decide to emigrate there, are said to be "making aliyah."

9. Some of the principles of the earliest settlements were later modified to enable the creation of religious kibbutzim.

10. Saul Tchernichowsky (1875–1943) was given a limited religious education. However, his devout but open-minded parents also exposed him to the philosophy and literature of the Haskalah (Enlightenment). Tchernichowsky ultimately rejected any association with religious life but became part of the Jewish national renaissance movement. Tchernichowsky trained as a physician and tried repeatedly to find work in Palestine before finally succeeding in 1931. The melody was composed by Tuvia Shlonsky (1874–1929) following Tchernichowsky's visit to the family and his reading of the poem for them. Shlonsky was not really a "composer"; his greater claim to fame was his paternity of poet Abraham Shlonsky (1900–1979).

11. Alone among the major world powers, Great Britain had evidenced some support for the idea of a Jewish state well before World War I. When Turkey (which had dominion over Palestine at the time) entered the war on the side of the Central Powers, sympathetic members of the British government began advocating for the detachment of Palestine from the Turkish empire and the encouragement of Zionist aspirations—in part as a way to attract American (and American Jewish) support for the war. The Balfour Declaration, issued on November 2, 1917, "view[ed] with favour [*sic*] the establishment in Palestine of a national home for the Jewish people" and vowed to use its best efforts to achieve that goal. With the defeat of Turkey (and its allies) in the war, Great Britain did, indeed, acquire control of the region. However, in light of its increasing rapprochement with Israel's Arab neighbors, Britain did little to realize the early promise of the Balfour Declaration.

12. Joseph Heftman (1898–1955), who wrote the lyrics, was among those whose first attempts at immigration were unsuccessful. Heftman arrived from Poland in 1920 and served as a member of the "National Committee," a group of leaders of the Jewish settlements, before returning to Europe. He returned to Palestine in 1934 and worked as a journalist until his death.

13. "Hammer," reminiscent of Judah Maccabee, who led the revolt against the Syrian-Greeks in 164 B.C.E. that is commemorated by Hanukkah.

14. The request came from one of the members of his group, Eliezer Lipa Sukenik (1889–1953), who, as professor of archaeology at Hebrew University, uncovered the famous ancient synagogue at Beit Alfa in northern Israel.

15. These words, set to an anonymous folk tune, were written by a young pioneer, Abba Shneller (1898–1969). Shneller changed his name to Abba Khoushi and was later elected mayor of Haifa.

16. The lyrics to "Numi, Numi, Yaldati" had actually been composed in Warsaw and become quite well known there. Upon arrival in Palestine, Heilperin changed some of the words to suit the new environment: "Market" changed to "field" and "vineyard"; the "shoes" and "socks" that Father would have brought from the market changed to "sheaves" and "grapes."

17. Noted critic Menashe Ravina later described Zeira as a troubadour who traveled the length and breadth of Israel, attempting to capture the spirit of his generation and to translate the experiences of his era into sound.

18. Hillel Avichanan arrived in Palestine from Russia in 1925 and worked as a journalist and as an actor at the avant-garde theater, Hamatateh (The Broom).

19. Ya'akov Fichman arrived in Palestine for good at the age of 41. (He had made a previous attempt at aliyah 12 years earlier.) In recognition of his own writing and his efforts at anthologizing important works, Fichman was awarded the Israel Prize for Literature in 1953. (The Israel Prize is like an Israeli Nobel Prize and is awarded for accomplishments in a range of fields.)

20. Yitzchak Shenhar arrived in Palestine in 1921 and wrote poetry, stories, and theatrical works. The language of "Shedemati" is somewhat esoteric, contributing, perhaps, to the exotic appeal of the song. It is interesting to note that according to the rules of Hebrew, the first word should be pronounced *shad'mati*. Admon's setting obviously attained its renown in spite of this grammatical error.

21. An agency established by the 1922 League of Nations Mandate for Palestine, the Jewish Agency provided a liaison between Jews in the Diaspora and those in the national homeland. It also served as a bridge between Mandatory and other powers. The Jewish Agency relinquished many of its functions with the establishment of the state, but continues to be involved with immigration, land settlement, youth work, and other activities funded by donations from Jewish communities around the world.

22. Aliyah to Israel continued in the period from 1940 to 1948, much of it illegal. Referred to variously as Sixth and Seventh Aliyot, or as Aliyah Bet, the entire period from 1934 to 1948 was also referred to as *ha-apalah*.

23. The text of "Olim" was written by Yitzchak Shenhar. Its composer, Shalom Postolski (1898–1949), received his early musical training in his native Poland and arrived in Palestine in 1929. Among the first composers from the kibbutz movement

(Postolski was a member of Kibbutz Ein Harod), he captured the upbeat spirit of the pioneers in most of his songs.

24. See "The *Eretz Israeli* Song and the Jewish National Fund" by Natan Shahar in *Modern Jews and Their Musical Agendas: Studies in Contemporary Jewry, An Annual, Vol. IX,* edited by Ezra Mendelsohn (New York, Oxford University Press, 1993).

25. One of the verses used in Hameiri's play spoke of a somewhat different reality than the idyllic image of blissful *kibbutz galuyot* (gathering of the exiles) that the Jewish Agency wanted to portray. Although it was eliminated from the version of the song promoted in 1930 and is little known today, it unfortunately remains a more accurate picture of the demographic tensions in Israel (then and now) than her promoters would like to paint.

> With a confident heart I came here to raise up your ruins
> But how will I build your Temple if there is no peace among your children:
> Sephardim, Ashkenazim, Yemenites, Ethiopians, Georgians, Orthodox, and secular.
> Jerusalem, Jerusalem, it is not that that I envisioned in my dream.
> Jerusalem, Jerusalem, inspire peace among your children.

26. Alterman arrived in Palestine at the age of 15 to study at the Herzlia Gymnasium in Jaffa. His first poetry was published in 1931 by which time the fame he would earn as a poet, translator, playwright, and newspaper columnist was already accumulating. Alterman ultimately won the coveted Israel Prize in 1967.

27. Zefira and Nardi were of widely disparate backgrounds and temperaments; the 11-year difference in their ages was also a factor in their divorce.

28. Boskovitch came to Palestine for a visit in conjunction with the performance of his *Chansons populaires juives* (popular Jewish songs) by the newly formed Palestine Orchestra. It was chiefly the warm reception he received at the time that induced Boskovitch to remain in the country. The decision likely saved his life and also afforded him a prominent position in Israeli musical society from the beginning.

29. Boskovitch was much less interested in preexisting folk materials. His collaborations with Bracha Zefira resulted in original songs, and, beyond his earliest arrangements, he focused on capturing the flavor of these songs without quoting them directly.

30. As a young musician writing in Germany, Ben-Haim had begun to work and write in the variety of genres that would characterize his later career. In addition to some 95 unpublished songs for voice (or chorus) and piano, Ben-Haim composed works for violin and piano, a string quintet, a piano quartet, and ballet music. His most important works of this period include *Pan* (Opus 17, 1931), a symphonic poem

for soprano and orchestra; and *Yoram* (Opus 18, 1932–1933), an oratorio for choir, soloists and orchestra, telling the story of a modern-day Job. This dramatic work, containing solos and choruses with full orchestral accompaniment, was completed in Munich in 1933, just before Ben-Haim left for Palestine.

31. The Palestine Orchestra was formed in 1936 under the visionary leadership of Bronislaw Huberman (1882–1947). With permission from the British authorities, Huberman imported leading Jewish musicians from orchestras across Europe. In most cases, those immigration permits probably saved the lives of the players and their families. The ensemble's premiere performance was conducted in December 1936 by Arturo Toscanini. Its name was changed to the Palestine Philharmonic Orchestra in 1946 and to the Israel Philharmonic in 1948, with the establishment of the Jewish State.

32. The catalogue of Ben-Haim's instrumental works continues with his *To the Chief Musician—Metamorphoses for Orchestra* (1958), inspired by Psalm 49; Concerto for Violin and Orchestra (Opus, 58, 1960); *Dance and Invocation for Orchestra* (Opus 59, 1960); Capriccio for Piano and Orchestra (Opus, 60, 1960); and Concerto for Cello and Orchestra (1962). In *The Eternal Theme: Music for Orchestra* (1963–1965), Ben-Haim created six interlinked segments based upon sayings of the Hasidic Rabbi Nahman of Bratzlav on the role of music.

Ben-Haim's later works included his Serenade for Flute and String Trio (1967); *Symphonic Metamorphoses on a Bach Chorale* (Opus 68, 1967–68); Rhapsody for Piano and Strings (Opus 71, 1971); Divertimento Concertante for solo flute, harp, glockenspiel, baritone, celesta and strings (1973); Prelude for String Quartet (1973); and Music for Violoncello (1977). His very last composition, *Three Studies* (1981), was a violin solo written for and dedicated to the famed violinist Yehudi Menuhin.

33. The poetry of Matti Katz came to Ben-Haim's attention after Katz fell in battle during the Six-Day War.

34. Modern composers have been most often drawn to the Books of the Prophets and the Writings, whose authorship is human (albeit with Divine inspiration).

35. This passage follows the Torah readings for Noaḥ, from the Book of Genesis, and Ki Tetze, from the Book of Deuteronomy. In the portion of Noaḥ the world is destroyed, but God promises to repopulate it through Noaḥ and, indeed, never to destroy the world again. The reading for Ki Tetze falls during the "Seven Weeks of Consolation" between Tish'a be-Av and Rosh Hashanah, promising that the barren Jerusalem, destroyed and robbed of her children, will see them grow in numbers and one day return to her.

36. In resorting to this rather archaic form, Ben-Haim followed the lead of many modern composers. "Neo-Classical" and "neo-Romantic" schools evolved as evidence of composers' tendencies to simultaneously test the limits of melodic invention and mollify their wary listeners by employing familiar musical structures.

37. The musical content of the bass line to a large extent predetermines, or at least limits, the potential melodies and harmonies that might be built on top of it, in much the same way that the size and/or depth of a building's foundation affects the type of structure that might ultimately be raised above it.

38. Noting the ethnomusicological work of scholars like A. Z. Idelsohn and Eric Werner, several Israeli composers have studied Christian chant, seeking the roots of Jewish music in the juxtaposition between the Eastern Jewish modes and the music of the church.

39. Orgad revised and rewrote this composition in 1958.

40. A rondo features a recurring "chorus" interspersed with passages that differ completely from each other. A typical rondo might be diagrammed ABACADA. . . .

41. His *Monologue* for viola was written for Ze'ev Steinberg and first performed by him in 1957 at the ceremonies marking Orgad's receipt of the ACUM Chamber Music Prize awarded for his *Out of the Dust* (Min he-afar) (1956) for mezzo-soprano, flute, and strings. (ACUM [Agudat Compositorim U'Mekhabrim, the Association of Composers and Writers] is the Israeli equivalent of ASCAP [the American Society of Composers, Authors, and Performers].) The sounds of the Middle East can be heard in his *Taksim* for solo harp (1962). Orgad also wrote several works with no particular programmatic agenda. Some of his compositions in this category include Seven Variations on C for piano, *Music for Orchestra* with Horn Solo, and Trio for Strings (all written in 1961); *Movements around A* for orchestra (1965); *Kaleidoscope* for orchestra (1966); and *Individuations* for clarinet and chamber orchestra.

42. Shmuel Yosef (Shai) Agnon (1888–1970) was one of the leading figures in modern Hebrew literature and won the Nobel Prize for Literature in 1966. Much of his work deals with religious concerns and features observant characters facing the disintegration of spirituality and tradition around them.

43. Orgad's *Songs without Words* for six instruments (1970) tell stories without text, while *The First Night Watch* (1969) for string orchestra and *Second Watch* for chamber orchestra (Ashmoret Shniya) (1973—reworked for full orchestra in 1982) both convey impressions of nights in old Jerusalem through music alone. *Hallel* for symphony orchestra (1978) offers praises, though again, without quoting texts. (The *Hallel* [praise] service, comprised of Psalms 112–118, is recited during morning prayers on the Pilgrimage Festivals, on Rosh Ḥodesh [the observance of the New Month], and on Hanukkah.)

44. Quoted by Peter Gradenwitz in *The Music of Israel: From the Biblical Era to Modern Times*, p. 405

45. Quoted by Gradenwitz, *The Music of Israel,* p. 406.

46. *Cantus I* for three oboes, *Cantus II* for string trio, and *Cantus III* for bass clarinet and orchestra were composed in 1984; *Cantus IV* for violin solo (1986) was succeeded by *Cantus V* (1990), a one-movement concerto for viola and orchestra.

47. The rabbis maintain that this person does not know that he must do good unto others without precondition or consideration of any potential payment or benefit to himself.

48. Notes by the composer appearing on the album jacket of the recording, *Israel Music Anthology, Vol. 9.*

49. The gala concert was conducted by Zubin Mehta in the courtyard of Toledo's Military Academy and hosted by Spanish actress Nuria Espert and American actor Gregory Peck. Metropolitan Opera star Placido Domingo was the work's principal soloist, and violinist Isaac Stern was a special guest soloist. French Chief Rabbi Joseph Sitruk led prayers, as did Christian and Muslim religious leaders in attendance. The audience of more than 2,000 included Queen Sofia of Spain.

Chapter 10

1. The popularity of Yemenite singer Shoshana Damari (b. 1918) and the songs written for her by Moshe Wilensky (b. 1910) were illustrative of this trend, but she sang an even larger number of entirely Western songs.

2. In an unfortunate chapter from which Israel's authorities only began to retreat more than 20 years later, efforts to make the new Oriental immigrants "proud Israelis" were tinged with an Ashkenazic ethnocentricity that denied the Eastern immigrants their own cultural heritage. While the larger communities were able to stand their musical ground, the absence of Oriental music from Israel's airwaves—and the fact that this was indicative of generalized negative attitudes toward Eastern immigrants—led to political and demographic tensions in the country that have not yet abated.

3. Despite the vaunted equality of Israeli women, who, like their brothers, are drafted into national service, there has always been a distinction between the roles of men and women on the battlefield. The defenders of kibbutzim and smaller settlements in outlying regions that became the front lines in the War of Independence did not have the luxury of segregating male and female fighters, though, and many women played critical roles in battle.

4. Raphael Klatshkin, an alumnus of the Herzliya Gymnasium, was a sometime actor in the Habimah theater, and also wrote poetry. Menashe Baharav reached immortality through this song, but is otherwise unknown.

5. Performing ensembles were formed in all military divisions and played several important roles. Foremost, they entertained the troops and released tensions by humorously pointing fingers at the military or national establishment. In addition, however, in a country where military service is still almost universal, they created a unifying cultural milieu of shared songs reflective of shared experiences.

6. American Colonel Mickey Marcus conceived of the Burma Road and volunteered to lead the brigade that built it. Tragically, the assimilated American knew no Hebrew at all and was shot to death by one of his own troops when he failed to acknowledge the soldier's warning.

7. Haim Guri was born in Tel Aviv. Inducted into the illegal Palmah in 1942, he was active in facilitating illegal immigration in the period before the declaration of the state in 1948. Guri studied at Hebrew University in Jerusalem and spent time in Paris. He published books of his poetry (many of his lyrics were later set to music) and had a column in one of Israel's daily newspapers. Guri won the Israel Prize for literature in 1988.

8. Moshe Wilensky was born in Poland and settled in Palestine in 1932. Almost immediately he became one of the leading writers of popular music, and has succeeded in crossing stylistic borders to suit the needs of each decade. Wilensky was awarded the prestigious Israel Prize in 1983 for his contributions to Israeli song.

9. Yehiel Mohar arrived in Palestine from Poland in 1937. He wrote two different types of poetry and used different names accordingly. To his lyrical, personal poetry he signed the name Yehiel Mar; he used Yehiel Mohar for the popular, strophic poetry that was so often set to music by Wilensky.

10. Alexander ("Sasha") Argov was born in Russia and settled in Palestine at the age of 20. The first of his songs to become popular were those performed by the army's Chizbatron, headed by Haim Hefer. Argov went on to write hundreds of songs (including many for the theater and for film) and to win the Israel Prize for Hebrew song.

11. The Parvarim began their career in the 1950s, with a diverse repertoire of popular songs of national interest, Ladino ballads, and traditional Sabbath songs. In the 1960s The Parvarim revitalized their career as Israel's answer to the popular American duo of Simon and Garfunkel. During the peak of the latter's popularity, the Parvarim recorded an album of their songs in clever Hebrew translations.

12. Yochanan Zarai was born and educated in Hungary and arrived in Israel in 1953 at the age of 24. In addition to writing many popular songs, Zarai composed scores for films and television.

13. Israel occupied the Gaza Strip and half of the Sinai peninsula during this campaign but was ultimately forced to withdraw by pressure from the United States and the Soviet Union. United Nations forces were stationed on the Egyptian side of the frontier and at Sharm el-Sheikh in order to guarantee the free passage of Israeli ships through the Straits of Tiran. Israel made clear that it would consider any deviation from this status quo an act of war. The Straits remained open until May 23, 1967, when Egypt unilaterally ordered the evacuation of the United Nations troops and closed the entrance to the Gulf of Eilat. This action precipitated the Six-Day War.

14. Written by Emanuel Amiran (1909–1993) for a play, *ha-Adamah ha-Zot* (This Land), presented by the Habimah theater company in 1942. Amiran was born in Russia and settled in Israel in 1924, discarding the family name Pougatchov. With the establishment of the state, Amiran became the first director of music education for the new Office of Education and Culture.

15. Written by Eli Gamliel (b. 1926) in 1952 during his days in a Tel Aviv school for music teachers.

16. "Vayiven Uziyyahu" (And Uziyyahu Built) by Yochanan Zarai became an enormous success, in spite of, or perhaps because of, being built on only three notes, making it especially easy for the popular, but not vocally gifted entertainer Arik Lavie to record.

17. Aryeh Levanon was born in Romania. A graduate of the Academy of Music, he wrote songs during his army service and has spent much of his career as an arranger and conductor.

18. Although Israel technically "threw the first stone," the blockade of the Straits of Tiran and the massing of hostile troops on all of her borders were viewed by Israel as acts of war that necessitated a preemptive response.

19. Israeli-born Shmuel "Shmulik" Kraus was one of the first to incorporate the new sounds of "rock" music into Israeli song. His popular band, ha-Ḥalonot ha-Gevohim (The High Windows), which included Arik Einstein and Josey Katz, embodied the sounds of the '60s generation—and along the way, earned the rancor of the "religious establishment" for its irreverent evocation of such biblical figures as Ezekiel in its music.

20. Naomi Shemer was born on Kibbutz Kinneret in 1930. Beginning with her first hit, "Anu Holkhim ba-Regel" (We Walk on Foot) in 1956, her songs have both reflected the national mood and revealed her own (often politically tinged) insights. In addition to receiving the coveted Israel Prize for Hebrew song, Shemer was awarded an honorary doctorate by the Hebrew University in 1994. The Zamir Choral Foundation, based in New York City, but representing singers from across North America, also recognized her achievements with its Niemat Z'mirot Yisrael (Sweet Singer of Israel Song)

award in 1996. Although most of her songs have appeared in a series of four song-books she published, and have been reprinted in a variety of other publications (some, apparently, without her permission), Ms. Shemer declined to have her music excerpted for this book.

21. Just weeks after the war, Israel hosted choirs from around the world at its pre-viously scheduled Zimriyah (song festival). Gil Aldema (b. 1928), who had produced choral arrangements of many of Shemer's earlier songs, hastily arranged a version of "Yerushalayim Shel Zahav," which was taught to delegates at the song festival and car-ried home with them later that summer.

22. In 1968 a play called *Ish Hasid Haya* (Once There Was a Hasid) brought tradi-tional Hasidic songs and stories to nontraditional audiences whose only contact with the Hasidic community was in the context of bitter arguments over control of traffic in Hasidic neighborhoods on the Sabbath. The enormous success of this small pro-duction gave rise to the thought that a secular public might enjoy hearing—and singing—new melodies in a Hasidic style (i.e., short, catchy tunes with equally short texts drawn from traditional sources). The Hasidic Song Festival was born the follow-ing year and continued to attract audiences in Israel (and North America, which hosted Israeli performing troupes) for nearly 20 years.

23. Israeli-born Dan Almagor has adapted and translated more than 100 plays for the Hebrew stage, including selections by Shakespeare and several major Broadway productions. He is also a researcher in the fields of literature and folklore and has taught Hebrew in Israel, Great Britain, and the United States. Nurit Hirsh, born in, is one of the country's premier songwriters.

24. Poet Dan Almagor collaborated with Effie Netzer to create this moving song. Netzer, born in Haifa, did his army service as a musician and went on to write many popular songs. He is best known, however, as a prominent song leader, presiding over large crowds at community gatherings, playing his accordion, and using slides to proj-ect song lyrics so that his entire audience could sing along.

25. Born in Kibbutz Shefayim, Rachel Shapira continues to live there and write her very personal poetry. "Mah Avarekh," written in memory of Eldad Kavek, a 21-year-old friend and fellow kibbutznik who died in the Six-Day War, became famous when it accidentally fell into the hands of composer Yair Rosenblum. The popularity of the song brought attention to her other poetry as well. While "Mah Avarekh" was written to memorialize one fallen soldier, it came to symbolize the nation's grief over all its losses.

Yair Rosenblum was born in Tel Aviv. Many of his songs were performed by the army and navy ensembles, for whom Rosenblum not only wrote the songs but also cre-ated the arrangements and conducted the accompanying ensembles. Rosenblum also wrote for films and television, and directed the annual Israel music festivals in Arad.

26. Yaakov Rotblit was born in Haifa and began writing poetry in the aftermath of the Six-Day War. He collaborated with Shmuel Kraus on many of his songs.

27. After "Shir le-Shalom" was endorsed by the Army's chief education officer and introduced by Rosenblum's military entertainment troupe, it quickly rose to the top of the hit parade. Soon, however, the song was banned from public performance because of pressure from other government offices (who felt that the song criticized their peace initiatives) and from the religious right (which objected to the implied criticism of the efficacy of prayer). Ironically, it was revived in the 1990s by the Labor government and used in an effort to secure support for the Oslo peace process begun in 1993 by then prime minister Yitzhak Rabin. The song was sung as the finale of a peace rally on Saturday evening, November 4, 1995, and the prime minister had joined in the singing. Moments later, Rabin was gunned down by a Jewish assassin opposed to the peace process. A sheet in his breast pocket bearing the words to the song was stained with the dying prime minister's blood. At a memorial concert organized a month later, the song was sung again as a remembrance of Rabin and the peace for which he—and the song—stood. Since then, "Shir le-Shalom" has become inextricably linked with the memory of Yitzhak Rabin and the continuing search for peace in Israel.

28. In the imagery of the High Holy Day season, God judges His people on Rosh Hashanah; then, following a ten-day period of repentance, that judgment is sealed on Yom Kippur. According to Jewish tradition, however, God is eager to receive the sincere repentance of His flock and to avert the evil decree. Thus the gates of Heaven are kept open until the last possible moment. The concluding service on Yom Kippur is called *Neilah* (Locking of the Gates [of Heaven]), and the text of Wilensky's song is taken directly from the *Neilah* liturgy.

29. The overarching question whose answer, according to tradition, is sealed on Yom Kippur.

30. Dov Seltzer arrived in Israel at the age of 17. He spent his army service as the first music director of the Naḥal Troupe and wrote many songs for them as well. In addition to the popular songs he composed, Seltzer has also written symphonic music, scores for films, and the music for such successful Israeli plays as *I Like Mike* and *Kazablan*.

31. Government inquiries implicated the Mossad, Israel's intelligence agency, for not adequately perceiving the threat to the nation's security. The careers of Army Chief of Staff Moshe Dayan and Prime Minister Golda Meir ended with their resignations in the wake of continuing investigations.

32. After army service in a military entertainment troupe, Israeli-born Uzi Hitman became a popular songwriter as well as a well-known television personality and performer.

33. The inadvertent scheduling of the Eurovision Festival on Yom ha-Shoah (Holocaust Remembrance Day) or Yom ha-Zikaron (Israel's Memorial Day) necessitated Israel's withdrawal from the competition in some years.

34. Israeli-born Ehud Manor has become a well-known lyricist and radio personality. Avi Toledano, born in Morocco, arrived in Israel at the age of 16 and signed his first recording contract that same year. He has appeared internationally as a performer and has been nominated for a variety of Israel music awards, including the prestigious Kinor Zion (Harp of Zion).

35. The winner of the Eurovision contest is determined by an international panel of judges. Like the Olympic sports competitions that appeared to suffer from partiality among judges during the years of the Cold War between the United States and the Soviet bloc, from time to time the Eurovision judging has seemed to suffer from political positions taken by some judges. The audience in the West German theater where the 1983 concert took place was visibly outraged by the poor estimation "Ḥai" received from two Arab panelists. Two extremely low scores (far below those awarded by the other judges) forced the song into second place in the competition, but it was apparent that "Ḥai" was the popular favorite that year.

36. Ofra Haza's world renown continued as she was heard as the voice of Moses' mother, Yokheved, in Hollywood's successful animated film, *The Prince of Egypt*. Tragically, Haza died of an undisclosed illness in February 2000.

37. Shlomo Gronich was born in Hadera, Israel, and educated at the Institute for Music Teachers in Tel Aviv. In addition to his popular music, Gronich has composed symphonic music as well as scores for film, theater, and dance.

Chapter 11

1. Politically oriented Zionists with attendant youth movements produced a core of Zionist fervor among groups like B'nei Akiva (Hapoel Hamizraḥi), Young Judea (Hadassah), and Habonim (Habonim Dror).

2. Alumni of the Ramaz Upper School who attended the modern Orthodox day school in Manhattan during the 1950s reminisced about their school experiences during interviews conducted in the late 1990s. They recalled being told quite clearly that the *kippot* (yarmulkes) they wore in school and during religious worship were "indoor garments" not to be worn in public. Observant boys who chose to keep their heads covered at all times were advised to wear baseball caps or other more "American" hats, lest they draw unnecessary attention to themselves and their religious beliefs.

3. Egalitarian Jewish prayer communities. The activities of these groups quickly spread beyond a purely ritual sphere to include holiday and life-cycle observances for

intergenerational celebrants. This new interest in a kind of "do-it-yourself" Judaism was evidenced by the publication and subsequent popular response to *The Jewish Catalog*, compiled and edited by Richard Siegel, Michael Strassfeld, and Sharon Strassfeld (Philadelphia, The Jewish Publication Society of America, 1973).

4. Ezrat Nashim (literally, the "arena of women," named after the area of the synagogue into which women are segregated, usually a balcony or behind the thick curtains of the *mehitzah*), was formed in 1971 by feminist activists to advocate for a greater role for women in public ritual. Philosophical differences among women of different denominations manifested themselves in a range of activities, but led ultimately to the ordination of women as rabbis and cantors in the more liberal communities and to the creation of women's prayer groups among the Orthodox.

5. Young people continue to be underrepresented in Federation-sponsored activities and, most glaringly, at the annual General Assembly (GA) of Jewish Federations. Recently, however, a new activism from the Hillel community of Jewish campus organizations and a desire to recruit young professionals to leadership positions in the Jewish community have begun to have an impact on Federation activity and on GA programming.

6. This profusion of Jewish studies in American academe led to, and was ultimately enhanced by, the 1975 establishment of the Association for Jewish Studies, a professional organization of American university faculty involved in research and teaching of Jewish studies. This organization was fueled, as well, by the new generation of American-born scholars whose first courses generally focused on Israel, American Jewish literature, and Holocaust studies.

7. There is no evidence that Peter Yarrow ever gave permission for the appropriation of "Puff, the Magic Dragon," which he wrote and sang with Paul Stookey and Mary Travers in the popular American folk trio, Peter, Paul and Mary. The small audience for the Ruach version did not pose any threat to the royalties due Yarrow or the trio.

8. The five Orthodox members of the group had difficulty choosing a name for themselves. In the midst of an argument that seemed to have no hope of resolution, one of them attempted to terminate the discussion by invoking the talmudic response *tayku,* an acronym meaning that when Elijah the prophet returns (to herald the coming of the Messianic era) he will also provide the answer to the problem. The discussion was effectively arrested, and the name stuck.

9. Some of these early recordings also included selected music from Israel, promoting those Israeli songs whose lyrics resonated with the musical tastes of the "pop" generation and the values of Reform Judaism. These included Arik Einstein's "Ani ve-Atah" ("You and I Will Change the World"); "Ten Shabbat ve-Ten Shalom" (Grant Sabbath and Peace to the City of Jerusalem) by Haim Hefer and Dov Seltzer; and "Shir le-Shalom."

10. Klepper's compositions also form the core of the repertoire of Kol B'seder, a folk/rock/pop duo consisting of Klepper and Rabbi Daniel Freelander (b. 1952). Singing together since their school days in the early 1970s, the duo has recorded several albums. Their performances of Klepper's *"Shalom Rav"* and *"Oseh Shalom"* have passed from the concert stage back to the synagogue from which the lyrics were taken and are now considered "standards" in the Reform community, which can now choose between the original melodies with simple harmony and guitar accompaniment or four-part arrangements for synagogue choir.

11. The opening line from a song by the same name in the recording and accompanying songbook and teachers' guide called *Sing a Song of Zionism*.

12. The group's nonmusical name means "mustache"—an accouterment that all of the members sported at one time.

13. Of course, we have already noted the creation of educationally oriented musical materials written in English. In most cases, though, these songs were sung exclusively in the controlled settings of schools (and some youth groups) and did not overlap into the "popular" arena.

14. Interestingly, at least some "inreach" reverted to Yiddish lyrics, even for some of the more modern strata of the Jewish community for whom Yiddish is not a particularly familiar language. Songs like Mordechai Ben-David's "Moshiaḥ" (Messiah) have become staples at his concerts and at wedding and bar mitzvah celebrations throughout the Orthodox community. The simple refrain *"Moshiaḥ, moshiaḥ, moshiaḥ, ay ay ay ay ay"* is sung enthusiastically, even though many of those listening—or dancing—to the tunes cannot sing along to any of the verses.

15. The liner notes of their recordings make no reference to or acknowledgment of the original songwriters and lyricists. It can only be assumed that, like Ruach at the start of the "Jewish parody" craze, Solomon and company considered their work highly unlikely to compete with the originals. This is certainly true in the cases noted, since all these songs had made millions for their creators and performers in their original, "authorized" versions before being appropriated.

16. Friedman's "Alef-Bet" has become a "classic" of the religious school curriculum and beyond. It was borrowed by the Neginah Orchestra for a recording aimed at Orthodox audiences (and sung as "Alef-Beis") and was parlayed by Barney, the purple dinosaur, into universal fame on public television and in a follow-up videocassette for the preschool set.

17. The biblical story in Genesis 12 has God appearing to a previously unknown figure named Abram, charging him to leave his homeland (and his father's house) and go "to a place that I will show you." Although God spoke directly only to Abram,

(soon to be renamed Abraham, the "father of a multitude" who would descend from him and become the Jewish people), it is obvious from the unfolding of the story that his wife, Sarai (later Sarah) was a partner in his mission—not to mention his progeny. Since Hebrew has no neutral gender, Friedman's song makes Sarai's role clear by adding a feminine rephrasing of God's charge, "*lekhi lakh*" to the masculine "*lekh lekha*" of the Bible.

18. In later years this song became a focal point of feminist seders devoted to celebrating the multifaceted role of women in sustaining Jewish culture (Moses and Miriam's mother, Yoḥeved), resisting Pharaoh (the midwives Shifra and Puah, Miriam, and Pharaoh's own daughter), and forging the free Jewish nation during its wilderness experience (Miriam and Moses' wife, Tziporah).

19. The settings by Fran Avni and Linda Hirschhorn of texts from Marcia Falk's 1998 *The Book of Blessings: New Jewish Prayers for Daily Life, the Sabbath, and the New Moon Festival* (HarperCollins, 1996) would seem to many to have reached a peak in this liberal feminist genre. Others find the texts clearly rooted in ancient Jewish practice and the music to retain a reverence typical of synagogue *nusaḥ* and to be superior to the venerated, but often insipid, music of tradition.

20. The greater prominence of female singers and subjects of special interest to women may represent a novel outgrowth of the American Jewish experience, but it is also a return to ancient practices still being followed in Oriental and Sephardic communities around the world. There, professional female singers continue to be the repository of traditional songs sung regularly at life-cycle ceremonies as well as the composers of modern ballads. For example, an ethnomusicological exploration of the varied Oriental styles of Israeli music recorded one Judeo-Arabic selection celebrating Israel's 1967 victory in reclaiming the old city of Jerusalem while lamenting the loss of the soldiers who fell in that battle.

21. Couples Benjie Ellen Schiller and Les Bronstein, and Billy and Ellen Dreskin were among the founding members of the group, together with David Wolfman and Kyla Epstein.

22. Wolfman and Epstein left the group when they returned to the United States. They were replaced by Erica (Riki) Lippitz and Leon Sher, who joined the group in 1983. Originally, Beth Sher joined the group in 1986 to replace Riki during her term of study in Israel that year, but she remained part of the group after Riki's return.

23. Richie Havens grew up in Brooklyn's Bedford-Stuyvesant section within a diverse community that exposed him to various musical styles. He gravitated toward the sounds of first-generation rock and roll and rhythm and blues. First playing in coffeehouses, Havens became one of the vital new voices of the mid-'60s folk-music scene. His 1969 appearance at Woodstock propelled him to international fame and he went

on to win gold records and a Grammy Award. His version of "Here Comes the Sun" was a hit in 1971. Havens appeared many times on television, his voice has been heard in radio and television commercials, and his songs have been used in the soundtracks of motion pictures.

24. The ensemble was born in Camp Massad in the summer of 1960 under the direction of Stanley Sperber (b. 1942), but the choir's members continued singing upon their return home to the New York metropolitan area. Joined by other high school and college-aged singers, the choir, renamed Zamir (Hebrew for "nightingale") Chorale, inspired a rebirth of American interest in avocational Jewish choral singing not seen since the heyday of the Yiddish choirs of the 1930s. Founding conductor Stanley Sperber was on staff at Massad as a tennis instructor but was transformed into a musician by the growing success of the ensemble. He earned a degree in choral conducting from the Juilliard School in 1969. Upon leaving Zamir in 1972, Sperber began a successful career in Israel, where he spent many years as conductor of Rinat: the National Choir of Israel and as music director of the Haifa Symphony.

25. The success of the Zamir Chorale resulted in the formation of similar choirs throughout America and the eventual evolution of the Zamir Chorale into the Zamir Choral Foundation, devoted to the promotion of Jewish choral music as a means to sustain Jewish culture and educate and unify the Jewish people across the denominational (and generational) spectrum. Founded and directed by Matthew Lazar (who had sung in the Zamir Chorale for many years and succeeded Sperber as conductor of the choir), the Foundation sponsors the annual North American Jewish Choral Festival, a five-day summer gathering of hundreds of singers from across the continent. Burger's "T'filah" quickly gained popularity among the assembled singers and became an anthem of that event as well.

26. Although not written until ten years later, the song tells the story of Burger's experiences singing with the Zamir Chorale on Mt. Scopus in the weeks following the 1967 Six-Day War. While the choir sang, bombs planted by the Jordanian army were being detonated by the Israeli army that now controlled the area.

27. Burger has received commissions from a number of individuals for Jewishly oriented choral and other works, often for the celebration of life-cycle events. The success of his Jewish music has also brought him commissions for secular works, including a series of choral settings for the Northeastern University Chorus.

28. The one selection that has achieved some success in a "folklorized" version is Burger's first choral effort, "T'filah." Although not intended for liturgical use, it has been welcomed into synagogues across America, where it is typically offered as a congregational prayer for Israel, without harmonization or accompaniment. The effort requires adaptation of the melodic line to accommodate group singing, as well as insertion of passages from the original text that Burger did not include. The end result

generally falls far short of the original setting, yet this has not deterred its use. Indeed, cantor-composer Charles Davidson has referred to the work as an "American classic." If adoption without attribution is the sign that a work has truly "arrived," then Burger's setting can be proud to join a long list of composed works that have been sung and even recorded under the heading of "traditional."

29. The New-York-based YIVO Institute for Jewish Research (from the Yiddish acronym for Yiddish Scientific Institute of Vilna) is the preeminent center for the study of Eastern European Jewry and their culture, including the Yiddish language.

30. The National Endowment for the Humanities was among the first to award research grants for rediscovery and documentation of the music of America's varied ethnic communities. More recently, institutions within the Jewish community have provided funding for doctoral research and other explorations of Jewish cultural traditions, including music.

31. In the early years of the twentieth century, companies competing for shares in the new market for 78 RPM recordings went after ethnic audiences. Thus, the catalogues of companies with no apparent connection to the Italian, Irish, or Jewish communities nevertheless featured recordings "guaranteed" to appeal to particular constituencies. In addition to hundreds of klezmer performances, American companies issued recordings by virtuoso *hazzanim* of the "Golden Age" and stars of the Yiddish theater.

32. Potok's novel focuses on a Hasidic boy whose interest in psychology and friendship with a modern Orthodox boy are inconsistent with the values of his father and their cloistered, traditional community. It was set in the 1940s, in the waning days of klezmer's popularity, but Hollywood's penchant for stereotyping communities was not deterred by the somewhat anachronistic inclusion of a klezmer ensemble. Ironically, Kapelye's appearance in the film did much to introduce the form to American Jewish audiences who had not grown up with klezmer music, and contributed greatly to its rebirth.

33. Ziggy Elman (né Henry Finkleman) was the star trumpeter for the band headlined by Benny Goodman and played the "Jewish" solos in the orchestra. Goodman, a clarinetist, did not play Jewish music, but his association with Elman led some to make that assumption.

34. Quoted by Joel Lewis in his article "Heavy Shtetl: The New, In-Your-Face Jewish Music," *Moment*, p. 48.

35. Lewis, Joel, "Heavy Shtetl," pp. 46–50.

36. Quoted in Lewis, "Heavy Shtetl," p. 49.

37. Ritual fringes required on four-cornered garments. The tallit (prayer shawl) worn by traditional Jews during morning prayers is the best-known example of such a garment, but many observant Jewish men also wear a *tallit katan,* a smaller garment worn as a kind of undershirt, whose tzitzit may be worn "in" (most often by the modern Orthodox) or "out" (by Hasidic and other ultra-Orthodox Jews). Some less-than-traditional Jews (including several musicians) have adopted the garment as a means of identifying in an overtly Jewish way, without taking on the other trappings of an observant lifestyle.

38. Sidran's complete lack of familiarity with Jewish liturgy or the sources of much of the music he chose led him to include Nurit Hirsh's setting of "Oseh Shalom," among others.

39. No relation to David Burger.

40. Disturbingly, none of the selections received any attribution at all, leaving the uninitiated listener to assume that all the compositions—and not merely the arrangements—were Burger's.

41. These reviews were excerpted on the *Rebbe Soul* web page.

42. Quoted in "New Jews: John Zorn, Mandy Patinkin, the Klezmatics, Hasidic New Wave and more" by Josh Kun.

Glossary

absolute music—music that exists for the sake of the music itself, without any programmatic agenda (see program music).

ad libitum—improvised.

aliyah—literally a "going up." Those who are called to the reading of the Torah usually ascend to a raised platform from which the reading takes place. Those who decide to settle in Israel are said to be "making aliyah," going up physically to Jerusalem, which is set in the Judean hills, and going up spiritually by living in and being inspired by the Holy Land.

anshe ma'amad—delegations sent to the Jerusalem Temple to represent the people in outlying regions. During their weeklong stays in Jerusalem they became immersed in the musical tradition there, returning as much as possible of the liturgical tradition to their home synagogue rituals.

antiphonal—a form of reciting (or singing) in which the leader alternates with the congregation (or choir), sharing the text between them. "Antiphonal" means literally "opposite sounds"; the portion that each participant recites is thus equal in (approximate) length and importance. In most congregations *Ashre* and other poetic passages are chanted in this manner.

art music—generally, a Western phenomenon; music written by a trained composer and usually conceived with harmonic accompaniment. Art music exists, at least partially, for the sake of the music itself, in addition to elucidating any text that it may set.

Ashkenazic (from the Hebrew word, *Ashkenaz*, designating Germany)—of, or relating to, the customs and rituals practiced by people living in Central and Eastern Europe.

badhan (pl. *badhanim*)—an Eastern European wedding performer, a kind of jester (or stand-up comedian) who acts as an "emcee" for the event while making up songs and stories about the bridal couple and their families.

Baroque—musical era extending from roughly 1685 to 1750. Best typified by the music of Bach, this period featured instrumental music of contrapuntal complexity as well as vocal music with homophonic textures.

bel canto—a style of "beautiful singing" popularized during the Renaissance, which contrasted with the highly embellished singing that became popular during the 19th century.

bimah—in the synagogue, a raised platform from which the precentor chants and the Torah is read.

Birkhot ha-Shahar—literally "dawn blessings," these are prayers of the early morning service. Unlike most Jewish prayers, these are mostly "self"-centered expressions of gratitude for the bounties with which God has blessed the individual worshiper, rather than communal prayers.

burmuelo—a taco-like food eaten by Sephardic Jews. Because it is fried in oil, it is popularly eaten on Hanukkah.

cantillation—the ritual public chanting of the biblical books according to prescribed musical patterns indicated by neumes in a punctuated text.

cantor—a professional synagogue prayer leader. Modeled after the position of the German *kantor,* whose position involved overall musical direction in the Protestant church, the term (and function) was co-opted by the Reform movement in the nineteenth century.

chironomy—a system in which an assistant to the Torah reader utilizes hand movements to prompt the reader's memory of the required chant.

chor-schul—literally, "choral synagogue." This Eastern European innovation merged the new choral tradition emerging in Central Europe with the more traditional synagogue sounds of Eastern Europe.

chromaticism—the use of notes (colors) foreign to the mode/scale on which a work (or portion thereof) is based.

coloratura—elaborate ornamentation of the melodic line in vocal music (and some solo instrumental works).

commedia dell'arte—a dramatic form that originated in Italy in the sixteenth century and flourished throughout Europe until the eighteenth century. The actors in this form devoted themselves to perfecting a personal interpretation of one of many stock characters that they always portrayed. The term can be roughly translated as "comedy of the professional players," because so much of the performance was dependent upon improvisation rather than predetermined dialogue.

Conservative—the movement founded to hold a "middle ground" between the radical new ideas of the Reform movement and the perceived rigidity of the Orthodox movement. Conservative Jews believe that *halakhah* should have a respected position in Jewish life but can be reinterpreted to respond to contemporary needs.

contrafaction—the utilization of a preexisting melody in conjunction with a new or different text. The body of what we call "Jewish music" was enriched by the process of (consciously or subconsciously) adapting popular tunes to liturgical (and other) texts. So-called internal contrafaction involves the adaptation of a melody already known in the community (although perhaps employed for secular purposes) for use with other (usually liturgical) texts. Contrafaction of "foreign" tunes occurs at least as frequently.

contrapuntal—making use of counterpoint, the combination of two (or more) independent musical lines, producing a harmonious texture.

Dhimmi—non-Muslim residents of Arab lands. Despite periodic outbreaks of violence, they are a tolerated presence, enjoying only second-class citizenship but (usually) protected by the government and allowed religious freedom. Jews (and Christians) benefited from this status during the Middle Ages and even through the nineteenth century.

Diaspora—the world outside the homeland (typically used to refer to the biblical land of Israel) into which the Jewish people have been dispersed over time.

Diwan—in the Yemenite community, a collection of traditional *piyyutim,* many by Shalom Shabazzi, the greatest of the Yemenite poets, who flourished during the seventeenth century. Passages from the *Diwan* are traditionally chanted by men during Sabbath and festival afternoons.

ethnomusicologist—one who studies the music of a particular community.

folk song—an anonymous composition, typically of limited range and without more than rudimentary accompaniment. Folk-song texts reflect the human condition in general through songs of work, childhood, love, death, and other aspects of the life cycle, as well as the particular details of the life and values of a given community.

folklorized—adapted into popular culture. The term is used for the appropriation of a composed song (either liturgical or secular) into common usage by the masses, generally in a somewhat simplified form and often without the original accompaniment.

Gemarah—Rabbinic commentary on the Mishnah.

genizah—literally a "hiding place" for old prayer books, Bibles, and other holy articles that can no longer be used. Although it is traditional to bury such items, in some places the act of storing them in a *genizah* (ostensibly until they could be buried) became sufficient.

Gregorian chant—the corpus of Catholic liturgical music, canonized during the reign of Pope Gregory during the sixth century but apparently evolved from the musical traditions of the ancient Jewish Temple. Jewish musicians seeking the "authentic" roots of their heritage assume it to be at the nexus between Gregorian chant and the traditions of the Babylonian and Yemenite Jews, who are direct descendants of the Jews who once worshiped at the First Temple in Jerusalem.

halakhah—literally, "the way;" the body of rabbinic law by means of which traditional Jewish life is led and on the basis of which legal decisions are rendered.

Hallel—service of "praises" taken from Psalms 112–118, recited at morning services on the Pilgrimage Festivals, the new moon, and Hanukkah. A special form of *Hallel* is also contained in the Passover haggadah.

Hanukkah—the Jewish "festival of lights," which lasts for eight days, beginning on the 25th of Kislev (generally some time in December). Hanukkah celebrates the defeat of the Syrian-Greeks who wanted to destroy traditional Jewish life. The lighting of candles for eight nights is the distinctive ritual of the holiday and recalls the legend of a miraculous cruse of oil that lit the Temple candelabrum for eight days, until more consecrated oil could be prepared.

Hasidic—of or relating to the movement known as Hasidism or its adherents, the Hasidim. Founded by Israel ben Eliezer (known as the Ba'al Shem Tov, the "owner of the good name"), Hasidism drew upon mystical teachings to advocate the innate worth of each individual and communion with God through music and other forms of joyous celebration.

Havdalah—a brief ceremony performed at the conclusion of the Sabbath (and other festivals), which separates the holy day from the rest of the week. The ceremony features blessings over wine, spices, and a multi-wicked candle, and traditionally concludes with an exchange of wishes for a good week.

ḥazzan (pl. *ḥazzanim*)—a "professional" prayer leader, generally with expert knowledge of synagogue music tradition and a very pleasing voice (although this last attribute is not a halakhic requirement).

Ḥazzaniyah—a form of *piyyut*, extemporaneously created by the *sheliaḥ tzibbur*. The requirement that a prayer leader be able to improvise such texts led to the emergence of a specially skilled cadre of precentors known as *ḥazzanim*.

ḥeder—traditional Jewish elementary school.

heterophony—literally, "different sounds." Heterophony is characteristic of less-sophisticated musical communities in which exact unison of pitch and/or rhythmic motion are not valued. It is especially prevalent in Oriental Jewish communities, in which singers of varying ages and vocal ranges will all sing in ranges that are comfortable for them without concern for the key in which others are singing.

High Holy Days—the period bracketed by Rosh Hashanah and Yom Kippur, unified by related liturgical rites and distinctive music unique to the season.

homophony—literally, "same sound." In this style, all musical lines are related to a single, predominating melody, and horizontal movement of all parts is in unison.

Hoshana Rabbah—the last day of Sukkot and, according to tradition, the last possible moment to atone for transgressions of the past year. Synagogue rituals include the dashing of willow branches in symbolic destruction of one's sins.

Kabbalah—Jewish mystical teachings, some of which influenced the development of Hasidism. Kabbalah was traditionally treated as a body of esoteric texts that could not be studied by those who had not already attained worldly wisdom (students of Kabbalah were expected to be at least 40 years of age) and who were not well versed in traditional Jewish literature. In the late twentieth century, the Kabbalah attained a good measure of popular interest by those seeking alternate paths to Judaism and spirituality.

kehillah—literally, a Jewish community, especially in Eastern Europe. The *kehillah* was not only a physical and demographic entity, but had its own rabbinic and communal leadership, often imposing taxes to support local Jewish educational and philanthropic institutions. This leadership often served as liaison between the Jewish community and officials of the secular government.

kibbutz (pl. kibbutzim)—collective settlement, the first of which, Degania, was established in Israel in 1903. At Degania and most of the kibbutzim that followed, pioneers worked together and shared equally in the fruits of their labors. Since 1948, increasing numbers of kibbutzim have branched out into industries well beyond simple agriculture (from the manufacture of bathing suits to film animation). As the end of the twentieth century neared, many kibbutzim began to abandon their socialist philosophies, adopting capitalism in an attempt to stem the flow of young people away from the kibbutz and into the cities where they could more freely pursue their private interests.

klezmer—the name given to a form of instrumental folk music and to the European Jewish musicians (*klezmorim*) who performed it at weddings within (and outside) the Jewish community.

Ladino—the language of the Jews of Spain and the Sephardic diaspora; a form of fifteenth-century Castillian Spanish with Hebrew terms for Jewish ritual leaders and value concepts.

landsman—one who comes from the same geographic region (originally of Europe).

landsmanshaftn—organizations whose members all hail from the same (originally European) region. These groups organized synagogues, cemeteries, and benevolent societies to take care of the religious, social, and economic needs of new arrivals.

Levite—a member of the tribe of Levi, descended from Jacob's third son. The Levites were not assigned land in Canaan, but instead were placed in charge of all Temple functions. Moses and Aaron were members of the tribe of Levi.

makam (pl. *makamat*)—Arabic musical mode, typically employed in the performance of Islamic rituals. Similar in character to the music of the Jews, the music of the Arabic "Great Tradition" had a profound influence on the development of synagogue song in the Oriental communities.

Masoretes—literally "conservators of the tradition" who notated biblical grammar and accents, which do not appear in the traditional scrolls, but which had been transmitted orally throughout prior generations.

matbe'ah shel tefillah—literally the "core of prayer," the obligatory prayers of any Jewish service, typically comprising the *Barekhu,* the *Shema* and its blessings, and, the *Amidah.*

melisma—a musical passage that extends a single syllable over several pitches.

midrash (pl. midrashim)—Rabbinic stories composed to enhance understanding of (and/or explain) biblical texts.

minhag Ashkenaz—the liturgical and ritual customs of Ashkenazic Jewry.

minimalism—a school of composition based upon the utilization of limited thematic material that undergoes numerous repetitions and variations.

minyan—quorum of ten adult Jews required to hold statutory prayer services.

Mishnah—Rabbinic commentaries on the Five Books of Moses.

mi-Sinai melodies—tunes from the Ashkenazic liturgical tradition (most associated with the High Holy Days) so universally venerated that it is as if they came literally "from Sinai."

Mitnaggedim—literally "opposers," those of the mainstream Orthodox world who opposed the philosophy and activities of the Hasidim.

mitzvah (pl. mitzvot)—literally a "command," a religious obligation. There are said to be 613 mitzvot incumbent upon Jews to observe. (It is impossible for any one individual to observe all 613, since some are reserved for priests, some only for women, some only for those who own land in Israel, and so forth.)

mode—in Jewish musical tradition, a collection of pitches as well as characteristic motives (musical themes) that are typically employed to convey a distinctive, homogeneous sound to the section of the service that is chanted.

mohel—the individual who performs the ritual circumcision of a male Jew (usually on the eighth day of life) in recognition of the ongoing covenant between God and the Jewish people.

monophony—music that consists of melody only, without independent or supporting accompaniment. This texture is typical of Middle Eastern music, as well as early European song.

motive—a short musical idea on which more sophisticated compositions may be based.

movement—a discreet segment of a larger musical work. Movements usually have clear endings, and rarely bear any musical connection to each other.

musicologist—one who studies the nature and history of music.

nationalism—a populist movement drawing upon folk culture and ethnic traditions to manifest a form of patriotism and national pride. The nationalism that swept through Europe in the late nineteenth century inspired a reexamination by the

Jewish community of the roots of its own cultural and religious traditions (including the Hebrew language) and the incorporation of these elements into new forms of literature and arts.

neumes—symbols that stand for a particular pattern of sung notes.

nig'n—a wordless melody, favored by the Hasidim for its potential to express the full range of human emotions.

nusaḥ—the accepted style of chanting a Jewish religious service (or segment thereof) utilizing prescribed modes and distinctive musical motives. In discussions of liturgy, the term refers to the particular textual rite.

organum—an early form of harmony, based upon four or five degrees of separation between vocal parts.

Oriental—of, or referring to, Jews who live in Near Eastern (mostly Arab) countries.

Orthodox—advocating Jewish life and practice based upon strict adherence to traditional halakhic practice.

ostinato—a repeating musical figure (usually melodic but, alternately, rhythmic) typically appearing in the lowest voice.

Pale of Settlement—a region of northeastern Poland that passed to Russian sovereignty in 1772. Through this transfer, hundreds of thousands of formerly Polish Jews came under the authority of the Czar, who forced his unwelcome new Jewish population to remain within the region of their original settlement (and specifically out of the cities and other major centers of Russian population).

parallel fourths—the harmonic use of four degrees of separation between musical lines for successive pitches.

passacaglia—musical form popular during the late Renaissance and Baroque eras, in which the "melody" lies in the lowest voice (whereas the melody is normally found in the higher voices, where it can be heard best).

Passover (Heb. Pesaḥ)—the springtime festival, beginning on the fifteenth of Nisan, celebrating the Israelites' miraculous delivery from slavery in Egypt. It is so named because the Angel of Death "passed over" the Israelite homes on the fateful night when the firstborn male in every Egyptian home was slain. God's redemption of the Israelites affirmed His promise to Abraham and led to the cementing of the special relationship between God and the Israelite people. In acknowledgment of this special occasion, The Song of Songs—according to Rabbi Akiba, an allegorical treatment of the love between God and Israel—is read in the synagogue on the Sabbath that falls during this weeklong observance.

Pesaḥ (see Passover)

Pesukei de-Zimrah—literally, "passages of song," but referring to the early part of the morning service immediately prior to the arrival of the *matbe'ah shel tefillah*.

Pilgrimage Festivals—the three agricultural festivals of Pesaḥ, Shavuot, and Sukkot, on which Jewish males were required to bring sacrifices to the Jerusalem Temple. The historic and agricultural linkage of these festivals led to their shared traditions of liturgy and *nusaḥ*.

piyyut (pl. *piyyuttim*)—religious poetry. Many such texts were included as part of the regular liturgy, including such familiar passages as *Adon Olam* and *Yigdal*. Other *piyyutim* are added only on Sabbaths (e.g. *Lekha Dodi*) or particular festivals (e.g. *Akdamut*, on Shavuot). Some *piyyutim* have become part of the quasi-liturgical tradition of table songs sung at Sabbath meals. It is estimated that a count of all the *piyyutim* used in the liturgies of all the different Jewish communities would number 35,000, although most of these do not find their way into the regular tradition.

polyphony—literally, "many sounds." In this type of music, especially popular during the Renaissance, each musical line (vocal or instrumental) has its own independent function (although the coincidences of these multiple lines is designed to produce pleasing harmonies).

precentor—individual who leads the chanting of a worship service.

prescriptions—the brief, opening verses of most psalms. These short introductions place the psalms in historical or functional context, ascribe authorship, and/or indicate musical direction. It is believed that these verses may also constitute instructions regarding the tune to which each psalm is to be sung.

priest—a member of the tribe of Levi, specifically those descended from the line of Moses' brother, Aaron. In Hebrew, *Kohen*.

program music—music that has an agenda beyond simply creating pleasing sounds. Music with text is always programmatic, since it reflects the composer's interpretation of that text. Other, purely instrumental compositions may also be programmatic, telling a clearly defined story through music (Prokofiev's *Peter and the Wolf* is a good example of this) or simply establishing a mood or milieu. "Jewish music" is always programmatic in that it intends, at the very least, to provoke an association with the Jewish people and/or the stereotypical sounds one would expect from the particular community or setting generally described in the title of the composition.

Purim—a festival celebrating the deliverance of the Jews of Persia from the hands of a villain who would have murdered them all. The hand of God is not mentioned in the biblical book of Esther read at morning and evening services on this joyous holiday. God's Divine intervention is understood to be revealed through the ascension of a Jewish queen to the throne, the intervention of her uncle in a plot to overthrow the king, and the comeuppance received by the would-be murderer.

purimshpiel—an enactment of the Purim story, the only rabbinically authorized theatrical productions in the Jewish community prior to the nineteenth century.

Reform—a movement that advocates the contemporizing of Jewish practice to meet the needs of the modern era. Emerging in Germany in the early nineteenth century, the Reform movement deleted from the prayer book references to Israel as "Zion" and to wishes for a reconstitution of the ancient Jerusalem Temple. They also rejected *halakhah* as a set of universally binding obligations, leaving the question of personal practice to individual, autonomous choice and making room for the use of accompanied art music in the synagogue.

Renaissance—musical era extending from about 1500 to 1685, characterized by polyphonic music and exaggerated word painting attempting to illustrate the literal meanings of texts through their musical representation.

responsorial—a form of reciting (or singing) in which a leader (either an individual or a trained ensemble, such as a choir) chants most of the text, and the congregation "responds" with a simple, recurring refrain, such as "amen" or "for his mercy endures forever."

responsum (pl. responsa)—a recorded rabbinic answer to a halakhic question. Responsa literature sheds much light on the evolution of Jewish law and liturgy and on distinctions in practice among various ethnic and/or geographic communities.

romancero—a Sephardic folk ballad, typically devoid of Jewish content but sung in Ladino by Jews who retained a cultural attachment to the Iberian peninsula even in their dispersion.

rondo—a musical form featuring a recurring "chorus" interspersed with passages that differ completely from each other. A typical rondo might be diagrammed: ABACADA. . . .

Rosh Hashanah—literally the "head of the year," the anniversary of the creation of the world, and the beginning of the annual season of atonement. It is said that on this date God considers each Jew, measuring good deeds against bad and determining his or her fate for the coming year, including "who shall live and who shall die."

Rosh Ḥodesh—literally the "head of the month," the day on which the new moon is sighted. The minor festival is traditionally a women's holiday.

Seliḥot—penitential prayers begun not later than the Saturday night preceding Rosh Hashanah, ushering in the High Holy Day season and its distinctive musical traditions.

Sephardic (from the Hebrew word, *Sepharad,* referring to Spain)—of, or relating to, the customs and rituals of the Jews of Spain and Portugal and other areas of the Sephardic diaspora into which they were forced to flee following the expulsion of the Jews from Spain in 1492.

serialism (serial technique)—the utilization of all 12 half steps in a conventional Western octave in a predetermined order, a technique pioneered by Arnold Schoenberg early in the twentieth century. Rather than creating an evolving musical work based upon manipulation of a particular theme or melodic fragment, the composer relies upon a 12-tone "row" of his/her creation. The row may be manipulated by the composer in a variety of ways (inversion, retrograde [backward], and retrograde inversion) and may be produced in various keys—even simultaneously—but the sequence of notes in the row may not be violated (although consecutive notes may be played in clusters).

Shabbat Shirah—literally, "the Sabbath of Song," on which Moses' "Song of the Sea" is included in the weekly reading of the Torah (in the portion known as Beshallaḥ, which is normally read during late January or early February). This Sabbath is often an occasion for elaboration of the normal synagogue ritual with choral and other festive singing. In twentieth-century America, this Sabbath initiated a declared "Jewish Music Season" during which special concerts and lectures on Jewish musical tradition were held.

Shaḥarit—morning services (the name derives from the Hebrew word meaning "dawn").

Shavuot—literally "weeks," this festival celebrates the giving of the Torah on Mt. Sinai and is held exactly 49 days (seven weeks) following the Passover celebration (corresponding to the sixth of Sivan). In the synagogue, the book of Ruth is read, paralleling the acceptance of the Torah by Ruth (a convert to Judaism).

sheliaḥ tzibbur (**pl.** *sheliḥei tzibbur*)—literally an "emissary of the community" who serves as a leader of prayers. This person is not required to have special training other than to be an upstanding member of the community who is knowledgeable about Jewish ritual practices. This is not a "formal" position but rather a designation for the person who officiates at any given service.

Shema—the Jewish "credo." "Hear, O Israel, the LORD our God, the LORD is one," recited during every prayer service and by Jews facing death.

shund—the earliest, popular form of Yiddish theater, featuring stock characters in contrived plots; considered "literary trash" by more sophisticated observers.

Simḥat Torah—literally, "rejoicing of the Torah." On this joyous holiday (which also marks the conclusion of the autumn festivals) the yearlong cycle of Torah readings is completed and immediately begun again. The celebrations feature festive dancing with the Torah scrolls at evening and morning services (this is the only time of the year at which the Torah is traditionally read during evening services) and repeated reading of the penultimate verses of Deuteronomy so that all may be called to the Torah.

singerl—literally a "little singer." The *singerl* was a young boy with a beautiful (usually soprano) voice who starred in synagogue choirs and/or as accompaniment to an itinerant *ḥazzan*. These boys often became *ḥazzanim* themselves, learning their trade by studying formally with their mentor and/or simply absorbing the synagogue traditions through constant exposure to them.

sonata—musical work for solo instrument (or solo with accompanying piano).

strophic—based upon patterns of musically—or, in the case of a poem, rhythmically—repeating verses.

suite—a grouping of musical works, generally too short to be perceived as "movements" but related to each other in much the same way.

Sukkot—the final agricultural festival, beginning on the 15th of Tishre, marking the conclusion of the "winter harvest." The ironic book of Ecclesiastes *(Koheleth)* is read, whose purported author, wise King Solomon, seems to have had second thoughts about the efficacy of Jewish study and prayer. (The rabbis have always concluded that apparent heresies should be resolved in favor of the tradition.)

symphony—composition for full orchestra, generally in multiple movements. The classical symphony consisted of four movements following a stereotypical pattern: fast; slow; moderate, but in triple meter; fast. Modern symphonies may have any number of movements whose structure, tempo, and meter do not necessarily follow consistent patterns.

synagogue—a Greek term denoting the local house of worship in which Jews who did not live near the Jerusalem Temple offered their prayers. With the destruction of the Temple and the establishment of Diaspora communities, the synagogue became the center of Jewish religious life and over time took on other functions as a house of meeting *(beit keneset)* or school *(beit midrash).*

tallit—ritual prayer shawl.

Talmud—the "oral law" composed of the Mishnah (Rabbinic commentaries on the Bible) and the Gemarah (Rabbinic commentaries on the Mishnah).

tefillin—phylacteries, comprised of leather straps and boxes containing parchment on which passages from the Torah are inscribed. Tefillin are donned by traditional Jews during morning prayers, bound around one arm (with the box mounted on the muscle of the left upper arm) and around the head (with the box between the eyes). The origin of the practice derives from the biblical instruction (Deut. 6:8) to "bind them (the Torah laws) as a sign on your hand and let them serve as a symbol on your forehead."

Temple—the center of Jewish worship, first built on Mount Moriah in Jerusalem during the reign of King Solomon. That First Temple was destroyed in 586 B.C.E. by the Babylonians but later rebuilt (and referred to, therefore, as the Second Temple) only to be destroyed again in 70 C.E. by the Romans. Sacrifices could only be brought to Jerusalem, and so all male Jews were required to make a pilgrimage to the Temple at least three times each year (see Pilgrimage Festivals). In modern times "temple" (with a small "t") is the term typically used by Reform Jews to identify their local house of worship.

through-composed—composed all the way through without utilizing repeated passages or themes.

Tish'a be-Av—the ninth day of the Hebrew month of Av, the unhappy anniversary of the date on which both the First and Second Temples were destroyed. Observed with fasting and the reading of the biblical Book of Lamentations, the date has also coincided with other tragedies for the Jewish community, including the expulsion of the Jews from Spain in 1492, pogroms throughout Europe, and the start of World War I (which led, indirectly, to additional Jewish suffering and, ultimately, to the murder of six million Jews during World War II).

tone poem—a musical work, especially popular in the nineteenth century, that attempted to tell a story through music.

trio sonata—an instrumental form pioneered by Salamone Rossi and popular during the Renaissance and Baroque eras. It features two high melody instruments (typically violins) and a low melody instrument (usually cello) together with a harmony instrument (harpsichord).

twelve-tone—a musical system using all 12 available pitches rather than just the 8 ordinarily used in traditional Western scales.

tzitzit—ritual fringes required to adorn any four-cornered garment. The tzitzit are tied to the corners of the tallit but in addition, special four-cornered "undershirts," themselves colloquially referred to as "tzitzit" are designed for observant Jews to wear so that they may always wear the required fringes.

wunderkind—literally, "wonder child," a prodigy.

yeshivah—academy of higher Jewish learning. Its students devote their time to study of the Talmud and *halakhah* (Jewish law).

Yiddish—the language of the Jews of Central and Eastern Europe, a combination of German and Hebrew.

Yishuv—the name used to refer collectively to the entity that comprised the pre-state settlements of early Israel.

Yom ha-Atzma'ut—a modern festival commemorating the establishment of the State of Israel on 5 Iyar 5708 (May 14, 1948).

Yom ha-Shoah—the date (28 Nisan) set aside for Jews around the world to remember the victims of the Holocaust.

Yom ha-Zikaron—Israel's Memorial Day, set aside to remember those who fell in defense of the Jewish state, observed on the fourth of Iyar, the day immediately prior to Independence Day.

Yom Kippur—a day of atonement (the 10th of Tishre) marked by fasting and communal prayers requesting forgiveness for sins of the past. It is said that God sits in judgment during this period, and that one's fate for the coming year is sealed on this day.

Zionist—one who supports the idea of a Jewish homeland in Israel. Religious Zionists believe in Israel as the spiritual center of Jewish life and creativity and aspire to observe those commandments (mitzvot) that can only be fulfilled in the Holy Land. Other Zionists simply support the right of the Jews to lead lives of self-determination in their own sovereign state.

Key Figures in the History of Jewish Music

JOSEPH ACHRON (1886–1943)—Virtuoso violinist, composer of the Society for Jewish Folk Music, and teacher.

SAMUEL ADLER (b. 1928)—American-born son of Cantor Hugo Hayim Adler, Samuel Adler has divided his professional time between writing Jewish music (including contemporary settings of *mi-Sinai* tunes), composing secular works, and serving as chairman of the composition department at the Eastman School of Music at the University of Rochester.

YEDIDYAH ADMON (1894–1985)—Russian immigrant of the Second Aliyah whose songs were much influenced both by his teacher, A. Z. Idelsohn, and by the Arab and Bedouin songs he heard around him.

CHAVA ALBERSTEIN (b. 1948)—Popular interpreter of Yiddish and Hebrew songs who began composing some of her own material in the 1980s.

SAMUEL ALMAN (1877–1947)—Russian-born composer whose career flourished following his emigration to London.

AMI (AMINADAV) ALONI (1928–1999)—Israeli-born composer who emigrated to the United States. After spending the early part of his career writing non-Jewish music, in 1970 he turned to music of the synagogue and thereafter divided his time between writing for Hollywood and composing for the synagogue.

ALEXANDER (SASHA) ARGOV (b. 1914)—Composer of hundreds of popular songs for the Israeli army's Chizbatron, for film, and for theater, and winner of the coveted Israel Prize.

BA'AL SHEM TOV (RABBI ISRAEL BEN ELIEZER, ca.1700–1760)— Founder of Hasidism and an advocate for the use of music to enable a closer relationship with God.

PAUL BEN-HAIM (1897–1982)—A member of the Oriental-Pastoral-Mediterranean school of composition who pioneered the merger of Eastern melodies with Western harmonies and forms, which characterized Israel's earliest art music.

LEONARD BERNSTEIN (1918–1990)—American-born and educated pianist, conductor, teacher, and composer of works for the classical concert hall and musical theater. Bernstein was knowledgeable about his Judaism and strongly committed to it, and included several Jewish-themed works among his diverse output.

ABRAHAM WOLF BINDER (1895–1966)—American-born choral conductor, composer, and teacher, he redacted the German tradition of cantillation and was the first to teach it at Hebrew Union College.

ERNEST BLOCH (1881–1959)—Swiss-born composer and teacher whose numerous "Jewish-themed" works for voice, chamber ensemble, and/or orchestra, as well as his *Sacred Service* for cantor, chorus, and full orchestra, earned him a reputation as a "Jewish" composer—despite his larger number of completely "secular" works.

NISSAN BLUMENTHAL (1805–1903)—Cantor of the first choral synagogue in Eastern Europe, who brought four-part music to synagogues there and whose simple, beautiful singing purged Eastern European *ḥazzanut* of the excesses that had lowered standards in the region.

ALEXANDER URIAH BOSKOVICH (1907–1964)—Among the primary exponents of Israel's Eastern Mediterranean school and the first to give it its name.

DAVID BURGER (b. 1950)—Composer and guitarist who worked with Richie Havens before turning to Jewish music and both popular and more sophisticated (especially choral) forms.

ABRAHAM CACERES—Composer of choral and instrumental music for the Jewish community of Amsterdam (flourished in the first half of the eighteenth century).

SHLOMO CARLEBACH (1925–1994)—Charismatic composer and performer who adopted Hasidism and its musical style as a means of doing outreach to

Jews of all backgrounds. Many of his melodies are considered "folk songs" because they have become so ubiquitous.

MARIO CASTELNUOVO-TEDESCO (1895–1958)—Italian-born composer and teacher who wrote several Jewish-themed works throughout his career, including a Sabbath evening service for cantor, mixed choir, and organ.

BARUCH CHAIT—A member of The Rabbis' Sons and an early composer of American Jewish popular music.

AARON COPLAND (1900–1990)—Quintessentially American composer whose brief foray into Jewish music included *Vitebsk: Study on a Hebrew Theme* for piano, violin, and cello, and a setting of the Palestinian (pre-Israel) "folk song," "Banu," by Joel Walbe, commissioned by the Jewish Agency.

CHARLES DAVIDSON (b. 1929)—Conservative cantor, teacher, and composer of synagogue music and Jewish-themed concert works.

DAVID EDELSTADT (1866–1892)—Poet and composer whose songs galvanized the labor movement, even after his untimely death.

JOEL ENGEL (1868–1927)—Composer and ethnographer whose early work helped inspire the creation of The Society for Jewish Folk Music.

ISADORE FREED (1900–1960)—Synagogue composer and theorist whose *Harmonizing the Jewish Modes* remains an important contribution.

DEBBIE FRIEDMAN (b. 1952)—Popular composer and educator whose music has become a staple in many American synagogues and religious schools.

HERBERT FROMM (1905–1995)—Prolific composer of a wide variety of Jewish works for the synagogue and the concert stage. Fromm was born in Bavaria but arrived in the United States in 1937, serving as organist and music director at synagogues in Buffalo, New York, and Boston, Massachusetts.

ELIEZER GEROVITSCH (1844–1914)— A cantor and composer of synagogue music. A product of the St. Petersburg Conservatory, Gerovitsch combined the Russian nationalist style of composition he learned there with Ashkenazic traditions.

SRUL IRVING GLICK (1939–2002)—Canadian composer and choral director who began his career in secular music before devoting himself to Jewish music for the synagogue and the concert stage.

ABRAHAM GOLDFADEN (1840–1908)—A playwright, impresario, and melodist who is regarded as the "Father of the Yiddish Theater."

SHLOMO GRONICH (b. 1949)—Innovative composer of popular Israeli music as well as symphonic music and scores for film, theater, and dance.

CARLO GROSSI (1634–1688)—A Christian singer, organist, and composer commissioned to write music for the Italian Jewish community.

ANDRE HAJDU (b. 1932)—A 1966 immigrant to Israel who studied gypsy tunes in his native Hungary and Hasidic music in his adopted homeland. Hajdu's compositions have been strongly influenced by his ethnomusicological interests, as well as by the enigmatic traditional texts he has chosen to set.

JACQUES FROMENTHAL HALEVY (1799–1862)—Jewish composer of French grand opera and a contributor to synagogue music via Naumbourg's *Zemirot Yisrael.*

LINDA HIRSCHHORN (b. 1947)—California-based cantor, songwriter, performer, and community educator.

NURIT HIRSH (b. 1942)—One of Israel's most prolific composers of popular song.

UZI HITMAN (b. 1952)—Popular Israeli songwriter and performer.

ABRAHAM ZEVI IDELSOHN (1882–1938)—Teacher, composer, and musicologist whose pioneering examination of the music of the many Jewish communities gathered in Israel remains a seminal contribution to the study of Jewish music.

MICHAEL ISAACSON (b. 1946)—American composer of music for various Jewish settings.

MAX JANOWSKI (1917–1991)—Chicago-based cantor and composer whose accessible melodies and recurring refrains made it possible for cantors, choristers, and congregants to feel equally invested in his music.

HANINA KARCZEWSKI (1873–1926)—Music teacher of the Second Aliyah whose songs were among the earliest new compositions to galvanize the *yishuv.*

JEFF KLEPPER (b. 1952)—Reform cantor and composer of many songs that have entered the popular vernacular as "classics" for the synagogue as well as the concert stage.

SHMUEL ("SHMULIK") KRAUS (b. 1932)—One of the first to incorporate the new sounds of "rock" music into his native Israeli song.

MARK KOPYTMAN (b. 1929)—A Russian-born and trained musician whose 1972 arrival in Israel inspired him to revisit the traditional folk materials of the Eastern communities and create new bridges between East and West, though in a much more contemporary idiom.

MARC LAVRY (1903–1967)—A German immigrant to Palestine in 1935 and one of the exponents of the Eastern Mediterranean school.

LOUIS LEWANDOWSKI (1821–1894)—First Jewish choral conductor and a leading composer of the nineteenth-century Reform movement. Many of his melodies and other choral compositions remain standards in the ritual of Jews of all denominations.

CRISTIANO GIUSEPPE LIDARTI (1730–after 1793)—A Christian composer commissioned to write music for the Jewish community of Amsterdam.

JACOB (GIACOMO) MEYERBEER (1791–1864)—Jewish composer of French opera who also wrote some Jewish-themed "secular" works and contributed selections for the synagogue through Naumbourg's *Zemirot Yisrael.*

DARIUS MILHAUD (1892–1974)—French composer and teacher (and long-time United States resident) who utilized the distinctive *nusah* of his native region in a variety of Jewish-themed compositions for the concert stage, as well as a *Sacred Service* for cantor, mixed chorus, and organ (or orchestra).

MOSES MILNER (1882–1953)—Composer from The Society for Jewish Folk Music, one of the few whose entire career was spent in Russia.

PINCHOS MINKOWSKY (1859–1924)—A rabbi and scholar as well as cantor. The 1890 installation of an organ and mixed chorus in his synagogue in Odessa firmly established the music of reform in Eastern Europe.

LEON MODENA (1571–1648)—An Italian rabbinic leader whose 1605 responsum on the permissibility of choral music in the synagogue made possible acceptance of Rossi's art.

NAHUM NARDI (1901–1977)—Pianist and composer who collaborated with Bracha Zefira in arranging Eastern tunes for Western consumption, as well as a writer of songs and other works of his own.

SAMUEL NAUMBOURG (1815–1880)—Leading reformer of French synagogue ritual and editor of the first modern edition of Rossi's music.

DAVID NOWAKOWSKY (1841–1921)—Choirmaster of the Broder Synagogue in Odessa under Nissan Blumenthal and Pinchos Minkowsky. The reforms instituted during the latter's tenure allowed Nowakowsky to emerge as one of the most "Europeanized" of the Eastern composers who contributed much to the Westernization of Russian synagogue music.

BEN-ZION ORGAD (b. 1926)—A German immigrant who arrived in pre-state Israel at the age of nine, Orgad was among the first composers of his generation to develop an intimate knowledge of modern Hebrew. Works setting passages from the Bible and other texts dominate his output, but some of his most successful compositions are settings for solo instruments or small ensembles.

OEDOEN PARTOS (1907–1933)—A Hungarian immigrant to Palestine and a member of the Eastern Mediterranean school.

SHALOM POSTOLSKI (1898–1949)—A Polish immigrant of the Fourth Aliyah, whose songs captured the upbeat spirit of the pioneers he met as a member of Kibbutz Ein Harod.

STEVE REICH (b. 1936)—American composer and exponent of the minimalist school who utilized this technique in his setting of *Tehillim* for four female vocalists and chamber orchestra.

STEPHEN RICHARDS (b. 1935)—American Reform cantor and composer of synagogue music and settings of other Jewish texts.

YAIR ROSENBLUM (1944–1996)—Tel Aviv–born composer of songs popularized by Israel's army and navy ensembles as well as for film and television, who also served as director of the annual Arad music festival.

MORRIS ROSENFELD (1862–1923)—Poet and composer whose songs captured the sorrow of American immigrant sweatshop workers at the turn of the twentieth century.

SOLOMON ROSOWSKY (1878–1962)—Composer of The Society for Jewish Music and a redactor and teacher of the Eastern European school of cantillation.

SALAMONE ROSSI (ca.1570–ca.1628)—A leading musician in the Gonzagan Court in Mantua beginning in 1587 and the first to write choral art music for the synagogue. His 33 settings for combinations of three-to-eight voices were published in 1623 in a collection called *Hashirim Asher li-Shelomo*.

LOUIS SALADIN—French composer of the late seventeenth century, commissioned to write music for the celebration of a circumcision ceremony.

DANIEL SAMBURSKY (1909–1975)—A 1933 arrival in Palestine whose songs for adults and children were as popular as his appearances leading "community singing."

LAZARE SAMINSKY (1882–1959)—An early, active member of The Society for Jewish Folk Music who utilized cantillation motives in his "secular" music (in Russia and later in America), regarding it the "truest" form of Jewish music.

HENRY SAPOZNIK (b. 1950)—Ethnomusicologist and klezmer musician.

HEINRICH SCHALIT (1886–1976)—Viennese-born composer, organist, and teacher who settled in Germany but immigrated to the United States in 1933, and wrote for the synagogue and the stage.

ARNOLD SCHOENBERG (1874–1951)—Viennese-born composer best known for his advocacy of 12-tone and serial techniques. Schoenberg composed several settings of Jewish texts and other Jewish-themed compositions, albeit utilizing his trademark, avant-garde methods.

BARUCH SCHORR (1823–1904)—Cantor/composer of Eastern Europe who brought the music and style of Sulzer to Orthodox synagogues he served in Eastern Europe.

FRANZ SCHUBERT (1797–1828)—A friend of Cantor Solomon Sulzer, Schubert, a well-known composer of art songs, symphonies, and other works, contributed a setting of Psalm 92 to Sulzer's collection of new music for the synagogue.

DOV SELTZER (b. 1932)—After arriving in Israel at the age of 17, Seltzer spent his army service as music director of the Naḥal Troupe and later wrote symphonic music and film scores, as well as music for such successful Israeli plays as *I Like Mike* and *Kazablan*.

NAOMI SHEMER (b. 1930)—A prolific writer of often politically tinged songs, this native of Kibbutz Kinneret has won widespread acclaim and worldwide renown for her "Jerusalem of Gold" and hundreds of other songs.

NOAM SHERRIF (b. 1935)—A native Israeli and student of Paul Ben-Haim, Sherrif is a highly regarded conductor and composer, with special skill in producing colorful orchestrations.

EPHRAIM SKLIAR (1871–1943)—atypical student at the St. Petersburg Conservatory (given his traditional Jewish upbringing) whose work for composition teacher Nikolai Rimsky-Korsakov led the master to urge his Jewish students to explore the roots of their own musical tradition.

ROBBIE SOLOMON (b. 1946)—Cantor/composer and member of the pop/rock group Safam.

NISSAN SPIVAK (1824–1906)—A leading exponent of the "classical" Eastern European synagogue song.

BEN STEINBERG (b. 1930)—Prolific Canadian composer and choral director. Many of his works have become contemporary "classics," especially within the Reform movement.

SOLOMON SULZER (1804–1890)—Chief Cantor of Vienna from 1826 to his death and the leading composer of the nineteenth-century Reform movement. Many of his melodies continue to be standards for Jews of all denominations.

CRAIG TAUBMAN (b. 1957)—Producer, performer, and composer of (secular) music for children and for Jewish prayer and educational settings.

AVI TOLEDANO (b. ca. 1950)—Moroccan-born Israeli performer and composer of prize-winning Israeli songs.

LAZAR WEINER (1897–1982)—Pianist, conductor, teacher, and composer of works for the synagogue and the concert stage, he is most closely associated with settings of Yiddish poetry by American writers of the twentieth century.

MOSHE WILENSKY (b. 1910)—After arriving from Poland in 1932, Wilensky almost immediately became one of the most successful composers of popular song in Israel, winning the coveted Israel Prize for his efforts.

MAX WOHLBERG (1907–1996)—*Ḥazzan*, composer, and teacher. His encyclopedic knowledge of traditional Ashkenazic *nusaḥ* influenced generations of Conservative *ḥazzanim* whom he taught at the Jewish Theological Seminary for more than 40 years.

MOSHE YESS (b. 1944)—Orthodox performer/composer who uses his music to convey traditional Jewish values.

DAVID ZAHAVI (1910–1975)—Israel's first native-born songwriter, whose tunes alternately capture the Eastern flavor of the Oriental immigrants and the European horah, which typified the music of his home kibbutz.

BRACHA ZEFIRA (1911–1990)—Born in Israel, but trained musically in Germany, Zefira resolved to bring the Oriental melodies of her youth to a wider audience by encouraging Western-trained composers to provide them with accompaniments.

MORDECAI ZEIRA (1905–1968)—Fourth Aliyah immigrant to Israel, considered one of the "fathers of Israeli song." Many of his tunes were influenced by the Eastern music to which he and the other immigrant composers were exposed upon their arrival.

ELIAKUM ZUNSER (1836–1913)—A *badkhan* and composer.

Selected Bibliography

Binder, Abraham Wolf, *Biblical Chant* (New York: Philosophical Library, 1959).

Bugatch, Samuel, "The Yiddish Folk Song and Its Importance to Jewish Music," in *The Historic Contribution of Russian Jewry to Jewish Music* (New York: National Jewish Music Council).

Cohen, Debra Nussbaum, "Crossover Dreams: Does Folksinger Debbie Friedman Have the Cure for Our Spiritual Blues?" in *Moment Magazine,* June 1996, vol. 21, no. 3, pp. 50–53ff.

Cohen, Robert L., "Reb Shlomo—Jewish Soul Man" in *Moment Magazine,* August 1997, vol. 22, no. 4, pp. 59–64ff.

Davidowicz, Lucy, *The Golden Tradition: Jewish Life and Thought in Eastern Europe* (New York: Holt, Rinehart and Winston, 1967).

Edelman, Marsha Bryan, "Some Thoughts on Identity and Jewish Music" in *Sh'ma, A Journal of Jewish Responsibility*, 27/518, October 4, 1996.

Freed, Isadore, *Harmonizing the Jewish Modes* (New York: The Sacred Music Press, 1958).

Gerber, Jane S., *The Jews of Spain: A History of the Sephardic Experience* (New York: Free Press, 1992).

Gottlieb, Jack, "Symbols of Faith in the Music of Leonard Bernstein" in *The Musical Quarterly,* vol. X, April 1980, pp. 45–53.

Gradenwitz, Peter, *The Music of Israel, From the Biblical Era to Modern Times* (Portland, OR: Amadeus Press, 1996).

Grout, Donald J., and Claude V. Palisca, *A History of Western Music,* 4th edition, (New York: W. W. Norton & Company, 1988).

Harrán, Don, *Salamone Rossi: Jewish Musician in Late Renaissance Mantua* (Oxford: Oxford University Press, 1999).

Heller, Charles, "Traditional Jewish Material in Schoenberg's *A Survivor From Warsaw,* op. 46" in *Journal of Synagogue Music,* vol. IX, no. 4, March 1980.

Heskes, Irene, *Passport to Jewish Music: Its History, Traditions and Culture* (Westport, CT: Greenwood Press, 1994).

————, editor, *Studies in Jewish Music: Collected Writings of A. W. Binder* (New York: Bloch Publishing Company, 1971).

Hirschberg, Jehoash, "Alexander U. Boskovitch and the Quest for an Israeli National Musical Style" in *Modern Jews and Their Musical Agendas: Studies in Contemporary Jewry, An Annual, vol. IX,* edited by Ezra Mendelsohn (New York: Oxford University Press, 1993).

Hundert, Gershon David, *Essential Papers on Hasidism: Origins to Present* (New York: New York University Press, 1991).

Idelsohn, A. Z., *Jewish Music in Its Historical Development* (New York: Holt, Rinehart and Winston, Inc., 1929).

————, *Thesaurus of Hebrew Oriental Melodies* (Leipzig: Friedrich Hofmeister, 10 volumes, 1914–1933).

Jacobson, Joshua R., "Choral Compositions in the 'Eastern Mediterranean' Style" (Cincinnati, OH: University of Cincinnati, unpublished, 1984).

————, "A Possible Influence of Traditional Chant on a Synagogue Motet of Salomone Rossi" (*Musica Judaica,* vol. X, no. 1, 1987–88), pp. 52–58.

Jacobson, Robert, in liner notes for the Columbia recording *Dybbuk,* M33082, Leonard Bernstein, New York City Ballet Orchestra, 1974.

Keren, Zvi, *Contemporary Israeli Music: Its Sources and Stylistic Development* (Israel: Bar Ilan University Press, 1980).

Kun, Josh, "New Jews: John Zorn, Mandy Patinkin, the Klezmatics, Hasidic New Wave, and More" (*The Boston Phoenix,* October 8–15, 1998).

Kushner, David Z., "The 'Jewish' Works of Ernest Bloch," in *Journal of Synagogue Music,* vol. XIV, no. 1, pp. 28–40.

Levine, Joseph A., *Synagogue Song in America* (Crown Point, IN: White Cliffs Media Company, 1989).

Lewis, Joel, "Heavy Shtetl: The New, In-Your-Face Jewish Music," *Moment,* vol. 20, no. 4 (August, 1995), pp. 46–50.

Liszt, Franz, *The Gypsy in Music,* translated by Edwin Evans (London: William Reeves, 1926).

Maclaren, Alexander, *The Book of Psalms,* vol. 1 (New York: Eaton and Mains, 1893).

Mendelssohn, Ezra, "On the Jewish Presence in Nineteenth-Century European Musical Life" in *Modern Jews and Their Musical Agendas,* vol. IX (New York: Oxford University Press, 1993).

Meyer, Michael A., *Response to Modernity: A History of the Reform Movement in Judaism* (New York: Oxford University Press, 1988).

Milgram, Abraham, *Jewish Worship* (Philadelphia: Jewish Publication Society, 1971).

Milhaud, Darius, *Notes Without Music: An Autobiography,* translated from French by Donald Evans and Arthur Ogden, eds. Roll H. Meyers and Herbert Weinstock (New York: Knopf, 1953).

Modena, Leon, *Hayyei Yehudah,* translated and edited by Mark R. Cohen as *The Autobiography of a Seventeenth-Century Venetian Rabbi* (Princeton: Princeton University Press, 1988).

Nulman, Macy, editor, *Concise Encyclopedia of Jewish Music* (New York: McGraw-Hill Book Company, 1975).

Rosenfeld, Lulla, *Bright Star of Exile: Jacob Adler and the Yiddish Theatre* (New York: Thomas Y. Crowell, Company, 1977).

Roth, Cecil, *The Jews in the Renaissance* (Philadelphia: The Jewish Publication Society of America, 1959).

Rothmuller, Aron Marko, *The Music of the Jews: An Historical Appreciation* (Cranbury, NJ: A. S. Barnes and Co., 1967).

Sandrow, Nahma, *Vagabond Stars: A World History of Yiddish Theater* (New York: Limelight Editions, 1986).

Sapoznik, Henry, *The Compleat Klezmer* (Cedarhurst, NY: Tara Publications, 1987).

———, *Klezmer: Jewish Music from Old World to Our World* (New York: McMillan Books, 1999)

Scherman, Rabbi Nosson, *The Complete Artscroll Machzor for Rosh Hashanah* (Brooklyn, NY: Mesorah Publications, Ltd., 1985).

Sendrey, Alfred, *Music in Ancient Israel* (New York: Philosophical Library, 1969).

———, *The Music of the Jews in the Diaspora, Up to 1800* (New York: Thomas Yoseloff, 1970).

Shahar, Natan, "The Eretz Israeli Song and the Jewish National Fund" in *Modern Jews and Their Musical Agendas: Studies in Contemporary Jewry, An Annual,* vol. IX, edited by Ezra Mendelsohn (New York: Oxford University Press, 1993).

Sheriff, Noam, liner notes for *Noam Sheriff "La Folia:" Variations for Orchestra; Music for Woodwinds, Trombone, Piano and Bass; Adkamoth Lemoed,* Gary Bertini, Jerusalem Symphony Orchestra, Israel Music Anthology, vol. 9, ATD 8601, Music in Israel, 1985.

Slobin, Mark, *Chosen Voices: The Story of the American Cantorate* (Urbana: University of Illinois Press, 1989).

Spector, Johanna, "The Role of Ethnomusicology in the Study of Jewish Music," *Musica Judaica,* vol. IV, no. 1, pp. 20–31.

Strassburg, Robert, *Ernest Bloch: Voice in the Wilderness* (Los Angeles: University of California Press, 1977).

Weisser, Albert, "Jewish Music in Twentieth-Century United States: Four Representative Figures" (New York: Jewish Theological Seminary of America, unpublished, 1980).

———, "Lazar Weiner: A Tribute," *Congress Bi-Weekly* 34, New York, November 20, 1967.

———, *The Modern Renaissance of Jewish Music: Events and Figures, Eastern Europe and America* (New York: Bloch Publishing Company, 1954).

Werner, Eric, *A Voice Still Heard: The Sacred Songs of the Ashkenazic Jews* (State College: Pennsylvania State University Press, 1976).

Wertheimer, Jack, *The American Synagogue: A Sanctuary Transformed* (New York: Cambridge University Press, 1987).

Sources for Music Materials Referenced in this Book:

Although some of the music excerpted in this volume does not appear in print, many of the selections were published in their entirety. Original sources are provided for items that are no longer in print; these may be available in libraries devoted to Jewish music or in private collections. While several songs appear in more than one volume, the following list provides selected sources from recent American and Israeli publications:

Chapter 2 (pages 11–38)

"La Rosa Enflorece" (aka "Los Bilbilicos")—*The Nico Castel Ladino Song Book,* arr. Richard J. Neumann (Cedarhurst, NY: Tara Publications, 1981).

"Durme, Hermozo Hijico"—*The Nico Castel Ladino Song Book,* arr. Richard J. Neumann (Cedarhurst, NY: Tara Publications, 1981).

"Scalerica De Oro"—*The Nico Castel Ladino Song Book,* arr. Richard J. Neumann (Cedarhurst, NY: Tara Publications, 1981).

"Cuando El Rey Nimrod"—*The Nico Castel Ladino Song Book,* arr. Richard J. Neumann (Cedarhurst, NY: Tara Publications, 1981).

"Unter dem Kind's Vigele"—*A Treasury of Jewish Folksong,* selected and edited by Ruth Rubin (New York: Schocken Books, 1950).

"Bulbes" (aka "Zuntig-Bulbe")—*A Treasury of Jewish Folksong,* selected and edited by Ruth Rubin (New York: Schocken Books, 1950).

"Tum Balalaika"—*A Treasury of Jewish Folksong,* selected and edited by Ruth Rubin (New York: Schocken Books, 1950).

"Gey Ikh Mir Shpatsirn"—*The Yiddish Song Book,* edited by Jerry Silverman (Briarcliff Manor, NY: Scarborough House, 1983).

"Nig'n" attributed to the Ba'al Shem Tov—*Songs of the Chassidim,* vol. 2, compiled, edited, and arranged by Velvel Pasternak (Plainview, NY: Harold Branchy Publishing, Inc., 1971).

"Az Der Rebbe" (aka As Der Rebe Tantst)—*Pearls of Yiddish Song,* compiled by Eleanor Gordon Mlottek and Joseph Mlotek (New York: Workmen's Circle, 1988).

Chapter 3 (pages 39–52)

Halleluyah (Psalm 146) by Salamone Rossi—*HaShirim Asher Lish'lomo,* vol. I, edited by Fritz Rikko (New York: The Jewish Theological Seminary of America, 1967).

Barekhu by Salamone Rossi—*HaShirim Asher Lish'lomo,* vol. I, edited by Fritz Rikko (New York: The Jewish Theological Seminary of America, 1967).

Cantata ebraica in dialogo by Carlo Grossi (Tel Aviv: Israel Music Publications Limited, 1965).

Ḥishki, Ḥizki by Abraham Caceres (Tel Aviv: Israel Music Publications Limited, 1965).

Canticum Hebraicum by Louis Saladin (Tel Aviv: Israel Music Publications Limited, 1965).

Chapter 4 (pages 53–70)

Tov le-Hodos by Franz Schubert—*Schir Zion* by Solomon Sulzer, reprinted as part of the *Out of Print Classics Series of Synagogue Music,* vol. 8 (New York: Sacred Music Press, 1954).

Shema—Schir Zion by Solomon Sulzer, reprinted as part of the *Out of Print Classics Series of Synagogue Music,* vol. 8 (New York: Sacred Music Press, 1954).

Ki mi-Tziyon—Schir Zion by Solomon Sulzer, reprinted as part of the *Out of Print Classics Series of Synagogue Music,* vol. 8 (New York: Sacred Music Press, 1954).

Psalm 92 —Todah W'Simrah by Louis Lewandowski, reprinted as part of the *Out of Print Classics Series of Synagogue Music,* vol. 10 (New York: Sacred Music Press, 1954).

Se'u Shearim—Z'mirot Yisrael by Samuel Naumbourg, reprinted as part of the *Out of Print Classics Series of Synagogue Music,* vol. 15 (New York: Sacred Music Press, 1954).

El Erekh Apayim—N'ginoth Baruch Schorr, by Baruch Schorr (New York: Bloch Publishing House, 1906).

Avinu Malkenu—Immortal Synagogue Choral Music for Cantor and Choir, vol. 3, series 2 (Toronto: Mydas Music Company, 1981).

Ḥatsi Kaddish—Cantorial Anthology, vol. IV (Shabbat), edited by Gershon Ephros (New York: Bloch Publishing House, 1953).

Pesaḥ Lonu Sha'ar—Schlussgebet—Jom Kippur by David Nowakowsky, reprinted as part of the *Out of Print Classics Series of Synagogue Music,* vol. 23 (New York: Sacred Music Press, 1954).

*Tel Ten—*by Eliezer Gerovitsch—*Shire T'filoh* by Eliezer Gerovitsch, reprinted as part of the *Out of Print Classics Series of Synagogue Music,* vol. 3 (New York: Sacred Music Press, 1954).

Chapter 5 (pages 71–94)

"Farn Obsheyd" by Ephraim Skliar (St. Petersburg, Society for Jewish Folk Music *[Gesellschaft für jüdische Volksmusik],* 1914).

"Lomir Zikh Iberbetn"—arranged by Solomon Rosowsky, in *The St. Petersburg Society for Jewish Folk Music,* edited by Velvel Pasternak (Cedarhurst, NY: Tara Music Publications, 1998).

"In Ḥeder" by Moses Milner—in *The St. Petersburg Society for Jewish Folk Music,* edited by Velvel Pasternak (Cedarhurst, NY: Tara Music Publications, 1998).

"Unter dem Kind's Vigele"—*A Treasury of Jewish Folksong,* selected and edited by Ruth Rubin (New York: Schocken Books, 1950).

"Hebräische Vieglied" (Hebrew Lullabye) by Joseph Achron (St. Petersburg: Society for Jewish Folk Music *[Gesellschaft für jüdische Volksmusik],* 1914).

"Hebräische Tanz" (Hebrew Dancc) by Joseph Achron (St. Petersburg: Society for Jewish Folk Music *[Gesellschaft für jüdische Volksmusik],* 1914).

"Schir Haschirim" by Lazare Saminsky, in *Songs,* op. 28. Polyglot (Vienna: Universal-Edition, c. 1928).

"Haftarah" by Samuel Alman (Paris, Edition Salabert, c. 1934).

Chapter 6 (pages 95–124)

"Rozhinkes mit Mandlen" by Abraham Goldfaden in *The Yiddish Song Book* edited by Jerry Silverman (Briarcliff Manor, NY: Scarborough House, 1983).

"A Brivele der Mamen" by Solomon Shmuelvitz in *Songs of the American Jewish Experience*, compiled and arranged by Neil Levin (Chicago: Board of Jewish Education of Metropolitan Chicago, 1976).

"Mayn Rue Platz" by Morris Rosenfeld in *The Yiddish Song Book* edited by Jerry Silverman (Briarcliff Manor, NY: Scarborough House, 1983).

"Mayn Yingele" by Morris Rosenfeld in *The Yiddish Song Book* edited by Jerry Silverman (Briarcliff Manor, NY: Scarborough House, 1983).

"Leb'n Zol Kolombus" by Arnold Perlmutter and Herman Wohl in *The Yiddish Song Book* edited by Jerry Silverman (Briarcliff Manor, NY: Scarborough House, 1983).

"Die Grine Kuzine" by Jacob Leiserowitz and Abe Schwartz in *Songs of the American Jewish Experience,* compiled and arranged by Neil Levin (Chicago: Board of Jewish Education of Metropolitan Chicago, 1976).

"Vakht Oyf" by David Edelstadt in *Songs of the American Jewish Experience,* compiled and arranged by Neil Levin (Chicago: Board of Jewish Education of Metropolitan Chicago, 1976).

"In Kamf" by David Edelstadt in *Songs of the American Jewish Experience,* compiled and arranged by Neil Levin (Chicago: Board of Jewish Education of Metropolitan Chicago, 1976).

Chapter 7 (pages 125–148)

Borkhu by Abraham Wolf Binder in *Ḥibbath Shabbath (Love of the Sabbath) Friday Evening Service* by A. W. Binder (New York: Transcontinental Music Publications, 1957).

Shaḥar Avakeshkha by Isadore Freed for Cantor, SATB Choir and Organ (New York: Transcontinental Music Publications, 1956).

Avodat Ha-Kodesh (Sacred Service) by Ernest Bloch (New York: Broude Brothers Limited, 1962).

Mekhalkel Ḥayim be-Ḥesed by Max Wohlberg in *Azamer be-Odi (I Will Sing While I Am Here): Congregational Melodies by Max Wohlberg,* edited by Cantor Sheldon M. Levin (New York: Cantors Assembly, 1990).

Yismeḥu by Max Janowski for Cantor and Unison Choir (Chicago: Friends of Jewish Music, 1968).

Shiru L'Adonai by Ben Steinberg from *Pirchay Shir Kodesh* by Ben Steinberg (New York: Transcontinental Music, 1964).

Anim Zemirot by Herbert Fromm, from *Six Short Anthems* for soloists, SATB Choir and Organ (New York: Transcontinental Music, 1966).

Ashamnu by Charles Davidson, from *The Hush of Midnight* by Charles Davidson (Elkins Park, PA: Ashborne Music, 1970).

"Esa Einai" by Shlomo Carlebach, in *The Shlomo Carlebach Songbook,* arranged by Milt Okun (New York: Zimrani Records, Inc. 1970).

"ve-Ha'er Einenu" by Shlomo Carlebach, in *The Shlomo Carlebach Anthology* compiled and edited by Velvel Pasternak (Cedarhurst, NY: Tara Publications, 1992).

"Erev Shel Shoshanim" by Yosef Hadar in *The International Jewish Songbook,* compiled, edited, and arranged by Velvel Pasternak (Cedarhurst, NY: Tara Publications, 1994).

"Ahavat Olam " by Aminadav Aloni, for Cantor, SATB Choir and Keyboard (New York: Transcontinental Music Publications, 1986).

Chapter 8 (pages 149–186)

"Tzela-Tzeldi" by Lazar Weiner in *Album of Eleven Songs for Voice and Piano* (New York: Metro Music, 1948).

"Volt Mayn Tate Raykh Geven" by Lazar Weiner in *Six Yiddish Art Songs for Voice and Piano* (New York: Transcontinental Music Publications, 1968).

"A Gebet" by Lazar Weiner in *Six Yiddish Art Songs for Voice and Piano* (New York: Transcontinental Music Publications, 1968).

"Ergetz Vayt" by Lazar Weiner in *Five Yiddish Songs for Voice and Piano* (Transcontinental Music Publications, 1953).

"A Bord" by Lazar Weiner in *Album of Eleven Songs for Voice and Piano* (New York: Metro Music, 1948).

"Di Reyd Funem Novi" by Lazar Weiner in *Five Jewish Art Songs for Solo Voice and Piano* (New York: Mercury Music Corportation, 1961, currently available through Transcontinental Music Publications).

"Yiddish" by Lazar Weiner, in *Album of Eleven Songs for Voice and Piano* (New York: Metro Music, 1948).

A Survivor From Warsaw, op. 46 by Arnold Schoenberg (Los Angeles: Belmont Music Publishers, 1977).

Symphony no. 1 *(Jeremiah)* by Leonard Bernstein, for full orchestra and mezzo-soprano soloist, (New York: Boosey and Hawkes, 1942).

Chichester Psalms by Leonard Bernstein, for mixed choir, boy solo, and orchestra (New York: G. Schirmer, Inc., 1965).

Tehillim by Steve Reich, for solo voices and orchestra (New York: Boosey and Hawkes, 1981).

Chapter 9 (pages 187–220)

"Di Sokhe" by Eliakum Zunser in *Anthology of Yiddish Folksongs,* vol. IV, edited by Aharon Vinkovetzky, Abba Kovner, and Sinai Leichter (Jerusalem: Mount Scopus Publications by the Magnes Press, 1987).

"Ya Hai Li Li," in *Songs of Zion,* compiled and edited by Harry Coopersmith (New York: Behrman House, 1942).

"Birkat Am" (aka "Tehezaknah") in *Songs of Zion,* compiled and edited by Harry Coopersmith (New York: Behrman House, 1942).

"Hushu, Ahim, Hushu" in *Sefer ha-Shirim la-Talmid,* vol. II, compiled by Gil Aldema and Dr. Natan Shachar (Tel Aviv: Culture and Education Enterprises Ltd. [The Nissimov Music Library], 1995).

"Hatikvah" in *The International Jewish Songbook,* compiled, edited, and arranged by Velvel Pasternak (Cedarhurst, NY: Tara Publications, 1994).

"ve-Taher Libenu" in *Songs of Zion,* compiled and edited by Harry Coopersmith (New York: Behrman House, 1942).

"El Yivneh ha-Galil" in *Sefer ha-Shirim la-Talmid,* vol. I, compiled by Gil Aldema and Dr. Natan Shachar (Tel Aviv: Culture and Education Enterprises Ltd. [The Nissimov Music Library], 1995).

"Po be-Eretz Ḥemdat Avot" in *Sefer ha-Shirim la-Talmid,* vol. I, compiled by Gil Aldema and Dr. Natan Shachar (Tel Aviv: Culture and Education Enterprises Ltd. [The Nissimov Music Library], 1995).

"Ani Ma'amin" (aka "Saḥki, Saḥki") in *Songs of Zion,* compiled and edited by Harry Coopersmith (New York: Behrman House, 1942).

"Anu Nihyeh Harishonim" in *Sefer ha-Shirim la-Talmid,* vol. I, compiled by Gil Aldema and Dr. Natan Shachar (Tel Aviv: Culture and Education Enterprises Ltd. [The Nissimov Music Library], 1995).

"El Rosh ha-Har" (aka "ha-Ma'apilim") by Hanina Karczewski in *Sefer ha-Shirim la-Talmid,* vol. I, compiled by Gil Aldema and Dr. Natan Shachar (Tel Aviv: Culture and Education Enterprises Ltd. [The Nissimov Music Library], 1995).

"Numi, Numi Yaldati" by Joel Engel in *Sefer ha-Shirim la-Talmid,* vol. I, compiled by Gil Aldema and Dr. Natan Shachar (Tel Aviv: Culture and Education Enterprises Ltd. [The Nissimov Music Library], 1995).

"Pakad Adonai" (aka "le-Moladeti") in *Songs of Zion,* compiled and edited by Harry Coopersmith (New York: Behrman House, 1942).

"Havu Levenim" by Mordechai Zeira in *Songs of Zion,* compiled and edited by Harry Coopersmith (New York: Behrman House, 1942).

"Sa'enu" in *Sefer ha-Shirim la-Talmid,* vol. II, compiled by Gil Aldema and Dr. Natan Shachar (Tel Aviv: Culture and Education Enterprises Ltd. [The Nissimov Music Library], 1995).

"Orḥah Bamidbar" by David Zahavi in *Sefer ha-Shirim la-Talmid,* vol. I, compiled by Gil Aldema and Dr. Natan Shachar (Tel Aviv: Culture and Education Enterprises Ltd. [The Nissimov Music Library], 1995).

"Shedemati" by Yedidyah Admon in *Sefer ha-Shirim la-Talmid,* vol. II, compiled by Gil Aldema and Dr. Natan Shachar (Tel Aviv: Culture and Education Enterprises Ltd. [The Nissimov Music Library], 1995).

"Olim" (aka "Ha'apilu") by Shalom Postolski in *Songs of Zion,* compiled and edited by Harry Coopersmith (New York: Behrman House, 1942).

"Me'al Pisgat Har ha-Tzofim" (aka "Yerushalayim") in *Songs of Zion,* compiled and edited by Harry Coopersmith (New York: Behrman House, 1942).

"Shir ha-Emek" (aka "Ba'ah Menuḥa) by Daniel Sambursky in *Songs of Zion,* compiled and edited by Harry Coopersmith (New York: Behrman House, 1942).

"Yesh Li Gan" in *Songs of Zion,* compiled and edited by Harry Coopersmith (New York: Behrman House, 1942).

Roni Akara by Paul Ben Haim, © Israel Music Institute, 1956, available through Theodore Presser Music, 588 North Gulph Road, King of Prussia, PA 19406.

"Mi Nishikani" in *Saperi Tama: The Diwan Songs of the Jews of Central Yemen,* by Naomi and Avner Bahat (Tel Aviv: Beth Hatefutsoth, 1995).

Chapter 10 (pages 221–248)

"Ha'amini Yom Yavo" by Menashe Baharav in *Sing Along with Effie Netzer,* vol. II, edited by Henry Klausner and Sami Zur (Tel Aviv: Culture and Education Enterprises, Ltd., 1988).

"ha-Finjan" in *The International Jewish Songbook,* compiled, edited and arranged by Velvel Pasternak (Cedarhurst, NY: Tara Publications, 1994).

"Bab El Wad" by Shmuel Pershko in *Sing Along with Effie Netzer,* vol. II, edited by Henry Klausner and Sami Zur (Tel Aviv: Culture and Education Enterprises, Ltd., 1988).

"Hayu Zemanim" by Moshe Wilensky in *Sing Along with Effie Netzer,* vol. I, edited by Henry Klausner and Sami Zur (Tel Aviv: Culture and Education Enterprises, Ltd., 1983).

"la-Midbar" by Sasha Argov in *Sing Along with Effie Netzer,* vol. I, edited by Henry Klausner and Sami Zur (Tel Aviv: Culture and Education Enterprises, Ltd., 1983).

"ha-Sela ha-Adom" in *Sing Along with Effie Netzer,* vol. II, edited by Henry Klausner and Sami Zur (Tel Aviv: Culture and Education Enterprises, Ltd., 1988).

"Mul Har Sinai" in *Sing Along with Effie Netzer,* vol. I, edited by Henry Klausner and Sami Zur (Tel Aviv: Culture and Education Enterprises, Ltd., 1983).

"Erev Ba" by Aryeh Levanon in *The International Jewish Songbook,* compiled, edited, and arranged by Velvel Pasternak (Cedarhurst, NY: Tara Publications, 1994).

"Yerushalayim Sheli" by Nurit Hirsh *in Jerusalem in Song,* compiled, edited, and arranged by Velvel Pasternak (Cedarhurst, NY: Tara Publications, 1995).

"Mah Avarekh" by Yair Rosenblum in *Sing Along with Effie Netzer,* vol. II, edited by Henry Klausner and Sami Zur (Tel Aviv: Culture and Education Enterprises, Ltd., 1988).

"Shir le-Shalom" by Yair Rosenblum in *Sing Along with Effie Netzer,* vol. II, edited by Henry Klausner and Sami Zur (Tel Aviv: Culture and Education Enterprises, Ltd., 1988).

"Petaḥ Lanu Sha'ar" by Moshe Wilensky in *Tamid Kalaniyot Tifraḥnah* (Hakibbutz Hameyuḥad, 1979).

"ha-Milḥamah ha-Aḥaronah" by Dov Seltzer in *The International Jewish Songbook,* compiled, edited, and arranged by Velvel Pasternak (Cedarhurst, NY: Tara Publications, 1994).

"Noladeti le-Shalom" by Uzi Hitman in *The International Jewish Songbook,* compiled, edited, and arranged by Velvel Pasternak (Cedarhurst, NY: Tara Publications, 1994).

"Ḥai" by Avi Toledano in *The International Jewish Songbook,* compiled, edited, and arranged by Velvel Pasternak (Cedarhurst, NY: Tara Publications, 1994).

"ha-Masa le-Eretz Yisrael" by Shlomo Gronich in *Sing Along with Effie Netzer,* vol. II, edited by Henry Klausner and Sami Zur (Tel Aviv: Culture and Education Enterprises, Ltd., 1988).

Chapter 11 (pages 249–278)

"Rabos Maḥashovos" by Baruch Chait in *Rejoice: Songs in Modern Hassidic Style,* compiled, edited, and arranged by Velvel Pasternak (Cedarhurst, NY: Tara Publications, 1973).

"Ura Kevodi" by Moshe Greineman in *Rejoice: Songs in Modern Hassidic Style,* compiled, edited, and arranged by Velvel Pasternak (Cedarhurst, NY: Tara Publications, 1973).

"Am Yisrael Ḥai" by Shlomo Carlebach in *The Shlomo Carlebach Songbook,* arranged by Milt Okun (New York: Zimrani Records, Inc. 1970).

"Yah Ribon Olam" in *Z'mirot Anthology: Traditional Sabbath Songs for the Home,* compiled and edited by Neil Levin (Cedarhurst, NY: Tara Publications, 1981).

"Or Zaru'a" by Jeff Klepper in *The Kol B'seder Songbook* by Jeff Klepper and Dan Freelander (Cedarhurst, NY: Tara Publications, 1996).

"Kippah" by Susan Nanus and Jeff Klepper in *Songs for Growin'* by Jeff Klepper and Dan Freelander (Cedarhurst,NY, Tara Publications, 1991).

"Master of All Things" by Craig Taubman in *Craig Taubman Songbook* (Los Angeles: Best Printing, 1987).

"Ana Adoshem" by Robbie Solomon in *Songs of Safam: 1976–1983* by Safam (Newton Centre, MA: Safam, 1983).

"World of Our Fathers" by Robbie Solomon in *Songs of Safam: 1976–1983* by Safam (Newton Centre, MA: Safam, 1983).

"Miriam's Song" by Debbie Friedman in *And You Shall Be a Blessing* (San Diego: Sounds Write Productions, Inc., 1988).

"T'filah Lishlom Medinat Yisrael" by David Burger (New York: Transcontinental Music, 1990).

"A Nakht in Gan Eydn" in *The Compleat Klezmer* by Henry Sapoznik (Cedarhurst, NY: Tara Publications, 1987).

List of Musical Illustrations

Note: Illustrations followed with an "asterisk" (*) are excerpted on the accompanying CD. For a separate listing of CD contents, see page 378.

Chapter 2 (pages 11–38)

2.1   Syllabic chant for weekdays from the Babylonian Jewish community*

2.2   Melismatic improvisational chant from the Babylonian Jewish community*

2.3   "La Rosa Enflorece" love song from the Sephardic tradition*

2.4   "Tzur mi-Shelo," Sabbath table song adapted from "La Rosa Enflorece"*

2.5   "Durme, Hermozo Hijico," lullaby from the Sephardic tradition

2.6   "Scalerica D'Oro," wedding song from the Sephardic tradition

2.7   "Cuando el Rey Nimrod" from the Sephardic tradition*

2.8   "Mama, Mirame Las Gambas" from the Sephardic community*

2.9   "Avot," *mi-Sinai* tune for Sabbath *amidah,* from the Ashkenazic tradition

2.10   "Kol Nidre," *mi-Sinai* tune for Yom Kippur from the Ashkenazic tradition

2.11   *mi-Sinai* tune for the High Holy Day *Ma'ariv* service in the Ashkenzic tradition*

2.12   Arabic Makam *Bayat*/Ashkenazic *Magen Avot* mode

2.13   Nonmetrical Arabic tune in Makam *Bayat*

2.14   "Debka Daluna" popularized in Israel

2.15   Arabic Makam *Siga*/ Ashkenazic *Hashem Malakh* mode

2.16   Arabic Makam *Sasgar*/Ashkenazic *Viddui* mode

2.17   Arabic Makam *Hijaz*/Ashenazic *Ahavah Rabbah* mode

2.18   Excerpt from "Unter dem Kind's Vigele," traditional Yiddish lullaby

2.19   "Bulbes," Yiddish folk song*

2.20   "Tum Balalaika," Yiddish folk song

2.21   "Gey Ikh Mir Shpatzirn," Yiddish folk song*

2.22   Nig'n, wordless Hasidic song attributed to the Ba'al Shem Tov*

2.23   "Az Der Rebbe," traditional Yiddish song

Chapter 3 (pages 39–52)

3.1 Opening "Halleluyah" from *Halleluyah, Halleli Nafshi* (Psalm 146) by Salamone Rossi

3.2 Traditional nusaḥ for *Barekhu* on Sabbath evening

3.3 Traditional congregational response to *Barekhu* on Sabbath evening

3.4 Opening (melismatic) passage from Rossi's setting of *Barekhu**

3.5 Rossi's (syllabic) treatment of God's name as it appears in his setting of *Barekhu**

3.6 Rossi's (syllabic) treatment of the "congregational response" in his setting of *Barekhu**

3.7 Excerpt from "Sova Semaḥot" chorus from *Cantata ebraica* by Carlo Grossi*

3.8 Copy of the original manuscript for "Ḥishki, Ḥizki" by Abraham Casseres

3.9 Excerpt from "Yeled ha-Yulad" in *Canticum Hebraicum* by Ludovico Saladin

Chapter 4 (pages 53–70)

4.1 Facsimile of "Allgegenwart" from Stuttgart hymnal of 1836

4.2 Excerpt from *Tov le-Hodos* by Franz Schubert

4.3 Opening motives of *Shema* and *Ki mi-Tziyon* by Salomon Sulzer*

4.4 Concluding section from setting of Psalm 92 by Louis Lewandowski*

4.5 Excerpt from *Se'u Shearim* by Samuel Naumbourg

4.6 Excerpt from *El Erekh Apayim* by Baruch Schorr

4.7 Excerpt from *Avinu Malkenu* by Nissan Blumenthal

4.8 Excerpt from *Ḥatsi Kaddish* for Friday evening by Pinchos Minkowsky

4.9 Excerpt from *Pesaḥ Lonu Sha'ar* by David Nowakowsky

4.10 Excerpt from *Tal Ten* by Eliezer Gerovitsch

Chapter 5 (pages 71–94)

5.1 Excerpt from "Farn Obsheyd" by Ephraim Skliar*

5.2 Excerpt from "Lomir Zikh Iberbetn" by Solomon Rosowsky*

5.3 Traditional folk song "In a Kleyner Shtibele"

5.4 Excerpt from Joseph Achron's setting of "In a Kleyner Shtibele" for voice and piano*

5.5 Traditional *lernsteiger* utilized in Milner's setting of "In Ḥeder"*

5.6 Excerpt from "Unter dem Kind's Vigele," traditional Yiddish lullaby*

5.7 Excerpt from Joseph Achron's setting of "Hebräische Viglied" for violin and piano*

5.8 Traditional source material utilized by Achron in "Hebräische Tanz"

5.9 Excerpt from "Hebräische Tanz" for Violin and Piano by Joseph Achron

5.10 Excerpt from "Schir Haschirim" (The Song of Songs) by Lazare Saminsky

5.11 Excerpt from "Haftarah" for cello and piano, by Samuel Alman*

Chapter 6 (pages 95–124)

6.1   Excerpt from "Rozhinkes Mit Mandlen" by Abraham Goldfaden
6.2   Excerpt from "A Brivele Der Mamen" by Solomon Shmuelvitz*
6.3   Excerpt from "Mayn Rue Platz" by Morris Rosenfeld
6.4   Excerpt from "Mayn Yingele" by Morris Rosenfeld
6.5   Excerpt from "Leb'n Zol Kolombus" by Arnold Perlmutter and Herman Wohl*
6.6   Excerpt from "Die Grine Kuzine" by Jacob Leiserowitz and Abe Schwartz
6.7   Excerpt from "Vakht Oyf" by David Edelstadt
6.8   Excerpt from "In Kamf" by David Edelstadt*

Chapter 7 (pages 125–148)

7.1   Excerpt from *Borkhu* by A. W. Binder*
7.2   Excerpt from *Shaḥar Avakeshkha* by Isadore Freed
7.3   Four themes from *Avodat ha-Kodesh* by Ernest Bloch
7.4   Except from *Mekhalkel Ḥayim be-Ḥesed* by Max Wohlberg
7.5   Excerpt from *Yismeḥu* by Max Janowski
7.6   Excerpt from *Shiru L'Adonai* by Ben Steinberg*
7.7   Excerpt from *Anim Zemirot* by Herbert Fromm
7.8   Excerpt from *Ashamnu* from *The Hush of Midnight* by Charles Davidson*
7.9   Excerpt from "Esa Einai" by Shlomo Carlebach
7.10   Excerpt from *Anim Zemirot* set to the tune of Carlebach's "Esa Einai"
7.11   Excerpt from *ve-Ha'er Einenu* by Shlomo Carlebach
7.12   Excerpt from "Erev Shel Shoshanim" by Yosef Hadar
7.13   *Mimekomo* adapted to "Erev Shel Shoshanim"
7.14   Excerpt from the conclusion of *Ahavat Olam* by Aminadav Aloni*

Chapter 8 (pages 149–186)

8.1   From the introduction to "Tzela-Tzeldi" by Jacob Glatstein and Lazar Weiner*
8.2   From andante of "Tzela-Tzeldi"*
8.3   Opening bar of "Volt Mayn Tate Raykh Geven" by Aaron Nissenson and Lazar Weiner*
8.4   Next phrase of "Volt Mayn Tate Raykh Geven"*
8.5   Opening excerpt of "A Gebet" by Jacob Rolnick and Lazar Weiner
8.6   From the opening of "Ergetz Vayt" by H. Leivick and Lazar Weiner
8.7   Excerpt from "A Bord" by Aaron Lutzky and Lazar Weiner* compared with haftarah chant
8.8   "Comfort, oh comfort My people" from "Di Reyd Funem Novi" by L. Magister and Lazar Weiner
8.9   Excerpt from "Yiddish" by Jacob Segal and Lazar Weiner
8.10   Traditional Hasidic melody used in the overture to *The Dybbuk*

8.11   "Shema" from *A Survivor from Warsaw* by Arnold Schoenberg*
8.12   Sulzer "Shema" compared with "Shema" from *Survivor*
8.13   First movement theme from Symphony no. 1 *(Jeremiah)* by Leonard Bernstein
8.14   *Haftarah* chant according to A. Z. Idelsohn
8.15   Second movement theme from *Jeremiah* symphony*
8.16   Opening line of traditional Eykha chant
8.17   Opening line of "Lamentation" from third movement of *Jeremiah*
8.18   "Hari'u L'Adonai Kol ha-Aretz" from *Chichester Psalms* by Leonard Bernstein
8.19   Excerpt from "Adonai Ro'i" from *Chichester Psalms,* second movement
8.20   Excerpt from "Lama rageshu" from *Chichester Psalms,* second movement
8.21   "Hiney Mah Tov" from *Chichester Psalms,* third movement
8.22   Excerpt from *Tehillim* by Steve Reich*

Chapter 9 (pages 187–220)

9.1   Excerpt from "Di Sokhe" by Eliakum Zunser
9.2   Excerpt from "Ya-Ḥai-Li-Li," folk song, lyrics by Noach Shapira *
9.3   Excerpt from "Birkat Am," folk song, lyrics by Chaim Nachman Bialik
9.4   Excerpt from "Ḥushu Aḥim Ḥushu," Russian folk song, lyrics by Yehiel Michael Pines
9.5   Excerpt from "Hatikvah," folk tune, lyrics by Naftali Herz Imber
9.6   Excerpt from "ve-Taher Libenu," traditional Ḥasidic folk song*
9.7   "El Yivneh Hagalil," folk song
9.8   Excerpt from "Po be-Eretz Ḥemdat Avot" by Yisrael Dushman and Herman Tzvi Erlich
9.9   Excerpt from "Ani Ma'amin" by Tuvia Shlonsky
9.10   "Anu Nihyeh ha-Rishonim," Russian folk melody, lyrics by Joseph Heftman *
9.11   Excerpt from "El Rosh ha-Har" by Levin Kipnis and Hanina Karczewski
9.12   Excerpt from "Shir al Trumpeldor," folk song
9.13   Excerpt from "Numi, Numi Yaldati" by Yehiel Heilperin and Joel Engel
9.14   Excerpt from "le-Moladeti" by Hillel Avichanan and Mordechai Zeira
9.15   Excerpt from "Havu Levenim" by Alexander Penn and Mordechai Zeira
9.16   Excerpt from "Sa'enu," traditional Bedouin song, lyrics by Alexander Penn
9.17   Excerpt from "Orḥa Bamidbar" by Ya'akov Fichman and David Zahavi
9.18   Excerpt from "Shedemati" by Yitzchak Shenhar and Yedidyah Admon*
9.19   Excerpt from "Olim" by Yitzchak Shenhar and Shalom Postolski
9.20   Excerpt from "Yerushalayim," folk song, lyrics by Avigdor Hameiri
9.21   Excerpt from "Shir ha-Emek" by Natan Alterman and Daniel Sambursky"*
9.22   Excerpt from "Yesh Li Gan," sung by Bracha Tzefira, lyrics by Chaim Nachman Bialik *

9.23   Opening theme from *Roni Akara* by Paul Ben-Haim*
9.24   Passacaglia theme, "Harḥivi" from *Roni Akara* by Paul Ben-Haim
9.25   Traditional Babylonian "Shema," and use of it as "Ki yamin u'Semol" in *Roni Akara* by Paul Ben-Haim
9.26   "Ki Vo'alayikh Osayikh" from *Roni Akara* by Paul Ben-Haim
9.27   "Mi Nishikani," traditional Yemenite melody
9.28   "Na'ale le-Artzenu," traditional Yemenite melody

Chapter 10 (pages 221–248)

10.1   Excerpt from "Ha'amini Yom Yavo" by Raphael Klatshkin and Menashe Baharav*
10.2   Excerpt from "ha-Finjan,"Armenian folk melody, lyrics by Haim Hefer
10.3   Excerpt from "Bab El Wad" by Haim Guri and Shmuel Pershko*
10.4   Excerpt from "Hayu Zemanim" by Haim Hefer and Moshe Wilensky*
10.5   Excerpt from "Horah Mamterah" by Yehiel Mohar and Moshe Wilensky
10.6   Excerpt from "la-Midbar" by Haim Hefer and Sasha Argov
10.7   Excerpt from "ha-Sela ha-Adom" by Haim Hefer and Yochanan Zarai*
10.8   Excerpt from "Mul Har Sinai" by Yehiel Mohar and Moshe Wilensky*
10.9   Excerpt from "Erev Ba" by Oded Avisar and Aryeh Levanon*
10.10   Excerpt from "Yerushalayim Sheli" by Dan Almagor and Nurit Hirsh
10.11   Excerpt from "Mah Avarekh" by Rachel Shapira and Yair Rosenblum*
10.12   Excerpt from "Shir le-Shalom" by Ya'akov Rotblit and Yair Rosenblum
10.13   Excerpt from "Petaḥ Lanu Sha'ar" by Moshe Wilensky
10.14   Excerpt from "ha-Milḥamah ha-Aḥaronah" by Haim Hefer and Dov Seltzer*
10.15   Excerpt from "Noladeti le-Shalom" by Uzi Hitman
10.16   Excerpt from "Ḥai" by Ehud Manor and Avi Toledano*
10.17   Excerpt from "Horah" by Yoram Tohar-Lev and Avi Toledano*
10.18   Excerpt from "Shuvi Harmonikah" by Yoram Tohar-Lev and Nurit Hirsh
10.19   Excerpt from "Ḥad Gadya," adapted by Chava Alberstein*
10.20   Excerpt from "Masa le-Eretz Yisrael" by Haim Idisis and Shlomo Gronich*
10.21   Excerpt from "Shir Yisraeli" by Ehud Manor and Shlomo Gronich*

Chapter 11 (pages 249–278)

11.1   Excerpt from "Rabos Maḥashovos" by Baruch Chait*
11.2   Excerpt from "Urah Kevodi" by Moshe Greiniman
11.3   Excerpt from "Am Yisrael Ḥai" by Shlomo Carlebach
11.4   Excerpt from "Yah Ribon," traditional Sabbath table song*
11.5   Excerpt from "Or Zaru'a" by Jeff Klepper*
11.6   Excerpt from "Kippah" by Susan Nanus and Jeff Klepper
11.7   Excerpt from "Master of All Things" by Craig Taubman*

11.8   Excerpt from "Ana Adoshem" by Robbie Solomon*
11.9   Excerpt from "Lekha Dodi" by Robbie Solomon
11.10   Excerpt from "Coming to America" by Robbie Solomon*
11.11   Excerpt from "I've Got the 'What Page Are We On in the Prayer Book' Blues" by Moshe Yess*
11.12   Excerpt from "Miriam's Song" by Debbie Friedman*
11.13   Excerpt from "Sarah and Hagar" by Linda Hirschhorn
11.14   Excerpt from "Adonai, Adonai" by Leon Sher*
11.15   Excerpt from "Tefilah Lishlom Medinat Yisrael" by David Burger*
11.16   Excerpt from "A Nakht in Gan Eydn," traditional Klezmer tune *

Recorded Selections Appearing on Accompanying Compact Disc

Track 1 **Psalm 148—Syllabic chant for weekdays from the Babylonian Jewish community**
Sung by Ezekiel H. Albeg from the recording entitled *Babylonian Biblical Chants,* Folkways 08930, provided courtesy of Smithsonian Folkways Recordings. © 1959. Used by permission.

Track 2 **Psalm 148—Melismatic improvisational chant from the Babylonian Jewish community**
Sung by Ezekiel H. Albeg from the recording entitled *Babylonian Biblical Chants,* Folkways 08930, provided courtesy of Smithsonian Folkways Recordings. © 1959. Used by permission.

Track 3 **"La Rosa Enflorece," love song from the Sephardic tradition**
Recorded as "Los Bilbilicos" by Yehoram Gaon on the recording entitled *Romansot ba-Ladino: Romantic Ballads from the Great Judeo-Espagnol Heritage,* arranged and conducted by Dov Seltzer, CBS 63379 (undated). Used by permission.

Track 4 **"Tzur mi-Shelo," Sabbath table song adapted from "La Rosa Enflorece"**
As recorded on *Shabbath Songs in the Sephardic Tradition,* CBS 82760 produced 1978 CBS Inc. Used by permission.

Track 5 **"Cuando El Rey Nimrod" from the Sephardic tradition**
Sung by Yehoram Gaon on the recording entitled *Romansot ba-Ladino: Romantic Ballads from the Great Judeo-Espagnol Heritage,* arranged and conducted by Dov Seltzer, CBS 63379 (undated). Used by permission.

Track 6 "Mama, Mirame Las Gambas" from the Sephardic community
Sung by The Voice of the Turtle on *Circle of Fire: A Hanukah Concert* (Songs of the Sephardim, vol. V), Titanic Records, produced and © 1987. Used by permission.

Track 7 *mi-Sinai* tune for the High Holy Day *Ma'ariv* service in the Ashkenzic tradition
Recorded by the Western Wind Vocal Ensemble as Rosh Hashanah Nusaḥ from *Birthday of the World Part I, Rosh Hashanah* (Western Wind Records WW1854). For info: www.westernwind.org or 800-788-2187. Used by permission.

Track 8 "Bulbes," Yiddish folk song
Sung by Abe Brumberg and ensemble on *Of Lovers, Dreamers and Thieves: Yiddish Folk Songs from Eastern Europe* (Troubadour TR-8) produced and © Troubadour Music, Inc., 1977. Used by permission.

Track 9 "Gey Ikh Mir Shpatzirn," Yiddish folk song
Sung by Raasche from the recording entitled *Jewish Folk Songs of Europe,* Folkways 08712, provided courtesy of Smithsonian Folkways Recordings. © 1960. Used by permission.

Track 10 "Nig'n," wordless Hasidic song attributed to the Ba'al Shem Tov
Recorded as "Nigun Besht I" on *Song of the Baal Shem*, chorus and orchestra conducted by Rafael Adler, Union of American Hebrew Congregations UA 0623 (undated). Used by permission.

Track 11 *Barekhu* by Salamone Rossi
Recorded by SELAH, Matthew Lazar, conductor, on *The Song That Transforms: Sounds, Names, and Places in The World of Synagogue Music,* produced and © 1986, Cantors Assembly. Used by permission.

Track 12 Excerpt from *Cantata ebraica* by Carlo Grossi
Recorded by Cantor Charles Osborne and SELAH, Matthew Lazar, conductor, on *The Song That Transforms: Sounds, Names, and Places in The World of Synagogue Music,* produced and © 1986, Cantors Assembly. Used by permission.

Track 13 *Ki mi-Tziyon* by Salomon Sulzer
Recorded by SELAH, Matthew Lazar, conductor, on *The Song That Transforms: Sounds, Names, and Places in The World of Synagogue Music,* produced and © 1986, Cantors Assembly. Used by permission.

Track 14 Excerpt from Psalm 92 by Louis Lewandowski
Recorded by SELAH, Matthew Lazar, conductor, on *The Song That Transforms: Sounds, Names, and Places in The World of Synagogue Music,* produced and © 1986, Cantors Assembly. Used by permission.

Track 15 **Excerpt from "Farn Obsheyd" by Ephraim Skliar**

Sung by Cantor Louis Danto; Natasha Tyomkina, piano, on *Masters of the Jewish Art Song/The St. Petersburg School (1908–1924)*, Cadenza Records, LRC 109. Used by permission.

Track 16 **Excerpt from "Lomir Zikh Iberbetn" by Solomon Rosowsky**

Sung by Cantor Louis Danto; Natasha Tyomkina, piano, on *Masters of the Jewish Art Song/The St. Petersburg School (1908–1924)*, Cadenza Records, LRC 109. Used by permission.

Track 17 **Excerpt from Joseph Achron's setting of "In a Kleyner Shtibele" for voice and piano**

Recorded by Leon Lishner, bass; and Lazar Weiner, piano on *The Yiddish Art Song*, Omega Classics, OCD 3010, Compilation produced and © 1992 Omega Record Group, Inc.

Track 18 **Excerpt from Milner's setting of "In Ḥeder," including traditional *lernsteiger***

Recorded by Leon Lishner, bass and Lazar Weiner, piano on *The Yiddish Art Song*, Omega Classics, OCD 3010, Compilation produced and © 1992 Omega Record Group, Inc.

Track 19 **Excerpt from "Unter dem Kind's Vigele," traditional Yiddish lullaby**

Sung by Rose Padden on *A Mama Sings a Lidele: Yiddish Lullabies*, Apollo Records, APL 492 (undated).

Track 20 **Excerpt from Joseph Achron's setting of "Hebräische Viglied" for violin and piano**

Recorded by Yuval Waldman, violin; and Cathy Waldman, piano on *The Russian Jewish Composers*, vol. II, Musique Internationale, MQI 7502 (undated). Used by permission.

Track 21 **Excerpt from "Haftarah" for cello and piano, by Samuel Alman**

Recorded by David Sella, cello; and Paul Posnak, piano, on *Russian Jewish Composers*, vol. IV, Musique Internationale, MQI 7504 (undated). Used by permission.

Track 22 **Excerpt from "A Brivele der Mamen" by Solomon Shmuelvitz**

Recorded by The Klezmer Conservatory Band on *A Jumpin' Night in the Garden of Eden*, produced and © Rounder Records Corporation, 1988. Used by permission.

Track 23 Excerpt from "Leb'n Zol Kolombus" by Arnold Perlmutter and Herman Wohl
Recorded by The B.J.E. Childrens' Choir, Jonathan Wasserman, soloist on *The American Jewish Experience in Song,* arranged and directed by Neil Levin, Board of Jewish Education of Metropolitan Chicago, 1976. Used by permission.

Track 24 Excerpt from "In Kamf" by David Edelstadt
Sung by Cantor Abraham Lubin on *The American Jewish Experience in Song,* arranged and directed by Neil Levin, Board of Jewish Education of Metropolitan Chicago, 1976. Used by permission.

Track 25 Excerpt from *Borkhu* by A. W. Binder
Recorded by Temple Emanu-El Choir of Dallas, Texas on *We Worship: Contemporary Hebrew Liturgical Music,* Samuel H. Adler, conductor, Unicorn Records 1026 (undated).

Track 26 Excerpt from *Shiru L'Adonai* by Ben Steinberg
Sung by Cantor Richard Allen with the choir and instrumentalists of Reform Congregation Keneseth Israel of Elkins Park, Pennsylvania, on *A Ben Steinberg Concert* (undated).

Track 27 Excerpt from *Ashamnu* from *The Hush of Midnight* by Charles Davidson
Sung by Cantor Ray Edgar and the Zamir Chorale, Stanley Sperber, Director, on *The Hush of Midnight,* Amim Records 425-A (undated). Used by permission.

Track 28 Excerpt from the conclusion of *Ahavat Olam* by Aminadav Aloni
Sung by Cantor Nathan Lam on *Legacy: A Mosaic of Jewish Music*, The National Symphony of Israel, conducted by Michael Issacson, produced and © 1987, Stephen S. Wise Temple. Used by permission.

Track 29 Excerpt from "Tzela-Tzeldi" by Jacob Glatstein and Lazar Weiner
Sung by Bianca Sauler on *Lazar Weiner Songs: Musical Settings of Yiddish Poetry* with Lazar Weiner, piano, Naomi 10001 (undated).

Track 30 Excerpt from "Volt Mayn Tate Raykh Geven" by Aaron Nissenson and Lazar Weiner
Sung by Bianca Sauler on *Lazar Weiner Songs: Musical Settings of Yiddish Poetry* with Lazar Weiner, piano, Naomi 10001 (undated).

Track 31 "A Bord" by Aaron Lutzky and Lazar Weiner
Sung by Bianca Sauler on *Lazar Weiner Songs: Musical Settings of Yiddish Poetry* with Lazar Weiner, piano, Naomi 10001 (undated).

Track 32 "Shema" from *A Survivor from Warsaw* by Arnold Schoenberg
Recorded on *Boulez Conducts Schoenberg*, B.B.C. Symphony Orchestra, Pierre Boulez, conductor; Gunther Reich, speaker, CBS M35882, produced 1978, CBS Records, Inc. Used by permission.

Track 33   Second movement ("Profanation") theme from Symphony no. 1 *(Jeremiah)* by Leonard Bernstein
Recorded by the New York Philharmonic, Leonard Bernstein, conductor, Columbia Records MS6303 (undated). Used by permission.

Track 34 Excerpt from *Tehillim* by Steve Reich
Recorded by Steve Reich and Musicians on *Tehillim*, conducted by George Manahan, ECM-1-1215, produced and © 1982 ECM Records GmbH.

Track 35 Excerpt from "Ya-Ḥai-Li-Li," folk song, lyrics by Noach Shapira
Sung by Hillel Raveh and the Tzadikoff Choir on *Anu Nihyeh Harishonim: Songs of Israel's First Pioneers* CBS S70041 (undated). Used by permission.

Track 36 Excerpt from "ve-Taher Libenu," traditional Ḥasidic folk song
Recorded by the Tzadikoff Choir on *Anu Nihyeh Harishonim: Songs of Israel's First Pioneers* CBS S70041 (undated).

Track 37   "Anu Nihyeh ha-Rishonim," Russian folk melody, lyrics by Joseph Heftman
Recorded by the Tzahal Choir and Orchestra on *Amud HaEsh*, CBS 22201, ©1982. Used by permission.

Track 38 "Shedemati" by Yitzchak Shenhar and Yedidyah Admon
Sung by The Parvarim on *The Parvarim: Favorite Israeli Folk Songs,* CBS 62898 (undated). Used by permission.

Track 39 Excerpt from "Shir ha-Emek" by Natan Alterman and Daniel Sambursky
Sung by The Parvarim, on *Amud HaEsh*, CBS 22201, © 1982. Used by permission.

Track 40 "Yesh Li Gan" sung by Bracha Tzefira, lyrics by Chaim Nachman Bialik
Recorded by Bracha Tzefira as "Jai Un Verger," arranged by Nahum Nardi, on *Trente Ans de Musique en Israel,* Les Industries Musicales et Électriques Pathé Marconi, MSTX 147 (undated).

Track 41 Excerpt from first movement of *Roni Akara* by Paul Ben-Haim
From a live performance by the Instant Choir conducted by Matthew Lazar at the thirteenth annual North American Jewish Choral Festival, Matthew Lazar, Founder and Director, 2002. Used by permission.

Track 42 **Excerpt from "Ha'amini Yom Yavo" by Raphael Klatshkin and Menashe Baharav**
Sung by Shoshana Damari on *25 Years of Song from Israel*, CBS 67286, produced CBS Records, Inc., 1982. Used by permission.

Track 43 **Excerpt from "Bab El Wad" by Haim Guri and Shmuel Pershko**
Sung by Yaffa Yarkoni on *25 Years of Song from Israel*, CBS 67286, produced CBS Records, Inc., 1982. Used by permission.

Track 44 **Excerpt from "Hayu Zemanim" by Haim Hefer and Moshe Wilensky**
Sung by Shoshana Damari and the Naḥal Entertainment Troupe on *Thirty Years of Song from Israel*, CBS 22064 produced 1978. Used by permission.

Track 45 **Excerpt from "ha-Sela ha-Adom" by Haim Hefer and Yochanan Zarai**
Sung by Arik Lavie in the collection *Gadalnu Yaḥad: Osef ha-Yovel shel Yisrael* (Israel's 240 Greatest Songs in Celebration of Its Fiftieth Anniversary), produced and © 1998, Hed Arzi Ltd.

Track 46 **Excerpt from "Mul Har Sinai" by Yehiel Mohar and Moshe Wilensky**
Performed by the Naḥal Entertainment Troupe on *Thirty Years of Song from Israel*, CBS 22064 produced 1978. Used by permission.

Track 47 **Excerpt from "Erev Ba" by Oded Avisar and Aryeh Levanon**
Performed by Shimon Bar and Aliza Kashi on *Thirty Years of Song from Israel*, CBS 22064 produced 1978. Used by permission.

Track 48 **Excerpt from "Mah Avarekh"by Rachel Shapira and Yair Rosenblum**
Performed by Lehakat Ḥel ha-Yam (The Navy Variety Ensemble) in the collection *Gadalnu Yaḥad: Osef ha-Yovel shel Yisrael* (Israel's 240 Greatest Songs in Celebration of Its Fiftieth Anniversary), produced and © 1998, Hed Arzi Ltd. Used by permission.

Track 49 **Excerpt from "ha-Milḥamah ha-Aḥaronah" by Haim Hefer and Dov Seltzer**
Sung by Yehoram Gaon on *Songs of the Yom Kippur War*, CBS 65907, produced 1973 CBS, Inc. Used by permission.

Track 50 **Excerpt from "Ḥai" by Ehud Manor and Avi Toledano**
Sung by Ofra Haza on *Pre-Eurovision Festival 1983*, produced 1983, Hed Artzi Ltd.

Track 51 **Excerpt from "Horah" by Yoram Tohar-Lev and Avi Toledano**
Sung by Avi Toledano in the collection *Gadalnu Yaḥad: Osef ha-Yovel shel Yisrael* (Israel's 240 Greatest Songs in Celebration of Its Fiftieth Anniversary), produced and © 1998, Hed Arzi Ltd.

Track 52 **Excerpt from "Ḥad Gadya," adapted by Chava Alberstein**
Sung by Chava Alberstein on *London,* CBS 465470-2, produced 1989 NMC Music Ltd./CBS.

Track 53 **Excerpt from "Masa le-Eretz Yisrael" by Haim Idisis and Shlomo Gronich**
Sung by Shlomo Gronich and the Sheba Choir on *Agudat Achsaniyot Noar be-Yisrael* (Hostelling International), CD 15615, distributed by Hed Artzi (undated).

Track 54 **Excerpt from "Shir Yisraeli" by Ehud Manor and Shlomo Gronich**
Sung by Shlomo Gronich and the Sheba Choir on *Agudat Achsaniyot Noar be-Yisrael* (Hostelling International), CD 15615, distributed by Hed Artzi (undated).

Track 55 **Excerpt from "Rabos Maḥashovos" by Baruch Chait**
Sung by The Rabbis' Sons on *The Rabbis' Sons: Hallelu,* Emes ES-101 (undated). Used by permission.

Track 56 **Excerpt from "Yah Ribon," inspired by a traditional Yemenite song**
Performed by Tayku on *Tayku,* WSD 5729, 1974, Windblown Music. Used by permission.

Track 57 **Excerpt from "Or Zaru'a" by Jeff Klepper**
Sung by Kol B'Seder on *Shalom Rav: Kol B'Seder in Concert,* produced and © 1992, Dan Freelander and Jeff Klepper. Used by permission.

Track 58 **Excerpt from "Master of All Things" by Craig Taubman**
Sung by Craig Taubman on *Moment to Moment,* Torah Aura Productions, © 1985. Used by permission.

Track 59 **Excerpt from "Ana Adoshem" by Robbie Solomon**
Sung by Safam on *Sons of Safam,* produced 1980 Safam. Used by permission.

Track 60 **Excerpt from "Coming to America" by Robbie Solomon**
Sung by Safam on *Sons of Safam,* produced 1980 Safam. Used by permission.

Track 61 **Excerpt from "I've Got the 'What Page Are We On in the Prayer Book' Blues" by Moshe Yess**
Sung by Megama on *Megama: Farewell,* produced and © 1988 Gold Bar Productions. Used by permission.

Track 62 **Excerpt from "Miriam's Song" by Debbie Friedman**
Sung by Debbie Friedman on *Debbie Friedman at Carnegie Hall,* produced and © 1996, Sounds Write Productions, Inc. Used by permission.

Track 63 Excerpt from "Adonai, Adonai" by Leon Sher
Sung by Beged Kefet on *Beged Kefet: Lifeline,* © 1987, Beged Kefet. Used by permission.

Track 64 Excerpt from "Tefilah Lishlom Medinat Yisrael" by David Burger
Performed by the Zamir Chorale, Mati Lazar, director, on *T'filah,* WSD 5735, produced 1978, Windblown Music. Used by permission.

Track 65 Excerpt from "A Nakht in Gan Eydn," traditional Klezmer tune
Performed by The Klezmer Conservatory Band on *Oy Chanukah!* Rounder 3102, produced and © 1986 Rounder Records Corporation. Used by permission.

Index of Musical Illustrations

A

A Bord, 158
A Brivele der Mamen, 109
A Gebet, 156
A Nakht in Gan Eydn, 272
Adonai Ro'i, 179
Adonai, Adonai, 269
Ahavah Rabbah, 31
Ahavat Olam, 146
Allgegenwart, 55
Am Yisrael Ḥai, 253
Ana Adoshem, 258
Ani Ma'amin, 194
Anim Zemirot, 138, 141
Anu Nihyeh ha-Rishonim, 195
Ashamnu, 139
Avinu Malkeinu, 67
Avodat ha-Kodesh, 133
Avot, Sabbath morning, 29
Az der Rebbe, 37

B

Bab El Wad, 223
Barekhu, 45, 46, 47
Birkat Am, 189
Borkhu, 131
Bulbes, 33

C

Cantata ebraica, 49
Cuando El Rey Nimrod, 26

D

Debka Daluna, 30
Di Sokhe, 188
Die Grine Kuzine, 111
Durme, Hermozo Hijico, 24

E

El Erekh Apayim, 66
El Rosh ha-Har, 196
El Yivne Hagalil, 192
Erev Ba, 230
Erev Shel Shoshanim, 143
Ergetz Vayt, 157
Esa Einai, 141
Eykha, 175

F

Farn Obsheyd, 76

G

Gey Ikh Mir Shpatzirn, 34

H

Ha'amini Yom Yavo, 222
ha-Finjan, 222
ha-Masa le-Eretz Yisrael, 245
ha-Milḥamah ha-Aḥaronah, 237
ha-Sela ha-Adom, 227
Ḥad Gadya, 243
Haftarah, 93
Haftarah (Traditional), 174
Ḥai, 240
Halleluyah, Halleli Nafshi, 44
Harḥivi, 212
Hari'u l'Adonai kol ha'aretz, 178
Hashem Malakh, 31
Hatikvah, 191
Ḥatzi Kaddish, 68
Havu Levenim, 200
Hayu Zemanim, 224
Hebräische Tanz, 88, 90
Hebräische Viglied, 87
Hiney mah tov, 181
Hishki Hizki, 50
Horah, 241
Horah Mamterah, 225
Ḥushu, Aḥim, Ḥushu, 189

I

I've Got the 'What Page Are We On in
    the Prayer Book' Blues, 263
In a Kleyner Shtibele, 82, 83
In Ḥeder, 85
In Kamf, 112

J

Jeremiah Symphony, 173, 174, 176

K

Ki mi-Tziyon, 58
Ki Vo'alayikh Osayikh, 213
Ki Yamin u'Semol, 212
Kippah, 256
Kol Nidre, 29

L

La Rosa Enflorece, 22
la-Midbar, 226
Lama Rageshu, 179
Lamentation, 176
le-Moladeti, 199
Leb'n Zol Columbus, 111
Lekha Dodi, 259
Lomir Zikh Iberbetn, 81

M

Ma'ariv, High Holy Day, 29
Magen Avot, 30
Mah Avarekh, 234
makam Bayat, 30
makam Hijaz, 31
makam Sasgar, 31
makam Siga, 31
Mama, Mirame Las Gambas, 27
Master of All Things, 257
Mayn Rue Platz, 110
Mayn Yingele, 110
Mekhalkel Ḥayim be-Ḥesed, 136
melismatic passage, 19
Mi Nishikani, 215
Mimekomo, 143
Miriam's Song, 265
Mul Har Sinai, 229
*Music for Woodwind, Trombone, Piano,
    and Double Bass,* 219

N

Nig'n, 36
Noladeti le-Shalom, 239
Numi, Numi Yaldati, 198

O

Od Yenuvun, 62
Olim, 203
Or Zaru'a, 255
Orḥah ba-Midbar, 201

P

Pesaḥ Lonu Sha'ar, 68
Petaḥ Lanu Sha'ar, 237
Po be-Eretz Ḥemdat Avot, 193

R

Rabos Maḥashovos, 251
Roni Akarah, 211
Rozhinkes mit Mandlen, 105

S

Sa'enu, 200
Sarah and Hagar, 266
Scalerica de'Oro, 25
Schir Haschirim, 91
Se'u Shearim, 64
Shaḥar Avakeshkha, 132
Shedemati, 202
Shema, 58, 169, 212
Shir al Trumpeldor, 197
Shir ha-Emek, 204
Shir le-Shalom, 236
Shir Yisraeli, 246
Shiru L'Adonai, 137
Shuvi Harmonikah, 242
Survivor from Warsaw, 169
Syllabic passage, 18

T

T'filah Lishlom Medinat Yisrael, 270
Tal Ten, 70
Tehillim, 184
Tov le-Hodos, 57
Traditional Hasidic melody, 166
Tum Balalaika, 33
Tzela-Tzelda, 153, 154
Tzur mi-Shelo, 23

U

Unter dem Kind's Vigele, 32, 86
Urah Kevodi, 253

V

Vakht Oyf, 112
ve-Ha'er Einenu, 142
ve-Taher Libenu, 192
Viddui, 31
Volt Mayn Tate Raych Geven, 155

W

World of Our Fathers, 260

Y

Ya-Ḥai-Li-Li, 188
Yah Ribon, 254
Yeled ha-Yulad, 51
Yerushalayim, 204
Yerushalayim Sheli, 232
Yesh Li Gan, 206
Yiddish, 161
Yismeḥu, 136

Index

A

absolute music, 163
Achron, Joseph
  Hebräische Tanz, 88–90
  In a Kleyner Shtibele, 82–83
  Unter dem Kind's Vigele, 86–88
Akdamut Le'Moed, 217–218
Alberstein, Chava, 243, 276
Alman, Samuel, 92
Aloni, Ami, 145–147
Amsterdam synagogues, beginning of
  art music, 51
anti-Semitism in America, 249–250
antiphonal worship, 6–7
art music
  definition, 39
  folk music as source of, 80–84
  incorporating traditional music, 92
  Israeli, 205–220
  origin among Jews, 40
  Sephardic origins, 48–51
  Society for Jewish Folk Music, 77–80
Ashkenazic community, art music
  evolution of, 80–84
  lack of, 53
Ashkenazic music. *see also* klezmer music
  first ethnography, 72–77
  origins, 28–29

B

Ba'al Shem Tov, 36
Bab-El-Wad, 223
badḥ'n, 99
Barekhu, 44–48
Beged Kefet, 267–268
Ben-Ami, Jacob, 121–122
Ben-Haim, Paul, 207–214
Bernstein, Leonard
  Dybbuk, 181–182
  Hashkivenu, 176
  Kaddish Symphony, 176–177
  Symphony No. 1 (Jeremiah), 173–175
Biblical music. *see also* Psalms
  antiphonal worship, 6–7
  First Temple period, 2–3, 8
  instruments, 2–3, 4
  in Israeli music, 210, 228
  Jubal, 1
  Lamekh, 1
  responsorial worship, 4–6
  Song at the Sea, 1–2
Bloch, Ernest
  as a Jewish composer, 162–163
  nature of Jewish music, 164–166
  synagogue music, 133–134
Blumenthal, Nissan, 65–66
Burger, Bruce, 275–276
Burger, David, 268–270

C

Cantata ebraica in dialogo, 48–50
cantillation
  differences on holidays, 15–17
  inspiration for compositions, 90–92
  origins, 12–13
cantorial schools, 134–135
cantors. *see also ḥazzanim*
  Blumenthal, Nissan, 65–66
  concert, recording engagements,
    128–130
  and congregational singing, 134–137
  Ephraim Skliar, 74–77
  Gerovitsch, Eliezer, 69–70
  impact on ritual, 130
  origin, 56
  Pinchos Minkowsky, 66–67
  Schorr, Baruch, 65
  Solomon Sulzer, 56–59
Carlebach, Shlomo, 141–142, 253
Castelnuovo-Tedesco, Mario, 171–172
Catholic mass, 9
Chichester Psalms, 177–180
Children's Song Festival, 242
chironomy, 13
Conservative Judaism
  adaptation of new music, 143–144
  Cantors Institute, 135
  congregational singing, 136
  influence on modern music, 256–258
contrafaction, 7–8
Copland, Aaron, 166–167

D

Davidson, Charles, 139–140
Diwan, 19

E

Eastern Mediterranean School, 208–211
Egypt, peace with, 238–239
Emancipation. *see also* Enlightenment
  differences in Western and Eastern
    Europe, 71–72

Engel, Joel
  activity during Fourth Aliyah, 198
  association with Lazar Weiner, 151
  ethnography of folk songs, 73–74
English, as language of Jewish music,
  259–264
Enlightenment. *see also* Emancipation
  affect on nusaḥ, 54–56
  causes, 53–54
Ethiopian influence, 245
Ethnography of Jewish music, 72–77
Eurovision Festival, 239–240
Ezra, 12

F

Fifth Aliyah, 202–205
First Aliyah, 187–191
First Temple period, 2–3, 8. *see also*
  Psalms
Fourth Aliyah, 198–202
French Revolution, 53
Friedman, Debbie, 142, 255, 264–265

G

Gerovitsch, Eliezer, 69–70
Gesellschaft für Jüdishe Volksmusic, Die.
  see Society for Jewish Folk Music
Ginsburg, Saul, 72–74
Goldfaden, Abraham
  early years, 100–101
  educational value of theater, 102–103
  final years in America, 107–108
  Shulamis, 103–106
  success in Russia, 106
Gordin, Jacob, 113–115
Gregorian chants, 9, 21–22
Grodner, Yisroel, 101–102
Gronich, Shlomo, 245–246

H

Ha-Shirim Asher li-Shelomo, 41, 42
Hajdu, Andre, 216–217
Hashkivenu, 176

Hasidic music
    modern form of, 252–253
    nature of, 36–37
    Nissan Blumenthal, 65–66
    Shlomo Carlebach, 141–142, 253
Hasidic Song Festival, 141–142, 232,
    253
Hasidism, origins, 35–36
Hatikvah, 190–191
Haza, Ofra, 241, 244
ḥazzanim. *see also* cantors
    adopting new music, 59
    in colonial America, 125
    demand for, 128
    early American, 126–127
    importing from Europe, 128
    prior to Emancipation, 54
    and recording industry, 128–130
Hefer, Haim, 222, 224, 226
hero songs, 25–26
Hirschhorn, Linda, 266–267

Hanina Karczewski, 193, 196
Hatikvah, 190–191
Jewish Agency, 203–204
Joel Engel, 198
Mark Kopytman, 215–216
migration to international style, 240
Mordechai Zeira, 199
Moshe Wilensky, 224–225, 228, 237
Mt. Sinai, 229–230
Nahum Nardi, 206–207
Noam Sherrif, 217–219
Paul Ben-Haim, 207–214
Shlomo Gronich, 245–246
Sinai campaign, 228–230
Six-Day War, 231–233
Sixties, 230–231
Third Aliyah, 195–198
War of Attrition, 234–236
War of Independence, 221–225
Yom Kippur War, 236–238
Yosef Trumpeldor, 196–198

I

immigration to America, 109–112
instruments, First Temple period, 2–3, 4
intifada, 243
Israeli music
    Alexander Penn, 199–201
    Andre Hajdu, 216–217
    Avi Toledano, 240–241
    Ben-Zion Orgad, 214
    Bible, use of, 210, 228
    Bracha Zefira, 205–207
    diversity of, 246
    Dov Seltzer, 237
    early religious, 191–193
    early secular, 193–194
    Eastern Mediterranean School, 208–211
    Ethiopian influence, 245
    Fifth Aliyah, 202–205
    Fifties, 225–227
    First Aliyah, 187–191
    Fourth Aliyah, 198–202

J

Jeremiah Symphony, 173–175
Jewish Agency, 203–204
Jewish art music. *see* art music
Jubal, 1

K

Kaddish, 176–177
Kaiser, Alois, 126
Kapelye (band), 271–272
Karczewski, Hanina, 193, 196
Klezmatics (band), 274, 277
klezmer music
    Henry Sapoznik, 271–272, 274
    Kapelye (band), 271–272
    maintaining Jewish identity, 277
    modern forms of, 273–274
klezmorim
    origins of, 35
    performances at weddings, 99
Kopytman, Mark, 215–216

L

labor movement, songs of, 112–113
Ladino, 22, 23–24, 27
Lamekh, 1
Lewandowski, Louis
  domination by Sulzer, 61
  motivations and talents, 60–61
  relationship with Mendelssohn, 59
Lichtenstein, Abraham Jacob, 60
Lion, Asher, 59, 60

M

makamat (modes), 18, 30–31
Marek, Pesach, 72–74
Masoretes, 13
Mass, 180–181
matbeah, 14
mi-Sinai melodies, 28–29
Milhaud, Darius, 170
Milner, Moses, 84–85
Minkoff, Nahum Baruch, 151
Minkowsky, Pinchos, 66–67
Modena, R. Leon
  leader of music academy, 48
  permitting synagogue choral music, 41
Moslems, Jewish life under, 20–21
Mt. Sinai, 229–230

N

Nardi, Nahum, 206–207
Naumbourg, Samuel, 62–63
neumes *(te'amim),* 13
1950s, Israeli music, 225–227
1960s, Israeli music, 230–231
nusah
  evolution, 17
  innovations by Sulzer, 58
  origins, 14–15, 18
  reformulation during Emancipation,
    54–56
  uniformity of in America, 130

O

Orgad, Ben-Zion, 214
Oriental music
  art music, lack of, 40
  for females, 19–20
  influence on modern Israeli music,
    241
  for males, 19
  nature of, 18
  piyyut, 19
  precedence of, 8, 17–18
  zemirot, 19
Orthodox Judaism
  adopting English in music, 262–264
  Cantorial Training Institute, 135
  influence on modern popular music,
    251–254
  new music in liturgy, 143
  shlihei tzibbur, developing liturgy, 135

P

Parvarim, 226
Patinkin, Mandy, 275–276
Penn, Alexander, 199–201
performances, rabbinic prohibition of
  relaxation for synagogue choral music,
    40–41
  relaxation on special occasions, 34–35
  and Spanish music, 23
  start of, 11
piyyut, in Oriental music, 19
popular music
  English, use of, 259–264
  influence on Orthodox, Reform, and
    Conservative Judaism, 251–259
  klezmer, 270–276
  new forms of, 267–270
  origins of, 249–251
  in synagogue liturgy, 138–140
  women, influence on, 264–267
prescriptions, 7–8

program music, 163–164
Psalm 137, 42–43
Psalm 146, 44
Psalms. *see also* Biblical music
  Salamone Rossi, 42–44
  types of, 4–8
Purimshpiel, 97–99

R

Rabbi's Sons (band), 251
Reform Judaism
  adopting new liturgical music, 54–65,
    126–127, 131–134
  congregational singing, 136–137
  influence on modern popular music,
    254–255
  School of Sacred Music, 135
Reich, Steve, 183–184
responsorial worship, 4–6
Rimsky-Korsakov, Nikolai, 75
Rosowsky, Solomon, 80–82
Rossi, Salamone
  Barekhu, 44–48
  impact of, 48
  Psalm 137, 42–43
  Psalm 146, 44
  R. Leon Modena, endorsement by, 41

S

Safam (band), 257–262
Saminsky, Lazare, 92
Sapoznik, Henry, 271–272, 274
Schoenberg, Arnold, 167–170
Schorr, Baruch, 65
Second Aliyah, 191–194
Second Temple period
  ban on performances after, 11–12
  music of, 2–3
  sound of, 8–10
Seltzer, Dov, 237
Sheba Choir, 245

Shemer, Naomi, 231
Sherrif, Noam, 217–219
Shulamis (play), plot and analysis,
  103–105
Sidran, Ben, 275–276
Sinai campaign, 228–230
Six-Day War, 231–233, 250
Skliar, Ephraim, 74–77
social activism, 250–251
Society for Jewish Folk Music
  founding, 77–78
  goals, 78
  Moses Milner, 84–85
  original works, 149–150
  publications and concerts, 78–79
Solomon, Robbie, 257
Song at the Sea, 1–2
Southern France, beginning of art
  music, 51
Spanish *(Sephardic)* music
  effect of Expulsion on, 26–28
  for females, 23–24
  and Jewish music, 23
  for males, 23
  Noam Sherrif, 219
  and origins of art music, 48–51
  religious, 22
  secular, 22–23
  songs of heroes, 25–26
Stark, Edward, 126–127
Sulzer, Solomon, 57–58
synagogue music in America
  congregational singing, 134–137
  development, 131–133
  future of, 144–147
  Hashkivenu, 176
  music directors, 131–132
  popular music, incorporating,
    138–140

T

Taubman, Craig, 256–257
The Dybbuk
    ballet by Leonard Bernstein, 181–182
    play by Solomon Anski, 117–119
    reaction to play, 119
Theater. *see also* Yiddish Theater
    Jewish actors in ancient and
        Renaissance times, 96–97
    Purimshpiel, 97–99
    rabbinic dislike of, 95–96, 102
Third Aliyah, 195–198
Thomashefsky, Boris, 106–107
Toledano, Avi, 240–241
Trumpeldor, Yosef, 196–198

V

Vaudeville, 108
Vilna Troupe
    The Dybbuk, 117–119
    early years, 115–117

W

War of Attrition, 234–236
War of Independence, 221–225
wedding entertainers, 99–100
Weiner, Lazar
    attraction to Yiddish, 151
    A Bord, 158
    Central Synagogue, music director of,
        152–153
    Di Reyd Funem Novi, 158–160
    early years, 150
    Ergetz Vayt, 157–158
    Freiheit Gesangs Verein, 151
    friendship with Nahum Minkoff, 151
    A Gebet, 156–157
    later years, 153
    love of Yiddish, 151, 160–161
    Tzela-Tzelda, 153–155
    Volt Mayn Tate Raykh Geven,
        155–156
    Workmen's Circle Chorus, 152

Wilensky, Moshe, 224–225, 228, 237
women in popular music, 264–267

Y

Yerushalayim Shel Zahav, 232
Yiddish
    decline of in favor of English,
        259–260
    origins, 29, 32
    resurgence of, 271
    songs and music, 32–35
Yiddish Art Theater, 120–123
Yiddish theater
    Abraham Goldfaden, 100–106
    ban by czar, 106
    Ben-Ami, Jacob, 121–122
    Folksbienne, 120
    Jacob Gordin, 113–115
    Maurice Schwartz, 120–123
    Vaudeville, influence on, 108
    Vilna Troupe, 115–117
YIVO Institute for Jewish Research, 271
Yom Kippur War, 236–238

Z

Zamir Chorale, 268–269
Zefira, Bracha, 205–207
Zeira, Mordechai, 199
zemirot, in Oriental music, 19
Zevi, Shabbatai, 35